The Cambridge Companion to
Modern Arab Culture

Dwight F. Reynolds brings together a collection of essays by leading
international scholars to provide a comprehensive and accessible survey
of modern Arab culture, from the early nineteenth to the twenty-first
century. The chapters survey key issues necessary to any understanding
of the modern Arab World: the role of the various forms of the Arabic
language in modern culture and identity; the remarkable intellectual
transformation undergone during the *Nahda* or "Arab Renaissance"
of the late nineteenth and early twentieth century; the significant
role played by ethnic and religious minorities, and the role of law and
constitutions. Other chapters on poetry, narrative, music, theater,
cinema and television, art, architecture, humor, folklore, and food offer
fresh perspectives and correct negative stereotypes that emerge from
viewing Arab culture primarily through the lens of politics, terrorism,
religion, and economics.

DWIGHT F. REYNOLDS is Professor of Arabic Language and Literature in
the Department of Religious Studies at the University of California,
Santa Barbara. He is the author of *Heroic Poets, Poetic Heroes: The
Ethnography of Performance in an Arabic Oral Epic Tradition* (1995), *Arab
Folklore: A Handbook* (2007), co-author and editor of *Interpreting the Self:
Autobiography in the Arabic Literary Tradition* (2001), and co-editor of *The
Garland Encyclopedia of World Music, Volume 6: The Middle East* (2002).

Cambridge Companions to Culture

The Cambridge Companion to
Modern Arab Culture

Edited by

DWIGHT F. REYNOLDS

CAMBRIDGE
UNIVERSITY PRESS

CAMBRIDGE
UNIVERSITY PRESS

University Printing House, Cambridge CB2 8BS, United Kingdom

One Liberty Plaza, 20th Floor, New York, NY 10006, USA

477 Williamstown Road, Port Melbourne, VIC 3207, Australia

4843/24, 2nd Floor, Ansari Road, Daryaganj, Delhi - 110002, India

79 Anson Road, #06-04/06, Singapore 079906

Cambridge University Press is part of the University of Cambridge.

It furthers the University's mission by disseminating knowledge in the pursuit of education, learning and research at the highest international levels of excellence.

www.cambridge.org
Information on this title: www.cambridge.org/9780521725330

First published 2015
Reprinted 2016

A catalogue record for this publication is available from the British Library

Library of Congress Cataloging in Publication data
The Cambridge companion to modern Arab culture / edited by Dwight F. Reynolds.
    pages cm
Includes bibliographical references and index.
ISBN 978-0-521-89807-2 (hbk.) – ISBN 978-0-521-72533-0 (pbk.)
1. Civilization, Arab–19th century.   2. Civilization, Arab–20th century.
3. Civilization, Arab–21st century.   4. Arab countries–Intellectual life–
19th century.   5. Arab countries–Intellectual life–20th century.   6. Arab countries–
Intellectual life–21st century.   I. Reynolds, Dwight Fletcher, 1956– editor.
DS36.88.C36   2015
909.0974927–dc23   2014043081

ISBN 978-0-521-89807-2 Hardback
ISBN 978-0-521-72533-0 Paperback

Contents

Illustrations

Tables

Maps

Contributors

DINA AMIN is a stage director and Assistant Professor of Drama and Comparative Literature in the English Department, Cairo University. She is the author of *Alfred Farag and Egyptian Theater* (2008), co-editor of *Salaam: Anthology of Middle-Eastern-American Drama* (2009) and of *From Orientalists to Arabists: The Shifts in Arabic Literary Studies* (special issue), *Journal of Arabic Literature* (2010). She directs in both the USA and Egypt, in Arabic and English. Her latest production in Cairo was *Segn al-Nisaa* (Women's Prison) by Fathiya al-ʿAssal (Spring, 2013).

KRISTEN BRUSTAD is Associate Professor of Arabic in the Department of Middle Eastern Studies at the University of Texas at Austin. She received her PhD in Near Eastern Languages and Civilizations from Harvard University. She is the author of a comparative study of Arabic dialects, *The Syntax of Spoken Arabic* (2000), and is co-author of the *Al-Kitaab* Arabic textbook series. She teaches and writes on Arabic language and linguistics.

JUAN E. CAMPO is Associate Professor of Islamic Studies and the History of Religions at the University of California, Santa Barbara. He is the author of *The Other Sides of Paradise: Explorations in the Religious Meanings of Domestic Space* (1991) and *Encyclopedia of Islam* (2009). He is currently engaged in a comparative study of modern Muslim, Hindu, and Christian pilgrimages and, together with his wife, Magda, is doing research and teaching on religion and the culinary cultures of the Middle East.

MAGDA CAMPO is Lecturer of Arabic Language in the Department of Religious Studies at the University of California, Santa Barbara. She holds a BA from Cairo University and an MA in Teaching Arabic as a Foreign Language from the American University in Cairo. A gifted chef and avid collector of Middle Eastern cookbooks, she co-teaches a course on religion and the culinary cultures of the Middle East with her husband, Juan E. Campo.

CHRISTINA CIVANTOS is Associate Professor in the Department of Modern Languages and Literatures at the University of Miami, Florida. She specializes in nineteenth- and twentieth-century Spanish American and Arabic literary and cultural studies with a focus on migration and diaspora, postcolonial and gender studies, and the politics of literacy. She is the author of *Between Argentines and Arabs: Argentine Orientalism, Arab Immigrants, and the Writing of Identity* (2006).

YOAV DI-CAPUA is Associate Professor of History at the University of Texas at Austin, where he teaches modern Arab intellectual history. He is the author of *Gatekeepers of the Arab Past: Historians and History Writing in Twentieth-Century Egypt* (2009). He is currently at work on a new book, tentatively titled *The Arab Sartre: Inside the Intellectual History of Decolonization*.

ANDREW HAMMOND is an author and journalist specializing in Middle East political and cultural affairs. Former bureau chief for Reuters news agency in Riyadh, he authored *The Islamic Utopia: The Illusion of Reform in Saudi Arabia* (2012), *What the Arabs Think of America* (2007), and *Popular Culture in the Arab World* (2007). He is currently doing doctoral research at the University of Oxford in Turkish and Egyptian Intellectual History.

NUHA N. N. KHOURY, Associate Professor of History of Art and Architecture at the University of California, Santa Barbara, is a specialist in Umayyad architecture, whose research transcends geographical and temporal boundaries to encompass the histories of Islamic architecture and Arab modern art. Her publications appear in *Muqarnas*, *The International Journal of Middle East Studies*, and *Third Text*, among other locations. Her current research engages the formative period of Islamic architecture and transitional artists of the modern Arab World, particularly Lebanon.

JOSEPH E. LOWRY is Associate Professor of Arabic and Islamic Studies in the Department of Near Eastern Languages and Civilizations at the University of Pennsylvania. He has published articles on the Qur'an, Islamic legal thought, and Arabic literature, is the author of *Early Islamic Legal Theory* (2007), and editor and translator of *Al-Shāfiʿī: The Epistle on Legal Theory* (2013), a volume in the Library of Arabic Literature.

ANDREW D. MAGNUSSON is a Lecturer in the Department of History at California Polytechnic State University in San Luis Obispo. He earned a PhD in Islamic History at the University of California, Santa Barbara. His research interests include the history of non-Muslim communities in the medieval and modern Middle East. A forthcoming article based on his dissertation, "Muslim-Zoroastrian Relations and Religious Violence in Early Islamic Discourse," will appear in the *ARAM Periodical*.

SCOTT MARCUS is Professor of Ethnomusicology at the University of California, Santa Barbara, specializing in the musics of the Arab World and northern India. His dissertation, "Arab Music Theory in the Modern Period," and numerous articles focus on the Arab system of melodic modes. He authored *Music in Egypt* (2007), co-edited *The Garland Encyclopedia of World Music, Vol. 6: The Middle East* (2002), and directs the UCSB Middle East Ensemble, whose performances have included a 2010 tour of Egypt sponsored by the Egyptian government.

MUHSIN AL-MUSAWI is Professor of Classical and Modern Arabic and Comparative Studies at Columbia University. He is the author of twenty-eight books (four of which are novels) including *Scheherazade in England* (1981); *The Society of One Thousand and One Nights* (2000); *Anglo-Orient: Easterners in Textual Camps* (2000); *The Postcolonial Arabic Novel: Debating Ambivalence* (2003); *Arabic Poetry: Trajectories of Modernity and Tradition* (2006); *Reading Iraq: Culture and Power in Conflict* (2006); and *The Islamic Context of the Thousand and One Nights* (2009).

NASSER RABBAT is the Aga Khan Professor and the Director of the Aga Khan Program for Islamic Architecture at Massachusetts Institute of Technology. An architect and a historian, his scholarly interests include Islamic architecture and urbanism, Arabic history, and post-colonial criticism. Among his books are *Mamluk History through Architecture: Building, Culture, and Politics in Mamluk Egypt and Syria* (2010) and *Thaqafat al-bina' wa-bina' al-thaqafa* (The Culture of Building and Building Culture) (2002).

DWIGHT F. REYNOLDS is Professor of Arabic Language and Literature at the University of California, Santa Barbara. His research areas include Arabic literature, oral poetry, music, and folklore. He is the author of *Heroic Poets, Poetic Heroes: The Ethnography of Performance in an Egyptian Oral Epic Tradition* (1995) and *Arab Folklore: A Handbook* (2007), as well as co-author and editor of *Interpreting the Self: Autobiography in the Arabic Literary Tradition* (2001).

DEVIN STEWART is Associate Professor of Arabic and Islamic Studies at Emory University. He is the author of *Islamic Legal Orthodoxy: Twelver Shiite Responses to the Sunni Legal System* (1998). The areas of his research include Shi'ite Islam, Islamic legal education, biography and autobiography in the Islamic world, medieval Arabic prose literature, and Arabic dialects.

SHAWKAT M. TOORAWA teaches Arabic, comparative, and world literature at Cornell University. His areas of research include the Qur'an, the writerly culture of ninth- and tenth-century Baghdad, and modern poetry. His edition and translation of Adonis's *A Time between Ashes and Roses* appeared in 2004. An anthology of New York City poems titled *The City That Never Sleeps* appeared in 2015.

Acknowledgments

I would like to thank Anna Bond and Linda Bree for their patience and guidance throughout the lengthy process of compiling and editing this volume. In addition, I wish to express my personal appreciation to the contributors, who have managed to persevere through multiple drafts and my many requests for changes, cuts, and additions. I hope they will see the finished work as worthy of their labors. Finally, I wish to extend thanks to my assistants who have helped with various aspects of editing and proofreading, including Philip Deslippe, Corinne Kalota, and Matthew Wilson, with particular gratitude to Sohaira Siddiqui, who worked on the final stages of the manuscript's preparation.

A note on terminology and transliteration

Technical terminology has been held to a minimum, but a few terms are so commonly used that they have been retained. Thus the Eastern Mediterranean region of the Arab World is referred to as the Mashriq (Arabic for "the East"; in other works sometimes spelled Mashreq) and North Africa is at times referred to as the Maghrib (Arabic for "the West"; elsewhere sometimes spelled Maghreb), and the term Levant (roughly Lebanon, Palestine, Jordan, and Syria) also makes a few appearances. Since the term "Berber" (derived from the same origin as the term "barbarian") is increasingly deemed outdated and even offensive, we have opted for the terminology that is now being used internationally: Imazighen (for Berbers as a people), Tamazight (as a global term for the Berber languages), and Amazigh (for the adjectival form of Berber, e.g., Amazigh culture). These and other terms are found in the Glossary at the back of the volume.

Academics have developed various systems for writing Arabic in Latin script that involve a large number of diacritical markings both above and below many letters. In order to make these essays more accessible to the general public, these markings have for the most part been avoided here; speakers of Arabic usually have no real difficulty understanding transliterations even without these markings, and for non-Arabic speakers they only serve to make those words opaque and hard to grasp. Only in the cases of some Arabic technical terms and words that are unfamiliar to all but specialists have full transliterations been included in parentheses according to the system of the *International Journal of Middle East Studies* (IJMES).

A large number of singers, artists, writers, movie stars, and other known figures have adopted their own preferred westernized spelling of their names, and many songs and film titles are also found in certain common English spellings: when these are mentioned they are sometimes accompanied by transliterations in parentheses. Since some books are published in English translation with titles that differ substantially from their Arabic originals, literary works are cited by a literal translation of the Arabic title with the transliteration in brackets, followed by the title of the English translation. For example, Tawfiq al-Hakim's *Diary of a Public Prosecutor in the Provinces* (*Yawmiyyāt nāʾib fī al-aryāf*, 1937; English translation, *The Maze of Justice*, 1947).

Several of these essays make references to online sources. Since copying out URL addresses is time consuming, and such addresses are often short-lived, wherever possible a general site (such as www.youtube.com) and keywords are listed instead. Only in cases where keywords will not lead to the desired link (such as on Arabic-language sites), have full URL addresses been given instead.

Chronology

1798	French invasion and occupation of Egypt under Napoleon Bonaparte
1801	Surrender and withdrawal of the French after defeat by Anglo-Ottoman forces; birth of Rifa'a al-Tahtawi
1805	Muhammad 'Ali (Mehmet Ali) officially recognized as governor of Egypt
1820–22	Muhammad 'Ali invades and conquers Sudan
1820	A series of "truces" establish the Trucial States (modern-day United Arab Emirates) as a British protectorate
1823	Birth of 'Ali Mubarak, author, educational reformer, and champion of modernization
1826–31	Egyptians sent to study in Paris accompanied by their chaplain, Rifa'a al-Tahtawi
1830	French invade and conquer Algeria, ruling for 132 years until Algerian independence in 1962
1835	Rifa'a al-Tahtawi founds the School of Languages in Cairo; establishment of the Egyptian Museum of Antiquities (later the Egyptian Museum)
1839	British forces occupy Aden (South Yemen)
1848	Algeria annexed and declared an integral part of France
1849	Death of Muhammad 'Ali; birth of Muhammad 'Abduh, Muslim religious reformer
1860	Violence between Christians and Druze in Mount Lebanon leads to intervention by French, British, and Ottoman forces
1861	British take control of Bahrain; birth of Jurji Zaydan, author and historian, whose series of historical novels were influential in shaping the *Nahda* (Arab Renaissance) vision of the Arabo-Islamic past

1869	Opening of the Suez Canal; completion of the Khedival Opera House in Cairo, inaugurated with a performance of Verdi's *Rigoletto*
1870	Establishment of the Egyptian National Library (Dar al-Kutub)
1871	Premiere of Verdi's *Aïda* in the Khedival Opera House, Cairo
1872	Establishment of the Teacher's College (Dar al-'Ulum) in Cairo by 'Ali Mubarak, combining traditional Islamic learning with Western education
1881	French Protectorate of Tunisia established and lasts until Tunisian independence in 1956
1882	Britain invades and occupies Egypt, effectively controlling the country until the 1952 Egyptian Revolution; 'Ali Mubarak publishes *'Alam al-Din*, a novel-like work in which the main characters debate the advantages and disadvantages of Western and Eastern culture
1883	Birth of Jubran Khalil Jubran, poet and writer, in Lebanon, later known as Kahlil Gibran after his emigration to the United States, author of *The Prophet*
1899	Kuwait becomes a British protectorate
c. 1904	Birth of Umm Kulthum, Egyptian singer who became the greatest Arab musical figure of the twentieth century
1911	Libya invaded by Italy and ruled until 1943 when it is seized by the Allies; birth of Egyptian novelist Naguib Mahfouz
1912	Morocco divided into Spanish and French protectorates that end with Moroccan independence in 1956
1916	Beginning of the Arab Revolt against Ottoman rule (Lawrence of Arabia)
1919	Treaty of Versailles ends World War I and divides the Middle East among the Western powers
1920	Beginning of French Mandate of Syria and Lebanon; beginning of British Mandate of Iraq
1921	Hashemite Prince Faisal placed on the newly created throne of Iraq by the British
1922	British Mandate of Transjordan established by League of Nations; nominal end to British occupation of Egypt, though effective control lasts until 1952
1923	Publication of Kahlil Gibran's *The Prophet* in English
1926	Republic of Lebanon declared
1928	Unveiling of the statue *Nahdat Misr* (Egyptian Renaissance) by Mahmoud Mukhtar

1932   Ibn Saud completes conquest of most of the Arabian Peninsula and declares the Kingdom of Saudi Arabia; Cairo Congress of Arab Music

1934   Establishment of the Academy of the Arabic Language (Cairo)

1934   Establishment of Egyptian State Radio

1936   Iraq granted nominal independence from Britain, but British troops remain; establishment of Egyptian national film studio

1943   Control of Libya wrested from Italy by the Allied forces

1945   Foundation of the League of Arab States, originally with six members (Egypt, Iraq, Transjordan, Lebanon, Saudi Arabia, and Syria); now includes twenty-two states

1946   Transjordan becomes an independent monarchy; Lebanon achieves full independence from France

1948   The United Nations recognizes the establishment of the Jewish State of Israel in Palestine

1949   Transjordan is renamed the Hashemite Kingdom of Jordan

1951   Libyan independence from Allied control

1952   Egyptian Revolution topples the monarchy

1953   Independent Republic of Egypt declared

1956   Nasser (Gamal 'Abd al-Nasir) becomes president of Egypt; the Tripartite Alliance (Britain, France, and Israel) invades Egypt and seizes the Suez Canal; after an international outcry, including pressure from the United States, they withdraw their forces

1958   Iraqi monarchy overthrown in a military coup

1961   Kuwaiti independence from Britain

1962   Algerian independence from France

1967   The "Six Day War" with Israel

1969   Egyptian film *al-Mumiya* (The Mummy) is released

1970   Death of Nasser; Anwar Sadat becomes president of Egypt

1971   Bahrain and United Arab Emirates become independent from Britain

1973   The "October War" (or "Yom Kippur War") with Israel

1981   Sadat assassinated by Islamists; Mubarak becomes president of Egypt

1988   Egyptian novelist Naguib Mahfouz awarded Nobel Prize for Literature

1996   Qatari-owned Al Jazeera Arabic satellite TV channel begins broadcasting

2003   Saudi-owned Al Arabiya Arabic satellite TV channel begins broadcasting

2006   Al Jazeera English news service begins broadcasting

2010   Self-immolation of Mohammed Bouazizi in Tunisia sets off large-scale demonstrations that unleash the "Arab Spring"

2011   Massive demonstrations in Egypt lead to the intervention of the Egyptian military and the toppling of the Mubarak regime

Dwight F. Reynolds

Modern Arab culture: introductory remarks

"The Arab World" – the very term places the Arab Middle East and North Africa into a category of its own, for no other cluster of modern nation states is so commonly referred to as a "world" in English political parlance. It is not necessarily an inappropriate label if it is taken as an indication that these twenty or so countries are bound together by certain shared cultural ties and yet at the same time possess their own distinctive local identities and histories.[1] One of the key challenges to exploring modern Arab culture is understanding the interplay between the larger shared history of the region – in essence, what makes Arabs Arab – and the dynamic regional and local identities that make this such a culturally rich and diverse area of the world.

The bond that unifies Arabs is first and foremost the Arabic language (similar to the role of English in the "English-speaking world"), but Arabic is a language that provides both a connection to a shared cultural heritage and a vehicle for the construction of distinct local identities. In its standardized written form, Arabic is used and understood by educated people from Morocco to Iraq and from Syria to Yemen. At the same time, however, the many distinct spoken dialect forms attest to the uniqueness of different regions, social communities, and even economic classes.

Written Arabic has changed remarkably little over time, so educated Arabs have access to a rich literary heritage that extends back some fifteen centuries. It has its roots in what appears to have been a poetic koine in pre-Islamic times that included features of various spoken dialects (similar to the koine of the Homeric poems) and was used primarily as a special register for the composition of poetry that could be understood across dialectal boundaries. After its revelation in the early seventh century, the Qur'an was accepted as the most eloquent example of the Arabic language and greatly influenced the later development of the language. The rapid spread of Islam in the eighth century led to an increased need to teach Arabic to non-Arabic-speaking peoples, so formal Arabic was codified in a set of grammatical rules that to a remarkable extent are still accepted and applied today. But this formal register of the language is no one's mother tongue and is rarely used in daily life. Instead, it is learned in school, is now used primarily for written communication, and is essentially the same wherever it is taught.

In contrast, the spoken dialects of Arabic are nearly as diverse as the Romance languages of Western Europe. Although much vocabulary and grammar is shared, certain sound shifts and different stress patterns at times make it difficult to understand even closely related words. Indeed, if the Arabic dialects had developed on their own as written languages at some point (as Spanish, Portuguese, Catalan, French, and Italian did), we might well now refer to "Arabic" not in the singular, but in the plural, or perhaps even as a family of languages. However, historical developments in the Arab Middle East, took a different path than in medieval Europe. Instead of allowing the standard form of the language to be supplanted with a host of vernaculars, the classical form of Arabic, due in part to the prestige accorded to it as the language of the Qur'an, has retained its position as the sole written form of the language. The dialects, on the other hand, have led a parallel, symbiotic existence as the primary means of spoken communication. The dialects are regional, whereas written Arabic is universal. Indeed, for over a millennium written Arabic has also been used far beyond the borders of the Arab World as a language of religion, literature, philosophy, and science among Muslims around the globe. In the past few decades, however, the technological revolution in broadcast and electronic communications in the form of hundreds of new satellite television channels and the advent of the Internet and social media has now put the spoken Arabic dialects in contact with one another in an unprecedented manner. Signs of rapid linguistic and cultural change are everywhere in the Arab World, but where those changes will eventually lead will not be known for quite some time. Arabic, the bond that holds the Arab World together, is undergoing dramatic transformations.

The Arabic language does more than open the door to a rich literary heritage, for in the Middle East one's mother tongue is also one of the most important markers of ethnicity, and ethnic identities often over-lap or intersect with religious identities. For outsiders who have been led by the Western mass media to believe that all Arabs are Muslims, and that Jews and Arabs are two separate and opposing peoples, it can be more than a bit confusing to learn that there are Jewish Arabs and Christian Arabs, as well as Muslim Arabs. Put quite simply, Arab identity is not based on religion any more than British, American, or French identity is, despite the presence of a dominant religious tradition in each of those countries. The dominant religion among Arabs is Islam, but being Muslim is not essential to being Arab, nor does being Arab mean that one is necessarily Muslim. Islam, Christianity, and Judaism are the three main religions of the Arab Middle East, and members of all three are native speakers of Arabic, and thus are Arabs. Arabs of these and of a number of other smaller religious traditions are very much participants in the larger sphere of "Arab culture" that is addressed in this volume. Indeed, the contributions of both religious and ethnic minorities have had a substantial impact on modern Arab culture.

Although the political, economic, and religious dimensions of the Arab World are those most often featured in Western media, the topic of this volume is Arab *culture*, the rich concatenation of language, literature, cuisine, music, cinema, theater, folklore, humor, television, radio, art, architecture, and other elements that make Arabs Arabs, whether they live in the Middle East or in the diaspora in other regions of the world. The essays included here are designed to provide a deeper understanding of modern Arab societies, a necessary counterpoint to the shallow coverage and staccato pace of news headlines. Although the focus here is on *modern* Arab culture, that is, of the past century or so, there are several broad historical processes that are critical to understanding the present state of the Arab World:

(1) the original spread of the Arabic language and Arabian culture beginning in the seventh century; in other words, the "Arabization" of what we now call the Middle East and North Africa;

(2) the impact of European colonization and the subsequent emergence of the independent Arab nation states that exist today;

(3) a cluster of important trends in political, religious, and cultural thought over the last century and a half, including the *Nahda* (the Arab "Awakening" or "Renaissance") of the late nineteenth and early twentieth centuries, the emergence of Arab Nationalism and Pan-Arabism, and the spread of conservative Islamist movements.

The historical spread of Arab culture

Before the seventh century and the advent of Islam, Arab tribes inhabited the Arabian Peninsula (modern Saudi Arabia, Yemen, Oman, the United Arab Emirates, Qatar, Bahrain, and Kuwait) and what are now the southern regions of Palestine, Jordan, Syria, and Iraq. Some were Christians, some were Jews, some were Zoroastrians, but most Arabs were pagans who worshipped multiple divinities, often in the form of idols, in a manner similar to the religions of ancient Greece and Rome. Bedouin Arab tribes led a nomadic existence that took them on migratory routes through the deserts of the Arabian Peninsula, but a large percentage of Arabs were sedentary, living in agricultural areas such as Yemen or in urban areas that survived to a great extent on trade, such as Mecca and Medina. Muhammad's call to monotheism in the form of Islam in the early seventh century set in motion great societal changes that, over a period of a century or two, led to the formation of a new Islamic community, the *umma,* in which tribal identities were gradually replaced or overlaid with a sense of being Muslim, an identity that quickly expanded to include non-Arabs. This same time period also saw a massive geographic expansion of the nascent Islamic Empire. Muhammad died in 632 and within a hundred years of his death the new polity controlled territories stretching from Spain in the west to the borders of India and China in the east.

It is a common misconception that these conquests consisted of large numbers of Arabs pouring forth out of the Arabian Peninsula who then occupied these extensive lands. Pre-Islamic Arabia was a sparsely populated region and there simply were not millions of Arabs waiting to fan out over these vast newly conquered territories and settle them. Instead, the conquests were driven to a great extent by new converts to Islam, as well as some mercenaries, who were recruited into the Muslim armed forces as the empire expanded. As each new city or region came under Islamic control, whether by conquest or capitulation, a basic political structure was set up for governing the region and the army was replenished with new volunteers, usually from the ranks of recent converts. By the time these armies reached North Africa or Iran or beyond, they were in fact very diverse bodies that included speakers of Arabic, Aramaic, Tamazight (Berber), Coptic, Greek, Kurdish, Latin, Persian, and other languages, united by their shared affiliation with Islam and led by a rather small number of ethnic Arabs.

The early Islamic military conquests were impressive, but not unique. This same region had, after all, seen similar empires and conquerors come and go. The Babylonians, ancient Egyptians, Alexander the Great, and Rome, for example, had all conquered comparably extensive territories – and the spread of Islam was similar to that of a number of earlier religions, such as the worship of the Greco-Roman gods, Mithraism, Manichaeism, and Christianity. What is perhaps most unexpected in the case of the Islamic conquests is that the Arabic language, which at that point had little written literature to speak of other than the Qurʾan, eventually supplanted a number of well-established languages and their literatures including Aramaic, Greek, Latin, and, for a short period, Persian. Over the course of many centuries, and in the wake of the spread of the Arabic language, ethnic identification with "Arabness" began to take root, as well.

One of the reasons for the spread of Arab identity is that both Islam as a religion and Arab ethnicity were well suited for expansion. In Islam a Muslim man may lawfully marry a woman who is Muslim, Christian, or Jewish (the primary requirement is that she believe in the One God and not be a pagan), and, in addition, she is not required to forsake her own religion. Their children, however, are considered Muslim from birth and must be raised as such. The same is true of Arab ethnicity, which is understood to be inherited through the father's line. Thus if an Arab Muslim soldier in Spain, for example, married a Christian woman and they had five sons, those sons would all be considered both Arab and Muslim (and not "half Arab" or "part Arab" as we might think of them today). If those five sons then married five local Christian women, all of their offspring would be considered Arab and Muslim, and so forth.

Over the centuries, a large percentage of the population of the Middle East became speakers of Arabic as their sole language, and Aramaic, Coptic, Greek, and Latin ceased to exist as spoken tongues. However, some languages survived in minority usage, including Tamazight (Berber, which is in reality a family of related languages and not a single tongue), Kurdish, and Nubian (in southernmost Egypt). The eastern and northern limits of the Arab World in modern times are in fact most clearly demarcated by language: the borders of modern Iran and Turkey roughly correspond to the edges of Turkish- and Persian-speaking cultures (although there are small enclaves of native Arabic speakers in both of those countries).

In essence, in modern times, an Arab is generally someone who speaks Arabic as a mother or primary tongue, or, in the case of Arabs living in the diaspora, who identifies ethnically as Arab. Arabs can be of any religion. The Arab World is also home to a number of non-Arab ethnic groups, defined primarily by language, such as Imazighen (Berbers), Kurds, and Nubians. But the situation is complicated, for there are also many people who speak Arabic as their mother tongue who have a sense of historical connection to a different ethnicity. This is particularly common in North Africa where the majority of the population was in the past ethnically Imazighen (Berber) – after many generations, even centuries, of speaking Arabic as their mother tongue, some now identify as Arab, but some do not. In contrast, there are also many native speakers of Arabic who now identify primarily in national terms, especially in those countries that have ancient histories of their own, such as Egypt, Iraq, Lebanon, or Syria, and only think of themselves as "Arabs" when speaking about the broader cultural or political context of the Middle East or in international terms, if indeed even then. Like all identities, "Arab" is a fluid concept that changes according to context. As will be clear from a number of the essays of this volume, the interaction between various identities in the Arab Middle East is a major component of modern Arab culture.

The era of European colonization

By the seventeenth century, nearly all of the Arab World had come under control of the Ottoman Turkish Empire, and most regions were at least nominally governed from Istanbul, though different areas experienced varying levels of autonomy. The main exceptions were Morocco in the far west, which repeatedly managed to repulse Ottoman incursions, and the sparsely populated interior of the Arabian Peninsula, along with some of the small principalities of the Persian Gulf. Although internal changes and transformations were already occurring in Arab lands in the eighteenth century, Napoleon's invasion of Egypt in 1798 provides a convenient starting point for understanding the extraordinary transformation of the region in the nineteenth and early twentieth centuries. It marks not only the beginning of more direct contacts with European culture, but also the opening gambit of a power struggle among Western nations that was played out in the Arab Middle East and that has continued unabated into the present day. Modern Arab culture has emerged in tandem with an unending series of Western interventions, military and otherwise, on

Arab soil. One cannot understand the situation of the modern Middle East without an understanding of the role these outside forces have played.

Napoleon invaded Egypt and Syria primarily to establish a French trading presence in the Middle East and to impede Britain's access to India. Although the French occupation of Egypt ended after only three years, it almost accidently set in motion a series of new political forces. When the French retreated, the new governor of Egypt, Muhammad ʿAli (who was ethnically Albanian and is sometimes referred to by the Turkish version of his name, Mehmet Ali), embarked on a program of modernization, primarily of the military and economic infrastructures. To do so, he sent a series of "study groups" or missions to France and elsewhere in Europe, the members of whom were meant to return to Egypt and help modernize their country. Nominally under Ottoman control, Muhammad ʿAli soon acquired such power that Egypt became virtually independent and was perceived to be a potential economic threat to European nations. The members of those study groups returned with new ideas not only about the organization of the armed forces, weaponry, engineering, agriculture, and so forth, but also about culture and education, and they began to write and publish books about their experiences. Newspapers began to be published, the government began to sponsor translations into Arabic of works from European languages, and European professors and teachers were brought to Egypt to teach in newly founded secular government schools.

In North Africa, however, the French set a very different process in motion. In 1830, they invaded Algeria and within a few short years had conquered the country. In 1848, they annexed Algeria to France and declared it not merely a French colony, but a permanent part of France. This move was accompanied by government-encouraged programs of emigration that led to hundreds of thousands of French citizens acquiring land and settling in Algeria. The French regime pursued a policy of "divide and conquer." They awarded privileges to Algerian Berbers and Algerian Jewish Arabs that were denied to Algerian Muslim Arabs. Jews, for example, were granted full French citizenship, a status that was denied to Muslims, both Berber and Arab. With the establishment of French military and political control in Algeria, and the initiation of administrative policies aimed at fostering religious and ethnic divisions, the colonial era in the Middle East had begun in earnest.

Eventually Britain, France, and Italy took advantage of the decline in Ottoman power to carve up the Arab Middle East into a variety of mandates, protectorates, fully annexed territories, colonies, and regions administered through capitulatory treaties in which rulers surrendered control of their finances, military, and foreign relations. With the ratification of the Treaty of Versailles after World War I, European powers effectively controlled over 85 percent of the Arab population. Although Arab leaders had repeatedly been promised independence and told that they would have a voice in choosing their own political future, their hopes were dashed at Versailles, and the future of the Arab World was instead decided by the Western powers.

Much of the political history of the Middle East over the last century is closely linked to the redrawing of the map in the aftermath of World War I. France and Britain played a large role in the creation of an independent state of Lebanon, which they conceived of as a homeland for the region's Arabic-speaking Christians, ignoring the realities of the mixed population. A united Iraq was created from three separate Ottoman provinces, though the fault lines between southern, central, and northern Iraq are discernible even today from news headlines. Libya, too, was pasted together from what had previously been separate provinces. Transjordan, including historical Palestine as well as what is now modern Jordan, was first brought into being as a British mandate, and the Kingdom of Jordan was later created "out of thin air" to fulfill British commitments to the Hashemite family of Mecca. The Hashemite Sharif of Mecca, Hussein, who revolted against the Ottomans during World War I at British instigation (in the Arab Revolt of 1916 that was made famous by the film *Lawrence of Arabia*), and three of his sons were each eventually given thrones: 'Abdallah became king of Transjordan (now Jordan), Faisal briefly ruled as king of Syria, but was then made king of Iraq, and 'Ali ruled after his father in the Hijaz for a short period before being overthrown by the Saudi family. The political boundaries of many of the modern Arab nation states have their origins on the drawing tables of Western politicians who were, quite literally, designing a new Middle East in the wake of the collapse of the Ottoman Empire during World War I.

Two decades later, at the end of World War II when the European powers were greatly weakened, a new postcolonial world began to emerge with former colonies around the globe declaring or demanding their independence. But in 1948, the West redrew the map of the Middle East one more time when the United Nations voted to establish a Jewish homeland in Palestine, against the will of the indigenous people of the region and those of all the surrounding territories. By doing so, the

West managed to solve one of its own difficulties, namely, what to do with the hundreds of thousands of Jewish refugees who had survived the Holocaust, but set in motion a series of conflicts that are sadly still with us today. Given the long history of Western intervention in the Arab World, it is not surprising that for many Arabs, the modern state of Israel, which was populated by a flood of Jewish refugees from Eastern Europe, is scarcely more than the last surviving European colony on Arab soil. Whether that attitude will change over time has yet to be seen.

Below is a brief listing of the Arab countries (from west to east) and a summary of their recent political history:[2]

* * *

Morocco – divided into Spanish and French protectorates in 1912; independence declared in 1956.

Algeria – invaded by France in 1830; annexed in 1848; independence declared in 1962 after 132 years of French occupation.

Tunisia – invaded by France in 1881; governed as a protectorate until independence in 1956.

Libya – invaded by Italy in 1911; governed from 1912 to 1943 as three (later two) Italian colonies; governed by the Allies from 1943; unified as a single independent nation in 1951.

Egypt – occupied by British military forces in 1882; fully or partially administered by the British until the revolution of 1952; declared the independent Republic of Egypt in 1953.

Sudan – conquered by Muhammad 'Ali, ruler of Egypt, 1820–22; governed as an extension of Egypt until the British occupation of Egypt in 1882; the Mahdist Revolt established an independent regime for a decade that was then overthrown by the British in 1899; ruled by the British via Egypt until the Egyptian Revolution of 1952; independence declared in 1956; the non-Arab, non-Muslim region of South Sudan voted to secede and was declared independent in 2011.

Palestine – occupied by British military during World War I; administered under the British Mandate of Transjordan from 1922 to 1947; declaration of the State of Israel in 1948 split historical Palestine; negotiations for an independent state of Palestine still ongoing.

Jordan – subsumed into the British Transjordan Mandate in 1922; established as an independent monarchy in 1946; name changed to Hashemite Kingdom of Jordan in 1949.

Lebanon – after violence between Christians and Druze in Mount Lebanon in 1860, an international commission separated Lebanon from Syria; governed from 1861 to 1918 by a non-Lebanese Christian governor appointed by the Ottoman sultan, but approved by European powers; from 1920 administered as part of the French

Mandate of Syria and Lebanon; the French created the Republic of Lebanon in 1926 that achieved partial independence in 1943 when Hitler invaded France; French forces attempted to retain control, but eventually withdrew fully in 1946.

Syria – an independent Kingdom of Syria declared by Faisal of the Hashemite family in 1920, but was almost immediately deposed by French military forces; administered as a French Mandate from 1920; a treaty of independence negotiated in 1936, but not ratified by the French Parliament; de facto independence with the fall of France to German forces during World War II; full independence recognized in 1946.

Iraq – administered as a British Mandate from 1920; the British created a monarchy and placed Faisal on the throne in 1921 after he had been expelled from Syria, and granted the new kingdom nominal independence in 1932 though they retained a significant military presence; in 1958 the monarchy was overthrown in a coup.

Saudi Arabia – the British supported the Arab Revolt against Ottoman rule by the Sharif of Mecca during World War I beginning in 1916; in the years immediately following World War I, however, Ibn Saud conquered and unified most of the peninsula, establishing the Kingdom of Saudi Arabia in 1932.

Yemen – the British occupied Aden (South Yemen) in 1839; Northern Yemen went back and forth between Ottoman and local control, was invaded by Italy in 1911, but declared its independence in 1918; South Yemen established in 1967 upon the final withdrawal of the British; the two Yemens unified in 1990.

Gulf States – consist of Kuwait, Bahrain, Qatar, the United Arab Emirates, and the Sultanate of Oman: Kuwait became a British protectorate in 1899 and remained so until independence in 1961; Bahrain was overrun by the British and remained a protectorate from 1861 until independence in 1971; Qatar became a British protectorate in 1916 and achieved independence in 1971; the seven small sheikhdoms that became the United Arab Emirates (Dubai, Sharjah, Abu Dhabi, Ajman, Fujayrah, Umm al-Quwain, and Ras al-Khaimah) were the target of British military expeditions from the first decades of the nineteenth century and, eventually, via a series of treaties or "truces" starting in 1820, became British protectorates (hence their early name of the "Trucial States") and became independent in 1971; Oman, like the interior of the Arabian Peninsula, was never under effective European control during the nineteenth and twentieth centuries.

* * *

The impact of the colonial period on Arab culture was enormous. Perhaps the most egregious example is that of Algeria where the French government outlawed the use of Arabic in government schools. For over a century Algerian Arabs were not taught anything about their own history and culture, but instead studied Molière, Voltaire, and Balzac. The introduction of Arabic into the public school system did not take place until after independence in 1962. And that independence came after a horrifically bloody war with France in the 1950s during which tens of thousands of Algerians died in the fighting or from disease in the French-run concentration camps in which much of the population was forced to reside as part of the French "counterterrorism" campaign. Even today, most Algerians over a certain age are unable, or scarcely able, to read and write formal Arabic, and instead read and write only French, though they speak their native spoken dialect of Algerian Arabic fluently.

As a result of the deep influence of European colonization in the Middle East, many countries of the Arab World have a cultural tilt toward the language and culture of the country that colonized them. Over the past century educated Arabs in North Africa, Lebanon, and Syria were most likely to speak French as a second language, while Libyans spoke Italian, and Arabs in Egypt, Sudan, Iraq, and the Gulf were more likely to know English. In more recent years, however, the use of English as a second language has been on the rise throughout the region. Another very substantial effect of the colonial period can be seen in the legal systems and constitutions of modern Arab states. These are patterned either more on the French or more on the English model depending upon their colonial past, and the appropriate role of Islamic law, or *shari'a*, is a topic of ongoing debate throughout the region.

Major intellectual and religious movements

The second half of the nineteenth century and the first decades of the twentieth are known in Arabic as the *Nahda*, a term that literally means "getting up" or "rising" from a prone position, which is commonly translated into English as the Arab "Renaissance," "Revival," or "Awakening." Though it started primarily as a linguistic and literary movement, it soon evolved to become the most important Arab cultural movement of the modern period. Arab intellectuals began with a sense that the ornate Arabic literary style of the past was not capable of expressing the new concepts of the modern age, nor was it conducive to writing newspapers, novels, books on science, and other modern genres. Interestingly, however, they did not adopt European terms for new ideas, but instead used the Arabic language's innate capacity to generate new words or reuse old ones for new purposes. This feature of Arabic had allowed it during the Middle Ages to create a vast new body of vocabulary to accommodate the translation of ancient Greek texts and new scientific discoveries (hence the transmission into English of Arabic technical terms such as algebra, admiral, algorithm, alkali, magazine, nadir, and others). The period of the *Nahda* was a similarly innovative and productive period of linguistic transformation.

This led to the writing of new Arabic dictionaries, the publication of the first encyclopedia in Arabic to incorporate Western European culture alongside that of classical Arabic, Persian, and Turkish cultures, the printing of newspapers and journals, and the publication of new editions of masterpieces of medieval Arabic literature on government printing presses. Systems of education, government administration, and financial institutions were overhauled and reformed as well. But it soon became clear that there was a fundamental question underlying all of these rapid changes: which aspects of Western civilization should be adopted because they were "modern" and which aspects should be shunned because they would lead to "westernization" and a loss of Arab identity and culture? It is a question that continues to be hotly debated even today.

Part of this question involves the issues of secularization versus religious reform. Some social groups, particularly the educated upper classes and religious minorities, such as Christians and Jews, championed a vision of an almost entirely secular future for the Arab World, in which religion would be redefined as a small, essentially private sphere that publicly intersected with only a limited number of issues such as marriage, divorce, family law, and religious rites. For other, more religious, groups, particularly educated Muslim leaders, this was unacceptable, though they at the same time recognized the need for modernization. These groups instead embarked upon a project of religious reform that would bring Islam "up to date" and allow an authentically Muslim and Arab culture to flourish in the modern period. These two tendencies, however, also engendered a conservative reaction that led to the formation of groups that are now termed "Islamists" (i.e., those who believe that legal and governmental systems should be derived directly from the Qur'an and religious law) or "Salafis" (i.e., those who wish to return to the model of governance practiced in the time of Muhammad and the first generations of the Islamic era). These movements constantly refer back to the earliest Islamic texts and traditions in a manner very reminiscent of the way some Americans refer back to the writings and intent of the "Founding Fathers."

The twentieth century also saw the rise of new political ideologies, termed Pan-Arabism and Arab Nationalism, that argued that the Arabs constituted a single nation and should work toward political unification. In the face of increasing European colonization of the Arab Middle East, especially in the aftermath of World War I and the Treaty of Versailles, various thinkers and leaders worked to promote the sense of Arabs as a single people possessed of a single language and heritage. These movements reached the pinnacle of their popularity in the 1950s and 1960s in the form of Arab Socialism, championed by Gamal ʿAbd al-Nasir, commonly referred to in English simply as "Nasser." The newly independent Arab nations made several attempts to overcome the political boundaries that had been imposed upon them by the Western powers; however, the differences between monarchies and republics, socialist versus non-socialist political orientations, and diverse regional identities, eventually led to the collapse of the larger Pan-Arabist political program. Despite its failure in practical terms, the Pan-Arabist ideal still appeals to many Arabs who see the splintered nationalisms of the modern Arab World as an unnatural and regrettable product of the colonial age.

A rapid glance at maps of the Middle East from three periods demonstrates the remarkable changes that have occurred in the region:

(1) in the years before European colonization, almost all of the "Arab World" was under the rule of the Ottoman Empire (see Map 1);
(2) in 1920, nearly all Arabs were living under various European colonial regimes (see Map 2);
(3) in the present, Arabs live in some twenty different nation states, or, in the case of Palestinians, as a stateless people (see Map 3).

After the heyday of Arab Nationalism in the 1950s and 1960s, an uneasy calm settled across the region. Strongmen, dictators, authoritarian states, and absolutist monarchies held the forces of discontent at bay. A number of these leaders and parties were initially deemed heroes for their resistance to the former colonial powers and for a period of time after independence were considered beyond reproach. Despite the simmering issue of Palestine and the series of wars with the Jewish State of Israel, there was little in the way of major political change or dramatic social upheaval for several decades from the 1960s to the new millennium. The seeds of change, however, were being planted in the dramatic demographic transformations in the Arab World: the soaring population has tilted the social balance toward ever larger numbers of young

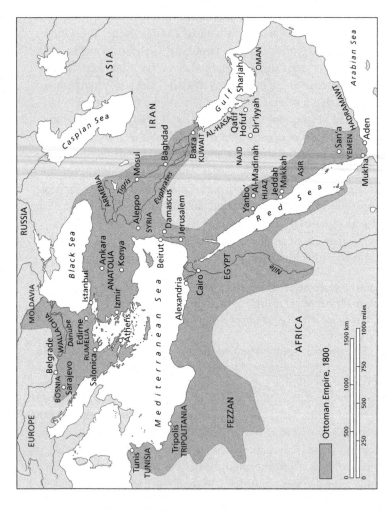

Map 1. The Ottoman Empire in 1800.

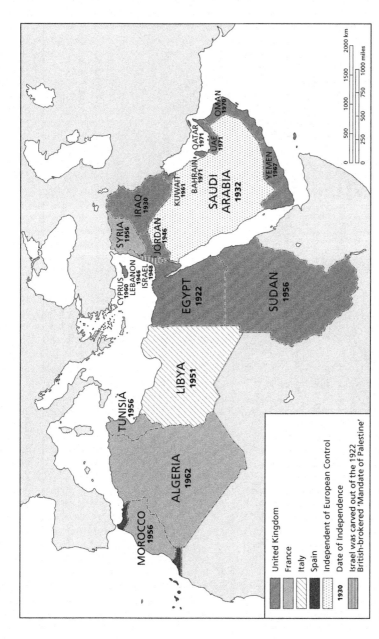

Map 2. European-controlled territories in the twentieth-century Middle East.

Legend:
- United Kingdom
- France
- Italy
- Spain
- Independent of European Control
- **1930** Date of Independence
- Israel was carved out of the 1922 British-brokered 'Mandate of Palestine'

MOROCCO 1956
ALGERIA 1962
TUNISIA 1956
LIBYA 1951
EGYPT 1922
SUDAN 1956
CYPRUS 1960
LEBANON 1946
ISRAEL 1948
SYRIA 1956
JORDAN 1946
IRAQ 1930
KUWAIT 1961
SAUDI ARABIA 1932
BAHRAIN 1971
QATAR 1971
UAE 1971
OMAN 1970
YEMEN 1967

0   500   1000   1500   2000 km
0   250   500   750   1000 miles

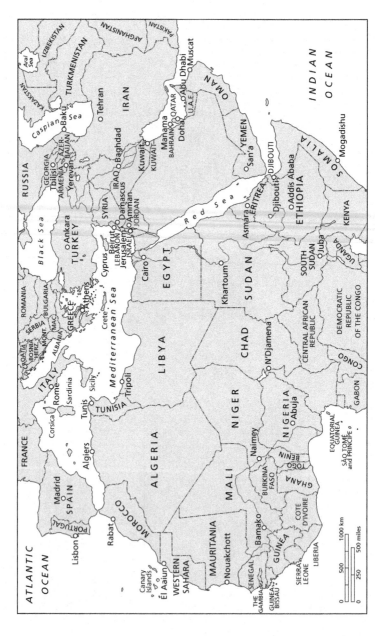

Map 3. Northern Africa and the Middle East.

people, often unemployed, discontented, and with little power to determine their own futures.

In the late 1990s, technological changes led to an explosion of new non-governmental satellite TV channels. For the very first time, Arabs had easy access to information and news broadcasts not produced or censored by the state. Music videos became one of the most widely consumed cultural products in the region. The spread of music videos was soon followed by the arrival of the Internet, social networks, and reality TV. A vibrant new "youth culture" emerged, at least among those affluent enough to be able to participate in it. But the licentious imagery of music videos, along with the open communication between the sexes now possible on the Internet, and other aspects of the new culture, drew the ire of conservative religious figures. In time, however, the conservative religious groups turned to those same media technologies and created religious satellite TV stations, religious music videos, and even religious game shows. The airwaves of the Arab World are currently filled with competing visions of Arab culture struggling to win the hearts and minds of the region's population, particularly of its young people.

In the midst of these dramatic cultural changes the events of 9/11 rewrote the relationship between conservative Islamic forces and the West, and, of course, sparked the invasion of Afghanistan and Iraq by the United States and its allies. Arabs throughout the region were glued to the broadcasts of the new satellite television stations, the most prominent of which are the Qatari-backed Al Jazeera (The Peninsula, a reference to the Arabian Peninsula) and the Saudi-backed Al Arabiya (The Arabic [Channel]). Westerners tended to focus entirely on the news broadcasts of these stations and, in particular, whether or not they supported American and European policies and military actions, but their true revolutionary characteristic was that they reached the entire Arab Middle East and were not directly linked to any one state apparatus. In some ways, the new technology is achieving the Pan-Arabist ideals of the mid-twentieth century. Among Arabs these stations became more widely known for talk shows and other formats in which issues that had never been mentioned on state-owned stations are openly discussed, including drug addiction, homosexuality, sexual satisfaction between married spouses, youth unemployment, sexual harassment in the workplace, and so forth.

Then, suddenly, in a series of events that no one had foreseen, starting in Tunisia in December 2010, the "Arab Spring" burst forth, fueled by deep-rooted feelings of discontent. Demonstrations, civil unrest, the toppling of regimes previously thought to be unchanging and unchangeable, open elections, new constitutions, counterrevolutions, and more, have all followed in quick succession. These political events will certainly produce dramatic transformations in Arab culture in coming years, though only the vaguest outlines of those changes are currently discernible.

* * *

It is against this background – of colonization, anti-colonial resistance, modernization, secularization, religious reform, conservative religious backlash, Pan-Arabism and Arab Nationalism, the imposed formation of nation states created on a European model, the sudden sweep of independence in the 1950s, the period of political stagnation, the events of 9/11, the invasions of Afghanistan and Iraq, the transformations of the media and the Internet, and now the Arab Spring – that modern Arab culture has emerged. The essays collected here are meant to provide an accessible introduction to some of the most important facets of that culture and to allow the reader to gain a deeper understanding of the cultural richness and diversity of one of the least well understood regions of the globe.

Although any of the chapters in the volume can be read in isolation, there is also a deliberate ordering to the initial chapters, designed to lay the groundwork for the later essays. Thus the opening chapter by Kristen Brustad, which tackles the social status of the Arabic language, is followed by Andrew Magnusson's discussion of ethnic and religious diversity in the Arab World. Next come Yoav Di-Capua's survey of the *Nahda* (the Arab Renaissance) and its impact on modern Arab culture and Joseph Lowry's examination of law and society in the modern Arab nation states. After this are essays on modern Arab poetry (Shawkat Toorawa), narrative (Muhsin al-Musawi), music (Scott Marcus), cinema and television (Andrew Hammond), theater (Dina Amin), art (Nuha Khoury), architecture (Nasser Rabbat), humor (Devin Stewart), folklore (Dwight Reynolds), food and cuisine (Juan and Magda Campo), and finally the impact of migration and the contribution of Arabs in the diaspora (Christina Civantos).

Notes

1 The League of Arab States, also known as the Arab League, currently includes twenty-two members: Algeria, Bahrain, the Comoros Islands, Djibouti, Egypt, Iraq, Jordan, Kuwait, Lebanon, Libya, Mauritania, Morocco, Oman, Palestine, Qatar, Saudi Arabia, Somalia, Sudan, Syria, Tunisia, the United Arab Emirates, and Yemen.
2 Not listed here are countries where Arabic speakers constitute only a small percentage of the population, even if they are members of the League of Arab States (such as the Comoros, Djibouti, and Somalia).

1

The question of language

Arabic is more than a tool for communication, it is an art form in its own right, a key element in Arab identity, and, as the language of the Qur'an, it has religious significance for all Arabic- and non-Arabic-speaking Muslims. This language has such a valued and venerated status in Arab culture that most Arabic speakers feel they have a stake in what happens to it. It would be unacceptable to millions of Arabic speakers for the language of the Qur'an and of a rich and diverse literary history to fall into disuse or lose touch with its past as it moves forward. And yet, Arabic must also serve the daily needs of its users and adapt to changing times. The question of language is closely related to questions of modernity: how can Arabic modernize without losing touch with its past? Centuries-old grammatical rules are closely tied to the Qur'an and are thus not easily discarded. The age of digital communication has opened up opportunities for public writing formerly reserved for the elite, and the resulting hybridity of form is of great concern to many. These are among the issues that concern many speakers and writers of Arabic.

Further complicating the situation is the significant contrast between spoken and written forms of Arabic. Some argue that spoken and written Arabic constitute different languages; however, this claim is based on impressions and feelings more than on linguistic facts and has to do largely with the way formal Arabic is taught in school. In general, school texts introduce a complex literary register of Arabic from the very beginning, so that the language of books is quite distant from the everyday language that children speak at home. There is also a relatively large degree of variation among spoken varieties across the Arabic-speaking region. The contact among these language varieties was previously quite limited, a factor that compounded the impression of insurmountable difference. Now, however, communication technologies have opened the airwaves, and the many varieties of Arabic are in contact with each other on a large scale for the very first time, changing their relationship to each other in ways we cannot yet fully appreciate.

Languages change over time, not just from contact with other languages, but through the internal dynamics of the language community itself. In any speech community, negotiation over the meaning and usage of words takes place constantly, and this is true of Arabic-speaking communities as well. However, in the Arab World this natural process of change conflicts with a deeply rooted belief that the modern versions of Arabic that people speak in everyday life are degenerate forms of a correct, pure Arabic language that has fallen into disrepair through the neglect of its speakers and must be restored.[1]

In this view, Arabic exists separately from its speakers in an ideal form which is of paramount importance. Arab culture thus tends toward what English linguist James Milroy calls a "standard language culture," which he defines as one in which speakers believe their language exists in "a clearly delimited perfectly uniform and perfectly stable variety."[2] In this worldview, when two or more forms exist, only one is deemed correct. Of course, this ideology exists to a certain extent in all cultures with a standardized language and is propagated to a great extent through formal education. In Arab culture, though, the ideal language has come to be defined in part by forms that are not used in the spoken idiom. Hence, "incorrect" forms abound and pose a danger to "correct" ones.

This essay explores the "question of language," that is, how Arabic can be both authentic and modern, as seen in public discourse over the past century or so, by identifying the various forms of Arabic, tracing their history, and touching on the recent impact of modern communication technology and the Arab Spring.

What do we mean by Arabic?

Arabic belongs to the Semitic family of languages and is thus closely related to Hebrew and Aramaic. Semitic languages share certain distinctive features, including a morphology based on consonantal roots used to derive word patterns with different syllabic patterns. For example, the root k-t-b has to do with writing and appears in words such as *aktub* (I write), *kitaab* (book), and *maktaba* (library, bookstore). English morphology, by contrast, relies heavily on prefixes (such as re- and pre-) and suffixes (such as –tion and –ing). Although Arabic was one of the last of the Semitic languages to emerge in writing, classical Arabic has many grammatical features that are considered to be very old, hence its grammatical system has played an important role in the reconstruction of the history of the Semitic languages.

Arabic inscriptions from the northwestern Arabian Peninsula (present-day Saudi Arabia, Syria, and Jordan) date to the early centuries of the Common Era and scholars trace a sophisticated and vibrant oral poetic tradition back to the fifth century. The seventh-century Qur'an, which Islamic tradition considers to have been revealed to the Prophet Muhammad orally, refers to itself as a "written text" (*kitaab*) in a context in which writing was known but not widely used, and in which the sacred books of Jews and Christians were a familiar category of writing. The Arabic writing system developed into its current form soon after the revelation of the Qur'an and the Arabic of this text and of the oral poetry was codified as a standard language in the eighth century, beginning with attempts to reconcile tribal variation into accepted norms of formal speech. The formal register was and is taught and learned through formal education and its religious importance and authoritative prestige have ensured its survival intact for some 1,300 years, not only among native speakers of Arabic dialects, but among Muslims everywhere.

Alongside the dissemination of formal Arabic, spoken Arabic spread widely and gradually via many waves of migration out of the Arabian Peninsula and surrounding areas into the Levant and North Africa, resulting in a fascinating and complex pattern of dialect variation. Unfortunately, we have no record of the everyday spoken language of earlier centuries, but early grammarians recorded some dialect forms. In addition, various "errors" found in written texts from the earliest periods indicate that formal Arabic has existed alongside the spoken dialects since the beginning of Arabic's recorded history. This evidence suggests that the variation found in Arabic today is not due to decline, but was the state of affairs from the very beginning. However, this view is not the one presented in most traditional accounts.

The existence of these two distinct language types or registers of Arabic, one used in writing and formal speech contexts and the other in spoken social communication, is often decried as an unfortunate state of affairs and a severe disadvantage to its speakers. Various labels for these two registers reflect their disparate status. Common terms for these two different registers include Classical Arabic or Modern Standard Arabic for the formal register and colloquial Arabic or dialect for the spoken. Classical Arabic refers to the language of the Qur'an and of the rich body of classical literature written in Arabic over more than a thousand years. Western scholars coined the term Modern Standard Arabic to designate the contemporary formal language variety used today in most forms of published writing as well as in formal speeches and media broadcasts. Those who distinguish between Classical and Modern Standard Arabic have in mind the rather obvious differences in vocabulary and style that have emerged over the centuries. Spoken forms of Arabic are often called "colloquial"; however, this term carries implications of inferiority that it is preferable to avoid. Collectively, we refer to them as Arabic dialects, but it proves difficult to separate and name them because political boundaries do not match linguistic ones. "Moroccan dialect" is thus a misleading term if one expects linguistic homogeneity – spoken Moroccan Arabic varies along regional and social lines, as all spoken languages do. As we would expect, the speech of educated people in capital cities (such as Cairo, Damascus, and Sana'a) serves in many regions as the most prestigious form of speech. We can best indicate the difference between these two types of Arabic by referring to them according to their social functions: as "formal Arabic" (primarily written, but also used in formal speaking) and as "spoken Arabic" (primarily oral, but occasionally used in informal writing).

Formal Arabic

Formal Arabic, which was originally called in Arabic al-'Arabiyya, is the literary register of the language. It was already a highly sophisticated poetic language in pre-Islamic times that was apparently widely understood while retaining some tribal and regional variation. Characterized by a complex case-inflected syntax and a rich vocabulary, it has lost little of either since grammars began to be written late in the eighth century CE. The golden age of literary and scientific production in al-'Arabiyya occurred in the ninth and tenth centuries, but it has remained in continuous use and still represents the ideal form of Arabic to speakers of the language. Its cultural value remains so high that words from this register are never considered to be "obsolete." Not only the Qur'an, but also many volumes on legal matters, theology, and literature continue to be read and studied today even though they were written hundreds of years ago. The contemporary term *al-Fusha* (pronounced "fus-haa") also refers to formal Arabic. The word *al-Fusha* itself means "the most elegant [language]," and reflects the continued cultural importance of being able to speak beautifully and correctly.

This is not to say that formal Arabic today is exactly the same language that was codified as *al-ʿArabiyya* centuries ago. Its Semitic morphological structure allows easy creation of new terminology to fit seamlessly into its grammatical system – something Arabic has done repeatedly throughout its history. And while the grammar remains fairly fixed, styles of writing have naturally varied and changed over time. Thus it is possible to say that the extent to which the classical and modern idioms differ is partly a matter of opinion and depends also on one's familiarity with the topic in question and its specialized vocabulary. The differences between Classical Arabic and Modern Standard Arabic have largely to do with changing cultural contexts and the expansion of human knowledge, both of which have necessitated the creation of large amounts of new vocabulary. The current upsurge in Islamist social and political movements in many areas has brought with it a revival of the classical heritage and one can find many medieval books posted on the Internet and discussed in various forums.

The western term "Modern Standard Arabic" refers to contemporary formal Arabic, especially the form of Arabic taught in many American universities and colleges. Modern Standard Arabic is sometimes used as a synonym for the language of journalism, which has itself shifted stylistically over the past century and continues to do so. These developments are sometimes, but not always, influenced by European languages. For example, the verb tense used in headlines in Arabic newspapers has shifted somewhat over the past decades from widespread use of the gerund ("Raising of the Euro's Value Yesterday") to the present tense ("University Signs Memo of Understanding"), but the most recent innovation of using the future tense ("Britain Will Help Algeria") is clearly an internal development. Here, as in other contexts, styles continue to evolve both locally and in parallel to international journalistic norms.

Lexical and stylistic variations notwithstanding, formal Arabic retains a high degree of uniformity throughout the Arabic-speaking world. Any educated Arab from Morocco to Iraq can open a newspaper or literary work from another Arab country and comprehend it. Formal Arabic has therefore played an important role in defining Arab Nationalism, the idea that all speakers of Arabic constitute a single people, for it is a mode of communication understood by all educated Arabs regardless of their geographic origin. In theory, educated elites from different countries or dialect regions rely on their knowledge of formal Arabic to communicate on issues of public or intellectual interest. In practice, few speakers of Arabic would ever attempt to use formal Arabic exclusively in a face-to-face conversation, because its degree of formality would be out of place in an interaction among peers. The degree of formality in a conversation between Arabic speakers from different regions depends on the topic and setting: a public conversation, such as might take place on a television program, will rely heavily on the vocabulary and style of formal Arabic; in a more private social context, on the other hand, speakers would simply use pronunciation and vocabulary they know to be widely understood and avoid local expressions and accents.

Formal Arabic is not "native" to any Arabic speaker and must be learned through formal education. Thus, someone will be a native speaker of her or his own dialect (e.g., some variety of Lebanese Arabic, or Moroccan Arabic), but her or his knowledge of formal Arabic depends on the level and type of education and exposure to formal Arabic that she or he has received. In most Arabic countries, speakers are also exposed to formal Arabic every day in the form of broadcasts of Qur'anic recitation, other religious programming and messages, news broadcasts, and other types of formal communication. Even speakers with limited ability to write or speak in formal Arabic can and do learn to understand much of what they hear around them in the way of sermons, announcements, and news reports on familiar, non-technical topics. However, Arabic speakers who have little or no exposure to this formal variety of the language, such as those who go to foreign schools in their own countries or live abroad, usually have a limited command of formal Arabic. The spread of private schools that teach in English or French contributes to the perception that knowledge of formal Arabic cannot be taken for granted for future generations.

In everyday life, an imperfect command of formal Arabic poses few problems, but the public sphere is more demanding. The ability to produce correct formal Arabic in the proper contexts carries with it intellectual and cultural prestige. It is important for intellectuals and political leaders to show solid command of formal Arabic, and failure to do so results in a degree of stigma. Use of formal Arabic is tied to expectations of correct grammar and style, meaning that the language form of any communication is judged as well as the content. Because of this great emphasis on form, eloquence, and conformity to an ideal, formal Arabic can be intimidating. The pressure of producing "correct" Arabic has led publishers to maintain in-house "language correctors," who do something comparable to the work of a western copy-editor, but in a much more exacting manner. This process can be illustrated by noting that the Arabic- and English-language networks of Al Jazeera differ in their treatment of language text editing. The Arabic network employs a group of language correctors in its Department of Language Accuracy. The English network, on the other hand, has no such department and the task of ensuring linguistic acceptability is the responsibility of the editor. Al Jazeera's administration knows that its Arabic programming will be judged not only on the accuracy of the content it reports, but also the correctness of the form.

Spoken Arabic

If formal Arabic is a fairly well-defined language register, spoken Arabic is the opposite, for it comprises all words and forms that are used by native speakers in their daily lives. Spoken Arabic itself is not uniform even for a single speaker, as she or he would most likely shift styles between work and leisure, family and strangers. Of course, this is not unique to Arabic; speakers of all languages use style to express social meanings. In Arabic, most of this variation centers on small pronunciation differences whose primary importance is social rather than linguistic. One of the most important functions of spoken Arabic (for which formal Arabic is utterly unequipped) is to carry information about geographical origin, social class, sectarian affiliation, and so forth. Arabic speakers have a keen awareness of this information, whether or not they can explain it, and this translates into a sense of wide dialect variation. Linguistically, the differences may be small, but, since they can communicate social, geographical, or sectarian identity, they are very important to both listener and speaker.

To what extent are dialects of Arabic mutually comprehensible? The answer to this question depends on many factors, some linguistic, most social. Arabic speakers who do not have contact with speakers from different regions are not always motivated to learn other dialects, especially when a higher prestige alternative such as English or French is available. One of the most important factors in the comprehension of

Table 1.1. *Arabic dialects compared*

	How are you?	I want	Government	Voice
Formal	*kayfa haaluk?*	*ureedu*	*hukouma*	*sawt*
Iraqi	*shlownak?*	*areed*	*hukouma*	*sowt*
Levantine	*keefak?*	*beddi*	*hukoume*	*sowt*
Egyptian	*izzayyak?*	*'aayiz*	*hukouma*	*sowt*
Moroccan	*la bas 'aleek?*	*bgheet*	*hkouma*	*sut*

different dialects is the speaker's education level: the more familiar-ity one has with formal Arabic, the easier it is to move among different forms of the spoken varieties. A few sounds are pronounced differently in different regions, but Arabic speakers learn to recognize these vari-ations merely by being exposed to them. Syllable patterns and word stress present more of a challenge for speakers trying to understand a new dialect, but this too can be overcome through exposure. This leaves vocabulary as the main challenge to cross-dialectal comprehension. The words that differ tend to be the most commonly used everyday expres-sions; thus one hears various expressions meaning "good," or "how are you?," or "I want," depending on locale, whereas the words for "govern-ment," "voice," and "to hear" are universal. The various expressions for "how are you?" and "I want" are all Arabic, but speakers of other dialects may not immediately recognize them as such (see Table 1.1). While it is true that original indigenous languages, such as Tamazight (Berber) in North Africa, Coptic in Egypt, and Syriac in the Levant, as well as the English, French, Italian, and Spanish of the European colonizers have all left traces in the local dialects, the Arabic character of the dialects is unquestionable.

Much scholarly attention has been devoted to the relationships among formal and spoken registers of Arabic. While most languages dif-fer in their written and spoken forms, some appear to differ more than others. In 1959, linguist Charles Ferguson hypothesized that a small group of languages including Arabic belonged to a special type of socio-linguistic situation that he named "diglossia."[3] He theorized that his-torical circumstances created these "diglossic" situations, which were characterized by a gap between the language of the educated and that of the lower classes. His study played a major role in shaping western aca-demic discourse on Arabic and has also been internalized by some Arab writers, who fear that "linguistic schizophrenia" is one of the major problems holding back the Arab World.

The idea that language variation was tied to social function was an important one and Ferguson's study launched a wave of investigations into functions of language variation. However, the characterization of Arabic as a "diglossic" language implies a bifurcation that is a vast oversimplification of linguistic reality. In Arabic, as in all languages, speakers use a range of forms that vary from the very formal to the very informal, and rarely remain at one end of the spectrum or the other. Semi-formal (and sometimes formal) contexts give rise to a mix of formal and spoken Arabic that contains features of both registers. Even when speaking about intellectual topics in a formal setting, speakers feel a certain unnaturalness about using "pure" formal Arabic in person-to-person communication and tend to mix it with some spoken forms that add an interactive touch. To put it another way, Arabic speakers often have choices in expressing meanings: they can choose more or less formal vocabulary, pronunciation, and grammar, including the literate forms of formal Arabic, the socially prestigious forms used in the capitals and among the middle and upper classes and on television, or the very local forms that express geographical, social, or sectarian identity. Terms such as "educated spoken Arabic" and "the Arabic of intellectuals" refer to a mix of spoken and formal Arabic often heard in formal contexts or on topics of public interest – and with the Internet and satellite television networks providing more and more contexts for public discourse, this type of Arabic is spreading. Thus the situation is far more nuanced than the binary relationship implied by the term "diglossia."

The characteristic most closely associated with Classical Arabic – and what school children focus on in Arabic classes – is the "case system" of grammatical endings. As in Latin, German, and Russian, nouns in Classical Arabic have endings that indicate their syntactic function. Thus the word for book is *kitaab* in both written and spoken Arabic, but in school children learn to write and read aloud *kitaab-un*, in which *-un* is an indefinite nominative ending (for example, the subject of a sentence), or *kitaab-an*, in which *–an* indicates that it is in the accusative (for example, the object of a verb), or *kitaab-in* in the genitive (for example, after a preposition or to indicate possession). These endings appear in print in the Qur'an, in school textbooks, and editions of classical texts, especially poetry; they are heard in news broadcasts and other formal speeches,

Table 1.2 *Levels of Arabic*

Classical Arabic (case endings superscripted):
  sa-yusaafir^u r-ra'ees^u l-yawm^a ila l-yaman^i
Modern formal Arabic (with no case endings):
  sa-yusaafir ir-ra'ees il-yawm ila l-yaman
Levantine spoken Arabic:
  rah ysaafir ir-ra'ees il-yowm 'a-l-yaman

---

usually when the speaker is reading from a text. Unlike German and Russian, these endings are not used in everyday speech in Arabic and thus are not part of most speakers' linguistic competence. The endings in Table 1.2 are classical, modern formal, and spoken Levantine versions of the sentence, "The president will travel to Yemen today" (the word order in Arabic is: will travel the president today to Yemen).

Does the existence of mixed registers threaten the existence of formal Arabic? Or does it, on the contrary, extend the reach of formal Arabic to new audiences and new speakers? Ferguson described diglossic situations as the result of a long period of time in which a formal language is quite limited in use to a privileged few. This certainly applies to the history of Arabic, in which literacy was quite limited until the latter part of the twentieth century when universal education was sponsored by newly independent Arab governments (many colonial governments limited access to education to a small number of elites). The spread of education and greater participation in public discourse has led to a spread of formal Arabic not as a closed system, but as a register available to more Arabic speakers than ever before.

Arabic and the West

Although many processes of language change are internal to a culture, the recent history of Arabic is also intertwined with the Arab encounter with the West. The European colonial powers made both language policy and language study an object of their attention, and Arab elites grappled with questions of language as they sought to modernize their own societies under colonial domination. The debate about the current state of Arabic as perceived by its speakers and what to do about it is in part the product of the colonial era. The question of language was first raised by Egyptian and Syrian writers in the late nineteenth century in the scientific digest *al-Muqtataf*. They asked whether the great distance between Classical Arabic and the language of the masses hindered the access of common people to knowledge. If so, might it not be prudent to use a more accessible form of Arabic for educational purposes, at least temporarily? Unfortunately, dialog on this question ended rather abruptly following a public lecture by British irrigation engineer Sir William Willcocks, in which he called for the abandonment of formal Arabic in favor of the spoken idiom. The idea of using the spoken dialects as written languages quickly became linked to colonial designs on dividing and ruling the Arab World, since the loss of formal Arabic as a uniting language would sever communications with each other as well as with the past.

During and after the struggle for independence, the Arabic language became entwined with Arab Nationalism. The consequence was that *al-'Arabiyya*, as the shared language of Arabic speakers in the larger unfulfilled Arab nation, came to represent the once and future dream of pan-Arab nationhood. As such it took on – and retains – a powerful symbolic worth. At the same time, aspirations for a pan-Arab state were denied as World War I ended. The denial of political unity was seen as parallel to the colonialist attack on formal Arabic. Willcocks's call for the use of colloquial Arabic in place of formal Arabic in the nineteenth century contributed to the abortion of an important discussion of the possible use of a spoken register of the language to help educate the masses.[4] Incidents such as this help us understand why westerners' interest in learning a dialect is sometimes met with mistrust and suspicion on the part of Arabic speakers.

The situation in Morocco, Algeria, and Tunisia deserves special mention here. French colonial governments promoted education in French and, in Algeria in particular, outlawed education in Arabic, resulting in an educated class illiterate in its mother tongue. Algerian Arabic in particular has a notable quantity of French lexical items, giving rise to the impression that "North Africans speak French, not Arabic." Despite the passage of nearly fifty years since independence and the establishment of Arabic language education, French still retains a great deal of social and professional prestige.

Increasingly, knowledge of English or French represents an important economic opportunity to job seekers. Tourism, international business, and technological expertise all demand knowledge of at least one of these languages. Formal Arabic skills are not in high demand among employers. This lack of currency/prestige is also reflected in college entrance requirements. Acceptance into a university is not universal but by department and is based on comprehensive high school examination scores. Admission to the Arabic department in most Arab universities has the lowest required scores of all subjects.

The colonial legacy in the Arab countries has left its mark on language use, most tangibly in expressions one hears repeatedly, such as *merci* in Egypt, *Hi, bonjour* and *bonsoir* in Lebanon, and *ça va?* in North Africa, to name a few common phrases that are part of the language of everyday exchange whether or not the speakers know French or English. It is not that these expressions have supplanted Arabic ones, but rather that the speakers use them to signal their own social and cultural identity. In the upper socioeconomic classes in many countries, a mix of Arabic with French or English expresses a complex code of identity politics. The mix of English and Arabic prevalent among youth in Jordan, Egypt, and the Gulf has even been named *Arabeezy* (from '*Araby*, Arabic plus Ingleezy, English). Knowledge of these codes implies a life of privilege, including private education, travel abroad, and sophistication. Among young people especially, to be confined to one language – especially if that language is Arabic – is backwards and perhaps even "hickish."

Arabic in danger

Is Arabic really in danger? For the past quarter century, a steady stream of articles, books, and television shows have been urgently raising this question. Why? Arabic is the official language of the twenty-two member nations of the Arab League. It has been in widespread continuous use as a spoken and written language for approximately 1,500 years. Today, with the spread of education and the subsequent increase in literacy, Arabic is used by more people and in more ways and venues than ever before. The recent proliferation of satellite television channels has put Arabic-speaking peoples in contact with each other across political and geographical divides. People are being exposed to dialects from distant regions. The Internet has opened the door for millions of Arabs from different regions to communicate with each other through the public sphere.

Yet, despite this linguistic renaissance, the second half of the twentieth century saw a steady increase in the number of news articles and television programs warning of the demise the Arabic language. The danger described by these articles is twofold: first, the encroachment of

European languages, especially English and French; second, the spread of the use of spoken forms of Arabic. This danger is so great, claim some authors, that Arabic may suffer irreparable damage and Arabs as a result would lose touch with their heritage.

The first danger is easy to perceive and to understand. English and French are more widely known and used now than ever before. In addition, knowledge of formal Arabic does not provide the kind of job opportunities that knowledge of English or French does. The most desirable employment opportunities are those connected with tourism and business, and generally require either English or French (and in some places, both). English and French are associated with and reflect modernity, education, and a high socioeconomic status. For many Arabic-speaking students (and their parents), the question of language is one tied more directly to earning a living and status than it is to cultural or national identity. Learning English or French (or both) is far more important than mastering the complex grammar of formal written Arabic.

Also, as language mixing gains ground across the Arabic-speaking region, it has also contributed to a renewed sense of the danger. Can Arabic in any form survive in the face of not only the economically dominant English and French languages, but also language mixing? The perception that foreign languages pose a danger to Arabic has been a recurring theme since the nineteenth century. It should come as no surprise that a renewed sense of danger has emerged at a time when the economic future of the Arab World is increasingly dependent on the West and when many Arab economies are stagnating.

The danger posed by the dialects of spoken Arabic is a more complex question and reflects in part the view that contemporary dialects are the result of generations of imperfect learning. Seen in this light, spoken Arabic represents a very real threat to formal Arabic, because these "mistakes" have become internalized and fossilized, and even the spread of formal education does not seem to be succeeding in erasing them. In addition, danger lies in the perception that spoken forms are encroaching upon written contexts to a greater degree than ever. Dialect forms of Arabic have appeared in literary written contexts for centuries (a fact that many speakers of Arabic do not know), but only to a limited degree and, in modern times, under a censor's control. A few literary writers made use of some dialect forms to convey humor, social criticism, and political satire in the nineteenth and twentieth centuries, and even this limited usage was not quickly or universally accepted. The Internet has, of course, transformed the nature and accessibility of writing itself. Until very recently, writing in the public sphere was under the tight control of autocratic regimes, in whose interest it was to promulgate the ideology of correctness. Few people had incentive to write.

Language usage on television is noticeably different now than it was thirty years ago, with more programming shifting from formal Arabic to spoken. News broadcasts have traditionally been the bastion of pure formal Arabic; recently, however, some networks have begun presenting parts of their news broadcasts in a mixed register that incorporates elements of spoken Arabic. For decades, television series (soap operas) made in the United States and Mexico were subtitled or dubbed into formal Arabic, but the early 2000s saw a reversal of this practice. Now, for example, Moroccans watch Mexican series in Moroccan dialect, and people from Morocco to the Gulf watch Turkish series dubbed into Damascene dialect. The United Arab Emirates, which has been home to dialect mixing on a large scale since the 1970s due to its large non-native population, has started producing serials with multiple dialects interacting on screen. The exposure of audiences to, and their engagement with, wide varieties of spoken Arabic at a previously unseen level will have lasting effects on Arabic, most importantly a shift in ideology that is more accepting of variation within the Arabic language.

Finally, educational systems whose goal it was to enable their pupils to function competently in formal Arabic have done poorly in many areas. The estrangement of Arabic speakers from formal Arabic often begins with the way it is taught in school, dominated by traditional ways of teaching that stress form over function and rely on examples largely divorced from real life. Memorization is stressed at the expense of comprehension. This kind of approach has led many young learners of formal Arabic to dislike the experience and consequently the language itself. It is also worth noting that articles have appeared in some newspapers in recent years protesting that (government-run) final examinations in Arabic language are too difficult, citing complaints of students' parents, who seem not to believe that the kind of Arabic competency being taught in public schools has value for them.

Arabic in the twenty-first century

Two developments at the end of the twentieth century and the beginning of the twenty-first have contributed to the demise of the state's erstwhile control of language in the public sphere and initiated access to and motivation for public participation. First, the rise of satellite television opened up the airwaves to the public for the first time with real forums for the discussion of important and urgent topics: the war on Iraq, the Palestinian Intifada, unrest in Cairo. These kinds of topics were not the subject of debate in public forums until Al Jazeera started asking people on the street about their opinions and perspectives on what was happening. In addition, youth programming on popular culture brought hosts from Tunisia, Egypt, Lebanon, and elsewhere, and listeners became familiar with new accents. Different dialects as well as formal and spoken Arabic first coexisted, then interacted.

The international and inter-Arab nature of satellite television has had several key consequences for the language of broadcast and also its effect on audience. After years of government-controlled television, audiences in countries such as Egypt and Syria can now watch programming from around the world. Arabic networks like MBC (Middle East Broadcasting Center) broadcast from Europe to pan-Arab audiences and their programming reflects the broad spectrum of taste and demand: soap operas from Syria, Kuwait, and Egypt; American films; pop culture shows with Tunisian, Egyptian, and Lebanese hosts. The "Star Academy" talent show aired by LBC (Lebanese Broadcasting Corporation) brings together aspiring young performers from across the Arab World with their mix of dialects and has them live together (belying the theory that Arabic speakers communicate with each other using formal Arabic). Al Jazeera, LBC, and other satellite networks provide opportunities for interaction among Arabic speakers from Morocco to the Persian Gulf. Interactive programming, including unrehearsed interviews and live audiences, provides a kind of linguistic democracy that allows participants to respond in the register or mix of their choice.

Soon after the proliferation of satellite television, writing took a quantum leap with the rise of the Internet. The salient characteristics of this new space include its international, inter-Arab, nature, the difficulty of censoring and blocking access to it, and the democratizing nature of satellite media and the Internet. As one might expect, the opportunity to express oneself to a large group of potential readers and sympathetic interlocutors with no censors in the way has been a powerful incentive to write. Writing conventions in forums and chat rooms are still evolving. The comments section on these and other websites contains an interesting mix of register, as do many internet forums. Chat rooms and social media have given rise to new transliteration systems that allow communication in a mix of registers and demonstrate that contemporary language use continues to evolve, and technology is playing a key role in pushing us further from the old ideological terms of the debate.

Thus it appears that the "internet generation" has a rather different relationship with Arabic than previous generations. While Classical Arabic remains important to them as the language of Islam, many do not seem to buy into the ideology that other forms of Arabic are somehow less worthy, degenerate forms of that language. The collapse of the authority structure includes at least a partial collapse of standard language ideology.

In other words, there was a revolution in language going on even before the youth took to the streets in Tunisia, Egypt, and elsewhere. This revolution was not so much about new language forms being used, but rather about a shift in speakers' views of language itself. To what extent should Arabic exist and be used in public space only in its standard "correct" form? Can there be linguistic plurality? Increasingly, Arabic speakers are answering that in the affirmative through their usage and this subtle ideological shift is where the real "danger" to Arabic lies.

What all this means is that the young generation has more power than ever to affect language use. Responses to the question "Is Arabic in Danger?" on an Al Jazeera online comment page were polarized, with a majority still defending formal Arabic. On the other hand, several voices blamed the state of formal Arabic on the fact that its own guardians had made it irrelevant.

As a language without native speakers, formal Arabic will continue to live a life dependent in part on the spoken varieties. But spoken Arabic is equally incomplete without the vast vocabulary reserves and structures of formal Arabic. So-called "educated spoken Arabic," which is appropriate for use in a public context, is spreading as more speakers are educated and are gaining access to such a platform. The hope during the Arab Renaissance (*Nahda*) that a revival of formal or Classical Arabic could eradicate the degenerate forms of spoken Arabic seems to be of little concern to the Arab Spring generation, who communicate with each other and the world with all the linguistic tools they have available. The sophisticated competence of these speakers to control multiple registers of language demonstrates the powerful flexibility of Arabic to respond to new challenges. In the end, the two realms will remain intertwined, as they have long been, and this may be one of the best arguments that Arabic is alive and well, and not in danger at all.

Notes

1 One way this belief manifests itself is in the reluctance of many Arabic language programs, especially in the Middle East, to teach students spoken forms of the language, preferring to give instruction to foreigners only in "correct" (i.e., formal) Arabic.

2 James Milroy, "Language ideologies and the consequences of standardization," *Journal of Sociolinguistics*, 5 (November 2001), pp. 530–55.

3 Charles Ferguson, "Diglossia," *Word*, 15 (1959), pp. 325–40.

4 Sir William Willcocks, "Syria, Egypt, North Africa and Malta speak Punic, not Arabic," *Bulletin de l'Institut d'Egypte*, 8 (1925–26), pp. 1–37.

2

Ethnic and religious minorities

It is appropriate, although perhaps not intuitive, that a volume dedicated to Arab culture – a culture defined by ethnicity and usually associated with Sunni Islam – should include a chapter on ethnic and religious minorities. For, contrary to popular belief, the population of the Arab World is remarkably diverse both ethnically and religiously, and even those who do not identify with the dominant ethnicity or religion contribute to Arab culture. Indeed, ethnic and religious minorities are among the leading producers, consumers, and critics of Arab culture. It is best to appreciate their contributions within this cultural framework rather than in isolation.

The term "ethnic and religious minorities" refers here to any segment of the indigenous population that does not identify as Arab or Sunni Muslim. The largest non-Arab ethnicities in the region are Armenian, Imazighen (Berber), Kurd, and Nubian, though there are also a number of smaller ethno-linguistic groups, especially in Sudan. Within the Arab World, language is the primary marker of ethnic identity, meaning that ethnic minorities are most often distinguished by the fact that they do not speak Arabic as their mother tongue. Members of minority ethnic groups use their own languages, especially within their communities, though they increasingly speak Arabic too, particularly in urban areas. Conversely, those who speak Arabic as their main language often identify ethnically as Arabs; some North Africans, for example, are of Amazigh (Berber) descent but consider themselves Arabs because they primarily speak Arabic.

Shiʿite Muslims are by far the largest religious minority in the Arab World. They actually outnumber Sunni Muslims in Bahrain, Iraq, and Lebanon. Most Arab Shiʿites are Twelvers, meaning that they recognize the Twelve Imams, descendents of the Prophet Muhammad, as the heirs of his spiritual and political authority. The Alawi and Druze sects also recognize Imams, each claiming that a particular Imam was a divine incarnation. Christians constitute the second largest group of religious minorities in the region. The Coptic Orthodox Church has the most adherents and is an independent church led by the Coptic Patriarch. Arab Catholics are the next most numerous: some follow the Latin Rite, but most, such as Maronites and Chaldeans, belong to churches that have distinct ecclesiastical hierarchies and liturgical languages, yet are in communion with Rome. The ecclesiastical leader of the Greek Orthodox Christians, the third largest denomination, is the Patriarch of Constantinople. Finally, there are the smaller independent Eastern Syrian, Armenian, and Assyrian churches, each with its own patriarch. The independent Eastern, Catholic, and Orthodox churches split from one another during the first centuries after Jesus' death over jurisdictional disputes or doctrinal controversies about the nature of Christ. Before 1948, Jews were a significant religious minority in the Arab World. Most have since migrated to Israel, where they are known as the "Sephardim" or "Mizrakhim." A few thousand Arab Jews remain in Arab countries, with the largest concentration in Morocco. In addition to Shi'ites, Christians, and Jews, there are a number of smaller groups of religious minorities scattered throughout the Arab World.

This chapter examines the role of minorities in the formation of Arab culture over the last century. In particular, it focuses on their contributions to politics, literature, music, and cinema. The chapter concludes with a discussion of the historical vulnerabilities of ethnic and religious minorities in the region, the challenges they face at present, as well as their prospects for the future.

Intellectual and political movements

Ethnic and religious minorities have been at the forefront of many major intellectual and political movements in the Arab World, including the Arab Renaissance (*Nahda*), Arab Nationalism, and Islamism. The Arab Renaissance was a late nineteenth and early twentieth century effort to revive Arabic as a language of intellectual and political discourse, for which Arab Christians deserve much of the credit. They produced the first modern Arabic encyclopedia, dictionary, grammar, and thesaurus.[1] Aided by the spread of literacy and print technology, Arab Christians wrote books, published newspapers, and translated European literature into Arabic. Adherents of all faiths participated in the production and consumption of print media during the Arab Renaissance, but Lebanese Christians disseminated much of this material because they owned the first commercial printing presses, publishing houses, and newspapers. For example, Catholic immigrants from Lebanon started one of Egypt's most famous daily newspapers, *al-Ahram* (The Pyramids), in 1875.

The main centers of the Arab Renaissance were Beirut and Cairo, cities with relatively large Christian populations. The schools built by American Protestant and French Catholic missionaries were a major source of inspiration and led to the establishment of the first Western-style colleges in the Arab World, including the Syrian Protestant College (now the American University of Beirut), the University of St. Joseph, and the American University in Cairo. Several of the leading figures of the Arab Renaissance were graduates of these institutions. Butrus al-Bustani, in particular, epitomizes the spirit of the Arab Renaissance. A Lebanese Maronite Christian, al-Bustani converted to Protestantism and produced a modern Arabic translation of the Bible. His conversion highlighted the social and political isolation of Arab Protestants in the Ottoman Empire. Christians were normally subject to the authority of indigenous church hierarchies, but al-Bustani was ostracized by the Maronites after his conversion. Effectively disenfranchised, he called for the separation of religion and politics. The sectarian violence that plagued Lebanon and Syria in 1860 troubled al-Bustani and he encouraged the inhabitants of the region to develop a patriotism that transcended religion. Lebanese dominance of the Arabic print industry ensured that secularizing messages like al-Bustani's reached a wide Arab audience.

Arab Nationalism was in many ways a natural outgrowth of the Arab Renaissance. Introduced to the idea of nationalism through European literature and missionary schools, Arab Nationalists sought the establishment of a secular Arab state. In fact, Arab Nationalism was a secular movement in part because so many of its leading proponents either were Christians or had been taught by Europeans to regard nationalism as a secular project, often both. At the same time, Arab Nationalists calculated that a secular state would deprive imperialists of an excuse to intervene in the region on behalf of religious minorities and that opposition to the Zionist colonization of Palestine would be more united when framed in national rather than religious terms. They likewise believed that a non-sectarian government would appeal to religious minorities, the best-educated segment of the Arab population and the one most comfortable petitioning European governments for support.[2] However, in the wake of World War I, Britain and France divided and colonized the region, confounding the aspirations of Arab Nationalists for a unified secular Arab state.

Once these colonies achieved independence after the end of World War II, and the beginning of the Cold War, the Arab Nationalist movement took a Marxist-socialist turn. Nevertheless, Christians remained in the vanguard. Michel Aflaq, a Syrian political philosopher of Greek Orthodox descent, formulated a socialist version of Arab Nationalism known as Ba'athism (Resurrection). It called for social justice and political revolution to unite the newly independent Arab states. Ba'athists seized power through military coups in Syria in the 1950s and in Iraq a decade later. Although political unification failed, Ba'athism remained the preferred ideology of military dictators such as Hafiz al-Assad and Saddam Hussein, who used its strict secularism to suppress religious dissent. Ba'athists still rule Syria over half a century after coming to power and the Ba'ath Party dominated Iraqi politics until it was banned after the US invasion in 2003.

Islamism is the most recent political trend to sweep the Arab World. Islamists are religious nationalists who seek to reorder politics and society around Islamic values. The popularity of Islamism has grown since the late 1960s at the expense of secular Arab Nationalism, which failed to sufficiently stimulate economic growth, provide social services, and confront Israel. To achieve these goals, Islamists seek a greater role for religion in society. They are not necessarily fanatical, violent, subversive, or anti-democratic; in the places where Islamists are allowed to participate openly in politics, they work within the system to shape society according to their religious views. However, fearing their growing popularity, many autocratic regimes have banned Islamist groups, thereby eliminating all but the most extreme avenues for religious dissent. This is beginning to change.

Shi'ites are among the Arab World's most successful Islamists. Shi'ites were underrepresented in Lebanon's parliament for decades until they began to clamor for political power in the 1960s with the help of a cleric named Musa al-Sadr. He founded the Higher Shi'a Islamic Council, which afforded the community independent political recognition for the first time. Al-Sadr also campaigned against poverty in southern Lebanon, a Shi'ite stronghold, and established a militia – as other sects did – to defend the community's interests during the Lebanese Civil War (1975–90). Al-Sadr disappeared in Libya in 1978, but the movement that he inspired, Amal (Hope), remains a powerful force in Lebanese politics. Nabih Berri, the current Speaker of Lebanon's parliament, is a member of Amal.

When Israeli forces invaded Lebanon in 1982, another Shi'ite militia, known as Hizballah (Party of God), arose to drive them out. Hizballah later became a political party led by the cleric Hasan Nasrallah. It is beginning to eclipse Amal in representing Shi'ite interests, caring for the poor, and defending Lebanon's borders. Hizballah's unwillingness to disarm its militia is a point of contention with the Lebanese government and causes some observers to fear the party's increasing influence. But many in Lebanon view Hizballah favorably, as an efficient distributor of social welfare, less corrupt than other political parties, and stronger than the national army. Hizballah appeared to earn that reputation in 2006 when its militia resisted another Israeli invasion and its representatives were the first on the ground with reconstruction aid. Thus, Hizballah represents the potential of Shi'ite Islamism in the Arab World.

Shi'ite Islamists have had mixed success in Iraq. Saddam Hussein did not tolerate political activism among Shi'ite clerics during the 1980s, fearing that Iran's Islamic Revolution would spread across the border. However, after an uprising by the Shi'ite majority in the wake of the 1991 Gulf War, Hussein realized that silencing the clergy had not led to Shi'ite quiescence. Saddam therefore sought to co-opt a popular Shi'ite cleric named Muhammad al-Sadr (a distant cousin of Amal's founder). Al-Sadr used the latitude given to him by the regime to amass a larger following. At the same time, he became increasingly critical and defiant of the government. Hussein had al-Sadr assassinated in 1999.

After the 2003 American invasion of Iraq, al-Sadr's son, Muqtada, assumed his father's mantle. While other clerics refused to denounce the occupation because it empowered Shi'ites, Muqtada was an outspoken critic. His Mahdi militia orchestrated an insurgency against the American troops, and when Sunni–Shi'ite violence spiraled out of control in 2006, Muqtada authorized, at least tacitly, the sectarian cleansing of religiously mixed neighborhoods in Baghdad. Despite his popular appeal, Muqtada lacked his father's religious credentials. He could call for a boycott of elections or condemn collaboration with the American-backed government, but his preaching had little religious sanction. In fact, Muqtada was forced to defer on several occasions to

Grand Ayatollah 'Ali Sistani, the leading Shi'ite cleric in Iraq. Sistani cleverly undercut Muqtada's popularity by condemning sectarian violence and attacks on American forces while maintaining a dignified detachment from politics. Nevertheless, Sistani emerged a real champion of democracy, encouraging Shi'ites to exercise their right to vote and forcing the Americans to hold elections when they preferred to appoint Iraqi officials. Sistani accomplished all of this without ever sanctioning the invasion or occupation of Iraq. Outmaneuvered in the religious arena, Muqtada laid down his weapons and joined the political process.[3] The contest between Shi'ite clerics in Iraq and Shi'ite political parties in Lebanon reflects a wider debate about the propriety of clerical activism in democratic politics, also known as Islamism.

Literature, music, film

Minorities are among the Arab World's leading authors, musicians, and filmmakers. Jewish playwright Yaqub Sanu is credited with introducing theater to Egypt in the 1870s. Saadallah Wannous, a Syrian of Alawi descent, was the foremost playwright of the late twentieth century. Adonis, another Alawi from Syria, is considered one of the best modern Arab poets. None of these artists emphasized their religious heritage, so it would be inappropriate, for example, to describe Adonis as an "Alawi poet." Yet their confessional identity is not negligible. Some of Wannous's politically charged plays likely escaped censorship in Syria because he belonged to the same Alawi community as President Hafiz al-Assad.[4] On the other hand, some minority artists do incorporate their identity into their works. The short stories and novels of the Egyptian author, Idwar al-Kharrat, often feature Coptic protagonists or are set in Coptic Upper Egypt. Other authors, such as Sudanese poet Muhammad 'Abd al-Hayy, are not minorities but write about them. For instance, his 1971 poem "Return to Sinnar" imagines the ethnic tolerance that existed between Arabs and ethnic minorities in the pre-colonial kingdom of Sinnar.[5] It is a nostalgic work that laments the ethnically inspired civil war that raged in Sudan after independence – hence 'Abd al-Hayy's longing for a "Return to Sinnar." While it is doubtful that ethnic relations were ever as harmonious as he portrays them, 'Abd al-Hayy's plea to end the conflict is nonetheless sincere. His poem illustrates that works about ethnic and religious minorities are part of the mainstream of Arab literary culture.

Religious minorities are quite prominent in Arab music, perhaps because Lebanon, the quintessential minority state, produces much of the popular music for the region. Fairuz, for example, is the most famous Lebanese singer of the second half of the twentieth century. She began her career by singing Lebanese folk songs but gained wider recognition when her lyrics began to address the loss of Palestine. Her deep, almost melancholy, voice fit the subject well, as did the themes of nostalgia, homesickness, and return which she incorporated from Lebanese folklore. The lyrics were always generic enough that songs about Lebanon could be applied equally well to Palestine and vice versa.[6] Consequently, her music had universal appeal. It resonated with refugees, expatriate workers, and rural migrants to cities who had been displaced by political and economic upheavals in the Arab World during the late twentieth century. Although a Christian, Fairuz's success was neither tied to nor hindered by her faith.

A number of current pop singers – Elissa, Haifa Wehbe, and Nawal al-Zoghbi – are also from minority communities in Lebanon, but the popularity of Arab singers still transcends religion to some extent. The current pop music sensation in the Arab World, Lebanese singer Nancy Ajram, seems never to have publicly disclosed her religious identity. Ajram's fan website divulges nearly every other detail about her personal life. Her silence on the matter is surprising, considering that she hails from confession-conscious Lebanon, but it may be a pragmatic choice not to limit her fan base or upset her international sponsor, Coca-Cola. After all, pop music in the Arab World is a "mainstream genre designed to score maximum success by offending no essential constituencies."[7] As a result, the Internet is abuzz with speculation about her faith. That Ajram has become so popular without disclosing her religious heritage is evidence that even as religion becomes more salient in the public sphere, popular Arab music has not become sectarian.

Minorities are equally well represented in Arab cinema. Egypt, the headquarters of the region's film industry, was a multicultural melting pot in the early to mid-twentieth century, and its cosmopolitan communities produced some of the Arab silver screen's biggest stars. Henri Barakat (Christian), Youssef Chahine (Christian), and Togo Mizrahi (Jewish) directed films while Farid al-Atrash (Druze), Omar Sharif (Christian), and Layla Murad (Jewish) acted in them. It should be noted, however, that both Sharif and Murad later converted to Sunni Islam. Though Arab cinema has always featured minorities, it now acknowledges their identities more readily and, occasionally, even addresses their concerns. Often this is done subtly, as in Coptic director Sandra Nashaat's 1999 action film, *al-Rahina* (The Hostage), in which the Muslim hero is saved by his Christian friends, or Eran Riklis's 2004 drama, *The Syrian Bride*, which is set in a Druze village on the Golan Heights. In other cases, the depiction of minorities and their struggles is quite overt. Moroccan directors, for example, are grappling with the flight of Jews from their country after the establishment of Israel.[8]

Painfully overt is *Turtles Can Fly* (2004) by Iranian-Kurdish director Bahman Ghobadi, that depicts the suffering of Iraq's Kurds under the rule of Saddam Hussein. The film's setting is a refugee camp on Iraq's northern border just before the American invasion of 2003. In the distressing opening scene, the young Kurdish protagonist, Agrin, slowly approaches a cliff, carefully removes her shoes, and then leaps over the edge. The film explores the sad existence that drove her to suicide. The audience discovers that Iraqi soldiers had raped Agrin and killed her parents during a raid on their village, presumably during Hussein's campaign to exterminate the Kurds. Her cross-eyed toddler is a constant reminder of the trauma of the night that she became an orphan. Although Satellite, the ringleader of the local boys, tries to court Agrin, she loathes herself too much to reciprocate.

As should be evident, *Turtles Can Fly* is not escapist entertainment. All of the actors are amateur Kurdish children, and many of them have some sort of real-life physical deformity, either from Hussein's depredations or the resultant deprivation. Agrin, the only visibly whole character, is emotionally broken. She lives with the other Kurdish refugees in communal tents in an army dump. The children clear landmines for a living. When a farmer protests that half of the children working on his fields have lost both arms, Satellite replies without sarcasm, "So what? They are not afraid of mines. They are our best!" The film's plaintive Kurdish soundtrack is appropriately haunting.

It is significant that films like *The Syrian Bride* and *Turtles Can Fly* were subtitled in English, distributed in the United States, and intended for an international audience. A recent Egyptian film suggests that there is an Arab market for at least lighthearted films about minorities. Rami Imam's 2008 comedy *Hasan wa-Marqus* (Hasan and Marcus) confronts the issue of interfaith relations in Egypt. The film begins with Bulus, a Coptic priest, addressing a conference on Muslim–Christian unity in Cairo. Bulus states that Christians who are not loyal to the state are not good Christians. When a disgruntled Christian attempts to assassinate him for that remark, the Egyptian authorities give Bulus a new identity and send him away from the city. Bulus becomes Hasan, a Muslim, and moves with his wife and son to rural Minya. Unfortunately, Hasan's reputation as an Islamic scholar precedes him. The town's Muslims, thrilled to have an urbane religious authority in their midst, bombard him with ethical questions at the mosque and line up at his door to be healed of various ailments. Hasan artfully dodges their questions and pronounces Christian benedictions over the sick as he struggles to keep his new identity straight and practice Christianity in secret, with humorous effect.

After inadvertently leading an Islamist revolution to overthrow the government, Hasan flees to a religiously mixed neighborhood in Cairo. His new neighbor, Marcus, is a Copt. The twist is that Marcus is really Mahmud, a pious Muslim living under an assumed identity. Unaware of each other's secret, they become friends and, predictably, Hasan's son falls in love with Marcus's daughter. The moment of truth arrives when Hasan's son admits to Marcus's daughter that he is really a Christian. Stunned and choking back tears, she admits to being a Muslim. Both instantly recognize that this revelation dooms their relationship. Islamic tradition holds that Muslim men can marry Christian women, but Muslim women cannot marry Christian men. Since religion is presumed to descend patrilineally, this arrangement preserves the supremacy of the dominant faith in the social order by ensuring that the children of mixed marriages are raised Muslim.[9] Resigning themselves to the fact that their budding romance is now forbidden, the star-crossed lovers sorrowfully part ways.

The film turns dark at this point, literally and figuratively, as the families revert to their true confessional identities and consider what this development means for their friendship. All of the opinions of Egypt are on display: the mothers demand there be no further contact with their neighbors, the children ask what difference their religious identity makes, and the husbands sit in ponderous silence. Meanwhile, Muslim and Christian preachers spew hate from their pulpits and a sectarian riot erupts in the street. Marcus saves Hasan's wife from the mob while Hasan rescues Marcus's wife and daughter from a burning building. Reconciled, the two families join hands and make their way defiantly through the melee. Suddenly a rioter rears up and strikes Hasan in the head. But Hasan presses forward, undeterred, with blood running down his face. Then a second rioter rears up and strikes Marcus in the same manner. He too marches on. At last, the six of them emerge from the crowd, still holding hands, as the scene fades.

The attractiveness of this film, particularly the ending, is that it does not paint an overly optimistic picture of interfaith relations in Egypt, nor does it advocate the defiance of social mores. Indeed, a sectarian brawl still rages in the street at the end of the film, and there is no indication that Hasan's son ultimately marries Marcus's daughter. The message of *Hasan wa-Marqus* is more personal: individual Muslims and Christians can forge friendships by resisting the siren song of extremists who preach hatred and incite violence. Those who swim against the sectarian current will not remain unscathed, but they can persevere hand in hand.

Historical vulnerabilities

As the opening scene of *Hasan wa-Marqus* illustrates, there is some suspicion of ethnic and religious minorities within the Arab World. The film indirectly addresses concerns that minorities are disloyal to the state, but minorities are also vulnerable to the accusation that they wield inordinate political power or precipitate foreign intervention. Such perceptions, if not entirely warranted, are rooted in the region's historical experience.

Minorities have served as a pretext for outside interference in the Arab World since the nineteenth century, when the Russians and the French appointed themselves stewards over the Ottoman Empire's Orthodox and Catholic subjects respectively. The ostensible purpose was to protect these minorities, but European governments were just as eager to claim a share of Ottoman territories should the empire fall. Britain and France later openly colonized the Arab World, privileging the ethnic and religious minorities who shared their faith or spoke European languages. To further divide and rule the population, imperialists sometimes inverted social hierarchies to empower ethnic and religious minorities. Hence French officials in Algeria stacked the colonial bureaucracy with Francophile Berbers and granted full citizenship to Jews but not to Muslims.[10] Though minorities did not invite imperialism, they often benefited from it.

Foreign intervention in the Arab World on behalf of minorities still occurs. In 1991 the United States enforced no-fly zones over Iraq to protect Kurdish and Shi'ite populations from massacre. The work of humanitarian groups and non-governmental organizations is increasingly perceived as outside interference. Christian activists urge governments around the world to exert diplomatic pressure on behalf of Christian communities in the region, sometimes to the detriment of those communities. For example, Copts living abroad were very vocal about the injustices that their co-religionists faced in Egypt during the Mubarak era, which embarrassed the Coptic Patriarch and threatened his entente with the Egyptian authorities.[11] The Patriarch bluntly asserted in 1997 that the welfare of Copts was an internal Egyptian matter. Similarly, the League of Arab States, the regional equivalent of the United Nations, rejected the International Criminal Court's 2009 indictment of Sudanese president Omar al-Bashir for war crimes against non-Arabs in Darfur. Albert Hourani warned long ago that if foreigners use minorities as a pretext for meddling in Arab affairs, or are perceived as doing so, the backlash against those minorities could be disastrous.[12]

Another common perception is that minorities wield inordinate political power. The current governments of Bahrain, Syria, and Lebanon are dominated by religious minorities. In Bahrain, minority rule in Bahrain is a relic of the colonial era. Although the island's population is predominantly Shi'ite, Britain placed the Sunni Al Khalifa family on the throne before granting Bahrain independence in 1971. Hafiz al-Assad seized power in Syria after an Alawi *coup d'état* in 1970. The Assad regime consolidated power by patronizing other religious minorities, much to the chagrin of the Sunni majority. The sectarian violence plaguing Syria after the Arab Spring illustrates an all-too-familiar pattern in the Arab World: an authoritarian ruler remains in power by suppressing the will of the majority but patronizing minorities. The minorities' support of the dictator earns the resentment of the majority and, when the regime falls, as it inevitably does, there is retribution.

The disproportionate political power of religious minorities in Lebanon is no secret. The Lebanese fought a devastating civil war from 1975–90 over this issue. At the insistence of France, Mount Lebanon was carved out of the Ottoman Empire as a semi-autonomous province for Maronite Christians in 1861. The Maronites lost their absolute majority when the French expanded Lebanon's borders to make it a viable mandate in 1922. According to the 1932 census, the ratio of Christians to Muslims in Lebanon was 6:5 and seats in parliament were allotted proportionally. The unofficial National Pact of 1943 stipulated that the President (the highest elected office) would be a Maronite Christian, the Prime Minister a Sunni Muslim, and Speaker of Parliament a Shi'ite

Muslim in perpetuity. Despite a well-known demographic shift in favor of Muslims, Maronites have refused to authorize a new census that would diminish their political power. To end the sectarian civil war that resulted, the Ta'if Agreement of 1989 split seats in parliament equally between Muslims and Christians – a step toward proportional representation that still favors the Maronites. Until there is a new census or a reallocation of parliamentary seats, the perception that minorities wield inordinate political power in Lebanon, as in other places, has some merit.

Minorities are sometimes perceived as disloyal to the state, though seldom with good reason. Concerns about the loyalties of Iraqi Shi'ites proved unfounded during the Iran–Iraq War (1980–88). Shi'ites were not a fifth column against Saddam Hussein's Sunni-dominated regime, despite having religious ties to Iran and facing discrimination at home. Yet in the last fifty years, there have been active separatist movements among the Kurds of Iraq and a coalition of ethnic and religious minorities in southern Sudan known as the Sudanese People's Liberation Movement (SPLM). Secession is less imperative now that the Kurds are represented in the Iraqi government and enjoy regional autonomy. The SPLM's war of attrition with the Arab-Islamist government of Sudan resulted in the creation of the Republic of South Sudan through referendum in 2011.

Zionism – a Jewish separatist movement of sorts – caused many Arab Nationalists to question Jewish loyalties in the mid-twentieth century. Zionist propaganda mischaracterized every Jew as a Zionist in order to boast maximum support for a Jewish state, which seemed to validate such suspicions, as did the fact that most Arab Jews subsequently immigrated to Israel.[13] Jews were not expelled *en masse* from the Arab World in retaliation for the establishment of Israel in 1948, although over decades and for a variety of reasons, most eventually left. There was considerable anti-Jewish sentiment throughout the region due to the situation in Palestine, but it should not be overstated as a factor driving immigration. Many communists and Zionists, for example, went to Israel voluntarily. Immigration incentives and better economic prospects lured other Arab Jews.[14] The xenophobic tenor of Arab Nationalist rhetoric, and the repressive regimes that spawned it, encouraged many ethnic minorities to emigrate, including Egypt's Jewish and Greek communities. Not all Arab Jews left the region, of course; Morocco and Tunisia still have small Jewish populations. Therefore, the notion that minorities are disloyal to the state should not be given unequivocal credence.

Prospects for the future

Ethnic and religious minorities face a number of challenges at present. Islamization, Arabization, and emigration threaten the vitality of minority communities in the Arab World. Islamization refers to the expanding reach of *shariʿa* (Islamic law) in society. Nearly every constitution in the Arab World already recognizes Islam as the state religion and *shariʿa* as a source of state law. Many Islamists want *shariʿa* to become the sole source of state law, forcing all citizens – even non-Muslims – to adhere to Islamic norms. Such is the case in Sudan where Christians have been punished for conduct that contravened *shariʿa* but was acceptable within their own communities. This incongruity was one of the grievances behind the establishment of an independent South Sudan in 2011. Copts unsuccessfully opposed a constitutional amendment that made *shariʿa* the principal source of Egyptian law in 1980 on the grounds that it inhibited their constitutionally guaranteed freedom of religion. They expressed similar concerns when Islamists drafted a new constitution in the aftermath of the Arab Spring.

Islamization affects Muslim minorities as well. According to the extremely narrow school of Sunni law that prevails in Saudi Arabia, Shiʿite Muslims are religious deviants. Their mere presence defiles the kingdom, the birthplace of Islam, by hindering the complete Islamization of society. Clerical fulmination against Shiʿites in Saudi Arabia is semi-official because the monarch sanctions the religious establishment insofar as it sanctions his rule. His legitimacy as "Defender of the Two Holy Sanctuaries" in Mecca and Medina is contingent on upholding the clerics' interpretation of Sunni Islam. Most Shiʿites in Saudi Arabia live atop the vast petroleum reserves along the kingdom's Persian Gulf coast; they have been subjected to sporadic persecution which have had the result of simultaneously bolstering the monarch's status among hard-line Sunni clerics and securing the kingdom's oil wealth. Shiʿites in Saudi Arabia endure special taxes, workplace discrimination, and state interference with their worship. In times past, they faced forced conversion.[15] Islamization thus threatens Muslim and non-Muslim minorities alike.

Arabization, forced linguistic and cultural assimilation, confronts ethnic minorities in countries like Sudan and Algeria. Years of drought in the arid Darfur region of Sudan and subsequent clashes between nomadic Arab tribes and sedentary Fur villagers erupted into large-scale violence in 2003. A group of Darfuris launched an armed campaign against the negligent, Arabophile government. In response, the government armed Janjaweed militias, drawn from the nomadic Arab tribes, to exterminate non-Arabs. The United Nations dispatched a peacekeeping force to quell the violence after more than a million people were displaced. The secession of South Sudan, which leaves Sudan's population more ethnically homogenous, almost certainly means that the government's policy of Arabization in Darfur and elsewhere will continue.

Imazighen (Berbers) have been fighting a half century of Arabization in Algeria. For decades, the dominant Arab nationalist party proposed legislation to make Arabic the exclusive language of state. Imazighen resisted such attempts through a combination of extreme patriotism, Francophilia, and violent protest. The career of Amazigh (Berber) musician Lounès Matoub highlights the trajectory of Arabization in Algeria to a striking degree. Matoub held his first concert in 1980, one week before the "Berber Spring," an uprising against government suppression of Amazigh culture, which he commemorated each year with an anniversary concert. Matoub was a staunch opponent of the regime's pro-Arab policies, composing songs in Tamazight – the primary Amazigh dialect – in protest. He was part of the Amazigh Cultural Movement, which promoted Tamazight as a medium of literary and artistic expression. Like most Imazighen, Matoub opposed Islamism on the grounds that it promoted Arabization, but he was also a religious iconoclast. He deliberately composed libertine lyrics that mocked Islam in order to shock conservative Muslims. Matoub was murdered by Islamists in 1998 during Algeria's civil war, just days before an Arabic-only law would have banned the use of Tamazight in public schools.[16] Rioting after his death encouraged the Algerian government to recognize Tamazight as a national language in 2002. Nevertheless, Arabization continues to challenge the cultural vitality of ethnic minorities in Algeria and elsewhere.

Lastly, emigration threatens the survival of many minority communities in the Arab World. Egypt, Palestine, Syria, and Iraq are rapidly losing their Christian populations to emigration. Several indigenous churches now have more congregants outside of the region than within. One indicator of this long-term trend is the relocation of the patriarchal seat of the Assyrian Church of the East from Baghdad to Morton Grove, Illinois, in 1978. Arab Christians emigrate at a higher rate than Muslims for many reasons. Like most migrants, they tend to be educated, urban, and middle class. Greater exposure to missionary schools provides them with the foreign contacts and language skills that they need to survive abroad. Arab Christians often find it easier to assimilate in the Christian-majority countries where they seek employment. More importantly, many Christian migrants already have a relative living abroad. The implication of that fact is considerable: as more Arab Christians emigrate, it is more likely that their family members will follow. As a result, Christian emigration has become self-perpetuating, a process that is devastating the Christian population of the Arab World. Proselytizing is forbidden in most places, so Christian communities must grow by natural increase. However, their birth rates are falling, especially relative to Muslim birth rates, so the number of Christians in the region and their proportion of the Arab population as a whole is shrinking.

The emigration of Palestinian Christians is relatively well documented. They leave Palestine at twice the rate of the general population.[17] The weak economy is the primary reason; political troubles are secondary. Christians emigrate first and foremost in search of employment since Israel's economic strangulation of the West Bank and Gaza Strip limits their opportunities at home. The hardships of life under occupation are also responsible for the flight of Christians. In 1993, when prospects for peace were bright, a survey conducted by Palestinian Christian scholar Bernard Sabella found that 65 percent of West Bank Christians would not emigrate if there was peace with Israel. Now that the peace process has stalled, some Israelis blame Islamist political parties like Hamas for pushing Christians out. Yet in a 2006 survey only 7 percent of West Bank Christians cited religious extremism as a major concern.[18] While it is fair to suggest that Islamization is one cause of Christian emigration, the dire economic situation in Palestine – caused by Israel's blockade of Gaza and its more subtle subordination of the West Bank economy – is the root cause. Until that issue is satisfactorily resolved, and the economic outlook improves for Christians throughout the Arab World, they will continue to emigrate.

Conclusion

Despite the challenges of Islamization, Arabization, and emigration, there is hope that the situation of ethnic and religious minorities in the Arab World will improve. Since 2003, the Kurds of Iraq have attained a degree of autonomy and political power that virtually guarantees their

Table 2.1 *Ethnic and religious minorities in the Arab World*

Ethnic minorities	Approximate population	Areas of concentration
Imazighen (Berber)	11,688,000	Morocco, Algeria, Libya, Tunisia
Kurd	7,628,000	Iraq, Syria
Nubian	300,000	Egypt, Sudan
Armenian	237,000	Lebanon, Syria

Religious minorities	Approximate population	Areas of concentration
Muslim		
Shi'ite (*Ithna 'Ashari*/ Twelvers)	20,011,000	Iraq, Saudi Arabia, Lebanon, Kuwait, Bahrain, United Arab Emirates, Qatar
Alawi (*Nusayri*)	2,047,000	Syria, Lebanon
Druze (*Muwahhidun*)	788,000	Lebanon, Syria
Christian		
Coptic Orthodox	6,138,000	Egypt
Catholic & Uniate	3,325,000	Egypt, Palestine, Jordan, Lebanon, Syria
Greek Orthodox	1,850,000	Egypt, Palestine, Jordan, Lebanon, Syria
Syrian Orthodox	250,000	Syria, Lebanon
Assyrian Church of the East	50,000	Iraq, Syria

Note: The numbers in Table 2.1 are purely estimates. No state in the region conducts a regular, reliable census, and minorities tend to overestimate their numbers while governments tend to underestimate. Few reference books provide information about all of the ethnic and religious minorities in every relevant country. Therefore, these numbers have been culled from a variety of sources including: *Europa World Yearbook 2012* (London: Routledge); *Europa Regional Surveys of the World: The Middle East and North Africa 2011* (London: Routledge); Colbert Held and John Cummings, *Middle East Patterns: Places, Peoples, and Politics*, 5th ed. (Boulder, CO: Westview Press, 2011); Betty Jane and J. Martin Bailey, *Who Are the Christians in the Middle East?*, 2nd ed. (Grand Rapids, MI: Eerdmans, 2010); Margaret Nydell, *Understanding Arabs: A Contemporary Guide to Arab Society*, 5th ed. (Boston: Intercultural Press, 2012); and *Oxford Encyclopedia of the Modern World* (Oxford University Press, 2008).

survival as a distinct ethnic group. Qatar approved the construction of its first church in 2008, where Christians can openly worship for the first time. Tamazight is now an official language of instruction for Berber students in Moroccan schools. Thus, there is no reason to suppose that minority communities are slated for inevitable decline (see Table 2.1). If minorities have enjoyed one advantage over the years, it is their considerable cultural influence, which ensures them a platform from which to articulate alternatives to or forge compromises with the movements and ideologies that excluded them in the past.

Notes

1   Kamal Salibi, "The Christian Role in the Arab Renaissance," *Theological Review of the Near East School of Theology*, 15:1 (1994), pp. 3–14.
2   Albert Hourani, *Arabic Thought in the Liberal Age, 1798–1939* (London: Oxford University Press, 1962), pp. 295–96.
3   Patrick Cockburn, *Muqtada: Muqtada al-Sadr, the Shia Revival, and the Struggle for Iraq* (New York: Scribner, 2008).
4   Judith Miller, "Saadallah Wannous, 56, Arab Playwright," *New York Times*, May 17, 1997.
5   Salma Jayyusi (ed.), *Modern Arabic Poetry: An Anthology* (New York: Columbia University Press, 1987), p. 26.
6   Christopher Stone, "Fayruz, the Rahbani Brothers, Jerusalem, and the Leba-stinian Song," in Tamar Mayer and Suleiman Mourad (eds.), *Jerusalem: Idea and Reality* (London: Routledge, 2008), pp. 155–67.
7   Andrew Hammond, *Popular Culture in the Arab World: Arts, Politics, and the Media* (American University in Cairo Press, 2007), p. 160.
8   Oren Kosansky and Aomar Boum, "The 'Jewish Question' in Postcolonial Moroccan Cinema," *International Journal of Middle East Studies*, 44:3 (August 2012), pp. 421–42.
9   Fuad Khuri, *Imams and Emirs: State, Religion and Sects in Islam* (London: Saqi Books, 1990), pp. 85–91.
10 Taoufik Djebali, "Ethnicity and Power in North Africa: Tunisia, Algeria, and Morocco," in Paul Spickard (ed.), *Race and Nation: Ethnic Systems in the Modern World* (New York: Routledge, 2005), pp. 135–54.
11 Mariz Tadros, "Vicissitudes in the Entente between the Coptic Orthodox Church and the State in Egypt (1952–2007)," *International Journal of Middle East Studies* 41:2 (2009), pp. 269–87.
12 Albert Hourani, *Minorities in the Arab World* (Oxford University Press, 1947), p. 112.
13 Reuven Snir, "'We Are Arabs Before We Are Jews': The Emergence and Demise of Arab-Jewish Culture in Modern Times," *Electronic Journal of Oriental Studies*, 8:9 (2005), pp. 38–39.
14 Tom Segev, *1949: The First Israelis* (New York: Free Press, 1986).
15 Yitzhak Nakash, *Reaching for Power: The Shi'a in the Modern Arab World* (Princeton University Press, 2006), pp. 42–71.
16 Paul Silverstein, "The Rebel Is Dead. Long Live the Martyr": Kabyle Mobilization and the Assassination of Lounes Matoub," *Middle East Report*, 208 (Fall 1998), pp. 3–4.

17 Bernard Sabella, "The Emigration of Christian Arabs: Dimensions and Causes of the Phenomenon," in Andrea Pacini (ed.), *Christian Communities in the Arab Middle East: The Challenge of the Future* (Oxford: Clarendon Press, 1998), p. 127.

18 Bernard Sabella, "Palestinian Christians: Historical Demographic Developments, Current Politics and Attitudes towards Church, Society and Human Rights," in *The Sabeel Survey on Palestinian Christians in the West Bank and Israel* (Summer 2006), p. 85. [Downloaded from www.sabeel.org/pdfs/the%20sabeel%20survey%20-%20 english%202008.pdf – accessed March 10, 2010]. My thanks to Michelle Magnusson for this reference.

3

Nahda: the Arab project of enlightenment

Three pieces of writing capture the distance that Arab thought and culture crossed from the early nineteenth to the early twentieth century. The first text was written in 1832 by the Egyptian shaykh Rifaʻa Rafiʻ al-Tahtawi (1801–1873) upon his return from a five-year sojourn in Paris. The second was published in 1882 by ʻAli Mubarak (1823–1893), an Egyptian bureaucrat, educator, and cabinet minister. The last was delivered in 1928 as a public lecture, a century after al-Tahtawi's book, by the Syrian-Egyptian Islamist Rashid Rida (1865–1935).

> **Rifaʻa Rafiʻ al-Tahtawi (1832):** One should note that the French have a natural propensity for the acquisition of learning and a craving for the knowledge of all things. This is why you see that all of them have a comprehensive knowledge of all things they have acquired. Nothing is alien to them, so that when you talk with one of them, he will talk to you in the words of a scholar, even though he is not one of them. For this reason, you can see ordinary French people examining and discussing a number of profound scientific questions. The same is true of their children; from a very early age they are proficient.[1]
>
> **ʻAli Mubarak Pasha (1882):** The nation now sheds her false ideas, frees herself from worthless conceptions and gets used to the new institutions. Within a short time, all has changed: attitudes, habits, customs, and institutions. This is what happening in Egypt today. Anyone who saw Egypt fifty years ago, and who now sees it again today, will find nothing he knew from former times. He will realize that it has experienced a revolution.[2]
>
> **Rashid Rida (1928):** In a time that is afflicted by ideological, intellectual, political, Communist and Bolshevik upheavals; in a time that is strained by religious, literary, and social chaos; in a time that is threatened by women's revolution, the violation of marital vows,

the disintegration of the family and the bonds of kinship; in a time
in which heresy and unaffected promiscuity have erupted, as well
as attacks on the nation's religion, language, and values, and its customs, dress, and origins, nothing remains stable [with which] to raise
our youths [and] to teach them respect.[3]

Between these lines lies the story of the "Arab Renaissance," or *Nahda*,
from curious cultural observation to optimistic implementation to skeptical retrospection and even regret. While in the Western academic tradition the *Nahda* is primarily a story of late nineteenth-century literary and
linguistic renaissance, in the Arab intellectual tradition it is a key concept that accounts for the Arab experience of the Enlightenment. This
essay approaches the *Nahda* from an expansive perspective that conceives
of both modernity (*hadatha*) and Enlightenment (*tanwir*) as two complementary aspects of the same phenomenon.

The sections below discuss the early encounters with modern Europe,
the emergence of an initial selective or defensive modernity focused on
state building, and the crucial roles of Lebanon and Syria where a host
of scholars experimented with cultural renewal and the translation of
European knowledge. The focus then moves to Egypt, the *Nahda*'s hub,
and the establishment of the sociopolitical and economic infrastructure
necessary for the emergence of the Arab Enlightenment, as well as the
attempts to institute an Arab modernity by way of sociopolitical and
legal reform. The discussion moves on to the response of Islamic modernism that sought synthesis and coexistence with the *Nahda,* and finally
to the nationalization of the *Nahda* through competing political and
ideological projects.

Early encounters with Europe and defensive enlightenment

Most accounts of the Arab Enlightenment consider the late eighteenth
century as a period of significant developments. Already during this era,
life in the Middle East was considerably challenged, enough to elicit two
kinds of reactions: one reformist and the other revivalist.

The reformists, even in a remote province of the Ottoman Empire
such as Yemen, struggled with how to instigate renewal and adapt to the
changing global circumstances of greater economic integration and intercultural influences. Operating from within the conventions of Islamic
culture, they responded to the changing times by rethinking the Islamic

legal tradition and its legal code (*shariʿa*). Due to the centrality of legal thought and practice in daily Islamic life, all attempts at reform had to be conceived of and executed in legal terms, in other words, by answering the question "Does religious law permit this?" In contrast with this intellectual response, revivalists such as Muhammad ibn ʿAbd al-Wahhab (d. 1787) of the Hijaz (in modern-day Saudi Arabia), founder of Wahhabism, created a movement of moral reconstruction and self-purification that fought behaviors it defined as representative of cultural decline (such as the veneration of saints, music, drinking coffee, and smoking) and deviations from a strictly interpreted scriptural tradition. However different these responses were, they both emphasized cultural continuity and their legacies would have important roles to play during the twentieth century.

In addition to incremental cultural and economic changes there was at least one modern "big bang": Napoleon's invasion of Egypt in 1798. Later, in 1830, a second trauma occurred when the French invaded and colonized Algeria. Napoleon's was the largest long-distance seaborne force the world had ever seen. Upon landing in Egypt, Napoleon – a self-declared Muslim – announced that he arrived as a "friend of Islam" in order to bring to it the values of the French Revolution (primarily liberty and citizens' rights) as well as the culture of the Enlightenment. The French claimed that the Enlightenment and its humanist standards were of universal value.

In 1801, after encountering much resistance during their three-year stay, the French withdrew from Egypt. The legacy of their expedition varied greatly over time. Yet it left behind the possibility of pursuing a new kind of political power and a new form of state, and two such states rapidly emerged: Egypt and a reformed Ottoman Empire. In Egypt, following the departure of the French, Muhammad ʿAli Pasha (r. 1805–48) established a powerful patrimonial regime which relied on skillful *ad hoc* application of modern power for its survival. The keyword for the institution of this power was "reform" and it came in all shapes and varieties: agricultural, economic, bureaucratic, and, first and foremost, military. By the 1830s, the Egyptian province was so powerful that it threatened the very existence of Ottoman rule. The common wisdom of this era was that, although modernity was a complete whole, it was the military and technological applications – its material aspects – that mattered most. This was the first Middle Eastern experience with selective, or defensive, modernity, in which aspects of modernity, especially those that were tied to technology, were seen as independent of more difficult questions concerning morality and creed.

The second example, in many ways more profound, was that of the Ottoman Empire itself. In 1839, due to direct European pressure, the Ottomans embarked on their own era of *Tanzimat* (literally, "reforms"). Unlike other selective reforms, the Ottoman ones had a significant political aspect, for they introduced the idea of citizenship and equality before the law. These measures reflected European liberal thinking and were thus dependent on the formation of a new elite for their success. In fact, both the Egyptian and Ottoman experiments saw a systematic state effort to train a new class of civil bureaucracy. These young conscripts of modernity studied in new schools, traveled to Europe in official state delegations, and were employed by new institutions such as the translation bureau, the medical school, the military academy, or the official *Gazette* upon their return. They identified the propagation of literacy and the expansion of a modern education system as crucial means for progress. Their rise, however, came at the expense of the religious elite and the clerics (*'ulama*), whose dependency on the state grew while the need of the state for their services significantly diminished. Impoverished and weakened, the *'ulama*'s role gradually shrank to that of guardians of values and morality. The general cultural attitude was that, whatever modern developments society would undergo, morality would remain a domain that was exclusively under clerical supervision. In other words, the first modern experiments in the Middle East envisioned a divided future in which the moral sphere would retain its authority and authenticity by remaining detached from the material sphere, the one governed by Islamic religious principles and the other by the modern secular state and its elites.

The previously cited al-Tahtawi is an exemplar of how some Egyptians became facilitators for, and at the same time were also products of, these defensive state projects. Al-Tahtawi was a member of the first Egyptian mission that Muhammad 'Ali sent to France (1825–32). While in Paris, he learned French, read extensively, and produced a travelogue *Refinement of Pure Gold in the Summarizing of Paris* (*Takhlis al-ibriz fi talkhis Bariz*) that described in detail the cultural differences between the Ottoman-Egyptian and French worlds. This book, written in the Islamic tradition of *rihla*, or travel literature, can be read as a roadmap for his future career as an administrator and education reformer.

Al-Tahtawi was an astute and comprehensive observer who commented critically on issues such as ethics, customs and manners, education, political philosophy, status and structure of knowledge, women and society, language, and science. Al-Tahtawi framed his observations in terms of the rise of civilizations and their decline into barbarity, and his work displays a clear sense that Islamic civilization was somewhat behind.

As a chronicler of cultural difference, al-Tahtawi's observations, such as "clarity of language is a pre-condition for sound reasoning," caused him to wonder about the foundations of Islamic learning. While modern knowledge prioritized science, philosophy and history, the Arabo-Islamic scholarly tradition favored "Syntax, inflection, prosody and vocabulary. Then derivation, poetry and composition. [And then] … semantics, rhetoric, calligraphy, rhyme and history."[4] Interestingly enough, al-Tahtawi never considered these two hierarchies of knowledge to be mutually exclusive.

This position was more difficult to maintain when it came to science. Perhaps the only indication of a certain tension between scientific reasoning and divinity was al-Tahtawi's reluctance to discard Islamic cosmology (*'ilm al-kawn*), the theocentric nature of which was inseparable from the Qur'anic notion of God. Thus, he never really embraced the mechanized law-bound world of Newtonian physics, which was free of the forces of divine authority and open for rational investigation. At the same time, however, he argued for a complementary relationship between reason and revelation. This ambiguity aside, it did not inhibit the school of translation that al-Tahtawi supervised from producing more than 2,000 translations of a technical-scientific character. This practical ambiguity, in which philosophical contradictions and tensions were overcome by avoiding clarity, characterized the first generation of defensive modernizers.

The enlightenment in Greater Syria: 1840–1870

While in Egypt the appropriation of modernity was primarily the official business of the state and its bureaucrats, in Lebanon and Syria the Enlightenment project was in the hands of individuals. Heavily influenced by the presence of missionaries, the impact of the abovementioned state projects in Egypt, the political and diplomatic activities of Americans and Europeans, as well as global commercial exchange, a circle of young Arab literati established modern institutions such as schools, libraries, daily and periodical presses, and theaters. By 1880, a hundred different schools belonging to a dozen Christian denominations operated in Syria, Lebanon, and Palestine. Jerusalem alone had forty such schools. Some of these institutions, such as the Maronite seminary of 'Ayn Waraqa and the Syrian Protestant College in Beirut (later, the American University of Beirut), functioned as advanced academic laboratories that, however selectively, celebrated and disseminated the achievements of the European Enlightenment, including the practice of educating girls. Distinguished by such novel habits of mind, this new educated class soon asserted its influence in public life.

The careers of several of the most significant figures of this period capture the scope of cultural reshuffling that took place during this era. The life of Faris al-Shidyaq (1804–1887), born a Maronite but later a convert first to Protestantism and then to Islam (upon which he took the name Ahmad), revolved around the role of language in public life. He began his scholarly career in the ranks of American missionaries from whom he learned about translation (first and foremost that of the Bible) and publication. He also worked at the American Protestant press in Malta, traveled extensively in Europe, and was aware of the public impact of publishing. In subsequent years, numerous books on all manner of subjects from Homer's *Iliad* to poems by Victor Hugo were independently translated by members of his generation.

Al-Shidyaq was particularly interested in linguistic change. This is because he and his colleagues realized that they had been translating and writing in an antiquated form of the Arabic language that drew heavily on classical forms of communication characterized by elaborate rhymed prose (*saj'*). Beautiful as it was, Classical Arabic stylistics, from a modern perspective, undermined the communicative capability of printed language and was often lacking in appropriate vocabulary. Equipped with the necessary publishing skill that he had acquired in Malta, al-Shidyaq founded *al-Jawa'ib,* one of the first independent newspapers in the Middle East. Through this newspaper al-Shidyaq and his peers revolutionized the usage of written language by expanding its vocabulary, as well as widening its expressive and syntactic scope. In doing so, he and others set in place the foundation stone for the subsequent creation of a new journalistic language that was precise, clear, and free from the complexities of Classical Arabic.

The working assumption of these individuals was that clarity in language is a pre-condition for clarity of thought. After all, despite its complicated Classical Arabic-style title, this was one of the elementary observations of al-Tahtawi's travelogue. The Christian Butrus al-Bustani (1819–1893), a contemporary of al-Shidyaq, had a similar career with American evangelists yet his work took a secular route that the American missionaries could not have anticipated. A man of multiple talents, Bustani left a rich cultural inheritance that touched upon many aspects of Lebanese culture. Perhaps his most enduring legacy was in the field of lexicography, as he concluded that, in its present form, the Arabic language fell short of accounting for the dramatic transformation of the contemporary world. As a revivalist who believed in the possibility of bridging gaps between civilizations, al-Bustani composed one of the first modern Arabic dictionaries (al-Muhit, 1867–70). In doing so he coined numerous new Arabic words and legitimized linguistic experimentation.

Beyond language, al-Bustani's quest for new forms of knowledge brought him to compose the first modern Arabic encyclopedia (Da'irat al-ma'arif, 1876–82). The western encyclopedia, a classic product of the Enlightenment's "Republic of Letters," was premised on the universality and objectivity of European knowledge as well as on the ability of all individuals to master it rationally. In the introduction to this work, al-Bustani wrote that his goal was to expand the knowledge of the "East" as a pre-condition for bringing the Arabs up to the level of European civilization.[5]

Unlike the earlier generation of al-Tahtawi, which did not view European culture in relativistic or competitive terms, al-Bustani's call for an awakening was conditioned by the understanding that Arab civilization should measure up to that of Europe. Put another way, cultural difference and the ways to abolish it became a major contemporary concern. Many, if not most, cultural entrepreneurs shared a similar view as they toiled to master new cultural practices. The joint careers of Yaqub Saruf (1852–1927) and Faris Nimr (1856–1951), two teachers from the influential Syrian Protestant College, marked a zenith in Lebanese journalism. Indeed, the two men capitalized on the linguistic and cultural achievements of previous generations and published al-Muqtataf, a scientific periodical that exposed a new generation of educated youth to the marvels of modern science and to its derivative social implications. Al-Muqtataf was read all over the Arab East but in 1884, in part due to the publishers' belief in Darwinism and its rejection by their home academic institution, they left for Egypt. By this point, other Lebanese cultural entrepreneurs, such as al-Bustani's former students the brothers Bishra (1852–1901) and Salim (1849–1892) Taqla, had already moved to Egypt where they published the influential political weekly *al-Ahram* (still in print today). Other pioneers such as Jurji Zaydan (1861–1914), author, editor, and publisher of the groundbreaking literary journal *al-Hilal* (still in print today), also moved to Egypt, further contributing to Egypt's dramatic emergence as the region's cultural hub.

With hardly any cultural opposition – a reality that would change during the 1880s – the emerging Syrian and Lebanese intelligentsia bypassed existing modes of indigenous knowledge such as biography, travel literature, and other classic genres. In their place, these writers experimented with European genres such as drama, the novel, the short story, as well as literary, political, and scientific journalism. Though influential, this cultural activity was not yet conceived of as a movement and hence did not have a name. They spoke of progress (*taqaddum*), civilization (*tamaddun*), fear of barbarity (*tawahhush*), and, metaphorically, about "entering the city." Yet, since the term *Nahda* appeared only later (see below), these modernistic developments remain nameless.

Whatever we might choose to call this yet nameless *Nahda* front, it was clearly committed to four fundamental traits of mid-nineteenth-century European thought: first, a belief in the idea of progress and its dependence on scientific and technological mindedness; second, an unflinching belief in the power of rationality and its positivist and empirical mindset; third, the adoption of a historicist habit of mind, or the realization that objects become intelligible only by grasping them as part of a causal process of development; and, fourth, acceptance of the notion that "civilization" exists in two fundamental states: rise or decline. Like Europeans, they distinguished between European civilization on the one hand and Eastern, Arab, and Islamic civilization on the other (all used interchangeably), and investigated the necessary conditions that might facilitate Arab progress. All four traits conjoined in the need to profoundly reform Arab civilization, which was now considered to be "lagging behind" Europe.

Though this generation understood that a European-style cultural revival necessitated direct political change, they rarely ventured into politics. Most of them, as members of Christian minorities who identified themselves as secular-minded Arabs, approached the question

of modernity exclusively from this ethnic perspective. Not to be confused with nationalism, they called this perspective "patriotism" (*hubb
al-watan*, lit. love of homeland) and yet it was remarkably apolitical. In
the last quarter of the nineteenth century, when political conditions in
Greater Syria proved hostile to their project, they initiated one of the
most remarkable intellectual migrations in Middle East history and left
for Egypt.

The state of culture: Egypt, 1860–1880

Khedive Isma'il (r. 1863–79) had a simple motto: "Egypt is no longer part
of Africa; it has become part of Europe." He built railways, telegraph
lines, roads, ports, bridges, irrigation canals, dams, hospitals, palaces,
and the Suez Canal. He hoped to "enlighten" black Africa. Isma'il's
great project of "becoming European" was premised on the modernistic
understanding that the machine is a civilizing force and that an influx
of technology could dramatically elevate living conditions and release
Egyptians from poverty and their alleged cultural backwardness. Yet, by
that time the limitations of material/technological modernization were
widely acknowledged and Isma'il therefore also invested heavily in cultural institutions such as professional societies, schools (including education for girls), higher training colleges, libraries, a museum, theaters,
an opera house, and a printing press. He generously patronized the arts
and the journalistic scene and increased the number of student delegations to Europe. This was the background for 'Ali Mubarak's sweeping
statement quoted at the beginning of this essay about profound changes
in urban life.[6] In other words, in place of the limited project of defensive
modernity, Isma'il envisioned a more holistic cultural process.

The magnitude of Isma'il's enterprises created a wave of migration
during which people from all over the Mediterranean flocked to Egypt in
search of economic opportunity and a better life. By the turn of the century there were 260,000 Italian, French, Maltese, Armenians, Ottoman
Jews, British, and Greeks living in Egypt. The successful reception of
these minorities created a new reality in which, by 1907, about a quarter
of the inhabitants of urban centers like Port Said and Alexandria were
foreigners. Thus, urban life and so-called cosmopolitan culture became
an integral part of the birth of Arab modernism.

Isma'il's actions provided the fundamental sociopolitical and economic infrastructure for the emergence of a viable Arab project of

enlightenment; a skeleton that was soon to be fleshed out with the secular outlook, literary sensitivity, and intellectual resourcefulness of the Syrians. This development also acquired a name: the *Nahda*. The term *Nahda* signifies "to rise," "to stand up," and has the connotation of "to be fit" and "to be ready for." It was most likely coined by Shaykh Husayn al-Marsafi (1815–1890), an educator in the progressive school of Dar al-ʿUlum (established 1872), which was founded by his friend and patron ʿAli Mubarak.[7]

In 1879 Ismaʿil's bid for making Egypt part of Europe ended with dramatic bankruptcy. From the outset, his project was heavily financed by European credit and, when Egypt defaulted on its loans, the Europeans collaborated in deposing him and taking over the country. In 1882, the British occupied Egypt, and, in one form or another, this occupation lasted until 1956. This was a far cry from the kind of cultural synthesis with Europe and the project of "closing gaps" to which Ismaʿil had aspired. Thereafter, whatever came from Europe also came with direct military and political domination to the degree that the next generation of culture makers was decidedly less naive and more political.

Putting enlightenment to work: the critical years, 1882–1900

In the last two decades of the nineteenth century a sustainable modern Arab culture emerged. It was inhabited by only a tiny fraction of the population, most likely under 10 percent, but was still influential enough to transform the wider cultural life. Since initially the British rulers of Egypt safeguarded the elementary political freedoms of association and expression, Egypt continued to function as the hub of this experimental new sphere. It was centered in Cairo, Alexandria, Port Said, and several other provincial cities, and from there it radiated as far as Basra in Iraq and Fez in Morocco, Greater Syria, and Palestine. Reading and writing were the necessary skills for participation. But what exactly was the nature of this sphere?

The structural transformation gave birth to a modern professional class of doctors, technicians, teachers, lawyers, journalists, state bureaucrats, and engineers, which formed an embryonic professional middle class, or, in Arabic, *effendiyya*. It was heavily dependent on the *effendiyya*'s experience of metropolitan Europe. Because they read, wrote, and formed opinions, sometimes in several languages, this class evinced greater willingness to translate its understanding of the world into action. With both collective and individualized reading on the rise, the new habits of mind with which the Syrian–Lebanese intelligentsia experimented achieved unprecedented presence.

At the heart of this sphere stood the modern Arab intellectual, a new type of activist-thinker who replaced the religious scholar and bureaucrat-scholar of previous generations. These intellectuals spoke in the new journalistic language of "public Arabic." Their business was to influence the public and hence their work had a built-in political aspect to it.

Intellectuals could do so only because by this point in time, as Shaykh Husayn al-Marsafi observed in his essay *A Treatise on Eight Crucial Words* (*Risalat al-kalim al-thaman*), this new form of the Arabic language, "Public Arabic," also stood for political modernity. An expert on giving names to abstractions, Marsafi elaborated on the new meaning which eight powerful words – indeed political concepts – had acquired since the 1870s. A review of these words – nation (*umma*), homeland (*watan*), government (*hukuma*), justice ('*adl*), oppression (*zulm*), politics (*siyasa*), freedom (*hurriyya*), and education (*tarbiya*) – illustrates that the *Nahda* was not merely a literary phenomenon but a fully fledged political force whose interest was the public good.

This great revolution in political expression was not simply a matter of quantity in writing. The most important aspect of this tide was the continuous acculturation of new disciplines and genres such as modern history, geography, the short story, the op-ed essay, and the historical novel. Jurji Zaydan, a Lebanese Greek Orthodox émigré to Egypt was a senior member in a circle of like-minded intellectuals, such as compatriot Greek Orthodox Farah Antun (1874–1922) and Shibli Shumayyil (1850–1917). Antun was a journalist, historical novelist, and playwright, and the first Arab translator of Nietzsche. Shumayyil was a physician and scientist who also wrote stories, poetry, and political criticism. He ultimately became a precursor of socialism.

Zaydan, the most prolific and versatile writer in this group, wrote twenty-three historical novels and the first modern history book on Islamic civilization. His extremely popular historical novels taught his readers how to "think with history," and were therefore important propagators of historical consciousness. Influenced by European Orientalist scholarship, Zaydan was the first Arab to treat the history of Islamic civilization as a secular rather than a divine story. His ambition in this field was bitterly opposed by mainstream Islamic scholars.

While the work of this generation of pioneers was hostile to popular culture (fiction, colloquial Arabic, and mass Islamic culture in general) it was particularly disruptive for the Islamic notion of what constitutes proper knowledge. This is why they were sometimes called "intruders." Thereafter, the disciplinary hierarchy that Tahtawi had elaborated existed no more. Science, philosophy, and history, three fields which had been at the bottom of the Islamic intellectual structure, were now at the top. All three preached secular reason. But, more importantly, all three conjoined to deliver a much more profound message. As Albert Hourani, the most integrative historian of this tradition, succinctly put it, the new knowledge propagated the realization that "from the discoveries of science there could be inferred a system of social morality which was the secret of social strength."[8]

The idea that the public good was backed by a force of moral, political, and social truth engendered a growing urban expectation to rationalize authority and the overall management of society. Positivism and multiple other ideologies of social betterment that relied on social Darwinism were readily available in Arabic. The ideas of Auguste Comte, Herbert Spencer, Henri Bergson, and Gustave Le Bon were understood within the specific social and historical context of the Arab World. Once intellectuals forged a connection between the scientific, the philosophical, and the political, the ground was conceptually ready for a new notion of political community. Thereafter, groups such as the confessional communities of culturally autonomous minorities, or rural communities, began their transformation into a unified territorial linguistic whole and the vague sentiment of patriotism that earlier generations had invoked began to be forged in terms of nationalism.

By then the experience of the Enlightenment touched upon so many aspects of Arab life that it was no longer possible to restrict it to one specific realm. The most noteworthy indication of this state of affairs was that morality and family structure – perhaps the most intimate aspects of Islamic life, which up until that point were the exclusive sphere of the clerics – became contested issues. The agents of this reformist attempt were a group of mostly Muslim women who, in clear, plain-spoken terms, demanded emancipation. In a move that was retrospectively dubbed the "Women's Renaissance," two generations of upper-class women joined hands to rethink the status of women in Arab society. Like the phenomenon of the *Nahda*, women's self-awareness and activism began with a high-culture literary and artistic sensibility. Polyglot literacy and the mingling with a growing number of European women in Egypt eventually brought Isma'il's niece, Princess Nazli Fazil (1840–1913), to establish the first multilingual salon. It was attended by women who made a point of lifting their veils, thus challenging an elementary gender division of the time. That fact did not inhibit powerful men from socializing with them on a regular basis.

Supported by the salon, a wave of female writers such as Maryam al-Nahhas (1856–1888), Zaynab Fawwaz (1860–1914) and 'Aisha al-Taymuriyya (1840–1902) began publishing critical writing, poetry, correspondence, and even, beginning in 1892, newspapers and magazines. 'Aisha's daughter, Hind Nawfal (1860–1920), launched the women's press with *al-Fatat* (Young Woman), a newspaper that declared that its "sole principle is to defend the rights of the deprived and draw attention to the obligations due ... we ask the gracious and learned ladies to consider *al-Fatat* their newspaper in the East."[9]

The main issues that these women sought to address were the patriarchic and polygamist structure of society, and the culture of the harem, or family compound, along with its intended consequences, namely, systematic isolation and discrimination. Thinking of gendered spaces in concrete physical terms, 'Aisha al-Taymuriyya wrote of her suffering in the harem ("this cave of isolation").[10] By focusing on patriarchy and male honor, an early feminist circle inevitably advanced the cause of the modern alternative: the nuclear family. Quite specific about the cause of women's problems, they argued that the contemporary interpretation of Islamic law was to blame. In Fawwaz's words:

> We have not seen in any of the divinely-ordered system of religious law [Islam] ... a ruling that [woman] is to be prohibited from involvement in the occupation of men. Nature has nothing to do with this ... woman is a human being as man is, with complete mental faculties and acumen, and equivalent parts, capable of performing according to her own abilities.[11]

By criticizing modern interpretations of religious law, these women crossed a moral Rubicon and showed that the *Nahda* claimed a moral sphere and could not be limited to the abstract principle of progress and sophisticated science-talk. At the same time, much of their discussion focused on everyday concerns such as marital relations, hygiene, child rearing, and breastfeeding.

Though a critique of patriarchy and Islamic law became the issues that galvanized Arab feminism and female activism, men with Western legal training also stepped into the same territory. In 1894, Murqus Fahmi published the play, *Woman in the East* (*al-Mar'a fi al-sharq*), that equated patriarchy with downright oppression. In 1899, following an invitation from Princess Nazli to attend her salon to discuss the condition of women with reformer Muhammad 'Abduh (see below), Muslim judge Qasim Amin published *The Liberation of Women* (*Tahrir al-mar'a*). A year later, he published his influential *The New Woman* (*al-Mar'a al-jadida*). He too attacked patriarchy and the abuses of divorce and polygamy. Because Amin chose to address the predicament of women from the delicate perspective of Islamic law, and because his goal was to advance the state of the nation as a whole rather than that of individual rights, over time his work was canonized as the official proclamation on these matters and entirely overshadowed the original female contributions to late-nineteenth-century feminism.

In sum, during this era Arabs established a space between the individual and the colonial state. Within this space, public opinion was formed and processed into civic action. By practice, if not by name, it was a secular sphere. This crucial development raised the question of what, precisely, should be the cultural role of thirteen centuries of Islamic erudition?

Islamic quest for synthesis: 1880–1900

Islam, as a cultural and religious practice, was glaringly absent from the Arab Enlightenment. A few individuals and a rapidly growing circle of devotees set out to change this reality by calling for religious reform. Their attempt to link Islam to the *Nahda* in a meaningful and deeply philosophical fashion gave birth to Islamic modernism. Since Islamic modernism is an enormous topic that lies outside the scope of this discussion, only its origins and early attitudes toward the *Nahda* are dealt with here.

Arab Islamic modernism developed in two consecutive stages under the leadership of two eccentric individuals. The first person was the political activist and imperial troublemaker Sayyid Jamal al-Din al-Afghani (1838–1897), who arrived in Egypt in 1871. Al-Afghani was an Iranian Shi'ite who, out of consideration for public opinion, took the identity of the Sunni majority. While traveling and living in India, Iran, and the Ottoman lands, he realized that the Islamic "gunpowder empires" were dying and came to think of this reality in the familiar terms of decline. To European imperialism – the well-known cause of this problem – al-Afghani ascribed a false unity of Christian purpose, thus describing imperialism as inherently Christian. As an antidote to Europe's allegedly religious imperialism he devised the doctrine of Pan-Islamic solidarity.

Though he came to the Arab World with Pan-Islamist action in mind, his primary impact was in the field of cultural self-reflection and action. Al-Afghani briefly taught philosophy at Al-Azhar University, the highest Islamic academy, but later quit and opened a salon/secret society/Masonic lodge of which journalist Adib Ishaq, satirist Yaqub Sanu (neither of whom was Muslim), as well as religious scholar Muhammad 'Abduh (1849–1905) were members. His activist ethos and nuanced understanding of global affairs were extremely compelling and he was an excellent oral communicator who preached in public as well as in the privacy of his close circle of coffee drinkers. But he wrote little. Like many other intellectuals of the time, he also tried to understand the causes and the possible remedy for Islamic inferiority vis-à-vis Europe. This is how his circle came to think more seriously of religious reform.

During the mid 1880s, al-Afghani was in exile in Paris where he and Muhammad 'Abduh published an experimental reformist journal. While there he entered into a famous debate with French philosopher and amateur observer of the Orient, Ernest Renan (1823–1892). Renan argued that Islam was incompatible with scientific rational thought. This was an emphatic argument that meant that Islamic civilization was condemningly unreformable. Particularly disconcerting was the fact that Renan's argument was supported at home by some key *Nahda* figures, such as Christian Lebanese writer Farah Antun. In response to Renan, al-Afghani argued that the reason for the poverty of scientific thought was not religion itself but the historical circumstances that surround all religions. He believed that if properly reformed, Islam would "catch up." Until its debunking by Islamic fundamentalists in the late 1940s, this "catching up" thesis formed the basis for the optimism of Islamic modernism.

But what did religious reform mean? How exactly should such reform be implemented and by whom? Though it was clear that the *shari'a* was the object of reform, al-Afghani never delved into specifics. In 1897, he died in Istanbul of either cancer or poisoning and left this gigantic task to

Muhammad 'Abduh, whose reformist project soon reverberated all over the Islamic world.

As an Islamic scholar who also participated in the modern intellectual world, 'Abduh understood that Islamic legal theory and methodology had become too entrenched to allow for social change. His idea, therefore, was to reform the legal code in a fashion that would make it compatible with the moral and philosophical standards of modernity. 'Abduh's process of rethinking Islamic law was based on a return to the unadulterated *sunna,* or "way of life," of the Prophet and his original community. Later termed the *salafiyya,* a movement that violently departed from 'Abduh's original notion, this philosophy maintained that in subsequent centuries the original *sunna* was corrupted and then subjected to centuries of blind and distorting legal imitation (*taqlid*). According to 'Abduh, this was the central cause for the present state of decline and he prescribed independent rational investigation, or *ijtihad,* as a cure.

Striving toward the development of a rational method, as the linchpin of *ijtihad,* 'Abduh sought to make more "room," so to speak, for rational inquiry by opening a discussion about the essence of faith and its metaphysical aspects. In his 1897 *A Treatise on the Oneness of God* (*Risalat al-tawhid*), he sought to redefine Islamic characteristics in modern times and thus create a brand of Islam that could be both authentic – that is, truthful to the original spirit of the faith – and modern. This theoretical and methodological formulation made 'Abduh the architect of Islamic modernism.

In 1888, he was finally admitted back to Egypt and a year later became the Grand Mufti (jurisconsult) of Egypt. He won the support of, and had close personal ties with, Lord Cromer, Egypt's de facto British ruler, who was impressed with 'Abduh's reformist agenda. But he also encountered bitter and personal opposition to his designs. Already in his lifetime it became clear that his agenda for reform was not a task for one gifted individual but a collective task that would require an extraordinary long-term commitment on behalf of several generations.

Initially, it seemed that a generation of intellectual leaders was responding to the challenge. 'Abduh's work legitimated experiments in legal reform in Syria, Iraq, and North Africa, and a close circle of devotees had emerged. Even prominent figures in the secularist *Nahda* joined, such as Ahmed Lutfi al-Sayyid (1872–1963). The general understanding was that if 'Abduh's project were to succeed, the barriers between the secularist modernizers and clerics would be removed. The young Syrian scholar Rashid Rida (1865–1935) came to Egypt in 1897 and became 'Abduh's most devoted disciple. Against all odds, he carried on this tradition until his death, when the relative failure of this platform was widely acknowledged. Indeed, 'Abduh's reformist platform disintegrated after his death. Because they were backed by emerging state institutions that were internationally recognizable, the devotees of the *Nahda* took the secular nationalist path to modernity while the clerics fell back on tradition and on politically defending Islam against imperialism, Christianity, and collaborating minorities at home. Hence, Islamic modernism fell between these two poles. A few Islamic reformers carried on, but, though intellectually important, their public weight was negligible.

The nationalization of the *Nahda*: 1900–1945

With the collapse of the Ottoman Empire in 1919, the *Nahda* became the business of the national movement, the *effendiyya* professional middle class, and the state. By this point, all the leading intellectuals of the first generation of the *Nahda* had already passed away and the ground was prepared for a new intellectual guard to take over. During this new stage, the *effendiyya* associated the *Nahda* with the ideological mechanism of nationalism and forged distinctive and exclusive national cultures (Iraqi, Lebanese, Syrian, Egyptian, Tunisian, and later Algerian, Palestinian, Jordanian, and so on). With the nationalization of culture and state building also came institutionalization, bureaucratization, disciplinization, and professionalization. Intellectuals began talking about national literature and national economy as two sides of the same coin. New universities and professional associations were established. Degrees were offered and academic specialties fortified their public status. The once private small enterprise of the printing press became a commercial publishing house and set a viable print market into operation. Concomitantly, the professional *effendiyya* class grew in number and ambition. They viewed intellectuals as cultural heroes and were proud of their free market of ideas and the culture of the mind. Self-satisfied with their achievements, members of the *effendiyya* positioned themselves as the guardians of liberal democratic rights and progress for all. Though Iraqi intellectuals chronically complained that they were not as productive and influential as their colleagues in the east, they too forged, despite sectarian differences, a pluralist middle-class *Nahda* culture which was alive in institutions such as the Iraqi Reform Club (Basra) and Scientific Club (Baghdad).

However, the intellectual leadership of the Arab East remained in Cairo. Taha Hussein (1889–1973), the so-called Dean of Arab Letters, embodied both the ideals and the promise of this era. Blind since childhood, Hussein first pursued a standard Islamic education but later revolted against it. He moved from his village to Cairo and from there to Paris. In 1919, he graduated from the Sorbonne. He was now a Francophone and a relentless promoter of European culture who held important university posts and even served as the Egyptian Minister of Education. Early in his career his research methods called into question the authenticity of the entire body of pre-Islamic poetry, which had been used by early scholars to interpret the language of the Qur'an. A cultural scandal ensued. At about the same time, Shaykh ʿAli ʿAbd al-Raziq (1888–1966), an Al-Azhar graduate, published a book which questioned the historical validity of the Islamic polity, thus practically calling for the separation of church and state. Another scandal broke out. With the abolition of the Islamic Caliphate in 1924, it seemed to individuals like Rashid Rida that the *Nahda* was out to defeat religion. This perception triggered Islamic fundamentalism and explains Rida's somber words quoted in the introduction to this essay.

Ironically, as the *Nahda* and the state became more closely intertwined, its limitations and paradoxes became more apparent and, by the mid 1930s, the entire project began to unravel. First, new grassroots movements such as the Muslim Brotherhood in Egypt criticized the *Nahda* as an inauthentic secular formulation that thrived at the expense of popular Islamic culture. Second, from the Iraqi prism of Marxism-Leninism, the *Nahda* was seen as derivative of colonial culture and hence could offer only second-rate mimicry of the West and the continuation of economic and political submission to it. Rooted in colonial modernity, the proprietors of the *Nahda* assumed that the masses lacked the elementary conditions for citizenship (literacy, erudition, hygiene, political maturity, familial structure). Accepting the notion that the lower classes were primitive, "traditional," and simply inadequate, the institutions of the *Nahda* – for example, the educational and political systems – offered only paternalistic liberalism which was devoid of true democratic participation. As a national culture that was closely associated with the state, it suffered the failure of the Arab liberal state to liberate its population from colonial rule, provide social mobility and justice, and secure adequate economic conditions for growth. Above all, however, the *Nahda* fell short of realizing its initial promise: the emergence of an authentic Arab subject. By 1945, the Arab World was ready to experiment with something else.

Conclusion: the *Nahda's* bifurcated modernity

As the defining Arab intellectual enterprise in recent centuries, the *Nahda* grew from a defensive and selective experiment to a fully fledged project that embraced the basic traits of modernity: autonomous and rational subjectivity, psychologism and self-reflectivity, dominance of secularism, nationalism with all its attendant socioeconomic structures and formulations, scientific and technological mindedness, urbanism and industrialism. As a new and highly integrated way of life, it also claimed a normative and moral space. A useful way of thinking about some aspects of this era is by considering them in terms of the German idea of *Bildung*: namely, a deep social transformation that collapses together several tendencies, such as the liberation of the mind from what was considered by the historical actors as "tradition and superstition," a journey of self-realization, rejection of pre-modern political systems, and, most importantly, the positivist realization that knowledge is gained only from experience.

As in the case of other "unfulfilled enlightenments" (Indian, Asian, Latin American, and even Russian), the *Nahda* was trapped in the paradoxes of colonial modernity.[12] Thus, while accepting the divided realities of East/West, rational/spiritual, Europe/Islam, rise/decline, and civilized/barbarian, it insisted that a harmonious singular and authentic Arab reality was indeed emerging. This bifurcated condition, indeed a deep cultural schism, shaped the *Nahda* and with it the lives of millions of Arab citizens. However, by the late 1940s, a sense of cultural strangeness caused a new generation of intellectuals to argue that Arab subjectivity was in a schizophrenic state of being. In this state of affairs, the Arab subject was alienated from her or his link to authentic Islamic culture as well as from their very own selves. This crisis of the Arab self was the vantage point for a new postcolonial stage in Arab culture. A long list of doubts circulated: Is there modernity without colonialism? How could Arabs liberate themselves as they go about imitating the culture of their oppressors? Could there be a *Nahda* without foreigners, minorities, and cosmopolitanism? Why was the *Nahda* a world of privilege closed to the majority of Arab citizens? Was the *Nahda* a Christian project? To what degree was the *Nahda* a project of historic continuity? Did the *Nahda* compromise the cultural authenticity of the Arab East? Was the *Nahda* responsible for Islamic reformism or was reformism intrinsic to Islam? Did it trigger a violent brand of Islamic radicalism?

Pondering these questions, philosopher Muhammad ʿAbid al-Jabiri recently wondered, "Are we still not free from the ambiguities of nineteenth-century thought?"[13] Indeed the *Nahda* is still relevant. After the spectacular failure of the *Nahda*'s alternatives – authentic Arab Socialism (Baʿathisim and Nasserism) and Islamism – the *Nahda*'s troubled legacy is once again up for reconsideration. The "Arab Spring" of 2011 gave a huge push for a renewed engagement and even revitalization of the *Nahda*. As summarized recently by a contemporary scholar of Arab thought, there is an acute need to comprehend, "Why did the first *Nahda*, and with it Enlightenment as a whole, disintegrate to the point of marginality and what is the right path for a second Arab *Nahda*?"[14]

Notes

1   Rifaʿa Rafiʿ al-Tahtawi, *An Imam in Paris: Account of a Stay in France by an Egyptian Cleric, 1826–1831* (London: Saqi Books, 2004), pp. 253–54.

2   Quoted in Sabry Hafiz, *The Genesis of Arabic Narrative Discourse: A Study In The Sociology of Modern Arabic Literature* (London: Saqi Books, 1993), p. 62

3   Rashid Rida, "Renewal, Renewing, and Renewers," in Charles Kurzman (ed.), *Modernist Islam 1840–1940: A Sourcebook* (Oxford University Press, 2002), p. 78.

4   Al-Tahtawi, *An Imam in Paris*, p. 183.

5   Butrus al-Bustani, *Kitab Dairat al-Maʿarif* (Beirut: n.p., 1876), p. 3.

6   Though Egypt was an important hub of these developments, they were not restricted to Egypt alone. Thus, by the mid 1880s, printing and publishing in the Arab World was quite established: presses were founded in Jerusalem (1847), Damascus (1855), Mosul (1856), Tunis (1860), Baghdad (1863), Sanaʿa (1877), Khartoum (1881), Mecca (1883), and Medina (1885). See "Publishing," in *Encyclopedia of Arabic Literature* (New York: Routledge, 1998), vol. II, p. 614.

7   G. Delanoue, "al-Marsafi, al-Husayn," in *Encyclopaedia of Islam* (Second Edition). [Available online from http://referenceworks.brillonline.com.]

8   Albert Hourani, *Arabic Thought in the Liberal Age, 1798–1939* (Cambridge University Press, 1989), p. 247.

9   Margot Badran, *Feminists, Islam, and Nation: Gender and the Making of Modern Egypt* (Princeton University Press, 1995), p. 15.

10   Badran, *Feminists, Islam, and Nation*, p. 14.

11 Ibid., p. 15.

12 Brenda Deen Schildgen, Gang Zhou, Sander L. Gilman (eds.), *Other Renaissances: A New Approach to World Literature* (New York: Palgrave Macmillan, 2006).

13 Muhammad 'Abid al-Jabiri, *Ishkaliyat al-Fikr al-Arabi al-mu'asir* (Beirut: Markaz Dirasat al-Wahda al-Arabiyya, 2005), p. 101.

14 Sharif Maher, *Rihanat al-Nahda fi-l-fikr al-'arabi* (Damascus: Dar al-Mada li-l-Thaqafa wa-l-Nashr, 2000), p. 23.

4

Law

Most modern Arab legal systems form a part of the civil law system that spread throughout the developing world as a result of the immense influence of French legal thought in the nineteenth century.[1] They therefore generally stand closer in their structure and spirit to continental European legal systems than to common law systems such as those of the United States and England. Codification of law in the Arab World is partly traceable to developments under the Ottoman Empire and partly to the impact of European colonialism and the subsequent imposition, adoption, and imitation of continental European models of legislation. While Arab legal systems remain united by a common language, broadly similar histories, and some shared cultural features (religion, for example), there is otherwise nothing quintessentially "Arab" about them. Islamic law (*shari'a*) plays a relatively minor role, usually limited to the realm of family law, even though it continues to exert a substantial political attraction as a symbol of cultural and religious authenticity. A small number of Arab states, mostly in the Gulf, claim to base their legal systems to varying degrees on Islamic law, though they nonetheless avail themselves of the legislative "technologies" of civil law.

One other thing that Arab legal systems share is that they are almost all found in states ruled by autocrats. This political fact may cause one to dismiss such legal systems as handmaidens of authoritarianism, so to speak, but such an assumption would be too broad. The Arab World's legal systems often represent one of the few institutional restraints on otherwise unchecked exercises of executive might.

Historical background: Ottoman legal system

Although the Ottoman Empire was neither ethnically nor linguistically Arab, it had a profound impact on law in the Arab World. From the early sixteenth century, the Ottoman state asserted its sovereignty through military conquest over lands that today comprise the territory of most Arab states (excluding Morocco and the central Arabian heartland of what is now the Kingdom of Saudi Arabia, with the exception of the Hijaz). The Ottoman legal system, while theoretically based on Islamic law, also exhibited certain key differences from premodern Islamic legal systems. In pre-Ottoman times, Islamic law had developed as a system in which independent scholar-jurists composed treatises on law and gave formal opinions (*fatwas*), and state-sponsored courts then applied that law.[2]

The scholar-jurists formulated the rules of Islamic law using sophisticated interpretive techniques for deriving rules from the Qur'an and the Prophetic traditions (short narratives, termed *hadiths*, that describe legally relevant acts or statements, *sunnas*, of the Prophet Muhammad, d. 632). The resulting doctrines were compiled in systematic collections covering both religious ritual and the entire range of legal subject matter that Western legal systems typically deem "secular": commercial law, contracts, penal law, torts, family law, the law of war, and so on. These legal doctrines were collectively termed *fiqh* (lit., "knowledge," or "understanding"), a word that emphasizes their status as variable, fallible, human interpretations of the invariable, infallible, divine will as expressed in the Qur'an and the Prophetic traditions. Although the jurists' authoritative formulations of legal doctrine were achieved largely independently from the state (a fact that contributed to their religious and moral authority), they were nonetheless patronized by rulers in various ways.

Under the Ottomans, previously private legal activities – higher education, legal opinion-giving, and the formulation of the law – were taken over in significant measure by the state. The state assumed control over law colleges (*madrasas*); created the position of Şeyhülislam (Ar. *shaykh al-Islām*), who became the empire's chief legal official; and, in the nineteenth century, began to promulgate law codes, some based on Islamic law and some based on French models.

The introduction of law codes represented a particularly far-reaching innovation. Although this development occurred in the second half of

the nineteenth century, Ottoman rulers had already begun to promulgate and codify administrative regulations, called *kanun* (Ar. *qānūn*), as
early as the late fifteenth century. These came to be considered a kind
of complement to the *shari'a*, but, unlike the *fiqh*, fell within the exclusive power of the executive branch of government. In the latter half of
the nineteenth century, codification gained momentum, and by 1858
Ottoman penal legislation had come to be based on the French Penal
Code of 1810, even though a few *shari'a* doctrines were retained (e.g., for
homicide). Soon thereafter, a code of criminal procedure, a commercial
code, and a code of maritime commerce were introduced, all based on
French models. From the mid-nineteenth century onward, a new court
system, separate from the religious *shari'a* courts, administered these
laws.

The most important of the Ottoman codes was the 1876 *Mecelle-i
Ahkam-ı Adliyye* (Ar. *Majallat al-aḥkām al-'adliyya*, the "Digest of Legal
Rules"), based on Islamic law according to the Hanafi school of legal
thought.[3] The *Mecelle* represented a laborious effort to codify laws of
contract and liability in a comprehensive literary form inspired by the
Napoleonic Code, while attempting to retain the substantive rules of
fiqh. As an enactment of the sultan, the *Mecelle* symbolically deprived
Islamic law's scholar-jurists of the ability to formulate legal doctrine,
notwithstanding the fact that important scholar-jurists participated
in its drafting. In addition, it had a profound impact on the subsequent legal history of the Arab World, surviving the dissolution of
the Ottoman Empire, remaining in force in Syria, Lebanon, Jordan,
Palestine and Israel, Iraq, Kuwait, and Tunisia through the early to
mid-twentieth century, and even contributing rules to some modern
Arab codes.[4]

These codes and the new court system, all clearly indebted to European
models, represented a stark departure from the earlier Islamic legal tradition. Law codes, as a legal technology, were alien to the world of classical
Islamic law. The new codes, especially in their totalizing literary form,
differed fundamentally from the sources and literature of Islamic law
and thus packaged legal doctrine in a profoundly different manner. The
melding of civil law and *shari'a* was thus, and remains today, a process at
once complex and fascinating. One undoubted consequence of codification, however, was that it allowed Muslims to imagine something new: a
codified, univocal *shari'a*.

Nineteenth-century Egypt

Legal developments in nineteenth-century Egypt – ruled by an Ottoman elite, but politically semi-autonomous – mirrored those in the Ottoman heartland. Egypt experienced a particularly intensive process of legal change during this time (as did Algeria, under direct colonial pressure from France) that had consequences for the subsequent history of Arab legal systems. Laws were increasingly codified, jurisdictions increasingly rationalized and regulated by statute, and courts and tribunals arranged into hierarchies.

In penal legislation, for example, a series of new codes was promulgated that described punishments with more specificity than before and spelled out which bodies could hear appeals from the rulings of Islamic law courts. *Shariʿa* punishments involving corporal or capital punishment were reviewed by higher authorities, though it appears that such punishments were less and less frequently applied. Convictions in the *shariʿa* courts were also infrequent, so that most punishments were meted out by secular courts according to the provisions of the code.

Of particular importance were the so-called "Capitulations," special jurisdictions established for foreigners. "Capitulations" had existed in the Ottoman Empire since the sixteenth century, giving foreign consular officials jurisdiction over legal disputes involving their own citizens. By the nineteenth century, however, they had become increasingly abused as a way for both foreigners (particularly merchants) and some Ottoman subjects (mostly non-Muslims) to avoid the Ottoman legal system and Ottoman taxes. In 1876 and 1883, the judiciary in Egypt was reorganized into two sets of courts, the Mixed Courts (*al-maḥākim al-mukhtaliṭa*), for civil cases involving Egyptians and foreigners as well as criminal cases involving foreigners only, and the National Courts (*al-maḥākim al-adliyya*), for all other cases involving Egyptians. The Mixed Courts used French-language codes drafted by a French jurist from Alexandria and the National Courts used a similar set of codes in Arabic, both based on the French-inspired Ottoman codes. These judicial reorganizations thus resulted in the existence of four separate court systems: the Mixed Courts, the National Courts, the various religious courts (for Muslims, Christians, and Jews) that retained jurisdiction over matters of family law, and consular courts with jurisdiction over certain non-Egyptian nationals.

The emergence of these new courts had significant longterm consequences for both Egypt and other Arab legal systems. A trained cadre of judges and lawyers (many educated in France) came into being, who became and remain advocates of liberalism and judicial independence. The administrative streamlining of the courts and codification of the law contributed further to the executive's centralization of control. The Mixed Courts, an outgrowth of European imperialism and the capitulations, came increasingly to be viewed as an affront to Egyptian nationalist aspirations. Finally, the early development of civil law expertise among Egyptians – judges, lawyers, and law professors – allowed Egypt to play a disproportionately important (and ongoing) role in the legal systems of other Arab states.

Developments elsewhere

Legal change in Egypt paralleled to some extent processes initiated from the Ottoman center in the Arab lands subject to Ottoman control: Syria, Lebanon, Transjordan, Palestine, Iraq, and Tunisia. In late nineteenth-century Iraq, for example, the French-based Ottoman codes of substantive and procedural law were applied. During World War I and the ensuing British Mandate in Iraq (1920–32), a more eclectic body of law was applied, culled from Ottoman, French, and Anglo-Indian colonial laws, while tribal customary law was applied in the countryside. In Transjordan, Ottoman legislation remained in effect under the British Mandate, but under the British Mandate in Palestine (1922–48), many Ottoman laws were replaced with British legislation and courts were empowered to apply British law.

Under the post-World War I French Mandate in Lebanon and Syria (1923–43 and 1923–46 respectively), Ottoman law continued to be applied until the adoption of the Lebanese Code in 1932 and the Syrian Code in 1949. Still in force today, the 1932 Lebanese Code was drafted by a French jurist, patterned after the joint French–Italian Code of Obligations and Contracts, which was then being developed but was never itself enacted into law, and then revised by Lebanese jurists to reflect local legal culture (including the incorporation of some provisions of Ottoman and Islamic law).

Arabia – outside the Hijaz, where Mecca and Medina are located – was less amenable to incorporation within the Ottoman legal bureaucracy. Various regions retained *shari'a* courts, administrative tribunals under the direct jurisdiction of local rulers, and in tribal areas distant from urban control, traditional tribally based dispute resolution mechanisms. The Hijaz, under Ottoman control until the Arab Revolt of 1916, retained its Ottoman-style system of courts and jurists after World War I and even for a time under Saudi rule.

By means of an 1830 treaty with France, Tunisia's ruler granted capitulatory privileges to the European powers and these were extended by European consuls (without any authority in the treaty itself) to cover cases in which the defendant was European and the plaintiff Muslim. Tunisia's relationship to the Ottoman Empire was slightly more attenuated than that of Egypt, so the Ottoman legal reforms of the later nineteenth century were not introduced or imitated to the extent that they had been in Egypt. Under British and French pressure, however, in 1857 the Tunisian ruler Muhammad Bey (r. 1855–59) promulgated a document entitled the Pledge of Security ('Ahd al-amān) that granted Muslims and non-Muslims equality before the law and allowed foreigners to acquire property in Tunisia. This was followed in 1860, under his successor, by the first constitution introduced in any Arab country (see below).

Tunisia's financial insolvency left it open to French occupation in 1881 and, with the establishment of a protectorate in 1883, French courts were introduced. Although land ownership disputes continued to be determined with reference to Islamic law, a joint French–Tunisian court was established in 1888 to hear such cases. In 1906, the Tunisian Code of Contracts and Obligations was adopted, drafted by David Santillana (d. 1931), a Tunisian-born Italian historian of Islamic law. This code was based on various European codes, but with an admixture of rules of Islamic law from the Maliki school of legal thought, long dominant in North Africa.[5]

Throughout the nineteenth century, Morocco avoided the kinds of "reforms" imposed by the French in Algeria (see below). However, an 1856 treaty gave British consular officials the right to try cases involving British subjects and in 1906 France and Spain gained the right to police and patrol ports, but under Swiss supervision. A French protectorate was established in 1912 and Santillana's Code of Contracts and Obligations, previously enacted in Tunisia, was adopted in Morocco the following year.

The situation in Algeria was in important respects unique because of the French invasion of 1830. France's annexation of Algeria in 1834 meant that all then-existing French legislation applied in Algeria. Islamic law continued to be applied to non-European Algerians, but the jurisdiction of *shari'a* courts was circumscribed and French courts with French judges had jurisdiction to interpret local customary law, which included but was purposefully not limited to Islamic law. French Arabists also studied Islamic law and in 1916 a commission headed by the Dean of the Law Faculty of the University of Algiers produced a code based on the Maliki school of legal thought, though it was never enacted.

Under both Ottoman and colonial rule or influence, then, many areas of the Arab World experienced the introduction or imposition of European-inspired codes, the emergence of secular legal institutions, the erosion of *shari'a*-related institutions, and a strengthening of executive power to varying degrees. These developments were most intensive in Egypt, but occurred also in other Ottoman provinces. The role of colonial interference in legal systems in Arab lands is subject to varying interpretations, but there is no doubt that such interference contributed in important ways, for better or worse, to momentous changes in legal culture in the nineteenth and early twentieth centuries.

Contemporary Arab legal systems

A key date in the emergence of contemporary Arab legal systems is the year 1949, when the new Egyptian Civil Code, drafted by the Egyptian legal scholar 'Abd al-Razzaq al-Sanhuri (1895–1971), was adopted into law. Sanhuri, a towering figure in the history of modern Arab legal thought who earned two doctorates from the University of Lyon, one on Islamic public law and one on English law, sought to produce a modern yet culturally authentic code. Sanhuri's Egyptian Civil Code of 1949, which became highly influential across almost the entire Arab World, was drafted in accordance with contemporaneous European legal ideas but attempted to reconcile those ideas with and assimilate them into the Islamic legal tradition. Its interpretation by Egyptian courts was considered important and the extensive commentary by its author is still considered persuasive authority by courts in the Arab World. Sanhuri's own influence was equally important: the Syrian Code of 1949 was closely patterned after Egypt's; Sanhuri played a substantial role in drafting the Iraqi Civil Code of 1951; he approved the Libyan Civil Code of 1954; he played a key role in drafting codes and reorganizing the courts in the Kuwaiti legal system beginning in 1959; and his code served as the basis for the 1971 Qatari Code. Sanhuri claimed to have made extensive (though by no means exclusive) use of Islamic legal doctrines in these codes and each of them refers to the *shariʿa* as a source of interpretation, though with differing emphases. Although it is tempting to divide contemporary Arab legal systems according to type of government (monarchies vs. republics) or according to the prominence accorded the *shariʿa* (*shariʿa* vs. civil jurisdictions), one might equally well divide such legal systems according to their adoption, or not, of codes drafted or inspired by Sanhuri.[6]

Courts and other institutions

Arab legal systems' judiciaries differ from each other principally in regard to the structure of appellate courts, constitutional review, and the role of *shariʿa* courts. In most Arab legal systems, courts that hear civil and criminal cases are organized regionally and a higher tier of courts reviews the decisions of courts of first instance. Such intermediate appellate review is usually a complete review of the entire case and can involve a new determination of the facts (unlike the US system, for example, in which appellate review is limited to certain areas). In regard to final courts of appeal, many Arab states have a court of cassation (*Maḥkamat al-naqḍ* or *Maḥkamat al-tamyīz*), modeled after the French *Cour de cassation*. Such courts stand at the apex of the regular judiciary; unlike intermediate appellate courts, they have a narrower scope of review, limited to the record established by the lower court. Also, unlike the Supreme Court in the US system, such supreme courts do not always have competence to review the legality of state action or the constitutionality of either state action or legislation. In some Arab states, the legality of state action is reviewed by a body patterned after the French *Conseil d'état*, a "Council of State" (usually *Majlis al-dawla*, but in Lebanon *Majlis shūrā al-dawla*), an administrative court system separate from the regular judiciary.

In Egypt, for example, the National Courts (*Maḥākim ahlīyya*) are organized regionally and divided into civil and criminal courts. Above these sit courts of appeal (*Maḥākim al-istiʾnāf*) and above those is the Court of Cassation (*Maḥkamat al-naqḍ*), which sits as a supreme court of appeal in civil and criminal matters. In addition, the Council of State (*Majlis al-dawla*) comprises a three-tiered system of administrative courts that hear cases contesting state action, at the apex of which sits the Supreme Administrative Court (*al-Maḥkama al-idāriyya al-ʿulyā*). In addition, and until very recently unique among all the Arab legal systems, Egypt has a dedicated constitutional court. Interestingly, Article 19 of the Lebanese Constitution grants to the heads of the recognized religious communities the right to request constitutional review of legislation that may infringe on their communities' rights. Typically, however, constitutional courts review the constitutionality of legislation pursuant to the request of certain specified officials.[7]

In legal systems in which the role of Islamic law is more conspicuous, the relationship between the *shariʿa* courts and other tribunals has been complex. In Qatar, for example, until recently, civil courts and *shariʿa* courts existed as parallel legal tracks under the authority of two different ministries: civil courts adjudicated cases under Qatar's various codes, and the *shariʿa* courts heard family law cases, tort cases, and cases pertaining to those few crimes governed by Islamic law. The 2003–9 reforms of the judiciary brought both courts under a common administration and made their decisions subject to appellate review by an appellate court (*Maḥkamat al-istiʾnāf*), with ultimate appellate review lodged in a Court of Cassation (*Maḥkamat al-tamyīz*), and created special Family Law and Supreme Constitutional courts. The latter has jurisdiction to hear, among other things, constitutional challenges to legislation and to resolve disputes among lower courts.

Saudi Arabia has undertaken judicial reforms similar to those of Qatar. Until recently, *shariʿa* courts heard the vast majority of civil and criminal matters, and a range of administrative tribunals under the authority of the executive exercised specialized competence in certain areas of commercial law, labor law, some criminal cases, and other matters. This bifurcated judicial structure rests on a doctrine of Islamic public law termed *siyāsa sharʿīyya*, "legitimate executive prerogative" (also the basis for the Ottoman *kanun*). New laws enacted in 2007 created a larger tier of courts of first instance, including both *shariʿa* courts and new courts to hear matters formerly within the purview of the administrative tribunals, all under the authority of the Ministry of Justice. Decisions of the expanded courts of first instance, including specialized commercial and labor courts, will be appealable to courts of appeal (*Maḥākim istiʾnāfiyya*), and those courts' decisions to a supreme court (*al-Maḥkama al-ʿulyā*). The Supreme Judicial Council (*Majlis al-qaḍāʾ al-aʿlā*), which formerly functioned as a supreme court of appeals for decisions of the *shariʿa* courts, will now instead become responsible for judicial administration. Notwithstanding the expansion of courts under the Ministry of Justice, the Saudi executive continues to employ a Board of Grievances (*Dīwān al-maẓālim*) for various matters deemed solely within the competence of the executive.[8]

The court system of the United Arab Emirates, a confederation of seven sovereign emirates (principalities), is of particular interest for its federal structure with a number of court systems that operate in parallel. Three emirates (Abu Dhabi, Dubai, and Ras Al Khaimah) maintain their own court system. A system of federal courts has jurisdiction to hear cases arising in the other four emirates as well as administrative cases involving the federal government and disputes between the member emirates. The Dubai courts, the federal courts, and the Ras Al Khaimah courts each have a division for *shariʿa* courts; by contrast, Abu Dhabi has no *shariʿa* courts. Legislation at the federal level in 1996 transferred jurisdiction over certain crimes including crimes under Islamic law, drugs cases, and cases involving juveniles, away from the federal criminal courts to the federal *shariʿa* courts.

Finally, in many Arab legal systems, judges may investigate crimes in tandem with the public prosecutor (*al-Niyāba al-ʿāmma*), as in France's "parquet" system. A court's power to pursue such a judicial investigation is generally conferred by statute.

Islamic law (*shariʿa*)

Although many Arab states proclaim in their constitutions that Islam is the official state religion, such constitutional provisions do not necessarily mean that a country's legal system is based on Islamic law. With the exceptions of Saudi Arabia (which had no direct legacy of colonial or, for the most part, Ottoman rule) and, until very recently, Oman (whose first civil code came into force in August 2013), nearly every Arab legal system is a recognizably civil law system, even those legal systems that grant a very prominent role to Islamic law, such as Qatar or the United Arab Emirates.[9] The status of Islamic law in a given legal system may be dealt with constitutionally (constitutions are discussed separately below). Also, as noted above, the Arab civil codes often refer to Islamic law as a source of law for matters unregulated by the codes. Article 1(2) of the Egyptian Civil Code of 1949, for example, provides that judges who cannot find a relevant provision in the Code should look to:

> custom (*ʿurf*);
> principles of Islamic law (*mabādiʾ al-sharīʿa al-islāmiyya*, lit.,
> "principles of the Islamic *shariʿa*");

principles of natural law and rules of equity (*mabādiʾ al-qānūn
al-ṭabīʿī wa-qawāʿid al-ʿadāla*).

The primary area of law in Arab states that continues to be based, to varying degrees, on Islamic law is family law, which includes marriage, divorce, and inheritance. In the small number of states (mostly in the Gulf) that claim to base their legal systems on the *shariʿa*, Islamic law may also furnish rules of penal law and/or tort law. Although Islamic law plays a relatively minor role in the regulation of financial services, its doctrines continue to inform some aspects of commercial law in the more *shariʿa*-leaning Arab legal systems.

Approaches to family law legislation have been diverse and reflect widely differing (and constantly evolving) policies toward religion, legal system, and gender equality in Arab countries. Codification of Islamic family law began with the Ottoman Family Law of 1917, one of the Ottoman codes that was based on Islamic rather than European law. Most Arab legal systems today have a "Code of Personal Status" that regulates family law. Law in this area remains politically highly symbolic and controversial. The wave of French-inspired codification after World War II included attempts to "reform" rules allowing polygamous marriage and unilateral male divorce, both largely unrestricted male prerogatives under Islamic law. Such regulation was accomplished in various ways. Tunisia, for example, prohibited polygamy outright and imposed a fine and imprisonment for anyone concluding a second marriage before dissolution of the first. Other countries required the judge's permission (e.g., Iraq) to conclude a second marriage or granted the preexisting wife certain limited remedies in case of a second marriage (e.g., Morocco). Still other areas expressly allowed the wife to stipulate in the marriage contract that no second marriage be concluded (Jordan, Morocco), or to require the husband to state in the marriage contract whether he was already married (Egypt).

Divorce, too, has been regulated in some jurisdictions in ways that modify the rules of Islamic law. In general, under Islamic law, men have the unilateral right to divorce their wives, without cause and without going before a court at all, but women can only obtain a divorce with the husband's consent or, under limited circumstances, by court order. The modern codes have sought to address this asymmetry in various ways, often by codifying those opinions of Muslim jurists that most restrict male prerogatives and by bringing all divorces within the competence of the courts, so that even exercises of the unilateral right of male divorce must be brought before a judge. Tunisian law, usually the most aggressive in its willingness to modify Islamic legal doctrine, even recognized a woman's right to petition the court for divorce without cause, and women's rights were further enhanced in a series of 1993 amendments to the Tunisian Code of Personal Status.

Male prerogatives in this area are often associated with Islamic practices, and any regulation or modification of rights granted under Islamic law runs a serious risk of being identified with Western or Western-supported elites' attempts to alter or abolish Islamic law. In 1979, Egyptian President Anwar Sadat issued a decree expanding women's rights in divorce and custody cases, but this was struck down by the Supreme Constitutional Court in 1985 on procedural grounds, amid Islamist opposition to its substance. In 2000, Egypt adopted a new law to reform some aspects of divorce which controversially granted women a unilateral right to divorce, in exchange for surrendering their dowry. The controversy stemmed in part from the fact that a divorce initiated by the wife under Islamic law requires the husband's consent and thus neither infringes male prerogative nor empowers women. Supporters of the new law saw it either as a needed reform of Islamic legal doctrine by the state or the revivification of a doctrine of Islamic law whose true interpretation had been long suppressed by male-dominated religious institutions. Opponents saw it as a completely unwarranted and substantively mistaken reformulation of religious law by a secular organ of government. The Moroccan Family Law of 2003 did not go quite so far in altering the traditional doctrine of divorce initiated by wives – it made it subject to mutual agreement – but it did provide relatively broad grounds under which a woman can petition a court for a divorce and raised the minimum age for marriage to eighteen for both sexes.

There is considerable variation in judicial structures and competences in the area of family law, for example, in regard to whether religious or other courts apply such law. In some countries religious courts are used and confessional communities such as Christians, Druze, and Jews may be empowered to handle such cases internally through their own religious institutions. In Egypt a 1955 law abolished such confessional courts and transferred their jurisdiction over all such matters to the National Courts, which now apply the various recognized religious communities' law in family law cases. Continuing a trend of family law reform, a law enacted in 2004 instituted a new family court with simplified and expedited procedures to avoid delays that could be detrimental in such cases.

For non-Muslims, separate jurisdiction over matters of family law amounts to legal recognition of their communal identity and autonomy, so they have no incentive to press for secularization of family law. In Lebanon, for example, a decree from 1936 grants the religious institution that conducted a marriage authority over any legal disputes related to that marriage; civil marriage in Lebanon is not deemed valid and mixed marriages therefore continue to pose problems of jurisdiction. Such considerations can also be relevant to Muslim sectarians. In Bahrain, where a Sunni monarchy rules over a Shiʿite majority, some Shiʿites have been leery of recent attempts at family law reform, which are perceived as Sunni encroachment on Shiʿite religious and legal institutions.

In countries that give an enhanced role to *shariʿa*, crimes and torts (the latter including intentional and accidental homicide, assault, and other personal injuries) continue to be governed to varying degrees by Islamic law. For a small number of Qurʾanically defined crimes, Islamic law prescribes capital or corporal punishment: amputation of the hand for theft; various physical punishments, including death, for so-called "brigandage" (*ḥirāba*); flogging or stoning for unlawful sexual intercourse; and flogging for false or unsupported accusations of unlawful sexual intercourse. In addition, based on the practice of the early community, unlawful intoxication is punishable by flogging and apostasy by death. Traditional Islamic jurisprudence on these topics, however, sets many obstacles to their enforcement. Not only did jurists define these offenses extremely narrowly and subject them to numerous exceptions, but they also imposed standards of evidence that were difficult to meet in practice (for unlawful sexual intercourse, for example, the requirement of four eyewitnesses to actual penetration). These barriers to convictions, together with the Qurʾan's dramatic imposition of these punishments, suggest that such punishments primarily served the purpose of denunciation more than deterrence, an interpretation that fits with the limited ability of premodern states to undertake widespread enforcement of penal law. Spectacular modern infliction of these punishments in some regions, both within and without the Arab World, is arguably ahistorical and aimed at pacifying domestic political constituencies.

Under Islamic law, homicide, assault, and personal injury form a group of offenses that remains analytically distinct from the small number of crimes listed above; one could think of them as torts. In general, serious intentional injuries and intentional killing give rise to a right of retaliation (belonging to the victim's heirs in the case of intentional homicide), which may be waived in favor of financial compensation or waived in full as a meritorious act of charitable forgiveness. Lesser injuries and accidental death or injury are generally subject to compensation. Thus, all such cases give rise to a private right, but it is one that premodern jurists generally felt should be enforced by the state, and one which modern states enforce.

Ottoman-period court records suggest that crimes such as adultery began to be punished with fines rather than death in the early modern period, and it has already been noted that punishments were generally increasingly limited by codified law in nineteenth-century Egypt. Such developments are often characterized as the results of "reform," but it might be that a change in sensibilities occurred that represented a natural, indigenous evolution of legal culture (reflecting that of Muslim and other societies more generally) away from corporal and capital punishment. Alternatively, one could also see in such developments the transition from severely exemplary punishment in the context of weak premodern states to punishments that were both less gruesome and increasingly rationalized and regulated in the context of early modern states with more effective techniques of surveillance, apprehension, and prosecution.

Saudi Arabia, the most committed *shari'a* jurisdiction in the Arab World, continues to apply Islamic criminal law, including the punishments specified in the Qur'an or otherwise developed in premodern Islamic jurisprudence. These punishments and the crimes for which they are imposed are traditionally referred to as *ḥudūd*, "limits." In Saudi Arabia, such punishments are inflicted publicly and witnessed, weekly, by large crowds. *Shari'a* courts also have jurisdiction over other non-specified crimes that receive lesser punishments; such discretionary punishments are referred to as *ta'zīr* (lit. "censure," or "chastisement") and are the counterpart under *shari'a* law to the *ḥudūd*. The premodern *ḥudūd* penalties continue to be applied in the Sudan as well. In Qatar, such cases can in theory be brought in *shari'a* courts, but seem now increasingly to be tried by the non-religious courts. The United Arab Emirates, a jurisdiction in which *shari'a* is important, but not always determinative, has combined torts and crimes governed by Islamic law into a single modern penal code in which Islamic legal doctrine is melded with modern approaches to penal legislation. Because there are so few crimes defined under Islamic law, *shari'a*-leaning jurisdictions usually find it necessary to define additional crimes by means of legislation, whether together in the same penal code with the *shari'a* -based crimes (as in the United Arab Emirates) or in separate legislation issued by the executive branch (as in Saudi Arabia, Qatar, or Sudan).

Given the increasing popularity of Islamic finance, one might expect it to feature prominently in recent legislation, but this has not been the case. On the other hand, Islamic law principles continue to inform doctrinal approaches to commercial law. For example, Islamic law tends to disallow commercial claims for lost earnings or lost future profits on the grounds that such claims are inherently speculative and uncertain; courts in Saudi Arabia will thus not normally entertain such claims at all. In other Gulf jurisdictions, statutes expressly permit claims for lost future profits but judges in those countries, operating within their cultural and educational frameworks, tend to be unsympathetic to such claims.

Usurious interest (Ar. *ribā*, in the context of Islamic law) is generally prohibited under Islamic commercial law and the mainstream view is that all interest is usury. Nonetheless, the Sanhuri codes, even in *shari'a* -based jurisdictions, provide for the paying of interest (*fā'ida*, in such contexts) in various situations. Throughout the Arab World, banks generally pay interest on deposit accounts and charge interest on loans (or, in both cases, a renamed equivalent). Certain jurisdictions, however, such as Kuwait, Qatar, the United Arab Emirates, and Saudi Arabia, impose restrictions of various kinds on the enforceability of interest obligations. For example, the charging of interest by persons (i.e., non-commercially) is a criminal offense and, although commercial interest is legal, the courts in Abu Dhabi will normally enforce only simple interest obligations, not compound interest. Courts in Saudi Arabia will normally not enforce any obligation to pay interest, though they may choose to enforce such clauses as a moral matter and then require that the interest be given to charity, so that the party entitled to receive it is not illegally enriched. Finally, although Islamic law recognizes only natural persons, statutes in the Arab World routinely recognize the artificial legal personality of various types of companies.

Constitutions

The earliest constitutions in the Arab World, from the late nineteenth and early twentieth centuries, aimed with only modest success to restrain executive authority, especially in decisions affecting economic policy.[10] Constitutions of the post-independence era (roughly after 1945), mostly produced through other than representative processes, have variously expressed national aspirations connected with independence: socialist and Arab Nationalist ideological orientations; liberal ideals of government and the rule of law; and sometimes a commitment to principles of Islamic government and/or law. Although actual constitutionalism and liberal practices of governance are not widespread in the Arab World, the blueprints for separation of and limitations on powers in the Arab states' constitutions and basic laws have led to a modest and possibly increasing measure of accountability. The last three decades have witnessed a heightened sense of constitutional purpose and intensive constitutional activity in which ideals of liberalism and accountability continue to gain ground, if slowly, and careful references to Islamic law are increasingly common.

Under the Ottoman Sultan Abdülhamid II (r. 1876–1909) a constitution (*Kanun-i Esasi*, "Basic Law") was promulgated in 1876. Drafted by a committee of senior statesmen and religious scholars led by Midhat Pasha (d. 1884) and modeled after the Belgian Constitution of 1831, it was quickly allowed to fall into desuetude by the Sultan in 1878 and then revived in 1908 by the "Young Turks," a reformist movement that opposed the absolutist powers of the Sultan. Although it did not really seek to restrain executive power, it did provide for appointed and indirectly elected legislative chambers (which included Arab delegates), and, echoing earlier proclamations, guaranteed certain liberties to Ottoman subjects irrespective of religion. The semi-autonomous Ottoman province of Tunisia also promulgated a constitution-like document in 1860 that confirmed the ruler's family in power and provided for an appointed legislative chamber. In 1882, a constitutional document (*Lāʾiḥa asāsiyya*, "Basic Regulation") was also promulgated in Egypt; it aimed primarily to reclaim control over budgetary matters from the executive and from European powers, but it was soon rendered irrelevant by the ensuing British occupation of the same year. The Egyptian Constitution of 1923, however, promulgated after the British granted Egypt conditional independence in 1922, ushered in a relatively liberal era of constitutional government that lasted until the Free Officers' revolt of 1952.

Many Arab constitutions promulgated in the post-independence period reflect their origins in anti-colonialist, nationalist struggles. The Syrian Constitution of 1973, for example, provides in Article 1 that Syria is "a democratic, popular, socialist state" (*dawla dīmuqrāṭiyya sha'bīyya ishtirākiyya*), part of the "Arab homeland" (*waṭan*), "whose people are a part of the Arab Nation [*umma*] that works and struggles for the realization of its complete unity." The 2007 amendments to the Egyptian Constitution, though retaining aspirational language about Arab unity (as does the 2011 Constitutional Proclamation, both in Article 1), removed the prominent reference to its "democratic-socialist political system." A recent amendment to Article 5 of the Moroccan Constitution represents a noteworthy departure from the earlier constitutional rhetoric of Arab Nationalism; the provision recognizes Tamazight (*al-Amāzīghiyya*), a Berber language, as an official language of the kingdom.

The nationalist, republican, and socialist aspirations of some post-independence constitutions have gradually evolved into potential constitutional bases for accountable government. Clauses describing or mandating the separation of powers are widespread (Lebanese Constitution of 1926, Arts. 16–21; Algerian Constitution of 1996, as amended, Ch. 2, Arts. 70–157) as are clauses insisting on judicial independence (e.g., Egyptian Constitution of 1971, Art. 65), and the importance of the rule of law (e.g., Iraqi Constitution of 2005, Art. 5). Such clauses are also found now in the constitutions of Arab monarchies as well (e.g., Moroccan Constitution, as amended, Chs. 4–7, Arts. 60–128). The UAE constitution is particularly interesting in that it effectively allocates power, responsibility, and authority between a federal government and the governments of the seven member emirates. To the limited extent that Arab constitutions provide for elected legislative assemblies, such assemblies' power to hold the executive accountable is usually carefully circumscribed – but elected legislatures in Egypt and especially Kuwait have demonstrated a measure of independence. Even the monarchs and/or ruling families in the Arab World have made themselves into constitutional monarchs, though in most cases without ceding much executive power. Article 4 of the Kuwaiti Constitution of 1962 provides, for example, that "Kuwait is an emirate in which rule is hereditary in the descendants of Mubārak al-Ṣabāḥ" (r. 1896–1915). Morocco has adopted a more eclectic rhetoric: its 1996 Constitution provides in Article 1 that its political system is "monarchical, constitutional, democratic, parliamentarian, and social." The monarchy is defined in Chapter 3 of the Constitution, which includes a list of the monarch's specific attributes (e.g., head of state, guarantor of religious freedoms, independence,

and territorial integrity, Arts. 41–42) and an enumeration of his powers (e.g., to legislate by means of decrees, *ẓahāʾir*, as provided for in the
Constitution itself, Art. 42).

Islam and Islamic law have become increasingly prominent features
of recent constitutional activity. Many Arab constitutions refer to Islam
as the state's official religion (as noted above) and even those states that
do not claim to base their legal systems on Islamic law have experimented
with constitutional expressions of Islamic legitimacy. Saudi Arabia has
made the most robust such bid; its "Basic Law" (*al-Niẓām al-asāsī lil-ḥukm*)
provides in Article 1 that "The Kingdom of Saudi Arabia ... has as its constitution God's Book and the Traditions [*sunna*] of His Messenger." What
this provision means as a legal matter – and the Basic Law is likely not
subject to modification – is very uncertain since the attitude of "God's
Book" (the Qurʾan) to earthly political power is arguably ambivalent, but
there is no doubt that this article represents an important ideological
assertion aimed at key political constituencies.

A noteworthy and ongoing experiment in inserting Islamic law into
a civil law system is Article 2 of the Egyptian Constitution of 1971 (paralleled by a corresponding provision in the UAE Constitution of 1971).
As originally drafted, Article 2 stated that "principles of Islamic law are
a principal source of legislation," but it was amended in 1980 to make
such principles "*the* principal source of legislation" (emphasis supplied).
As in the case of Saudi Arabia's Basic Law, broad assertions of theological
principle are difficult to implement, interpret, or test. They also mask an
enormously complex, contentious, and diverse set of currents in the history of Islamic legal and political thought.[11]

Over the years, political turmoil has led directly to constitutional
changes. A July 2011 constitutional referendum in Morocco occurred in
the wake of protests inspired by the toppling of autocratic rulers in Egypt
and Tunisia. In Egypt, the 1971 Constitution grew out of dislocations associated with the 1967 Arab–Israeli war and the accession of Anwar Sadat.
The Egyptian military suspended this constitution in 2011 after the resignation of Hosni Mubarak, Sadat's successor, and initially replaced it with
a sixty-three article Constitutional Proclamation (*al-Iʿlān al-dustūrī*) that
retained some provisions of the 1971 Constitution as amended, including Article 2 with its amended wording concerning the role of the *shariʿa*,
but also provisions proclaiming that Egypt is a democratic state (Art. 1)
and that freedom is a natural right (*ḥaqq ṭabīʿī*, Art. 8). Egypt has had an
eventful constitutional history, which perhaps furnishes some perspective on the prospects for a new Egyptian constitution. Organic laws,

constitutions, or similar documents were promulgated in 1866, 1882, 1883, 1913, 1923 (the first "constitution"), 1930, 1935 (reinstatement of the 1923 constitution, the 1930 constitution having been abrogated in 1934), 1952 (strictly, revolutionary decrees), 1956, 1958, 1962 (a National Charter), 1964 (Provisional Constitution), and 1971. Amendments to the 1971 Constitution variously made it more democratic, less democratic, more Islamic, less socialist, and more market-oriented. An interesting contrast is Syria, which has been ruled under emergency law since 1963 and where, consequently, the 1973 Constitution has (like its predecessor) mostly not been in force.

Even apart from recent events, there does seem to be a trend toward the use of constitutions to express, and in some cases to realize, ideals of liberal government. Although it is possible to criticize a document such as Saudi Arabia's Basic Law, it is a noteworthy development in a monarchy whose rulers have in the past publicly acknowledged their theological commitment to an anti-democratic form of government. The 1971 UAE Constitution is widely perceived in the region as a successful model to be emulated in that it has provided the framework for limited central authority and broadly autonomous emirate-level governments that have facilitated significant economic growth in a relatively open and tolerant environment. Other Gulf monarchies – Qatar, Bahrain, Oman – have recently produced, adopted, or amended constitutions or basic laws that define powers, limit authority, and express limited liberal ideals.

Conclusion

The above brief survey has concentrated on law in a narrow sense: legal history, codes, legislative and judicial institutions, and constitutions. Given the reality of authoritarian government in most Arab states, this may seem a cynical approach. The annual Country Reports on Human Rights Practices produced by the US Department of State cite, with depressing regularity, serious human rights abuses in many Arab states. Many such states are portrayed in very unflattering terms by Western and indigenous human rights organizations. Law can also be used for non-liberal purposes. Security and military courts are sometimes used, constitutionally or otherwise, to circumvent rights apparently guaranteed by constitutions or positive legislation. Domestic intelligence services can operate extralegally, sometimes with impunity. And even justice meted out according to law can violate international norms.

With a few notable exceptions, however, judiciaries in the Arab World do not simply rubber stamp executive policy and many in fact constrain executive authority, including in politically charged cases in countries with a minimum of democratic participation. The trend toward constitutionally defining and also limiting powers continues even in Arab monarchies that expressly invoke Islamic law as a key source of legislation – such trends cannot simply be dismissed as so much window dressing. Neither should it be assumed that Islamic ideals of government are necessarily authoritarian or uniformly inconsistent with constitutionalism. Positive legislation in Arab states, especially the Arab civil codes, routinely use language that evinces a respect for the rule of law. Substantive political change may be gradual, but legal frameworks that could accommodate and even encourage such change are to some extent in place or emerging. The political protests that spread across many Arab countries in 2011 may have been due in part to the communications revolution, but it would be wrong to underestimate the role of indigenous legal institutions in such events, whether through their failures or the expectations created by their successes.

* * *

Addendum

A chapter on law such as this one will inevitably be outdated soon after (or even before) publication; that is in the nature of legal scholarship. The events of the so-called Arab Spring continue to have legal ramifications. Since this chapter was first written a new president was elected in Egypt, Mohammed Morsi, who, after shepherding through a new constitution with a more conspicuous Islamic focus, was unceremoniously deposed by the Egyptian army and was initially held, ominously, at an undisclosed location. It seems possible that a new constitution with a more secular orientation will follow. Serious civil strife continues in Syria, and Libya's transition to a new political system has been beset by violence and an increasing lack of security. In all these cases, there has been far too much suffering and loss of life.

Notes

1 In writing this chapter, I have benefitted enormously from the comments and advice of Herbert S. Wolfson, Esq. and Dr. Leonard Wood.

2 The two best recent succinct introductions to Islamic law are Wael B. Hallaq, *An Introduction to Islamic Law* (Cambridge University Press, 2009) and Knut Vikør, *Between God and the Sultan: A History of Islamic Law* (Oxford University Press, 2006).

3 From the tenth century on, Sunni jurists have been divided into four schools of legal thought (*madhhabs*), named after four important early jurists who died between 767 and 855. The Hanafi school is named for Abu Hanifa (d. 767) and was the official school of the Ottoman Empire.

4 On the history and significance of the *Mecelle* for modern Arab legal systems (and on modern Arab legal systems generally), see Chibli Mallat, *Introduction to Middle Eastern Law* (Oxford University Press, 2007), pp. 244–61. See also George N. Sfeir, *Modernization of the Law in Arab States* (San Francisco: Austin & Winfield, 1988).

5 The Maliki school takes its name from Malik ibn Anas (d. 795).

6 On Sanhuri, see Enid Hill, "Al-Sanhuri and Islamic Law: The Place and Significance of Islamic Law in the Life and Work of 'Abd [sic] al-Razzaq Ahmad al-Sanhuri, Egyptian Jurist and Scholar, 1895–1971," *Arab Law Quarterly*, pt. 1 in 3:1 (1988), pp. 33–64, pt. 2 in 3:2 (1988), pp. 182–218; on his codes, see Nabil Saleh, "Civil Codes of Arab Countries: The Sanhuri Codes," *Arab Law Quarterly*, 8:2 (1993), pp. 161–67. The most recent work on Sanhuri is Guy Bechor, *The Sanhuri Code, and the Emergence of Modern Arab Civil Law (1932 to 1949)* (Leiden: Brill, 2008).

7 On Egypt's laws and courts generally, see Nathalie Bernard-Maugiron and Baudouin Dupret (eds.), *Egypt and its Laws* (The Hague: Kluwer, 2002).

8 On the Saudi legal system generally, see Frank E. Vogel, *Islamic Law and Legal System: Studies of Saudi Arabia* (Leiden: Brill, 2000).

9 For a trenchant critique of overstatements of the role of Islamic law in modern Arab legal systems, see Lama Abu-Odeh, "The Politics of (Mis)recognition: Islamic Law Pedagogy in American Academia," *American Journal of Comparative Law*, 52 (2004), pp. 789–824.

10 On Arab constitutions generally, see Nathan J. Brown, *Constitutions in a Nonconstitutional World: Arab Basic Laws and the Prospects for Accountable Government* (Albany: State University of New York Press, 2002).

11 On judicial interpretation of Egypt's Article 2, see Clark B. Lombardi, *State Law as Islamic Law in Modern Egypt: The Incorporation of the Shari'a into Egyptian Constitutional Law* (Leiden: Brill, 2006).

5

Poetry

The city of Medina in Saudi Arabia, where the tomb of the Prophet Muhammad is located, hosts between two and three million visitors during the season of the annual pilgrimage to nearby Mecca. Among the many shops that do brisk business there are bookstores. Their shelves are crammed with the kinds of books one might expect to find in the vicinity of a revered religious shrine: Qur'ans, biographies of the Prophet Muhammad, books on Islamic law, and manuals on religious practice. Remarkably, one can also typically find collections of poetry by Abu al-Tayyib, nicknamed al-Mutanabbi (915–965). This is remarkable because he is not a religious poet at all, but rather the *enfant terrible* of Arabic poetry, an individual whose very moniker signals this, since "al-Mutanabbi" means "the would-be prophet," or "the man who fancies himself a prophet." But then, poetry is inextricably linked to Arab identity and if one is going to stock a single poet in a bookshop, even if it is a religious bookshop adjacent to the tomb of the Prophet, then it is very likely that it will be al-Mutanabbi, often touted as the greatest of all Arab poets.

Among classical poets, that is, those who composed poetry in formal literary Arabic using classical poetic models, motifs, meters, and rhymes, only a few can rival al-Mutanabbi in fame. One of them, however, is the poet Imru al-Qays (sixth century), a pre-Islamic Arabian prince and bon vivant, who was reviled by Muhammad as a denizen of Hellfire. Despite the Prophet's personal condemnation, in a bookshop directly opposite the main entrance to the Grand Mosque in Mecca the only literature to be found are a few volumes of poetry, including a celebrated collection of pre-Islamic odes that includes Imru al-Qays's most famous poem, one that opens with a verse that may well be the single best-known line of Arabic poetry:

Halt, my two friends! Let's weep together in remembrance of the
beloved and the traces of her encampment, here by the edge of the
sand-dunes between Dakhul and Hawmal.

Nearly as famous is the thirteenth-century Egyptian mystical poet,
al-Busiri (1211–1294), whose "Mantle Ode" remains one of the most
widely circulated texts in Arabic in the world. Al-Busiri composed this
lengthy poem of praise to the Prophet after Muhammad appeared to him
in a dream, wrapped his mantle around him, and thereby miraculously
cured him of paralysis.

What do al-Mutanabbi, al-Busiri, and Imru al-Qays have to do with
poetry in the modern Arab World? For centuries, educated Arabs have
been exposed to and schooled in their poetic heritage from a very young
age, a heritage that extends back some 1,500 years. Almost all modern
educated Arabic speakers can quote the lines translated above, as well as
lines by modern poets writing in literary Arabic. For many Arabs, being
able to quote poetry by heart is not simply part of being cultured, it is
part of being Arab. The place that poetry occupies in the minds and lives
of Arabs is impossible to overstate – it is the single most prestigious literary form in Arab culture. Almost all medieval writers, scholars, intellectuals, and religious figures, for instance, routinely composed poetry
alongside their other works, and samples of their verse are nearly always
included in their biographies. And if a major modern prose writer such
as the Egyptian Nobel prizewinner Naguib Mahfouz (1911–2006) did not
write poetry or incorporate verse into his many novels and short stories, he nonetheless closed his Nobel Lecture by quoting verses of poetry
by the eleventh-century philosopher, poet, and prose writer, al-Ma'arri
(973–1058).[1] In the contemporary Arab World, classical poetry that is a
thousand years old exists side by side with the most recent literary and
colloquial verse.

Stop people in the street in Bahrain or Casablanca and they will
almost certainly be able to cite or recite some poetry – however, this is
more likely to be verses written in the local vernacular or poems that
have become famous as songs. It is only highly educated Arabs who know
more than a handful of verses by the canonical poets, because for those
who receive little or no formal education, al-Ma'arri and al-Mutanabbi
are not much more than names, recognizable perhaps, but rarely known
well enough to quote. This is in part because the classical form of Arabic
that these poets used in their compositions is nearly incomprehensible to
anyone who did not study it extensively in school. Thus, for many Arabs

the reference to the "traces of the encampment" would not be as recognizable from Imru al-Qays's ode composed 1,500 years ago as it is from the modern poem "The Traces" (al-Aṭlāl) by the Egyptian Romantic poet, Ibrahim Nagi (1898–1953), who reworked this ancient trope and which was subsequently made famous in song by the legendary female singer, Umm Kulthum (c. 1904–1975).

Poetry in vernacular Arabic

Written literary poetry plays an important role in modern Arab culture, but vernacular poetry is more widely known and appreciated. Various different terms are used in Arabic to refer to colloquial or vernacular poetry. One catchall term that is used to describe many forms is *zajal*, a name that was originally given to the principal vernacular poetic form in medieval Muslim Spain. Other umbrella terms from across the Arab World reflect the differing attitudes toward this poetry: popular poetry (Lebanon), "deviating" poetry (Morocco), colloquial (or "vulgar") poetry (Egypt), Bedouin poetry (Arabian Peninsula, the Gulf), and national poetry (Lebanon, Sudan). This last term, "national," captures a salient dimension of modern vernacular poetry, namely the role it plays in politics and in chronicling social and political realities.

The origins of vernacular poetry are not modern. Already in the fourteenth century, the historian Ibn Khaldun (1332–1406) noted the wealth of poetry produced in Arabic dialects and criticized scholars for dismissing this component of the Arabic literary heritage.[2] For Ibn Khaldun, poetry needed to be appropriate to the situation; if a poet needed to speak to the masses, then what better way than in their daily language, rather than in a formal, literary, or even artificial Arabic. This accounts for the fact that the vernacular is widely used in genres addressed to a broad public, such as folk poetry, epic poetry, laments, elegies, love songs, and poems of political protest.

Much of the poetry that Arabs know by heart, they have heard or listened to in person (in homes, at gatherings, at festivals), through recordings (records, cassette tapes, CDs, MP3s), on the airwaves (radio, TV), and, in recent times, via the Internet (audio- and video-sharing sites). Published collections of poetry in colloquial Arabic (previously a rarity) are increasingly becoming available, but the main mode of access to this repertoire remains listening. This is quite different from, for example, English-language poetry in England or the United States, where the populace does not typically interact with poetry through such media, but rather through print. Arabic poetry, whether in the vernacular or in the more formal literary language, is in this respect more akin to English folk, protest, or rap song than it is to English literary verse, as it is an art that exists primarily in aural form.

There is nonetheless a tradition of writing and publishing vernacular poetry. 'Abdallah al-Nadim (d. 1896), for example, was a major composer and performer of *zajals*. His peripatetic career included contributing to and founding satirical newspapers in the 1880s and 1890s and participating in the 'Urabi Revolt, an uprising against the ruler of Egypt – the Khedive Tawfiq Pasha – who was seen to be excessively influenced by European values.[3] Al-Nadim was imprisoned, exiled, and eventually given a sinecure in Istanbul.

Some vernacular poets, such as the nineteenth-century Algerians, Tahir ibn Hawwa' and Muhammad Bilkhayr, remain little known and receive virtually no scholarly attention.[4] The Sudanese colloquial poet, Muhammad Ahmad Abu Sinn Hardallu (d. 1917), on the other hand, became so famous that the couplet form in which he wrote (*dūbayt*) has come to be known as a *ḥārdallū*. Similarly, the Iraqi poet/composer Hajj Zayir (d. 1920) invented his own verse forms, which are still sung today.

Perhaps the most well-known vernacular poet across the Arab World is Bayram al-Tunisi (1893–1961), who wrote in both Egyptian and Tunisian vernacular Arabic. Like his predecessors, he founded satirical newspapers, criticized regimes and their lackeys, and was exiled, first to Tunisia and France and later to Syria. Besides political commentary, his poetry also described the trappings of modernizing technology and society (especially in the *maqama*, a virtuoso genre in rhymed prose), exposed the poverty of the working classes, and caricatured religious officials and clerics. The following are verses from a poem in which he faults a religious official for opposing the setting up of food cooperatives for the poor:

> In neither mosque nor cloister have I seen one like you prowl.
> You're known as "scholar," "Muslim," yet at doing good you scowl.
> As long as Your Grace dines so well on cutlets and fine fowl,
> You leave the maize and radishes to fill the sheep's foodpan.[5]

Al-Tunisi's achievements in vernacular poetry influenced revolutionary poets of the subsequent generation, especially Salah Jahin (1930–1986), who, like al-Tunisi, privileged the *zajal*, wrote for TV and radio, and composed songs; and Fu'ad Haddad (1927–1985), who explored other forms such as the *mawwal* (a genre filled with intricately rhymed puns) and who was influenced by French experimental poetry and Islamic mysticism. Like his compatriots, Haddad embraced political resistance, even outside of Egypt. It is not surprising, then, that the recent protests and revolutions in the Arab World have been accompanied, occasioned, and immortalized by poetry. Salah Jahin's poem, "Photograph," celebrating the end of the Suez Crisis of 1956, was sung by protesters in Tahrir Square in Cairo in early 2011. Another poem of his heard in Tahrir Square, and put to song, went as follows:

> If Injustice has enjoyed long nights
> Justice will mark the coming days.
> No matter how brutal injustice gets,
> It will someday be abolished.
> For how can it last,
> When only God is Everlasting?[6]

These lines are reminiscent of perhaps the most famous of all resistance verses, from the poem "Life's Will," written in the 1920s by the Tunisian Romantic poet, Abu al-Qasim al-Shabbi (1909–1934), and regularly reprised and repeated during times of protest, revolution, and revolt:

> When people choose
> To live by life's will,
> Fate can do nothing but give in;
> The night discards its veil,
> All shackles are undone.[7]

There is also a tradition of criticizing Western leaders and policies in verse, though now and again a Western personality is the object of praise. The poet, Muhammad Fanitil al-Hajaya, a Bedouin from a small village in Jordan, composes frequently about foreign politicians. In one poem, "A Bedouin Poem on the War in Iraq," he praises George Galloway, a British politician who, after being expelled by his party, successfully won a parliamentary seat on an anti-Iraq War, pro-Arab, anti-British government platform:

> So stick to your guns, you're a civilized voice
> And cock a deaf ear to the barking dogs' threats!
> The market their consciences soon overcame,
> Selling their honour for oil and hard cash;
> With skill and aplomb, George, you put them to shame,
> That hornets' nest, Congress, faced down with panache![8]

Song has been inseparable from vernacular poetry and some of the most famous vernacular poets owe a large part of their renown to musical versions of their works. In the case of Ahmad Fu'ad Nigm (b. 1929), his poetry was made famous by the blind Egyptian singer, Shaykh Imam (1918–1995), whose songs were banned for decades for their revolutionary content and circulated primarily on cassette tape, passed hand to hand, rather than being broadcast on the radio.

The most influential and the most widely known vernacular poetry across the Arab World has been from Egypt and North Africa, facilitated in large part by the robust music and film industries based there. But when it comes to modern poetry in literary Arabic, the laurels can be claimed by poets of the Fertile Crescent (Iraq, Syria, Lebanon, and Palestine). It is worth pointing out, however, that it is not particularly useful to think of Arabic poetry as bifurcated into two distinct categories (vernacular versus literary) for there are in fact many different registers of literary Arabic (think of the difference between a BBC news broadcast and the poetry of the late Cornish poet, Charles Causley) as well as regional variations (think of the difference between the poetry of the American Robert Frost and that of Derek Walcott from St. Lucia). What is more, there is poetry that straddles both, such as Yemeni *humayni* poetry, which is in literary Arabic but which does not conform strictly to traditional rules and takes its inspiration from vernacular forms. There is also the *muwashshah*, a complex, rhyming strophic form from medieval Muslim Spain that originally mixed literary Arabic, colloquial Arabic, and Romance dialect. The *muwashshah* has influenced vernacular poetry and music in many regions and also has a long history in Hebrew. So, while we may at times speak of literary versus vernacular poetry, it is more realistic to think of Arabic poetry as existing on a spectrum ranging from hip street verse to formal erudite poetry.

Poetry in literary Arabic

Like vernacular poetry, poetry in literary Arabic reaches back into the past, looks forward into the future, scrutinizes influences from within and without, and struggles with issues of identity. Importantly, the engagement with identity in the past century or so has been dominated by reflection on the nation (notably its formation in the wake of European colonialism and presence) and nationalism (in the ferment of Pan-Arabism, Pan-Turkism, and Zionism). As one social historian and cultural commentator has aptly observed, the "renaissance of Arabic literature began in the late nineteenth century and has paralleled the growth of Arab nationalism, inspiring it, sustaining it, hymning it, and mourning it to this day."[9]

The generally accepted phases in the history of modern literary Arabic poetry are: an age of Neoclassical poetry (roughly 1870–1930); an age of Romantic poetry (roughly 1910–50); and an age of Modernist poetry (roughly 1950–present).[10] These phases are by no means discrete and all three styles continue to be composed to this day, as is clear from submissions to contests and competitions, such as the Mirbad Festival of Poetry in Baghdad. In addition, many poets choose to write in more than one mode. So it is possible to think of poets operating in these three modes as looking to three different sources of inspiration. The Neoclassical poets looked back to the medieval heritage of the "golden age," the ninth to eleventh centuries, considered by many to be the pinnacle of Classical Arabic literature. They valorized this period above all others, a stance facilitated by the widespread view that cultural production and output had been in decline since then, a view espoused by educated Arabs in order to underscore the "Awakening" or "Renaissance" (*Nahda*) of the late nineteenth century. The Neoclassical poet, Mahmud Sami al-Barudi (1839–1904), for example, produced an anthology of classical poetry that stuck closely to medieval models. The bulk of "golden age" poetry had been produced for patrons and purse at the courts of rulers and high officials, and this was also true of the Neoclassical poets. Some became famous, such as the Egyptian "prince of poets," Ahmad Shawqi (1868–1932), who was retained by the Khedive of Egypt, while others equally skilled remained less well known, such as the Greek Catholic poet, Butrus Karama (1774–1851), who served an emir in Lebanon.

The Lebanese poet Khalil Mutran (1872–1949) is widely regarded as the figure who served as a bridge between the declining Neoclassical and the innovating Romantic modes in Arabic poetry. In this, Mutran was helped by his exposure to European literature (especially French), by his abiding interest in the theater (as both a producer and an accomplished translator of playwrights such as Shakespeare), and by his view that a poem should not be imitative, but rather should possess vision and unity. Given all this, it is no wonder that Mutran was all but revered by Ahmad Zaki Abu Shadi (1892–1955), a major painter, scientist, and poet of the Romantic movement. Abu Shadi is best remembered and lauded for his work with the Apollo Group, an Egyptian literary society devoted to the promotion of literature and to cooperation between Arab writers. Its monthly magazine, *Apollo* (1932–4), was shortlived but influential. Although poets such as Nagi and al-Shabbi (both already mentioned), and the Sudanese Muhammad al-Mahjub (1908–1976), published in *Apollo*, detractors attacked the Apollo Group for being excessively reliant on Western models and for being elitist, in spite of the fact that, in reality, they were cosmopolitan and inclusive.

Remarkably, it was a group of Romantic poets based in the West who were the real harbingers of the changes that modern and modernist Arabic poetry was to experience. These were mostly Levantine, mostly Christian, émigré (*mahjar*) poets working in North and South America at the turn of the twentieth century. Most notable among them were Kahlil Gibran (Jubran Khalil Jubran, 1883–1931) and Iliya Abu Madi (1889–1957), though there were many others. These writers too formed an association, known as the "Bond of the Pen" (*al-Rābiṭa al-Qalamiyya*). They founded Arabic newspapers, literary magazines, and an Arabic publishing house in New York, São Paolo, Rio de Janeiro, and Buenos Aires. At least one *mahjar* writer, Gibran, also became widely read and successful in English: his poetic prose book, *The Prophet* (1923), though not regarded by critics as his best work, has been translated into forty languages (including into Arabic, by Yusuf al-Khal [1917–1987]) and has never been out of print.

Modernist poets, like Adonis ('Ali Ahmad Sa'id, b. 1930), acknowledged the link between the innovative writings of Gibran and poets like himself. At a 1961 conference in Rome, Adonis famously described Arab poets as living for centuries in a closed world, always turning or returning to the past. For Adonis, the modern Arab poet had to be, in his famous formulation, a new flame from an old fire. This radical view makes the poet something of a prophet, an aspect that is evident in two of Adonis's most highly regarded works, a collection of psalmic poems titled, *Songs of Mihyar the Damascene* (*Aghānī Mihyār al-Dimashqī*), and the complex, multivocal intertext, "The Book" (*al-Kitāb*), a work Adonis attributes to al-Mutanabbi. Numerous poems from other collections also feature a prophetic character, including one of Adonis's earliest poems, and arguably a pivotal one in the history of modern Arabic poetry, namely "The New Noah" (1957). The second half of this bipartite poem reads:[11]

> If time started anew,
> and waters submerged the face of life,
> and the earth convulsed, and that god

rushed to me, beseeching, "Noah, save the living!"
I would not concern myself with his request.
I would travel upon my ark, removing
clay and pebbles from the eyes of the dead.
I would open the depths of their being to the flood,
and whisper in their veins
that we have returned from the wilderness,
that we have emerged from the cave,
that we have changed the sky of years,
that we sail without giving in to our fears –
that we do not heed the word of that god.
Our appointment is with death.
Our shores are a familiar and pleasing despair,
a gelid sea of iron water that we ford
to its very ends, undeterred,
heedless of that god and his word,
longing for a different, a new, lord.

Noah stands for the possibility of renewal after deluge. By speaking to, as, and through Noah, the poet can dispense with the need to stake any ethno-religious claim. The appeal of Noah thus also lies in the fact that he is antediluvian, living long before the existence of Jews, Arabs, Christians, and Muslims.

The symbolic use by many of the poets already mentioned of ancient Near Eastern figures, such as the Mesopotamian god of the harvest, Tammuz, is also an example of reliance on a Near Eastern mytho-poesis. Another such figure deployed to powerful rhetorical effect is Christ, and not just by Christian poets such as Gibran, Tawfiq al-Sayigh (1924–1971), or Khalil Hawi (1919–1982) – translator, incidentally, of Eliot's *Four Quartets* into Arabic – but also by non-Christians, such as the Iraqi ʿAbd al-Wahhab al-Bayati (1926–1999), another pioneer of free verse in Arabic.[12] If Bayati's use of masks or personas in his poetry reflects his need to find a way to channel his strong opposition to the social and political conditions in the Arab World, an opposition that also resulted in imprisonment and exile, this in no way diminished the poetry of one of the great voices in modern Arabic literature.

The use of symbolic language and imagery and the experience of exile is also apparent in the verse of Palestine's most celebrated poet, Mahmoud Darwish (1941–2008). Darwish was born near Acre and was active in the Israeli Communist Party as a young man before leaving Israel in 1971 for Beirut, Paris, and Tunis. In February 1983, when delegates of the Palestinian Liberation Organization met at a party congress being held in Algiers, Yasser Arafat – who had just escaped the 1982 siege and bombardment of Beirut – had serious concerns about his ability to retain leadership of the movement. The London-based *Sunday Times* reported as follows:

> Late one night after hours of speech making, the fog of revolutionary rhetoric lifted, briefly. Arafat suddenly rushed out of the hall, his bodyguards jogging beside him, and tore away in a motorcade. Rumours flew that he had resigned.
>
> The truth was more extraordinary. The world's most famous guerilla leader had gone to fetch a poet. He returned holding the hand of Mahmoud Darwish who began at midnight to declaim his latest poem, on the battle of Beirut. It went on until 2 a.m. The hundreds of delegates listened with rapt attention. Arafat stared at Darwish with almost childlike adoration. When after the final stanza Darwish slumped exhausted into his chair, Arafat went to the microphone and spoke a little poem of his own. "The revolution is not just guns; it is the pen of the poet, the needle of the woman who makes scarves for the fighters." He sat down to thunderous applause.[13]

The plight and cause of the Palestinian people is deeply felt by Arab poets, Palestinian and non-Palestinian alike. Darwish's poetry is a poetry now of loss, now of nostalgia, now of hope, and always in simple and beautiful literary Arabic, but one that is highly symbolically charged. Like so many who chose to mourn Palestine in verse, Darwish was haunted by the *Nakba* (Catastrophe) of 1947–48, which resulted in the displacement of some 700,000 Palestinians. But Darwish was both defiant and optimistic for a place he came to describe as "Eden." Darwish's recourse to religious imagery included a poem directly inspired by the Joseph story in the Qur'an, one in which the rejection of Joseph by his brothers was intended to mirror the rejection of Palestinians. Although the poem included words from the Qur'an, it was not controversial until the Lebanese singer Marcel Khalife (b. 1950) put it to music and performed it as a song, something commonly done with Darwish's and countless others' poems. Khalife was charged with blasphemy, but was eventually exonerated by the courts. The Muslim religious right may object to poetry that samples the Qur'an or that appears to challenge it[14] – it is also the case that much poetry is written on religious themes out of pious devotion, such as the countless panegyrics of the Prophet Muhammad in both literary and vernacular Arabic – but many with strong religious views will not tolerate music.

Modern/ist poetry in literary Arabic emerged from the discernible rupture that took place in the 1950s, one that included the abandoning of the formal constraints that characterized all earlier poetry (especially the use of a single end-rhyme that is a primary characteristic of Classical Arabic poetry), an attention to newer and modern themes, greater discussion about questions of modernity and modernism (ḥadātha), and a desire for experimentation with form. One poet credited with calling for a departure from traditional forms was someone whose early poems were decidedly Romantic and deeply indebted to the English Romantics in particular, namely the Iraqi poet, Nazik al-Malaʾika (1923–2007). Although she retained the two-part line of classical poetry (i.e., broken by a medial caesura), she sought to liberate Arabic poetry through free verse (shiʿr ḥurr), notably in a collection titled *Splinters and Ashes* (*Shazāyā wa-ramād*, 1949), though she remained attached to the classical foot (*tafʿīla*) as a metrical building block in her compositions. Her compatriot Badr Shakir al-Sayyab (1926–1964) for his part emphasized the need to break free from the constraints of the sixteen Classical Arabic meters and devise new metrical systems, such as the one he showcased in *Song of Rain* (*Unshūdat al-maṭar*, 1960), his signature collection and a signal collection in the history of modern Arabic poetry. It opens:

> Your eyes are two palm tree forests in early light
> Or two balconies from which the moonlight recedes
> When they smile, your eyes, the vines put forth their leaves
> And lights dance ... like moons in a river
> Rippled by the blade of an oar at break of day;
> As if stars were throbbing in the depths of them.[15]

Al-Sayyab's call for reform in poetics went hand in hand with commitment to political reform, activism, and opposition, a commitment (*iltizām*) that is a hallmark of almost all modern Arabic poetry. This commitment to political issues did not in al-Sayyab's case taint the beauty and symbolism of his poetry; in this he was by his own admission influenced by early Romantic poets in literary Arabic and by modernist European poets such as T. S. Eliot and Edith Sitwell.

The imprint of Eliot can be found everywhere in modern Arabic literary poetry, from the verse drama of the Egyptian poet and playwright Salah ʿAbd al-Sabur (1931–1981) – who defended Western influence on

Arab poets in his 1969 autobiographical work, *My Life in Poetry* (*Ḥayātī fī al-shiʿr*) – to the symbolist poetry and critical writings of Adonis and Yusuf al-Khal (1917–1987). Adonis and al-Khal were foundational figures for modernist Arabic poetry, not only with their oeuvres, but also as critics, translators, and as the founders of two major forums for modern and experimental poetry. Al-Khal ran the highly influential journal, *Poetry* (*Majallat Shiʿr*), and its associated publishing house, and later Adonis started *Stations* (*Mawāqif*), both of which were also platforms for experimental art. It should also be noted that although they wrote in, and translated foreign works into, literary Arabic, the editors of *Shiʿr* also approvingly published a vernacular poem by Michel Trad (1912–2009), "It's a Lie" (*Kizbī*) in which he mocks common tropes of literary poetry. It opens:

> Lies! What lies!
> They're saying the moon brought me a doll,
> Threw it like a bouquet through the window
>
> That with one hand he set
> Two daffodils in my hair,
> Exploring my chest with the other
> And said it was hot,
> Let's unfasten two buttons.[16]

This approbation for vernacular poetry by Adonis, al-Khal, and the *Shiʿr* group was not matched, however, by an interest in composing such poetry. In part this was because in order to break with the poetic conventions of literary Arabic they believed they needed to do so in literary Arabic itself.

Khalida Saʿid has characterized modern Arabic poetry as one of repudiation and questioning, and preoccupied with identity. Increasingly, poets of the avant-garde and of the "new generation," as they are called in Egypt, are looking beyond repudiation, questioning, and even identity.[17] This is not to say that social criticism and political critique have been abandoned or that contemporary poets are no longer decrying despotism, tyranny, and oppression, but rather that daily life and personal preoccupations have also come to the fore. Iman Mersal (b. 1966), an Egyptian poet who lives in Edmonton, Canada, and others like her are at the vanguard of this more personal poetry – for want of a more apposite characterization. Her poem, "Oranges," opens:[18]

> I face the mirror to scrub off
> the scent that two lips left on my neck.
> And though there is no need to document the sadness,
> I still indulge in counting tears
> by examining the paper tissues I threw in the wastebasket.
> I think my eyes are prettier than the image I have of them
> and decide that understanding is more beautiful than forgiveness.
> I was with you
> on a journey to a holy place.
> I am wearing a dress of a sixteenth-century French princess
> when you take me away from the convent.
> You push me to climb a staircase hanging in air.
> And since this is impossible with all those spangles,
> I begin taking off petticoats
> and climb,
> corsets,
> belts shaped like bows
> that turn into dead butterflies when I release them,
> and climb.

Another poet who engages with the personal is Salwa al-Neimi, for example in the following short poem, "Dracula," from the 1996 collection *Temptation of my Death*:

> Protruding, rebelling against the lips,
> the long, pointed, ill-fated fang stared at me,
> (in spite of awkward attempts to hide it).
>
> Stealing adolescent glances,
> I dreamed it pierced me, pushing deep in the base of my neck.
> I bit my lower lip, flushed,
> but not before blushing under its spell.
>
> Yesterday,
> Yesterday when he smiled at me, with teeth in perfect alignment
>   (dentistry can work miracles),
> I turned my apostate face,
> and squinting, pretended to watch passers-by.[19]

Arab(ic) poetry in English

Modern Arabic poetry in English translation was first published in a few multi-poet anthologies, all of which focused exclusively on poetry in literary Arabic – there are still no multi-poet anthologies of vernacular poetry in English translation. In 1974, Mounah Khouri and Hamid Algar edited and translated seventy-nine poems by thirty-five poets, sequenced chronologically from Gibran and Ameen Rihani (1876–1940) to Darwish and his compatriot Harun Hashim Rashid (b. 1930). In 1976, Issa Boullata published an English-only anthology of his translations of fifty-five poems by twenty-two poets, divided by country (Iraq, Lebanon, Syria, Egypt, Sudan, and Palestine).[20] In 1987, Salma Jayyusi commissioned and published an anthology consisting of 295 poems by eighty-six writers, and translated by tandems of eleven first translators (including Jayyusi herself) and seventeen second translators (including Naomi Shihab Nye, W. S. Merwin, and Richard Wilbur). Jayyusi divided her anthology into two chronological sections: "Poets before the Fifties" and "Poets after the Fifties." In 1988, John Mikhail Asfour published an anthology of his own translations of ninety-six poems by thirty-five poets, which he divides more instructively than his predecessors into "The free verse movement," "Tammuz rediscovered," and "Resistance movement." ʿAbdullah al-Udhari also used an explanatory organization in his 1986 anthology, dividing 101 poems by twenty-three poets into "Tafʿila Movement (Iraqi School): 1947–57," "Majallat Shiʿr Movement (Syrian School): 1957–67," "Huzairan Experience: 1967–82," and "Beirut Experience: 1982–."[21] In 2001, Nathalie Handal produced the first major anthology of women's poetry consisting of one or two selections each by eighty-three poets.[22]

Mahmoud Darwish is the most translated poet, not only in terms of his individual poems, but also in terms of individual collections, which is to say that a great number of his individual collections have been translated into English. In part this is because of the appeal of marketing and disseminating the poetry of Palestine, and in part because of the accessibility of his poetry. Someone like Muhammad ʿAfifi Matar (1935–2010), though critically acclaimed, is less well served in translation because he can be difficult to read, exhibiting what the Arab critics call "the (apparently) easy (but effectively) elusive."[23] Things are changing and many poets are now better served in English, often by translators who are themselves accomplished and award-winning poets in English as well as in Arabic, such as Fady Joudah and Khaled Mattawa. Indeed, the Anglophone Arab poetic voice is now a fundamental component of the Arab(ic) literary landscape.

Handal's anthology mentioned above includes Arabic voices such as al-Malaʾika and Mersal, but also Arab-American ones, such as Etel Adnan

(b. 1925) – who coined the term "Arab-American" – and Mohja Kahf (b. 1967), both of whom also write in English and in prose. One simply cannot think critically about Arab(ic) poetry in the twenty-first century without thinking about poetry by Arabs writing in languages other than Arabic.[24] In 2007, Fady Joudah won the Yale Series of Younger Poets Competition, a prize that has in the past gone to Adrienne Rich, W. S. Merwin, John Ashbery, and Carolyn Forché, who, like Joudah, is a translator of Darwish.[25] The Radius of Arab American Writers Inc. (RAWI) in North America has been an important forum and Arab writers writing in English also have two important English-language journals that promote their work and the critical study of it, namely *Al Jadid*, based in California, and, to a lesser extent, *Banipal*, based in London and also associated with major prizes and regular poetry readings. Though not a literary outlet, the independent e-zine, *Jadaliyya*, for which Sinan Antoon serves as a cultural editor, carries many important articles about poetry.

It is, of course, not possible to know what the future holds for Arabic poetry. It may be that technology will help blur the distinctions between the vernacular and the literary or that the political will give way to the lyrical and the personal. Whatever course or courses Arabic poetry takes, what is certain is that it will adapt to new circumstances and cyberways and will continue to be, in print and aurally, a vibrant tradition in world poetry.

Notes

1 In Sture Allén (ed.), *Nobel Lectures: Literature, 1981–1990* (Singapore: World Scientific, 1993), p. 125.

2 Cited in Marilyn Booth, "Poetry in the Vernacular," in M. M. Badawi (ed.), *Modern Arabic Literature* (Cambridge University Press, 1992), p. 463.

3 Ziad Fahmy, *Ordinary Egyptians: Creating the Modern Nation through Popular Culture* (Stanford University Press, 2011), pp. 55–59.

4 Booth, "Vernacular," p. 467, n. 12.

5 Marilyn Booth, *Bayram al-Tunisi's Egypt: Social Criticism and Narrative Strategies* (Reading, UK: Ithaca Press, 1990), pp. 602–3.

6 Noha Radwan, "Egypt's Revolution, in Verse," *The Chronicle Review*, 57/28 (March 18, 2011), p. B20; last line adapted from Radwan's translation.

7 Translated by Sargon Boulos and Christopher Middleton, in Salma Khadra Jayyusi (ed.), *Modern Arabic Poetry: An Anthology* (New York: Columbia University Press, 1987), p. 97.

8 Clive Holes and Said Salman Abu Athera, *Poetry and Politics in Contemporary Bedouin Society* (American University in Cairo Press, 2009), p. 188.

9 Basim Musallam, *The Arabs: A Living History* (London: Collins/Harvill, 1983), p. 33.

10 M. M. Badawi, *A Critical Introduction to Modern Arabic Poetry* (Cambridge University Press, 1975); Shmuel Moreh, *Modern Arabic Poetry 1800–1970* (Leiden: E. J. Brill, 1976); Salma Khadra Jayyusi, *Trends and Movements in Modern Arabic Poetry*, 2 vols. (Leiden: E. J. Brill, 1978); Roger Allen, *The Arabic Literary Heritage: the Development of its Genres and Criticism* (Cambridge University Press, 1998), pp. 103–217; Paul Starkey, *Modern Arabic Literature* (Edinburgh University Press, 2006), pp. 42–114.

11 Adonis, "The New Noah," trans. Shawkat M. Toorawa, *Poetry*, 190/1 (April 2007), pp. 21–23.

12 David Pinault, "Images of Christ in Arabic Literature," *Die Welt des Islams*, 27 (1987), pp. 103–25, esp. pp. 114–25.

13 Cited in Musallam, *The Arabs*, p. 25.

14 Shawkat M. Toorawa, "Modern Arabic Literature and the Qur'an: Creativity, Inimitability... Incompatibilities?," in Glenda Abramson and Hilary Kilpatrick (eds.), *Religious Perspectives in Modern Muslim and Jewish Literatures* (London: RoutledgeCurzon, 2005), pp. 239–57.

15 Translated by Lena Jayyusi and Christopher Middleton, in Stefan Sperl and Christopher Shackle (eds.), *Qasida Poetry in Islamic Asia and Africa*, 2 vols. (Leiden: E. J. Brill, 1996), vol. I, p. 132.

16 John Mikhail Asfour (ed. and tr.), *When the Words Burn: An Anthology of Modern Arabic Poetry 1945–1987* (Dunvegan, Ontario: Cormorant Books, 1988), p. 89.

17 M. M. Enani (ed. and tr.), *The New Arabic Poetry in Egypt* (Cairo: General Egyptian Book Organisation, 1988); M. M. Enani (ed. and tr.), *Angry Voices: An Anthology of the Off-beat Arabic Poetry of the 1990s in Egypt* (Cairo: State Publishing House [GEBO], 2001).

18 Iman Mersal, "Oranges," translated by Khaled Mattawa, *Blackbird*, 7/2 (Fall 2008). [Available at www. blackbird.vcu.edu/v7n2/poetry/mattawa__k/oranges.htm – accessed December 23, 2014.]

19 Salwa Al-Neimy, "Dracula," trans. Shawkat M. Toorawa, *Poetry*, 194/1 (April 2009), p. 62.

20 Issa J. Boullata (ed. and tr.), *Modern Arab poets: 1950–1975* (Washington, DC: Three Continents Press, 1976).

21 Abdullah al-Udhari (ed. and tr.), *Modern Poetry of the Arab World* (Harmondsworth, Middlesex: Penguin, 1986).

22 Nathalie Handal (ed.), *The Poetry of Arab Women: A Contemporary Anthology* (New York: Interlink Books, 2001).

23 But see Muhammad Afifi Matar, *Quartet of Joy: Poems*, trans. Ferial Ghazoul and John Verlenden (Fayetteville: University of Arkansas Press, 2001).

24 Munir Akash and Khaled Mattawa (eds.), *Post-Gibran: Anthology of New Arab-American Writing* (West Bethesda, MD: Kitab, distributed by Syracuse University Press, 2000).

25 Fady Joudah, *The Earth in the Attic* (New Haven, CT: Yale University Press, 2008); Mahmoud Darwish, *If I Were Another*, trans. Fady Joudah (New York: Farrar, Straus & Giroux, 2009).

6
_____

Narrative

Have the modern genres and sub-genres of Arabic narrative developed from the narrative genres of Classical Arabic literature, are they inauthentic imitations of Western literary genres, or have they developed from a combination of indigenous roots and the influence of Western culture? The question is both complex and hotly debated among scholars. There is a broad range of narrative writing in modern Arabic literature spanning many genres: novels, short stories, novellas, *maqamas* (picaresque tales), autobiographies, biographies, travelogues, and epistolary narratives are but the most commonly cited examples. Any answer to the question of their origins would require dealing with each genre separately. Instead, it is more productive to examine how these various genres have engaged with the most commonly recurring themes of modern Arabic literature: the encounter with the West, tensions between urban and rural life, the formation of the modern nation state, the Palestinian situation, gender relations, and the recent resurgence of Islamist thought and movements.

Nineteenth-century narrative

There was a rich tradition of Arabic travel literature in the pre-modern period, perhaps most famously exemplified by Ibn Battuta's (d. 1369) account of his journeys from Morocco to East Africa, India, China, and back again, but the colonial encounter with Europe created a new interest in various forms of narrative travelogues in the nineteenth century.[1] Rifaʿa Rafiʿ al-Tahtawi (1801–1873) gave readers a perspective on French society in his *Refinement of Pure Gold in the Summarizing of Paris* (*Takhlīṣ al-ibrīz fī talkhīṣ Bārīz*, 1834; English translation: *An Imam in Paris*, 2004), a work of lasting appeal that led to other travelogues such as that written by the Tunisian Ahmad ibn Abi Diyyaf (1804–1874), who recorded his visit to France in 1846 in the company of the ruler, Ahmad Bey. After his visit he concluded: "These people are ahead of us in civilization, which they have adopted as a way of life and conduct."[2]

Muhammad al-Muwaylihi's (1858–1930) *The Words of Isa ibn Hisham* (*Hadīth 'Isā ibn Hishām*) was first serialized from 1898 to 1903 under the Arabic title *Fatra min al-zaman* (published in English as *A Period of Time*, 1992) in the newspaper *Misbah al-sharq* (Lantern of the East) that was founded and edited by his father, before the work appeared in book form in 1907. This transgeneric narrative interweaves the author's journalistic skills, elements of travel writing, and the Arabic *maqāma* (picaresque) tradition, especially in its episodic narratives and masterful prose. Both the original narrative set in Egypt and its sequel, which takes places in Europe, bear evidence of an intellectual awareness of the political and social issues, as well as the hardships, that beset Egypt and the Ottoman Empire in the late nineteenth century. As a result of his father's support for the aborted revolt of the Egyptian Nationalist officer 'Urabi Pasha (1881–2), al-Muwaylihi lived with his father in exile for five years, during which he became acquainted not only with Istanbul, his primary residence, but also with Italy, Paris, Brussels, and London, before returning to Egypt in 1887. His double interest in addressing the growing Arab reading public and acquainting it with European politics and cultures was achieved not only in writings under his own name but also under various pseudonyms that included *al-Ṣādiq al-Amīn* (the truthful and faithful one) that recalls one of the epithets of the Prophet Muhammad.[3]

The Egyptian educator 'Ali Mubarak (1823–1893) also published a narrative travelogue in somewhat fictionalized form. His work *'Alam al-Dīn* (1882) in four volumes describes how an Azharite shaykh named 'Alam al-Din traveled through Europe accompanied by an Orientalist scholar to educate himself in European ways of life. These and other travel accounts, which at times mix the Arabic picaresque *maqāma* style and novel-like narrative, were quite popular until the advent of realistic fictional narratives that dealt with social and political dimensions and drew on styles then fashionable in Western Europe and Russia.

In the latter half of the nineteenth century, in addition to the popular travel narratives, a number of European novels and plays were translated into Arabic and helped provide an impetus for the emergence of the modern Arabic novel. Especially in Egypt, the nineteenth-century translation enterprise was first and foremost state oriented. The establishment of the Bulaq Egyptian Government Press (1819–20) and the founding of the School for Foreign Languages (1835) inaugurated a movement in science and literature that greatly influenced the rising classes and their potential for future leadership.[4] There were also, however, many individual translation projects in Syria and Lebanon that grew into sustained narrative works, especially in journals like *al-Jinān* (The Gardens), edited by Butrus al-Bustani from 1870 to 1886, where John Bunyan's *Pilgrim's Progress* and Daniel Defoe's *Robinson Crusoe* appeared alongside al-Bustani's own serialized narratives.

The historical novel in Arabic

The massive new flow of information associated with the rise of the Arabic-language press in the nineteenth century led to an increase in political and social awareness that was to find expression not only in political speeches and writings, but also in poetry and fiction. At this juncture, the role of the historical novel cannot be overlooked. Interestingly, Egyptians, Iraqis, and Lebanese or Syrian immigrants to Egypt played leading roles in what was then termed "Awakening" (*Iqāz*), which the Iraqi lawyer Sulayman Faydi (1885–1952) used as the name for his newspaper and was the subject of his work, *The Awakening Novel* (*al-Riwāya al-Iqāziyya*, 1919). The historical novel was most significantly developed by the Lebanese-Syrian immigrant to Egypt, Jurji Zaydan (1861–1914), who used his journal *al-Hilāl* (The Crescent Moon) (1892–) for the publication and dissemination of his novels, thus bringing the genre to a large reading audience and forging a recognizably novelistic tradition.[5] With a strong sense of Arab history across ethnic and religious boundaries, Zaydan brought key figures, controversial events, and also crucial historical periods to the attention of the growing reading public. In different historical novels he wrote about the Muslim conquest of Egypt, a ruthless ruler of Iraq in the Umayyad period (661–750), a powerful queen of medieval Egypt, the problematic rule of the Mamluk slave dynasty in Egypt (thirteenth to early sixteenth centuries), and a number of prominent female historical figures. Written in an accessible style, with straightforward structure and flowing narrative, these works marked the heyday of the historical novel in Arabic and continued to be popular for decades. At least two other thinkers and intellectuals from among Zaydan's compatriots participated in the proliferation of historical narratives. Yaqub

Saruf (d. 1927) and Farah Antun (d. 1922), both founders and editors of prominent journals also penned historical novels. Saruf published *Prince of Lebanon* (*Amīr Lubnān*, 1907) as a reflection on the religious strife that drove many to emigrate from Lebanon a few years after Antun wrote *New Jerusalem or the Arab Conquest of the Holy City* (*Ūrishalīm al-jadīda aw fath al-ʿarab bayt al-maqdis*, 1904).[6] These and many other historical narratives cannot be seen as outside the social and political concerns of their writers. Indeed, although writers of historical novels wrote novels of social criticism and protest set in the present, they also couched social criticism within their historical narratives, as can be seen in the oeuvre of Naguib Mahfouz (1911–2006), who started his career writing historical novels, a number of which were set in ancient Egypt and a few in later periods, though his later social novels are the ones that brought him widespread recognition.

Autobiographical dimensions to early novels

The Egyptian critic and writer Mahmud Taymur's (1894–1974) statement that *Zaynab* (1913) by Muhammad Husayn Haykal (1888–1956) was the first "real Egyptian novel" is now regarded as an over-simplification, but this work does provide a convenient starting point.[7] Haykal wrote *Zaynab* in Paris during the years 1910–11. Its significance lies primarily in its social context and the attention it pays to the peasantry within a growing Egyptian national consciousness; however, it is also a reflection of an emerging self-awareness among the literary elite and a broad spectrum of intellectuals all over the Arab World. The novel, set in the Egyptian countryside, recounts the romantic rivalry among three men for the favors of Zaynab, a beautiful peasant girl. Though she is in love with a handsome young man of her own class, she is married off to a richer peasant in an arranged, and ultimately deeply unhappy, marriage, all of which is observed and recorded by the landowner's son, who himself has strong feelings for her. The novel's protagonist, Hamid, bears a strong resemblance to the author and the work lays the foundation for a new tendency to translate personal experiences into novelistic narrative. This was an important element in the rise of a "new school" of writing, especially among short story writers like the Egyptians Yahya Haqqi (1905–1992), Mahmud Tahir Lashin (1894–1954), and Mahmud Taymur (1894–1973). Yahya Haqqi associated this new literary style with the growing interest in foreign literatures, attention to national realities, and an increased focus on the individual. Although speaking of the rise of the short story, Yahya Haqqi's evaluation of a trend that he himself participated in also applies to autobiography, memoirs, epistolary narrative, and a novelistic tradition that witnessed a stupendous growth in the eastern Arab countries in the 1930s. Almost every major writer published autobiographical narrative(s) of one sort or another, ranging from works that were publicly acknowledged as autobiographies to works that were ostensibly published as fictional novels.

Taha Hussein's (1889–1973) work *The Days* (*al-Ayyām*: Vol. 1, *An Egyptian Childhood*, 1932; Vol. 2, *The Stream of Days*, 1948), which first appeared serialized in Jurji Zaydan's journal *al-Hilāl* from 1926 to 1928, was long considered, and rightly so, the exemplary modern Arabic autobiography and it subsequently influenced generations of writers. One significant element is its portrayal of the bourgeois aspiration to attain higher social status through education. It speaks to the belief among the rising elite that they could and should lead their society through their education and struggle, and reject the privileges of lineage and nepotism. Another of Hussein's works, *A Man of Letters* (*Adīb*, 1935) is a combination of epistolary fiction and autobiography. It was preceded by a novel by the Iraqi Mahmud Ahmad al-Sayyid (1903–1937) *Jalal Khalid* (*Jalāl Khālid*, 1929), the first part of which relates the author's journey with an Iraqi Jewish family to Bombay in order, in the second part, to discuss the political situation in Iraq in an epistolary fashion.

The autobiographical element is conspicuous enough in these narratives to warrant an explanation. All over the Arab World, but primarily in Egypt (where the Syrian intelligentsia had already found a congenial habitat), there was a rising consciousness among Arab intellectuals. Although most obviously pitted against the colonial "Other," this sense of identity soon had to face multiple "Others," including cultural and class divisions within Arab society, especially pertaining to habits of thought and social customs, as well as regional rivals and puppet regimes. As participants in the formation of emerging nation states, Arab intellectuals had in mind the role of European intellectuals in the nineteenth century. This drove them to assign a large narrative role to intellectual heroes and protagonists in their writings.

Taha Hussein was an acclaimed pioneer in this regard. Other writers including the Syrian-Egyptian Yaqub Saruf (d. 1927) and the Egyptians ʿAbbas Mahmud al-ʿAqqad (d. 1964), Yahya Haqqi (d. 1992), Ibrahim al-Mazini (d. 1949), Salama Musa (d. 1958), Tawfiq al-Hakim

(d. 1987), Latifa al-Zayyat (d. 1996), the Syrian Muta' Safadi, the Moroccans 'Abdallah Laroui, Muhammad Barada (b. 1938), and 'Abd al-Majid Ben Jelloun, the Iraqis Dhu al-Nun Ayyub (d. 1988), and 'Aziz al-Sayyid Jassim (executed 1991), all of whom wrote narratives which, if not fully autobiographical, expressed the writer's social and political agenda by featured protagonists who were representatives of the intellectual elite.

Eventually, however, Arab writers reached an artistic impasse, which the half Iraqi, half South Arabian 'Abd al-Rahman Munif (1933–2004) expressed: "In a subsequent period, I discovered that the intellectual is not everything in the novel and life. Life is richer and broader than this category."[8]

The rural novel

After the success of national revolutions or liberation movements in Egypt (1952), Tunisia (1956), Iraq (1958), and Algeria (1962), a counterpoint emerged to the theme of the intellectual protagonist seeking to reform a society deemed backward and ignorant through the promotion of Western/colonial ideas of progress. Although neither a genre, nor a subgenre, the rural novel offers some departure from the bourgeois epic model. The Egyptian 'Abd al-Rahman al-Sharqawi's (1920–1987) *The Land* (*al-Arḍ,* 1954; *Egyptian Earth*, 1962) can serve the purpose of tracing this shift. The depiction of reform and the critique of the past are central to the mission of the 1952 revolution in Egypt, but al-Sharqawi brought something else to his writing about rural life. There is a valorization of peasant life – there is no longer a disdainful portrayal of peasants as ignorant and backward; rather, there is dignity, humor, and beauty, along with suffering and hard work. *The Land* portrays the struggles of the peasantry within a feudal system in Egypt prior to the 1952 revolution and is one among a series of novels in the Arab World that focus on life in the village, including the Egyptian Yusuf Idris's (d. 1990) *The Forbidden* (*al-Ḥarām* 1956; *The Sinners*, 1984), the Iraqi Dhu al-Nun Ayyub's (d. 1988) *Hand, Earth and Water* (*al-Yad wa-l-arḍ wa-l-māʾ*, 1948), and the Tunisian al-Bashir Khurayyif's (d. 1983) *The Dates in Their Palm Trees* (*al-Diqla fī ʿarājīnih,* 1969). Later novels dealing with peasants and rural life include the Moroccan Mubarak Rabi's (b. 1938) *The Moon of his Times* (*Badr zamanih*, 1983) and the Algerian Abdelhamid Ben Haddouga's (d. 1996) *The South Wind* (*Rīḥ al-janūb*, 1971).

A further series of rural novels that began in the late 1960s testi-
fies to a growing political awareness. Perhaps disturbed and shocked
by the failure of the nation state and its leading elite to deliver on its
promises and commitments, young writers embarked on taking the
rural not only as a setting, but also as the controversial space for the
production of Sufi, religious, and deviational politics. Protagonists in
political and existential novels, like Babil in the Iraqi ʿAziz al-Sayyid
Jasim's *The Militant* (*al-Munāḍil*, 1970) and ʿAbdul Rahman Majeed
al-Rubaie's (b. 1939) protagonist in *The Brand* (*al-Washm*, 1971) draw
on their rural origins to oppose and fight back against imposed party
politics. The tendency receives even more nuanced reading in a Sufi
context that takes the village as a space that can accommodate Sufism
before the encroachment of national politics through the invading
media, and the radio in particular, as in the Egyptian ʿAbd al-Hakim
Qasim's (1934–1990) *The Seven Days of Man* (*Ayyām al-insān al-sabʿa*, 1969;
The Seven Days of Man, 1996). Partly sharing the same title, the Iraqi ʿAbd
al-Khaliq al-Rikabi (b. 1946) wrote *The Seventh Day of Creation* (*Sābiʿ ayyām
al-khalq*, 1994). Like his other writings, it takes the rural as its landscape and motivating poetic in a manner that reminds the reader of
his other novels, such as *Who Dares to Decode the Riddle?* (*Man yaftaḥ bāb
al-ṭilasam*, 1982). The Iraqi Musa Kraidi (d. 1996) brings rural sensibility to the urban life of the holy city of Najaf, where the encroaching
cemetery envelopes the life of the urban center in contradictions and
diversity as it is attended every day by people from everywhere, either
to bury the dead or visit the holy shrines. Yusuf al-Qaʿid's (b. 1944) *War
in the Land of Egypt* (*al-Ḥarb fi barr Miṣr*, 1978; *War in the Land of Egypt*, 1986)
is a sharp and subtle critique of the double exploitation of peasants by
post-Nasserite regimes, which try to rob the common Egyptian of both
the honor of martyrdom in the war with Israel and dignity and labor.

In the Iraqi ʿAbd al-Sattar Nasir's (d. 2013) *The Madhouse*
(*al-Shammāʿiyya*, 2007), we find a land of strangeness and mystique,
agony and prospect, and sites where the boundaries of madness falter
and pale. It is a narrative that makes a logical conclusion to his other
harrowing narratives of disappointment and loss: *Half of the Sorrows* (*Niṣf
al-aḥzān*, 2000) and *Abū al-Rīsh* (2002). In these and in many other narratives, the usual paradigmatic binary of rural and urban disappears, and
narratives come out richer and with greater pictorial and psychological
depth.

Secular versus religious worldviews

One important element of the earlier narratives featuring intellectual protagonists is a deep faith in secular thought and a portrayal of more traditional and religious social classes as backwards and in need of enlightenment. Long narratives like Tawfiq al-Hakim's *Diary of a Public Prosecutor in the Provinces* (*Yawmiyyāt nā'ib fī al-aryāf*, 1937; *The Maze of Justice*, 1947) and shorter ones like Yahya Haqqi's *The Lamp of Umm Hashim* (*Qindī l Umm Hāshim*, 1946; *The Saint's Lamp*, 2004), explore areas of human feeling, behavior, and faith from a secular perspective that tends to focus on the seemingly negative side of traditional customs and beliefs. Whether produced as memoirs, autobiographies, stories, novellas, or novels, these narratives tend to focus on social criticism and the writer's mission to promulgate enlightened reforms that would lead to the formation of a nation state modeled on solid examples, while at the same time incorporating some empowering elements of ancestral spirit that could uplift low societal morale and usher the nation into a new age with confidence and vigor. Such was Tawfiq al-Hakim's message to the nation and its elite in *Return of the Spirit* (*'Awdat al-rūḥ*, 1933), which the Egyptian leader Nasser (d. 1970) found inspiring.

The national identities celebrated in these narratives are not Islamic ones, but are instead identities that are Pharaonic, espoused by al-Hakim and the early Naguib Mahfouz; Mediterranean, embraced by Taha Hussein; Syrian, in Shakib al-Jabiri's *Greed* (*Naham*, 1937); leftist, in Tawfiq Yusuf 'Awwad's (d. 1989) *The Loaf of Bread* (*al-Raghīf*, 1939), Dhu al-Nun Ayyub's (d. 1988) *Hand, Earth, and Water* (*al-Yad wa-l-arḍ wa-l-mā'*, 1948), and *Doctor Ibrahim* (*Duktūr Ibrāhīm*, 1936–38); and straightforwardly secular in the Iraqi Kazim Makki's *Safwan the Writer* (*Ṣafwān al-adīb*, 1939).

Modern Arabic fiction's association with European models entailed the absence of religion as a dynamic force until sometime in the 1960s. In Naguib Mahfouz's *Children of Our Alley* (*Awlād ḥāratinā*, 1959; *Children of Gebelawi*, 1981), for example, religion gives way to science and the narrative ends on a mixed note of armed resistance and a celebration of science. It is only with the growing disillusionment with the state bureaucratic apparatus that the Sufi element emerges shyly in Mahfouz's *The Thief and the Dogs* (*al-Liṣṣ wa-kilāb*, 1962; *The Thief and the Dogs*, 1984) to expose corruption in a land forsaken by God. This thin Sufi streak was taken up by Mahfouz's disciples such as Gamal al-Ghitani (b. 1946) in his *al-Zayni Barakat* (1971; *Zayni Barakat*, 1988) and 'Abd al-Hakim Qasim in

The Seven Days of Man (Ayyām al-insān al-sabʿa, 1969; *The Seven Days of Man,* 1996) and *The Mahdi (al-Mahdī,* 1977; *The Rites of Assent,* 1995). Al-Kuni's (b. 1948) *The Bleeding of the Stone (Nazīf al-ḥajar,* 1990; *The Bleeding of the Stone,* 2001) is a Sufi cry in the face of callousness and cruelty. It is only later in time that we come across narratives that give substantial space to organized Islamist politics and poetics, as in Alaa Al Aswany's *The Yaʿqubian Building (ʿImārat Yaʿqūbian,* 2002; *The Yacoubian Building,* 2004).

In the Algerian and Moroccan novel, however, Arabo-Islamic identity is stronger and the awareness of the colonial challenge enforced a combative identity that has remained rooted in traditional religious culture. One nevertheless comes across such novels as ʿAbd al-Majid Ben Jelloun's (b. 1944) autobiographical *In Childhood (Fī al-ṭūfula,* 1957) and Tahir Wattar's (1936–2010) *al-Lāz* (1974), where the secular element is prioritized against a backward tradition in Ben Jelloun's autobiographical narrative, and against an organized Islamic politic in Wattar's novel. Wattar's *The Earthquake (al-Zilzāl,* 1974; *The Earthquake,* 2000) is a nuanced narrative of opportunist politics that internalizes Islamist discourse and uses it as facade to counteract a hollow national one that nevertheless claims change and reformist politics. The protagonist, a schoolmaster who becomes a land proprietor through his family's alignment with the colonial administration, panics when the postcolonial administration announces its land reform plan. Hence his profuse use of Qurʾanic verse to debunk rising populism as no more than an omen of the Day of Judgment.

Even in war literature throughout the 1980s, in Iraq, Lebanon, Palestine, and Egypt, the secular tendency highlights individual survival and domestic issues within a broad national scene that used to be the center of earlier narratives of struggle and progress. Thus Ilyas Khuri's (b. 1948) *The Journey of Little Ghandi (Riḥlat Ghāndī al-Ṣaghīr,* 1989; *The Journey of Little Ghandi,* 1994) takes the Israeli invasion of Lebanon in 1982 as its pivotal point through the tale of the poor shoeshiner ʿAbd al-Karim, who is nicknamed "Little Ghandi." His vocation entails a solid and also ironic connection to the city and the poor fringes of Lebanese society, which, though seemingly falling apart, gathers strength from national awareness that shows forth through the chain of socially disadvantaged narrators. In this narrative of the dispossessed who carry the burden of national integrity, and hence reverse the modernist paradigm of the intellectual as the custodian of emancipatory discourse, women of the social fringes present a new model for national consciousness. Although

downtrodden, they are there at the center of the city not only to give identity and meaning to an otherwise meaningless death of Little Ghandi in
a deserted street run by an invading army, but also to occupy national
space and thereby inscribe new significations and markers for social and
national struggle.

Women's writing

Political upheavals and wars since 1967 have left, and continue to leave,
an enormous impact on Arabic writing that covers every perspective
and style. Shifts in women's writings are noticeable as in many other
categories of writing. Between the courageous and daring endeavors
of the Syrian Layla Ba'albaki (b. 1936) in her novel *I Live* (*Anā Aḥyā*, 1958)
and the Iraqi 'Alia Mamduh's (b. 1944) *Mothballs* (*Ḥabbāt al-naftalīn*, 1980;
Naphtalene, 2005), there is a difference, not only in daring to oppose,
but also in presenting lesbian and transgendered relationships within
a larger context of social and political struggle in the Iraq of the 1950s.
Another Syrian, Colette Khuri (b. 1937), presents the complex relationship between a young girl and an elderly man in order to drive home the
rights of women, but there is a difference between this and *The Story of
Zahra* (*Ḥikāyat Zahra*, 1980; *The Story of Zahra*, 1986) by the Lebanese Hanan
al-Shaykh (b. 1945). Al-Shaykh's novel presents Zahra's rebellious affair
with a sniper during the Lebanese Civil War as an act of revenge against
a body that is already intrigued, challenged, repressed, targeted, and
invaded. Her sense of the futility of love in war does not change the process or the outcome and her experience of her uncle's talk of nationalism
and the charismatic leader serves only as backdrop to an actual failure of
ideology in societies that have not come to terms with their social problems. The presence of the female body no longer connotes national honor
as in national discourse. It is brought down to earth, a human body
that may be part of a whole chaotic scene in a nation that is ravaged and
humiliated in contrast to its idealization in her uncle's discourse.

One cannot look at the civil war in Lebanon without recalling the
pioneering effort of Tawfiq Yusuf 'Awwad (d. 1989) in his *Beirut Mills*
(*Tawāḥīn Beirut*, 1972; *Death in Beirut*, 1976), which served as a prototype
for *The Story of Zahra*, not only in focusing on a southern Shi'ite heroine and her disenchanting experience of intellectual rhetoric in Beirut,
which was the Arab cultural center before the Israeli onslaught and
occupation in 1982, but also in pointing to the political transformation

that was bound to take place afterward. Women novelists and short story writers in Lebanon during the war had something distinct to say, however, and they looked at the war as a liberating experience without overlooking its devastating and demoralizing effects.[9] Hanan al-Shaykh (b. 1945) is one such writer, but there is also Emily Nasrallah (b. 1938), whose novelistic trajectory provides a map for this development in women's writing from a one-sided concern with the plight of women to a more complicated view of a nation under siege, wracked with misery and destruction. Her novels *The Pawn* (*al-Rahīna*, 1973), *Those Memories* (*Tilka al-dhikrayāt*, 1980), and *Flight Against Time* (*Iqlā' 'aks al-zamān*, 1981; *Flight Against Time*, 1987) no longer limit her vision to migrations and misfortunes. Her homeland assumes a different meaning through details and preoccupations which only a mind liberated from hegemonic discourse can engage. Readers may feel, however, that the Egyptian Nawal El Saadawi (b. 1931) is more daring than many in laying bare the plight of womanhood in specific circumstances, such as her heroine Firdaws in *Woman at Point Zero* (*Imra'a 'inda nuqtat ṣifr*, 1975; *Woman at Point Zero*, 1983) whose rejection of social demands for conformity leads to her death. More harrowing is the experience of her women in *Fall of the Imam* (*Suqūṭ al-Imām*, 1988; *Fall of the Imam*, 1988), where the leader, who could be any male figure, imposes a system that demands women's total subordination.

Women's short stories are no less diversified and powerful whenever they work within a larger canvas of engagement and experimentation. Thus one comes across a short story by the female writer Salma Matar Sayf (pseudonym) from UAE with her "The Sound of Singing,"[10] and its striking focus on discrimination, abuse, and women's resistance to hypocrisy and sham appearances, and "The Return of the Prisoner" by the Iraqi Buthayna al-Nasiri (b. 1947),[11] with her deft depiction of a wife's resumption of a male's role during his disappearance as a war prisoner whose return becomes superfluous. On the other hand, one may read of a lesbian relationship in 'Alia Mamduh's (b. 1944) "Presence of the Absent Man" to see how women writers have developed strident strategies and narrative styles that are far beyond the accustomed descriptive styles of the first half of the twentieth century.[12] Even when focusing on issues of state ideological apparatuses, as Salwa Bakr (b. 1949) does in her *The Shrine of 'Atiyah* (*Maqām 'Aṭiyah*, 1992; *The Shrine of Atia*, 1997), the traditional reservation of sainthood to men is reversed and women saints take over. At the same time, there is in the story the implication of some clandestine operations that are coordinated between the state apparatus and foreign companies.

Encounter with the West since the 1960s

Although the encounter with the West fluctuates in terms of focus on sociopolitical and cultural issues, a noticeable shift began in the 1960s towards a cultural dialog with more rigorous application and knowledge of the dynamics of cultural interaction and estrangement. Encounter narratives in the first half of the century were numerous and they often conveyed the experience of their writers who lived, studied, and traveled in France and England. Pivoting on an encounter with a European woman, these narratives often presented the female character as instructive, different, and separate, like Europe itself. Such are the women in Haqqi's *Saint's Lamp* (*Qindīl Umm Hāshim*, 1944), al-Hakim's *Bird from the East* (*'Usfūr min al-sharq*, 1938; *Bird from the East*, 1967), and the Lebanese Suhayl Idris's (d. 2008) *The Latin Quarter* (*al-Ḥayy al-Latīnī*, 1953). The Moroccan 'Abd al-Majid Ben Jelloun's *In Childhood* (*Fī l-Ṭūfula*, 1957) accommodates the West not as alien or "other," but as an enlightening experience that enables the protagonist to help in building up his nation against backwardness and traditionalism. The novel became part of the Moroccan curriculum as it catered to the aspiration of the nation state to forge a future away from tradition. Years later, the Sudanese Tayeb Salih (1929–2009) problematized this encounter in his monumental *Season of Migration to the North* (*Mawsim al-hijra ilā al-shamāl*, 1967; *Season of Migration to the North*, 1969), not only through an economic divide of north and south against a cultural one which was established through early colonialism, but through subtle parody of Orientalism and its stereotyping legacy that permeates the media and the common consciousness in Europe. Parodying late nineteenth-century anthropological views on Africa, the protagonist lives the encounter as a complex reality, which continues to be so in realistic situations in a Sudanese village.

The encounter with the West takes different proportions and receives different treatment when the onslaught comes as a barbaric and devastating war like the attack on Iraq in 1991 and its aftermath. In a sardonic narrative, *The Sultan of Sleep* (*Sulṭān al-nawm*, 1994), by the late Jordanian novelist Mu'nis al-Razzaz (d. 2002), Operation Desert Storm is presented in the trope of encompassing sands that leave no space untouched, including the narrator's room. The encounter takes on different dimensions in women's novels. In a novel by Raja' ʿAlim (b. 1970) from the Arabian Peninsula titled *Sitr* (lit. cover/sacral protection/chastity, 2006) there are a number of women whose experiences in love and divorce give a grim picture of an elite female society that meets Europe and America on terms of equality and reciprocity, whether in Jeddah, London, or Miami. All this takes place in a textual and spatial location where interaction is condoned and a life of intellectual exchange and erotic rendezvous is smooth and easy. The overall power of the narrative rests on its prose, with its erotic, humorous, satirical, and descriptive layers. Language lives the density of this experience and the emerging text relishes rich prose that negates everything else, for even the words of the character Badr, which intoxicate the woman protagonist and narrator, are like "fireworks" that suggest "revolution, but do not ignite real fire." He is the outcome of frustration and disappointment with a rampant anarchist mood, and to whom the Internet provides the outlet to "orally engage all ideas, bearded, veiled, belted with dynamite, and sharp knives that threaten the kidnapped in Iraq and Afghanistan, to end up spitting on all proclamations and banners."[13]

The Iraqi exile Haifa Zanqana (b. 1950) wrote *Women on a Journey* (*Nisā' ʿalā safar*, 2001; *Women on a Journey*, 2007), in which women live through recollections that occupy more than two-thirds of the text, which ostensibly covers their lives in London. In *Girls of Riyadh* (*Banāt al-Riyāḍ*, 2006; *Girls of Riyadh*, 2008) by the Saudi Raja' al-Saniʿ, we come across different encounters where the Internet provides communication that enlists the stories of a number of females from different regions in the Arabian Peninsula, who narrate their lives, marriages, and divorces while moving between the US, Europe, and their homeland. Political elements are scattered here and there to criticize outworn customs and tribal attitudes, but there are no master narratives or ideological positions to raise suspicions. In Hanan al-Shaykh's *This is London, My Dear* (*Innahā London, yā ʿAzīzī*, 2000; *Only in London*, 2002) an Iraqi immigrant, Lamis, asks a London teacher for private lessons in English in order to teach her to speak with a British accent. "I've realized I want to assimilate. I need to look for work. I think having an English accent could be the key."[14] In line with a significant portion of women's writing, the ideological dimension is minimized to allow more space for minute domestic details and economies. The ideological appeal to national aspirations is rarely touched on and, if it ever appears, it does so only to counterweigh and thereby efface its application in current discourse. Whereas early twentieth century women's writing was noticeably engaged with national issues, post-1967 women's writing witnessed a postmodernist shift to micro politics that is also in response to upheaval, wars, and national failures.

The impact of Palestine

The creation of Israel and the partition of Palestine in 1948, usually referred to as the *Nakba* (Catastrophe) in Arabic writing, served as the motivation for several military coups. Although the subject appears every now and then in writing before 1948, as in the Palestinian Khalil Baydas's (d. 1949) *The Heir* (*al-Warīth*, 1919), it assumes significant proportions only later when Palestinian writers who suffered the debacle engaged the issue. The whole climate, whether existentialist or leftist and nationalist, has been receptive to this mounting output that amasses a number of thematic patterns and styles to deal with a complex reality, not only of uprootedness, forced dislocation and exile, but also of corruption and abuse by Palestinians.

Ghassan Kanafani (assassinated by the Israeli intelligence service in Beirut in 1972), in his novels *Men in the Sun* (*Rijāl fī al-Shams*, 1963; *Men in the Sun*, 1999), and *What's Left to You* (*Mā tabaqqā lakum*, 1966; *All That's Left to You*, 1990), sets the plight of Palestinians in fierce metaphorical terms that provide scathing criticism of impotent nationals and borders created by colonial powers with strong endorsement from Arab governments that continue speaking of Palestine as their central concern. In *Men in the Sun*, the water-tank truck in which the impoverished, dislocated, unfortunate Palestinians suffocate to death is an apt metaphor for both colonial and national machinery that shamelessly cause so much havoc and destruction. This novella critiques a sordid reality and lays bare the whole dubious climate that will assuredly lead to the 1967 *Naksa* (setback), a phrase that connotes temporal regression in an otherwise forward movement. The politics involved in the phrase also suggests the predicament of both the leading intelligentsia and the nation state, and their inability to criticize a corrupt system of thought and practice.

The American–Lebanese author Halim Barakat wrote two novels that engage with the Palestinian question. One of them, *The Return of the Flying Dutchman to the Sea* (*'Awdat al-ṭā'ir ilā al-baḥr*, 1969; *Days of Dust*, 1974), captures the sense of a war that was fought in the air, where there is nothing heroic but death, mass killing, and misery, and leaves a sense of futility and repugnance in one's mouth. His other novel, *Six Days* (*Sittat Ayyām*,

1961; *Six Days*, 1990) engaged the events of 1948 and the Israeli siege of a seaside Palestinian town. These writings take place within a context that sets the terms of literary production in the 1960s–70s. The response to 1967 and the dismal failure of the nation state's ideological apparatuses draw writers to individual experience as more viable and foreseeable than the collective one, which has been monopolized by political regimes under the banner of nationhood and the masses. Edward Said was right in noting that "while it is true that the war [i.e., 1967] involved the Arabs as a whole, the very particularism spurring the writer to capture every detail of life also led to make precise differentiation between, say, local experience and collective experience."[15]

This particularism appears in a number of narratives, especially in the publication of autobiographies by Palestinian authors, including Edward Said's (d. 2003) *Out of Place* (2000). The Palestinian woman poet Fadwa Tuqan's (1917–2003) *Mountainous Journey, Difficult Journey* (*Riḥla Jabaliyya, Riḥla Saʿba*, 1985; *Mountainous Journey*, 1990) details her own experience and the impact of her nationalist brother and poet Ibrahim Tuqan. There are also Mourid Barghouti's (b. 1944) *I Saw Ramallah* (*Raʾaytu Rām Allah*, 1997; *I Saw Ramallah*, 2000); Jabra Ibrahim Jabra's (d. 1994) *The First Well* (*al-Biʾr al-ulā*, 1987; *The First Well: A Bethlehem Boyhood*, 1995), and, significantly, Mahmoud Darwish's (d. 2008) *Memory for Forgetfulness* (*Dhākira li-l-nisyān*, 1982; *Memory for Forgetfulness*, 1995), an autobiographical segment detailing the siege of Beirut by the Israelis in 1982. This piece rises to a standard of prose writing that is only matched by the beauty of his poetry. Between the Israeli occupation of his home, his village, his life, and his memory, the siege of Beirut is a journey in dispossession, persecution, danger, and catastrophe. His deft prose style captures the sense of catastrophe and disaster in the face of brutal powers and his commitment and sincerity gives his writing a tragic sense which is compatible with Ghassan Kanafani's *What's Left to You* (*Mā tabaqqā lakum*, 1966; *All That's Left to You*, 1990). It enables the reader to see and sense a recent history that has been made at the expense of another nation with its own people, memories, homes, culture, and history.

Somewhat different from these autobiographical narratives, is Emile Habibi's masterpiece *The Strange Events of the Disappearance of Saeed the "Pess-optimist"* (*al-Waqāʾiʿ al-gharība fī ikhtifāʾ Saʿīd Abī l-Naḥs al-Mutashāʾil*, 1974 and 1977; *The Secret Life of Saeed, the Ill-Fated Pessoptimist*, 1982), where the protagonist narrates and lays bare the entire experience of occupation as it touches an ordinary person who is misused, trifled with, tortured, imprisoned, and is held suspect by his countrymen for being a forced informer, and who finds, therefore, nowhere to go except an imaginary flight to heaven. Habibi's style is sarcastic in tone, hilarious, yet tragic, comical but agonized.

These works are complemented by Palestinian women's writings, especially Sahar Khalifa (b. 1941) and Lyana Badr (b. 1950). In Khalifa's *The Prickly Pear Cactus (al-Ṣubbār*, 1976; *Wild Thorns*, 1985), women's suffering under occupation in the West Bank is an important concern, but the novel explores the difficult trajectory of exploitation by both local Palestinian overlords and Israelis. On the other hand, Badr's feat lies in her preoccupation with Palestinian refugee camps and her novels and short stories, such as *A Compass for the Sunflower (Būṣla min ajl ʿabbā d al-shams*, 1979; *A Compass for the Sunflower*, 1989), use women narrators not only to acquaint readers with an arduous life under occupation and exploitation, but also to alert people to a situation created and sustained by the occupying power and regional and international alliances.

Alienation from the nation state

The defeat of 1967 and the inability of Arab power elites to alleviate the suffering of the Palestinians, led writings after the war with Israel to be more critical of the nation state, and the colonial experience rarely appears except as a backdrop to remind readers of the struggle of intellectuals and social forces for a future which has been claimed but never reached by the nation state. This struggle brings forth new narrative strategies. Pastiche, parody, and also reportage and collage receive more attention and are deployed to satirize the misuse of history and literary heroics. Rashid Abu Jadra's *Struggle in the Straits (Maʿrakat al-zuqāq*, 1986) draws attention to the gulf or the strait that separates the Muslim conqueror Tariq ibn Ziyad, who crossed the Straits of Gibraltar in 711 CE, from his namesake in the novel, whose Algerian father tries to model him on that hero. It also alludes to post-liberation leaders who are no less separated from the ideals of education that were celebrated in the early years of independence. History no longer serves the earlier purpose of building national consciousness through recollections of a glorious past, but instead allows novelists to expose repression and corruption. Between parody and subtle irony, Gamal al-Ghitani (b. 1945) wrote his *Zayni Barakat (Zaynī Barakāt*, 1971; *Zayni Barakat*, 1988), a work that makes brilliant use of Mamluk historical writing – large portions of the work consist of passages only slightly reworked from the chronicle of Ibn Iyas (d. after 1522). His criticism of the Nasser regime emerges through the parallels to modern Egyptian society, such as the massive use of spying, the murky nature of national politics, and the manipulation of media to deceive or intrigue the mass audience. Although with a different flare, the Libyan Ibrahim al-Kuni (b. 1948) draws on more recent history not only to celebrate the struggle against Italian occupation, but also to expose the local and national elites that participate in the extinction of old lifestyles, livestock, nature, and tradition.

Naguib Mahfouz produced *Karnak* (*al-Karnak*, 1974; *Karnak Café*, 2007), as a scathing critique of political corruption, coercion, and repression. His *Chatting on the Nile* (*Tharthara fawq al-Nīl*, 1966; *Adrift on the Nile*, 1993) deals with the other side of frustration in the face of repression: the increasing sense of disillusionment and alienation which overtook many intellectuals after years of imprisonments and torture, which Sunʿallah Ibrahim (b. 1937) also exposes in *That Scent* (*Tilka al-Rāʾiha*, 1966; *The Smell of It*, 1971) and which ʿAbd al-Rahman Munif depicts in gruesome detail in *East of the Mediterranean* (*Sharq al-Mutawassiṭ*, 1977). Even when writers approach these disappointments and troublesome realities in more aesthetic terms, such as Jabra Ibrahim Jabra in his multivoiced and dense narrative *In Search of Walid Masʿud* (*al-Baḥth ʿan Walīd Masʿūd*, 1978; *In Search of Walid Masʿud*, 2000), there is an ironic level of narration that pokes fun at the official discourse of the nation state as it speaks of the Arab nation from "the Arab Gulf to the Atlantic Ocean" while it at the same time tortures its people and turns the land into a horrible prison.

Cities as sites of nostalgia and loss

In medieval Arabic literature a genre called *faḍāʾil* (virtues) vaunted the virtues and superior qualities of great cities such as Granada, Cordoba, Baghdad, Cairo, and Jerusalem. Echoes of these medieval works reappear in modern writings of nostalgic longing. Andalusian cities in particular serve as sites for recollections of past glories, but they reflect also on the present situation of loss. The Palestinian Mahmoud Darwish (d. 2008) recollected cities in his poetry and Beirut in his memoir of the Israeli invasion of Lebanon in 1982, *Memory for Forgetfulness*, which depicts a wounded city, beleaguered, and under siege. Jabra Ibrahim Jabra has his own *Princesses' Street* (*Shāriʿ al-amīrāt*, 1993; *Princesses' Street*, 2005), in which a specific district where he used to live in Baghdad encapsulates for him the past and the present of his journey in life since his early exile in 1948. ʿAbd al-Rahman Munif (d. 2004), whose father was Saudi and his mother Iraqi, has his narratives of growing up in Amman. In *Story of a City* (*Qiṣṣat madīna*, 1994), Munif wrote of his childhood and his realization that "although they were separated from Baghdad by a great distance and different accent, Baghdad was also very close." The Iraqi poet Hamid Saʿid (b. 1941) narrates his natal city of Hilla and also Baghdad, after passing through Granada in *Space in the Topography of Memory* (*al-Makān fī tadārīs al-dhākira*, 1993). The Egyptian author, Gamal al-Ghitani, wrote his *Khiṭaṭ* (1980) in imitation of an earlier work of the same title by ʿAli Mubārak (d. 1893), both of which refer back to the work of the same name by Taqi al-Din al-Maqrizi (d. 1441). The title *Khiṭaṭ* (a word that can be translated as "lots" or "districts" or "layouts") indicates an encyclopedic description that moves geographically from place to place, citing all significant information about a city or region before moving on. Thus a medieval literary genre based on descriptions of towns, districts, neighborhoods, and major buildings has been revived and reinterpreted as a map of memories. Novels that take the name of cities as their titles are also numerous, although these cities range between middle-class locales like Mahfouz's *New Cairo* (*al-Qāhira al-jadīda*, 1945) to cities that emerge suddenly with the discovery of oil in the middle of deserts, as in Munif's *Cities of Salt* (*Mudun al-milḥ*, 1984; *Cities of Salt*, 1987), to cities that take over the role of the protagonist like Ahmad al-Madini's *Fez* (*Fās*, 2003). In all of these narratives, there is a mixture of autobiographical detail, memories and recollections, travelogues, character sketches, and insights into the careers and lives of individuals from all walks of social life that sum up the varieties of modern Arabic narrative.

Short story

The historical development of the Arabic short story runs a separate course in many ways than that of the novel. Long narratives, such as novels, are constrained by a spiral journey towards selfhood within a national identity. Even in polyphonic narratives like Mahfouz's *The Epic of the Rabble* (*Malḥamat al-ḥarāfīsh*, 1977; *The Harafish*, 1994), al-Ghitani's *Zayni Barakat*, and Fuʾad al-Takarli's (d. 2008) *Distant Echo* (*al-Rajʿ al-baʿīd*, 1980; *The Long Way Back*, 2001) that resist this focus, there is nevertheless a prominent character, a protagonist, and, at times, a hero. The short story has no such aspiration. The Palestinian Khalil Baydas (d. 1949) produced his collection *Domains of the Minds* (*Masāriḥ al-adhhān*, 1924) to narrate personal and intellectual intimations or engagements; Ibrahim al-Mazini (d. 1949) penned his comic and humorous short narratives to poke fun at traditional beliefs; Jaʿfar al-Khalili (d. 1984) in Iraq did the same with a more satirical and comical penchant; Dhu al-Nun Ayyub (d. 1988) turned the short story into a vehicle for social criticism. These story writers all have social criticism in mind and approach it through comical, satirical, reformist, and realistic representations. The short story took on a new literary status with the foundation of *al-Fajr* literary weekly (1925) by Mahmud Tahir Lashin (d. 1954), Mahmud Taymur (d. 1973), and Yahya Haqqi (d. 1992) in Egypt.

After World War II, the short story continued to provide sharp critiques of worn-out customs and social practices and miserable living conditions, such as in the masterful handling in Yusuf Idris's (d. 1991) many collections of short stories. Focused on the subtleties of human feeling and ambition, Idris gave the short story new depth that earlier practitioners were unable to reach. The Iraqis ʿAbd al-Malik Nuri (d. 1994) and Fuʾad al-Takarli (d. 2008) wrote in the same vein, as did the Egyptian Yusuf al-Sharuni (b. 1924) and the Syrian Zakariyya Tamir. They dealt with marginalized human beings, delved into their sensations and feelings, and reached their inner contradictions. Like painting, which witnessed an upsurge in Iraq, or poetry with its new concern with the common man, common language, and present experience, the short story finds in ordinary human beings and their lives a wealth of material worthy of investigation. Especially in the 1960s and the 1970s, a new focus on alienation, particular human experience, gender, and human desires and frustrations emerged.

The establishment in 1967 of the journal *Jālīrī* (Gallery) in Cairo as a platform for innovation and experimentation in short narrative and poetry is important, not only because it enlisted the contributions of most avant-garde Arab writers and translators, but also because it came soon after a major failure, the 1967 war, that exposed the worn-out rhetoric of fake heroism and sham appearances. The short story had a substantial presence there and the best story writers contributed to the journal. In Egypt, the contributors to *Jālīrī* were many and they are still among the avant-garde in Egypt, including Muhammad al-Bisati (d. 2012), Bahaʾ Tahir (b. 1935), Yusuf Abu Rayya (b. 1955), ʿAbd al-Hakim Qasim (d.1990), Mahmud al-Wardani (b. 1950), Gamal al-Ghitani (b. 1945), Saʿid al-Kafrawi (b. 1939) and Idwar al-Kharrat (b. 1926).

In Tunisia, a journal in the 1980s called *al-Qiṣṣa* (The Short Story) provided an important vehicle publishing short fiction, and in Morocco many writers such as Idris al-Khuri (b. 1939), Muhammad Zifzaf (d. 2001), and Ahmad al-Madini (b. 1947) wrote short stories that often focused on the role of a locale as it impacted the making of an individual. In Algeria, there was first a generation dominated by Muhammad Dib (d. 2003), followed by a second generation of writers, such as Tahir Wattar (d. 2010) and 'Abd al-Hamid Benhadouga (d. 1996), who were followed by such prolific novelists and short story writers as Rashid Boudjedra.

In recent decades, almost every theme and issue that was once treated as a social realist tract, a humorous anecdote, or a plain struggle between the old and the new, has taken a different direction and has received a new perspective that can be summed up as an awareness of individuality, and an interest in individuation. Even the issues of social climbing, opportunism, and departure from standard religious teachings take on a different level of discourse, whereby the economic factor takes over as a personal decision within a broad-based social competition. In what at first seems almost a nursery tale, for example, by the Egyptian Yahya Tahir 'Abdallah (d. 1981) titled, "Who'll Hang the Bell?," the young Sabir, whose mother aspires to see him as a village shaykh, instead uses his religious training as cultural and symbolic capital to outsmart the fishmonger, take over his business, and become thereafter the sole owner of a fleet of boats and a thriving business, at the expense of his customers and workers.

The Iraqi generation of the 1960s and 1970s achieved new heights in the short story as an independent genre. The Iraqi Musa Kraidi (d. 1996) recreated traditional milieus through the behavior of idiots, reprobates, and other aliens. Jalil al-Qaysi (d. 2006), 'Aziz al-Sayyid Jassim (executed 1991), Mahmud Jindari (d.1989), 'Abd al-Ilah 'Abd al-Razzaq (b. 1939), 'Abd al-Sattar Nasir (d. 2013), 'Abd al-Khaliq al-Rikabi (b. 1945), and Abdul Rahman Majeed al-Rubaie (b. 1939) and the women writers Buthayna al-Nasiri (b. 1947), Lutfiyya al-Dulaimi (b. 1943), and Maysalun Hadi (b. 1954) are among the many writers in Iraq of the late 1960s who made excellent contributions to the genre through diligent efforts to engage the rising social, economic, and psychological problems. Each reaches the depths of the human soul in moments of fear and duress. There is also the war generation, including Warid Badr al-Salim (b. 1956) and Hasan Mutlaq (executed 1989), who wrote war short stories of enormous depth and value. Despite the fact that many were asked to contribute to a warlike national agenda, the outcome is surprisingly engaged with human misery, suffering, loneliness, and despair, where a human soul is caught between the challenges of life and death. A distinguished writer like Muhammad Khudhayyir (b. 1940) from Basra uses visual language to let external reality betray its inside like the nation state itself. His "Clocks like Horses" portrays Basra through the watchmaker's vision of time as indicated by clocks that tell of time all over the globe, especially Asia. Basra reiterates its presence, but it also loses it through the dominance of other times, and other cities and lands. War has already turned it into a ghost city ravished by time.

Conclusion

Since the early 1990s, the Arab political scene has witnessed dramatic upheavals and massive migrations. Especially in the case of Iraq, sanctions, wars, and military occupation have spawned narratives of mourning that can rarely escape the recent past. Even in narratives that build on a mixture of parody, memory, and social criticism, such as those by ʿAli Badr (b. 1974) in *Papa Sartre* (2001) and *The Tobacco Keeper* (*Ḥāris al-tibgh*, 2008; *The Tobacco Keeper, 2011*), and Sinan Antoon (b. 1967) in *The Pomegranate Tree Alone* (*Waḥdaha shajarat al-rummān*, 2010), the past always has a nightmarish look. Another Iraqi, the woman writer Betool Khedairi (b. 1965), has published several novels, the most impressive of which is *How Close the Sky Appeared* (*Kam badat al-samāʾ qarība*, 1999; *A Sky So Close*, 2002), a novel that is partly autobiographical covering the protagonist's early years as the child of an Iraqi father and a Scottish mother during the war with Iran.

On the other hand, there is also an upsurge in narrative writing, especially in South Arabia where ʿAbdu Khal (b. 1962) and Rajaʾ ʿAlim, among others, have engaged in new explorations with language in fiction writing. Khal's novel *She Spews Sparks* (*Tarmī bi-sharār*, 2007; *Throwing Sparks*, 2012) focuses on the harrowing and nightmarish experience of absolutism and police states. Using a Qurʾanic reference to hell (Q 77:32) as its title, the novel digs deep into the structures of traditionalist authoritarianism under the veneer of modernity. The Lebanese Rabee Jaber (b. 1972) is very prolific and his novel *The Druze of Belgrade* (*Durūz Bilgrād*, 2010) is another tale of struggle for survival in the face of exile, deportation, and calamity. No less innovative is the Egyptian Yusuf Zaydan (b. 1958), especially in his masterly novel *Azazel* (another name for Satan) (2009; *Azazel,* 2012). The novel is unique in capturing the struggle among separate lines of thought in early Christianity, and also the struggle within each person between the earthly and the heavenly, the pagan and the religious. In part due to the sponsorship of organizations such as the International Prize for Arabic Fiction (the Arabic Booker Prize) and the Sheikh Zayed Award, both funded from Abu Dhabi, the last few years have witnessed an upsurge in the writing of long fiction that has pushed the short story into the background. Reflecting each other, and with their authors' eyes focused on the prize, these narratives have generated a register and rhetoric of their own. They thematically engage with terror, nightmares, and individual experience, as opposed to communal solidarity, erotic scenes, historicized accounts, oriental mystique, and so on. These innovations have helped to create an invigorating climate for the proliferation of narrative writing.

Notes

1 On the travels of Ibn Battuta, see Ross E. Dunn, *The Adventures of Ibn Battutah: A Muslim Traveler of the Fourteenth Century* (Berkeley: University of California Press, 1989), and Tim Mackintosh-Smith (ed.), *The Travels of Ibn Battutah* (London: Picador, 2002).

2 Aḥmad Ibn Abī al-Ḍiyyāf, *Ithāf ahl al-Zamān bi-akhbār Tūnis wa-ahd al-amān* (Tunis: al-Dār Tūnisiyya li-l-Nashr), vol. II, pp. 115–16.

3 See Roger Allen, *The Arabic Novel: An Historical and Critical Introduction* (Syracuse, NY: Syracuse University Press, 1995), pp. 29–30; 181.

4 J. Brugman, *An Introduction to the History of Modern Arabic Literature in Egypt* (Leiden: Brill, 1984), pp. 215–118, and 215, n. 1, on articles and books on translated material.

5 A series of Zaydan's novels is currently being translated and published with sponsorship from the Zaydan Foundation, including *Tree of Pearls, Queen of Egypt* (2012), and *The Conquest of Andalusia* (2010).

6 Muhammad Mustafa Badawi, *Cambridge History of Arabic Literature: Modern Arabic Literature* (Cambridge University Press, 2006), p. 188.

7 Brugman, *Introduction*, pp. 210–11. The view was made popular through H. A. R. Gibb's endorsement.

8 Iskandar Habash's interview with ʿAbd al-Rahman Munif, *L'Orient Express*, 1999. Translated by Elie Chalala in *Al Jadid*, 9/45, 2003.

9 See Miriam Cooke, "Women Write War: The Feminization of Lebanese Society in the War Literature of Emily Nasrallah," *Bulletin of the British Society for Middle Eastern Studies*, 14:1 (1988), pp. 52–67.

10 See Denys Johnson-Davis, *Under the Naked Sky: Short Stories from the Arab World* (American University in Cairo Press, 2000), pp. 100–107.

11 Ibid., pp. 211–18.

12 Johnson-Davis, *Under the Naked Sky*, pp. 223–33.

13 Rajaʾ ʿAlim, *Sitr* (Beirut: Al-Markaz al-Thaqāfī, 2007), p. 5.

14 Hanan al-Shaykh, *Only in London* (New York: Anchor Books, 2002), p. 53.

15 Edward Said, "Arabic Prose and Prose Fiction after 1967," in *Reflections on Exile and Other Essays* (Cambridge, MA: Harvard University press, 2000), p. 57.

7

Music

Music in the Arab World has a long dynamic history and a wealth of interacting, ever-evolving traditions. This essay highlights elements and issues within this musical world by focusing on six songs. The song with the oldest documented roots allows us to look briefly into the deep past, acknowledging the variety of influences that helped shape the modern Arab musical world. Through two other songs, we consider the vital presence of Islam and how it continues to influence musical traditions. Finally, from two additional songs, we can perceive how Sufism (Islamic mysticism) has interfaced with Arab music past and present.

All six of the songs demonstrate how forms of mass media have shaped the music of the region. Additionally, one song highlights a specific artistic aesthetic, *tarab* (ecstatic engagement), that has informed many musical traditions. Three of the songs help us see changes that have occurred in performance ensembles over the last century. Finally, through an examination of several of the songs, we can understand how musicians have negotiated the creation and furthering of their careers by reacting to a variety of societal forces, including newly emerging approaches to the commodification of the arts, conservative religious forces that have recently swept through the region, and changing understandings regarding socially acceptable presentations of the body and of sexuality. From these six songs, we can grasp some of the richness and vitality of the world of Arab musical traditions.

Ya man la'ibat bihi shamulu (O you whom the wine has played with)

Arab music has a long history dating to before the advent of Islam when music flourished among Arabian nomadic tribes and also in urban centers. With the dramatic spread of Islam, opulent courts based first in Damascus (661–750) and then in Baghdad (762–1258) provided lavish patronage for singers, poets, composers, and instrumentalists, and also scholars who wrote extensive treatises on music theory. The Arab World was not isolated from other cultures, however, and its music was also influenced by Persian and Greek musical instruments, styles, and theoretical traditions. Medieval Muslim (Andalusian) Spain also contributed a new poetic form, the *muwashshah*, that spread throughout the Arab World and has continued to have a major presence even in modern times.

Though it owes many crucial components (including melodic, rhythmic, and poetic structures, and musical instruments) to this distant past, contemporary Arab music has more immediate roots in nineteenth- and twentieth-century traditions. With no tradition of writing down the musical dimension of songs (melodic notation only became widespread with the adoption of Western staff notation in the twentieth century), the oldest surviving performed repertoire can only be dated for certain to the nineteenth century. Some modern musical pieces surely predate this period, but we have no way of knowing their age or origin. The lyrics of songs, however, have been preserved for centuries in songbooks that contain songs' poetic texts. As such, the modern period of eastern Arab music might best be signaled by Muhammad Shihab al-Din's *c.* 1840 songbook, *Safinat al-mulk*. Shihab al-Din's work offers an excellent view of the poetic component of the art music of Egypt of the time, providing the texts to over 350 *muwashshah* songs divided into thirty performance suites called *wasla*s. The *muwashshah*, a genre that first emerged in medieval Muslim Spain, had by that time become the dominant form of art song in the eastern Arab World. Each *wasla* in Shihab al-Din's collection contains a series of ten to fifteen *muwashshah*s, united by being set in the same melodic mode (*lahn* or *maqam*). The songs within a given *wasla* were also organized according to their rhythmic mode, following a progression from heavy to light rhythms. Songs in the heaviest, most serious, rhythms – *murabba'* (a thirteen-beat rhythm), *muhajjar* (fourteen), or *mudawwar* (twelve) – were presented first. These were followed by songs in somewhat lighter rhythms. Finally, each *wasla* concluded with songs in the liveliest rhythms, specifically, *sama'i darij* and *sama'i saraband*, both versions of 6/8 time.

While handwritten songbooks have a long history in the Arab World, Shihab al-Din's volume signaled a new element of modernity when it was printed in lithograph form in Cairo in 1892. In this new form,

Figure 7.1 The song, *Ya man la'ibat bihi shamulu*, as it appears in the 1892 lithograph edition of Shihab al-Din's *Safinat al-mulk*.

Shihab al-Din's work became widely available: we are told that the great art-music singers of the earlier twentieth century "all drank from one spout: the book of al-Sayyid Muhammad Shihab al-Din."[1]

One of the songs in Shihab al-Din's work is *Ya man la'ibat bihi shamulu* (O you whom the wine has played with) (see Figure 7.1).

As with the other songs in Shihab al-Din's volume, we do not know either the composer or the poet of this song. The first four of the song's fourteen verses, transcribed and translated here, are in a flowery language common to the *muwashshah* genre: prominence is given to wine, an enhancer which facilitates union with the Beloved (both human and divine); the body of the beloved is likened to a graceful willow branch; when love and beauty are concerned, the eyes are the primary organ for perceiving and also for sending messages; finally, one must be on the lookout for jealous friends and neighbors, ever a possible source of the evil eye.

Yā man laʿibat bihi shamūlu	O you whom the wine has played with,
Mā alṭafa hādhihi sh-shamāʾil	How charming are your features!
Nashwān yahuzzuhu dallālun	Exulted with all this flirtation,
Ka-l-ghuṣni maʿa n-nasīmi māʾil	Like a willow branch swaying in the breeze.
Lā yumkinuhu l-kalāmu lākin	He cannot speak and yet,
Qad ḥamala ṭarfuhu rasāʾil	His glance is laden with messages.
Mā aṭyaba waqtanā wa-ahnā	How sweet is our time together and how joyful!
Wa-l-ʿādhilu ghāʾibun wa-ghāfil	The jealous watcher is absent and unaware.[2]

Shihab al-Din included the song as the concluding segment of his third *wasla*-suite, set in a six-beat rhythm and in the melodic mode called *rast* (see below), but tells us that the song was also performed in the *sikah* mode: he gives the song again as the concluding section of his seventh *wasla*-suite, a *wasla* set in the *sikah* mode. A number of the songs in this collection are still performed by singers and groups who feature *muwashshah* songs and this is the case with this song. The version in *rast* in a 6/8 rhythm is performed widely in the eastern Arab World. The song was regularly featured, for example, by the Egyptian government's Arabic Music Ensemble (*Firqat al-musiqa al-ʿArabiyya*) during the 1970s and 1980s; it is also frequently performed by the famed Syrian singer, Sabah Fakhri.[3] The *sikah* version of the song is not known in the eastern Mediterranean countries (Egypt up through Lebanon and Syria), however, but is common in Iraq. This version was part of the repertory of the late Iraqi superstar Nazim al-Ghazali (d. 1963), set in the mode of *awshar*, a variety of *sikah*.[4]

The fact that the Iraqi version is unknown in the eastern Mediterranean coastal region speaks to the distinct music regions that have developed across the Arab World: Morocco, Algeria, Tunisia, and Libya all received the *muwashshah* genre from al-Andalus (medieval Muslim Spain), and placed *muwashshah* songs at the center of the distinct Andalusian traditions that developed in each country. The eastern Mediterranean countries are recognized as comprising a separate region, while Iraqi art music represents yet a third distinct regional tradition, separate in turn from other unique musical practices based in the Arabian Peninsula.

Umm Kulthum's *Ghanni li shwayya* (Sing to me sweetly)

The *wasla* tradition changed in the late nineteenth century with the introduction of Turkish instrumental genres (called *saz semai* and *peşrev*; *sama'i* and *bashraf* in Arabic) and new forms of Arabic song (especially the *dawr*, *qasida*, and *taqtuqa*). *Muwashshah* songs remained common, but their number dropped to perhaps two or three in each *wasla*-suite. Additional changes occurred with the development of musical theater, also in the late nineteenth century, and the spread of recorded music from the first decade of the twentieth century. In addition to introducing new performance venues and greatly expanding the numbers of people who could hear the music, musical theater and the recording industry also brought about changes in typical performance ensembles: the traditional *wasla* ensemble, called a *takht*, consisted of a solo singer, two to three male chorus members, two to four melodic instruments (a lute ['*ud*], a plucked zither [*qanun*], an end-blown reed flute [*nay*], and the Western violin [which had replaced an indigenous bowed spiked fiddle, the *kaman* or *kamanja*, even taking on its name]), and a single percussion instrument (a tambourine [*riqq*]). Over time, the ensemble, now called a *firqa*, was greatly expanded to include multiple violins and other Western instruments, including the cello and double bass.

With the development of radio beginning in the 1920s and musical films from 1932, newly emerging forms of mass media continued the changes first initiated by print media and recordings. Audiences expanded greatly; media stars were cultivated; copyright issues arose; issues of government control (including censorship) came to the fore; and technological restrictions specific to each medium effected changes in the music.

In 1945, the Egyptian superstar singer Umm Kulthum (*c.* 1904–1975) starred in her fifth film, *Sallama*, acting the part of a famous eighth-century slave singer who sang in the caliph's court in Damascus. *Ghanni li shwayya* (Sing to me sweetly) was one of nine songs that she sang in the film. Each song now appeared separately, not as a part of an extended *wasla*-suite form. This piece was composed by Zakaria Ahmad (1896–1961) as a setting for a poem by Bayram al-Tunsi (1893–1961). In the film, Umm Kulthum begins to sing the song in a rural setting, accompanied by a drummer and a shepherd playing a flute. An enthusiastic crowd of villagers gathers around, singing the song's refrain. The group begins to process to the city, with ever more people joining in, singing along, and dancing. Besides celebrating the past tradition of slave girls who were bought and sold on the basis of the beauty of their voices and the depth of their song repertoire, the song also brings to the fore contentious issues concerning the permissibility of music in Muslim society. Since the birth of Islam, many have considered music to be an unacceptable distraction from a proper religious life: music, they declare, is *haram* (unlawful, impermissible). Others, however, have celebrated music's ability to foster aesthetic pleasure, communal celebration, and even, if properly employed, a means of achieving union with the Almighty here and now, the latter a belief of Sufi mystics. In *Ghanni li shwayya*, music is unabashedly celebrated, lauded for its ability to affect nature, cure illness, soothe the heart, and bring girls to dance.

Refrain:

Ghannī lī shwayya shwayya	Sing to me sweetly, sweetly [or: softly, softly]
Ghannī lī wa-khud ʿaynayya	Sing to me and take my heart [lit. "my eyes"]

1st verse:

Khallīnī aʾūl alḥān	Let me sing melodies
Titmāyil lihā s-sāmiʿīn	That will move listeners
Wa-trafrif lihā l-aghṣān	And cause branches to sway,
Wa-n-narjis maʿa l-yāsmīn	Along with the narcissus and the jasmine,
Wa-tsāfir bihā r-rukbān	And that travelers will remember
Ṭāwiyīn il-bawādī ṭayy	As they cross the wide deserts.
Shwayya shwayya shwayya shwayya	Sweetly, sweetly, sweetly, sweetly,
Ghannī lī wa-khud ʿaynayya	Sing to me and take my heart (eyes).

[Refrain.]

2nd verse:

Il-maghnā ḥayāt ir-rūḥ	Singing is the life of the soul,
Yismaʿhā l-ʿalīl tashfīh	It cures the illness of he who hears it,
Wa-tdāwī kabid majruḥ	And it heals the wounded heart
Tihtār it-tibbā fīh	That doctors cannot cure;

Wa-tkhallī zalām il-layl   It turns the dark of night,
Fī ʿayūn il-habāyib ḍayy   In lovers' eyes to light!
Shwayya shwayya shwayya shwayya   Sweetly, sweetly, sweetly, sweetly,
Ghannī lī wa-khud ʿaynayya   Sing to me and take my heart
(eyes).

[Refrain.]

3rd verse:
L-aghannī wa-aʾūl li-ṭ-ṭīr   If I sing and say to the birds,
Min badrī ṣabāh il-khayr   "Good Morning" in the early
morn,

Wi-l-ʾamarī maʿa l-khaḍīr   The turtledoves and greenfinches
Wayyāhā yaraddū ʿalayya   Will sing with me and reply.
Shwayya shwayya shwayya shwayya   Sweetly, sweetly, sweetly, sweetly,
Ghannī lī wa-khud ʿaynayya   Sing to me and take my heart
(eyes).

[Refrain.]

4th verse:
Ahlif lak bi-rabb il-bayt   I promise you, by the Lord of the
House
(i.e., of the Kaʿba in Mecca, thus,
God),
Yā muṣaddiq bi-rabb il-bayt   O you who trust in the Lord of the
House,
L-asḥirkum idhā ghannayt   That if I were to sing, I would
charm you,
Wa-ʾaraʾ ʾaṣ banāt il-ḥayy   And make the neighborhood girls
dance.
Shwayya shwayya shwayya shwayya   Sweetly, sweetly, sweetly, sweetly,
Ghannī lī wa-khud ʿaynayya   Sing to me and take my heart
(eyes).

[Refrain.]

5th verse:
L-aghannī w-aghannī w-aghannī   I will sing and sing and sing,
Wa-arwī il-khalāyiq fannī   I will transmit my art to all
creatures.

Il-insī yiʾūl li-l-jinnī   Men will pass it on to the Jinn,
Wa-r-rāyiḥ yiʾūl li-l-jāyy   To those going and those coming.
[Repeat 2nd verse; refrain.][5]

In the film, the song lasts over five minutes. When Umm Kulthum later performed the song in public concerts, however, she employed one of the crucial resources of live performance: improvisation. Above all, eastern Arab art music values the emotional and aesthetic engagement of performers and audience members alike as a performance unfolds. In order to create the desired state, *tarab*, characterized by a shared state of ecstasy, many elements of the music are left to be decided at the time of the performance itself. Individual phrases of a song and entire sections may be repeated any number of times in order to fully evoke the aesthetic qualities of the text and melodies. Each repetition can be performed with new melodic and rhythmic ornaments, with the levels of variation ranging from very small to extensive. Additionally, whenever the singer wants, he/she can temporarily stop the song and perform an extended improvisation using one or two lines of the song's poetic text. A single word or short phrase can be sung over and over, with ever new melodies, the audience roaring approval with each new rendition. A five-minute song easily expands to twenty minutes or more, often much more. Live performances by Umm Kulthum and other superstars occurred in large halls, were broadcast on radio and later on television, sold on records and then cassettes and CDs. Most recently, music has become a mainstay on satellite TV stations and is widely distributed on internet sites.

Throughout her long career (extending from her early childhood until her death in 1975), Umm Kulthum included nationalist songs in her repertoire, singing for royalty when Egypt was a kingdom and for the post-monarchy Republic of Egypt (from 1953), including numerous songs in response to specific events: the 1952 revolution, the 1956 Suez Crisis, the 1967 war with Israel, and so on. She was also active as the head of the musicians' union and a member of government committees, all serving to highlight the engagement of music and musicians with issues of government cultural policies and national and international politics.

During Umm Kulthum's lifetime, eastern Arab art music experienced many changes, including the institutionalization of music education. Music conservatories were opened in countries throughout the region, teaching both Western classical and Arab music. A new music theory was formulated to teach the latter, firmly grounded in Western staff notation. A music tradition that had been passed down aurally came to have a major written component: students now learned the music by reading staff transcriptions.

Saber el-Robaei's *Sidi Mansur*

In addition to believing in the power of music, as evidenced in the song
Ghanni li shwayya, Sufi mystics also believe in the efficacy of prayer
directed to recognized Sufi saints. Saints' birthdays are celebrated with
a variety of festivities. While some celebrations, such as those for the
birthday of the Prophet Muhammad, are observed across the region,
many occur only in particular locales, for example, by the tomb of a saint
whose fame might be restricted to the immediate vicinity. In the coastal
city of Sfax in Tunisia, a shrine housing the tomb of Sidi Mansur, is the
place of worship, including annual pilgrimages by the saint's devotees.
Celebrations include the singing of a specific song of praise for the saint.
This song, recorded widely in Tunisia by ensembles that perform traditional repertoire, is understood to be a part of the culture's historic heritage. The development of the mass media, however, created the potential
for such locally based songs to travel beyond their usual confines and
achieve much wider notoriety. Such was the case with the song for Sidi
Mansur. Ethnomusicologist Richard Jankowsky writes:

> The praise song for Sidi Mansur … traditionally performed by a
> chorus of men accompanied by traditional percussion … and the *gasba*
> (traditional reed flute), is perhaps the most widely recognizable song
> for a Tunisian saint in the country. Its melody and lyrics have made
> their way from Sidi Mansur's local *zawiya* in … Sfax to a national
> listenership via broadcast of the … 45 rpm recordings of Mohammed
> Jerrari, then to the pan-Arab satellite music television stations and
> beyond, popularized by Tunisian singer Saber el-Robaei's 1990s pop
> version.[6]

Saber el-Robaei's (Sābir al-Rubāʿī, b. 1967) music video that helped spread
the song is light-hearted and upbeat with no explicit visual references
to Sidi Mansur other than the fact that the singer processes along with
his entourage in a manner reminiscent of pilgrimage to a saint's shrine.
While this might indeed signal the annual pilgrimage ritual to those who
understand the traditional context for the song, this was not clear across
the Arab World. Indeed, from the video, it is clear that el-Robaei and his
managers had another goal: to place the song in the realm of the sexualized music videos that have dominated Arab pop music since the 1990s. As
we will see, they succeeded in their goal. The video begins with el-Robaei
sleeping comfortably outdoors on a bed luxuriously appointed with

traditional colorful fabrics and an oversized pillow.[7] A moment later, the song begins with a short percussion introduction played on the Tunisian version of castanets (the *shqashiq*). Visually, we see close-ups of six young women, one after another, each playing one cycle of the rhythm on the large metallic instruments. Sexuality is immediately brought to the fore: we see the first woman in a tight shot that shows only the pair of *shqashiq*, a bare arm holding one of the instruments, and the woman's body from her chin to her belly button. She is wearing a small bright yellow top that shows off her midriff and much skin at and below the neck. The second woman is similarly dressed, but we see her entire upper body. Her small top is red, and she, like the following four women, is looking directly at the camera. The close-up of the third woman features her blond hair, her red top with spaghetti straps, and her bare arms and shoulders. This percussion introduction wakes up el-Robaei, who rises from the bed and immediately starts singing, and then energetically walks down a narrow path surrounded by lush green foliage. The shot quickly changes to el-Robaei, now singing and dancing in place on a small second-floor balcony, followed by quick alternations between the path and balcony shots. Two close-ups, one of a young woman with bare neck and shoulders, the other a repeat of the chin to midriff that we have seen earlier, are inserted to maintain the video's aspect of titillation.

Finally, fifty-two seconds into the video, we see a group processing. For those familiar with the song's function as a Sufi praise song, it might be clear that they are going to visit Sidi Mansur's shrine; indeed, the refrain includes the words, "Sidi Mansur, O father, we are coming to visit you, O father." Visually, however, the procession does not feature religiosity, but, rather, pretty women, the earlier *shqashiq* players, now without their instruments, dancing along behind el-Robaei, the leader. Some six male frame drummers wearing bright red caps are shown now and again, sometimes behind el-Robaei, sometimes in front of him. For a number of extended sections in the 4'17" video, the procession theme is given up in favor of celebratory scenes of the women dancing in various formations in a courtyard, with el-Robaei occasionally featured and the frame drummers in the background. These sections of the video match similar moments in countless pop music videos in the Arab World, Bollywood, and the West, where women's bodies are brought to the fore, with the seemingly obligatory occasional pelvis close-ups.

The video succeeded, as Jankowsky mentioned above, in popularizing the song across the Arab World. However, outside of Tunisia, the song's Sufi associations were lost. Egyptians have reported that the song was extremely popular in Egypt, but that there was little or no under-standing of the song's Sufi context. Others of Lebanese background commented that the song is a pop song, widely used in wedding celebrations. They are stunned to hear of the traditional context of the song. No one knew. "We had no idea. When I mentioned it to my parents, they also had no idea."

The words of el-Robaei's version of the song do contain traditional lines that reference the pilgrimage ritual, such as going to visit Sidi Mansur's shrine and carrying traditional candles. However, many lines feature an ambiguity that is common in much Arabic poetry: is the beloved for whom the singer longs a worldly lover or is it the Divine?

Refrain:
Allāh Allāh yā bābā	Allah, Allah, O Father,
wi-salām ʿalek yā bābā	Peace be upon you, O Father,
sīdī Manṣūr yā bābā	Sidi Mansur, O Father,
wi-njīk nzūr yā bābā	We are coming to visit you, O Father.

1st verse:
ashhad bi-llāh yā bābā	I swear by God, O Father,
mā ʿshigt siwāh yā bābā	I've never loved any but him, O Father,
jarḥ il-ḥabīb yā bābā	The wound [caused by] the beloved, O Father,
ʿalāj iṣʿīb yā bābā	Is difficult to cure, O Father,
wish ḥālī fīh yā bābā	What is my situation with him, O Father?
malhūf ʿalayh yā bābā	I am longing for him, O Father,
wa-shhad bi-llāh yā bābā	I swear by God, O Father,
mā ʿshigt siwāh yā bābā	I've never loved any but him, O Father,
wi-njīk yā sīdī (x2)	I'll come to you, my master,
bi-shamū ʿfī īdī (x2)	With candles in my hands,
wi-n-nār fī galbī (x2)	And a fire in my heart
taḥrig warīdī (x2)	That scalds my veins.
[Refrain.]	

2nd verse:
wi-kaḥīl il-ʿayn yā bābā	The one with black eyes, O Father,
ḥilw il-khadayn yā bābā	With beautiful cheeks, O Father,
ḥilw wi-mabhūr yā bābā	Beautiful and fascinating, O Father,
wi-ʿuyūnuh bhūr yā bābā	His eyes are like the sea, O Father,
wi-kharigt maʿāh yā bābā	I drowned with him, my Father,
ʿaṣṣibnī jfāh yā bābā	His absence torments me, my Father,

wi-kaḥīl al-ʿayn yā bābā	The one with black eyes, my Father.
khada galbī li fayn	Where did he take my heart?
sīdī wasīnī (x2)	My master, ease me!
aḥkī wi-ḥakīnī (x2)	Speak and tell me!
ṣabbarlī ḥālī (x2)	Give me the patience to accept my state,
ʿallī nāsīnī (x2)	Concerning the one who has forgotten me!

[Refrain.][8]

The song *Sidi Mansur* stands as a vibrant example of the numerous regional traditions that flourish throughout the Arab World. While Cairo-based Egyptian art and pop music traditions have spread throughout the Arab World, Egypt itself is also home to distinct music and dance traditions in southern (Upper) Egypt, in the western oases, in the Suez Canal region, and in the Sinai. Lebanon and Syria are similarly rich in unique regional music and dance traditions. The legendary singer Fairuz (b. 1935), dubbed the "Voice of Lebanon," is understood to have a style that is uniquely Lebanese, while Syria's Sabri Mudallal (1918–2006) and Sabah Fakhri (b. 1933) have performed repertoire specific to Syria during their long and illustrious careers. Arab culture is not monolithic in nature: diversity reigns throughout the region.

Hisham ʿAbbas's *Asmaʾ Allah al-husna* (The Beautiful Names of God)

Up through the early decades of the twentieth century, the prevailing form of childhood education occurred in the *kuttab* (Qurʾan school). Housed at the local mosque, *kuttab* training focused on learning to recite the holy Qurʾan, following rigorous rules of pronunciation, and, in its more elaborate form, adhering to the patterns of melodic improvisation specific to the Arab system of melodic modes, the *maqamat* (singular, *maqam*). With this training, and living in "[a] predominantly religious society [that] favored performance of spiritual poetry not only for specifically Islamic occasions (such as Ramadan nights, the two Feasts, or the Prophet's Birthday), but also for festive social occasions such as … weddings,"[9] singers often emphasized religious repertoire, while also including secular songs. For this reason, singers were referred to as *shaykh*, a title applied to individuals with a widely varying range of religious education.[10] Thus, among the famous singers of the late nineteenth and early twentieth centuries were Shaykh Salama Hijazi (1852–1917), Shaykh Sayyid Darwish (1892–1923), and Shaykh Zakaria Ahmad (1896–1961), the composer of the Umm Kulthum song above.

This intermingling of religious and secular songs continued throughout much of the twentieth century. Umm Kulthum, for example, continued to include religious songs along with secular love songs in concerts throughout her long career, such as the religious song *al-Qalb ya ʿshaq kull gamil* (The Heart Loves All that is Beautiful), debuted in 1971. However, two developments contributed to a separation of the religious and secular realms in music performance. First, the Islamic training provided by the *kuttab* experience became less and less common, especially in urban centers like Cairo where a modern form of secular public education became the norm. Second, the marketing strategies of the newly developing mass-mediated music industry (with commercial records from 1904) required a clear separation between the religious and the secular, so that profits in the latter realm could be maximized by emphasizing the sensual and the sexual. "Subject to different values, religious and popular domains became increasingly differentiated."[11]

Ideas about the boundaries between the religious and the secular gained new impetus in the last decades of the twentieth century with the growth of movements across the region towards a more conservative interpretation of Islam. Indeed, numerous musicians, actors, and dancers felt compelled to retire from the world of secular entertainment, an act that was commonly referred to as "repenting." After a period of reflection, a number came back to performance with repertoire that was explicitly religious in nature. Karim Tartoussieh's article, "Pious Stardom: Cinema and the Islamic Revival in Egypt," provides an insightful look at this phenomenon in the realm of Egypt's film industry from the early 1990s. Tartoussieh quotes a *Wall Street Journal* article: "In a country that proudly calls itself the 'Hollywood of the East,' a group of actresses has touched off a furor by appearing on television and in movies with a new look: the conservative Islamic veil."[12] The best-known example in the West of this phenomenon in the realm of music is the case of Cat Stevens, who retired from a performing career after converting to Islam in 1977, only to come back years later as Yusuf Islam with an exclusively religious repertoire.

While this extreme stance is common enough to be known to one and all in the Arab World, many popular singers took another approach, maintaining the intermingling of religious and secular repertoire that had been common throughout Arab music's long history. Thus a modern pop singer might insert one or two religious songs into an album (cassette or CD) that otherwise featured a series of love songs. An example of this phenomenon that met with great success was the 2000 CD by the Egyptian singer, Hisham ʿAbbas (b. 1963). Within a progression of love songs was a song by the Egyptian composer Sayyid Makkawi (1927–1997) that sets the Ninety-Nine Names of God, *Asma' Allah al-Husna* (The Beautiful Names of God) to music. Islamic tradition holds not only that God possesses ninety-nine names (or attributes), but that they occur in a standard progression, starting with *al-Rahman* (The Merciful) and *al-Rahim* (The Compassionate, or Beneficent), and ending with *al-Rashid* (The Righteous) and *al-Sabur* (The Patient). See Table 7.1 below. This list is found in many art forms, including in paintings, on cloth, and etched in metal plates. An internet search for "Ninety-Nine Names of God" will call up dozens of examples (see Figures 7.2 and 7.3 below).

During the 1980s, prior to Hisham ʿAbbas's recording, the *Asma' Allah al-Husna* song was regularly performed in Cairo every other Thursday evening during concerts by the Arabic Music Ensemble. In the middle of the ensemble's concerts, a separate group, the Religious Song Ensemble (*Firqat al-inshad id-dini*) would perform a set, invariably including this song. The song was received with great enthusiasm each and every time, with the audience requesting a repeat performance with a characteristic circular waving of the printed program. The ensemble's conductor would inevitably oblige, thus the audience would hear this song twice in each concert.

Hisham ʿAbbas's decision to include this song in his 2000 album was a shrewd one. In the context of the increasingly conservative religious atmosphere that spread throughout Egypt, ʿAbbas's version of the song was adopted by DJs throughout Cairo as the obligatory starting item for their wedding performances. This became the tradition in both lower class, "folk" weddings, where the DJ would wheel out his equipment on a small wooden cart, and also in elaborate weddings in five-star hotels. Hisham ʿAbbas's version of the "Ninety-Nine Names of God" became a constant presence, universally recognized throughout the city. The superstar singer of love songs had yet another super hit. Thus, ʿAbbas managed to confirm his identity as a pop star with an appropriately righteous character.

Table 7.1. *The Ninety-Nine Names of God in their standard order*[43]

1	Ar-Rahman	The All-Merciful	51	Al-Haqq	The Truth
2	Ar-Rahim	The All-Beneficent	52	Al-Wakil	The Trustee
3	Al-Malik	The Absolute Ruler	53	Al-Qawi	The Possessor of All Strength
4	Al-Quddus	The Pure One	54	Al-Matin	The Forceful One
5	As-Salam	The Source of Peace	55	Al-Wali	The Governor
6	Al-Mu'min	The Inspirer of Faith	56	Al-Hamid	The Praised One
7	Al-Muhaymin	The Guardian	57	Al-Muhsi	The Appraiser
8	Al-ʿAziz	The Victorious	58	Al-Mubdi	The Originator
9	Al-Jabbar	The Compeller	59	Al-Muʿid	The Restorer
10	Al-Mutakabbir	The Greatest	60	Al-Muhyi	The Giver of Life
11	Al-Khaliq	The Creator	61	Al-Mumit	The Taker of Life
12	Al-Bari'	The Maker of Order	62	Al-Hayy	The Ever Living One
13	Al-Musawwir	The Shaper of Beauty	63	Al-Qayyum	The Self-Existing One
14	Al-Ghaffar	The Forgiving	64	Al-Wajid	The Finder
15	Al-Qahhar	The Subduer	65	Al-Majid	The Glorious
16	Al-Wahhab	The Giver of All	66	Al-Wahid	The Only One
17	Ar-Razzaq	The Sustainer	67	Al-Ahad	The One
18	Al-Fattah	The Opener	68	As-Samad	The Satisfier of All Needs
19	Al-ʿAlim	The Knower of All	69	Al-Qadir	The All Powerful
20	Al-Qabid	The Constrictor	70	Al-Muqtadir	The Creator of All Power
21	Al-Basit	The Reliever	71	Al-Muqaddim	The Expediter
22	Al-Khafid	The Abaser	72	Al-Mu'akhkhir	The Delayer
23	Ar-Rafiʿ	The Exalter	73	Al-Awwal	The First
24	Al-Muʿizz	The Bestower of Honors	74	Al-Akhir	The Last
25	Al-Mudhill	The Humiliator	75	Az-Zahir	The Manifest One

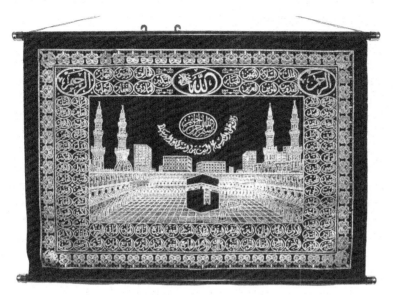

Figure 7.2 A cloth presentation of the Ninety-Nine Names of God.

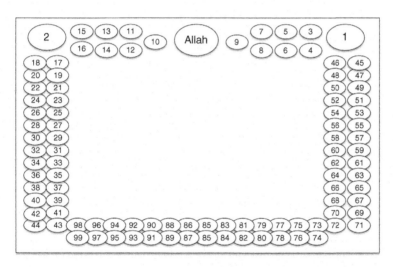

Figure 7.3 A chart showing where the Ninety-Nine Names of God occur in Figure 7.2 above. Note: The name "Allah," the "Greatest Name," is not included in the Ninety-Nine; the eighty-fifth name is a compound name that takes up two oval spaces.

Hakim's *is-Salamu ʿalaykum* (Peace be upon you)

The Egyptian pop singer Hakim (b. 1962) released his first album in 1991, subsequently releasing over a dozen more. In the period after the death of the eastern Arab World's three great twentieth-century superstar singers (Umm Kulthum in 1975, ʿAbd al-Halim Hafiz in 1977, and Farid al-Atrash in 1974), a new type of pop music began to appear, with Hakim and Hisham ʿAbbas being among the top singers. The new music came to be conceptualized as comprising two contrasting styles: *shababi* and *shaʿbi*. Both emphasized short songs for dancing (perhaps four minutes in length) with catchy lyrics and melodies. But *shababi*, understood to favor lyrical ballads, garnered a middle-class following, whereas *shaʿbi*, featuring faster driving rhythms and often edgy street-derived lyrics, attracted a lower class fan base. Hakim rose within the *shaʿbi* style (Hisham ʿAbbas within the *shababi* style), although individual songs often blurred the distinction between the two. Significantly, however, armed with a carefully constructed classy image (wearing tailored Italian suits for wedding performances, for example), Hakim succeeded in attracting people of all social groups, including the upper class. Indeed, he and his managers labeled his unique version of *shaʿbi* as "*shaʿbi chic*."

The performance ensemble for the new musics was decidedly Western influenced, featuring electric keyboards, electric bass, a trap drum set and, commonly, a small brass section of trumpets and trombone. Traditional Arab elements remained, including an Arab percussion section and a few "traditional" Arab melody instruments (the *kawala* reed flute, violins, and accordion, for example).[14] From the 1990s, Arab pop music has prominently featured a video component, with new releases appearing as slick "video clips," the Arabic term for the art form (without the letters "v," "p," and "o," the Arabic language renders the term as *fidiyu klib*.) *Shaʿbi* scholar, James Grippo, comments that *shaʿbi*'s image as the music of the everyman, as the music of the street, is explicitly and exemplarily manifested in the music video that accompanied the 2002 release of Hakim's song, *is-Salamu ʿalaykum*.[15]

In the video, Hakim playfully morphs through a series of personas. He *is* the everyman: he first appears when a car mechanic slides out from under the car he is working on and we realize that the mechanic is Hakim. Singing and dancing, he proceeds to an outdoor cafe and takes a seat. When a waiter places a cup of tea in front of him, we find that the waiter is again Hakim. Next, we see him, still a waiter, in the back of the cafe, singing and dancing while pouring tea in the small space among the water pipes that are an ever-present feature in Egyptian tea/coffee shops. Then, distracted by a passing girl, he goes out onto the street, following her. Dressed with a black cloth covering her modest dress and a flowery reddish band of cloth in hair, she is a neighborhood girl from the working class (a *baladi* girl). In his distraction he walks in front of one of Cairo's ubiquitous taxis and falls onto the taxi's hood before rolling to the ground, adopting a slapstick pose of someone seriously injured, with his tongue extended far out of his mouth. A passerby, again Hakim, comes over and, greatly shocked, calls an ambulance. Next, we see Hakim on a stretcher in the ambulance, being administered to by a nurse. Hakim sings and flirts with the nurse as she repeatedly tries to place an oxygen mask on his face. Next we find him, still on the stretcher, being wheeled down a hospital's corridors, still singing and gesticulating repeatedly. Then, a doctor appears with an oversized needle and syringe, the latter filled with a liquid playfully colored orange. Hakim, the patient, faints when he sees the size of the needle and syringe. The doctor, it turns out when we see his face, is again Hakim.

Next, we see the doctor filling and closing his briefcase, preparing to leave work. The next shot has Hakim dressed as a worker, slightly lower class than the doctor, running alongside a bus, waiting for the opportunity to jump on, an endeavor that all in Cairo are well familiar with. He is bringing home the daily paper and also a watermelon, a favorite food of the "average" Egyptian. However, while jumping abroad the moving bus, the watermelon is knocked out of his hand. We see it explode on the street and then we see Hakim looking back at it, helplessly. In the following sequences Hakim appears as the bus attendant, the bus driver, a gas station attendant, a fast-food delivery person, and a policeman who, dancing, singing, and motioning with his arms, is directing traffic. The traffic gets progressively worse until there is complete gridlock. Seeing the absolute futility of the situation, Hakim simply leaves his post, gesturing repeatedly that there is nothing one can do to alleviate Cairo's legendary traffic problems.

Clearly, Hakim, the *sha'bi* singer, is presented as the common man: a car mechanic, a waiter at a coffee shop, a passerby, a doctor, a worker returning home, a ticket collector in a bus, a bus driver, a gas station attendant, a fast-food delivery person, and a traffic patrolman. In each case, he is dressed in the clothes that typify that class and occupation.

The song is an ardent love song, the singer repeatedly trying to bring back a now distant lover. The title line of the song, *is-salamu ʿalaykum,* is perhaps its most brilliant line: *is-salamu ʿalaykum* (peace be upon you) is surely the most common greeting in the Arab World. By framing the entire song and also each verse with multiple repetitions of this greeting, the greeting "became Hakim's" for a period of time after the song and video's release. You could not say hello to a family member, friend, or colleague without thinking of Hakim. By starting and ending the song with a playful repetition of the greeting's first syllable (*is-, is-, is-salamu ʿalaykum*), equivalent to saying "hel-, hel- hello," Hakim invited one and all to mimic this playful phrase whenever they offered someone a greeting. Indeed, many took Hakim up on this, and thus Hakim became a part of many everyday conversations.

Refrain:

is- is- is- salā mu ʿalaykum (x4)	Greetings ("Peace be upon you").
is-salāmu ʿalaykum (x4)	Greetings ("Peace be upon you").
baʿdi s-salām yiḥlā l-kalām	After the greetings, our talk will be sweet
nishar nidūʾ ḥubbi wi-gharām	We stay up late and taste love and passion
di-l-hayāt halā yallā binā yallā naḥḍun il-ayyām	Life is bright, come on, let's embrace the days.
w-is-salāmu ʿalaykum, is-salāmu ʿalaykum (x2)	Greetings ("Peace be upon you").

1st verse:

ana ʾalbī sallim yā ḥabībī rudd is-salām	My heart greets you. Please answer!
w-iftah lī ʾalbak yā ḥabībī w-insā l-khiṣām	Open your heart to me, my love, and forget our disagreement
ḥibbi w-urʾuṣ ghannī	Love, dance, and sing!
uwʿā tibʿid ʿannī	Don't go far from me!
[Refrain.]	
hāt īdik yallā	Give me your hands.
dā s-salām li-llāh	This greeting is for God.
lā kifāya ʿinād	Enough of your stubbornness!

w-is-salāmu ʿalaykum, is-salāmu ʿalaykum (x2)	Greetings ("Peace be upon you")

2nd verse:

mā tḍumm shōʾak ʿalā shōʾī ʾarrab yā wād	Add your passion to mine and come closer, boy!
w-aḥlawwi yā dunyā wa-rūʾī baʿd il-biʿād	May the world become sweet and clear after our separation
bayn rumūshak khudnī	Take me between your eyelashes
aw taʿālā fī ḥuḍnī	Or come into my embrace

[Refrain.]

ḍaḥka maʿa ghamza	A laugh with a wink
naẓra maʿa hamza	A look with a whisper
kulluh yibʾā tamām	Everything will be alright
wi-s-salāmu ʿalaykum, is-salāmu ʿalaykum (x2)	Greetings ("Peace be upon you")

3rd verse:

anā bass ʿāyzak tiddīnī ḥabbit ḥanān	I just want you to give me a bit of kindness
wi-b-aḥlā ḥubb tnassīnī murr iz-zamān	And, with the sweetest love, to make me forget the bitter time
law ghiliṭṭ ʿātibnī	If I've made a mistake, talk to me!
mish tirūḥ wi-tsībnī	Don't just go and leave me!

[Refrain.]

yallā yā wāḥishnī	Oh, I've missed you so
ʿaysh wi-ʿayyishnī	Live and let me live!
leh tibāt zaʿlān	Why spend the night angry?
w-is-salāmu ʿalaykum, is-salāmu ʿalaykum (x2)	Greetings ("Peace be upon you")[16]

The importance of the video clip component of the modern Arab pop music has grown exponentially over the last many years as satellite

television stations have spread throughout the region. Accessible internationally, the songs are featured on a number of stations that broadcast non-stop music videos. An additional layer of mediaization occurs
when short excerpts of hit songs are sold as downloadable ringtones.
When a video is playing, instructions are given on the television screen
for the number to call to obtain the ringtone on your phone. Similarly,
the J-cards on cassettes or CDs include instructions for obtaining the
songs' catchy lead melody as the ringtone. Indeed, this was the case with
is-Salamu ʿalaykum in the 2002 cassette that included the song.

The commodification of pop music and pop singers is seen in a number of other ways. Hakim has been featured on TV ads for one of Egypt's
main mobile phone companies, Mobinil, and also for a tea company.[17] In
these commercials, Hakim sings versions of his own songs, thus blurring
the line between the music and the commercial's stated product: both are
being promoted. Hakim (and many other pop singers) has also appeared
in commercial films, including the 2005 release, *Ali Spicy*, in which he is
the lead actor. The publicity narrative begins, "'Ali' is a young man whose
father wants him to be a doctor, but 'Ali' loves singing and has the dream
of becoming a famous singer."[18]

Modern-day pop singers actively seek to reach out to the Arab World
beyond Egypt, to Arabs in the diaspora, and to audiences outside the
Arab World. Hakim is no exception. He has performed in several Arab
countries and has toured the United States and Europe a number of
times. In addition, he gave a number of his hit songs to the London-based
Transglobal Underground for remixing (see his 1998 album, *Remix*), part
of a larger effort to reach audiences in the West. Hakim acknowledged an
awkward aspect of this project: in Egypt, "people liked [the songs] as they
were, and didn't understand the need to remix them."[19] Many felt, however, that the remix element was needed to catch diasporic and Western
audiences. Thus, on many levels, *shaʿbi* and *shababi* musics exist in highly
commodified worlds. Hakim is one of dozens of singers over the last
three or more decades who have become stars in, and by means of, these
processes of commodification.

Nancy Ajram's *Ah wa-nuss*

For many in the Arab World today, the biggest issue concerning the
modern music scene is the greatly expanded levels of sexuality that per-
vade the music. Patricia Kubala reports that many view the ubiquitous

suggestive clothing and sexualized dance moves that accompany the music as having "crossed the line of public propriety and respectable artistic presentation."[20] A complex array of factors have contributed to the present situation, including the growth of the "video clip" as an obligatory component in the production of a modern-day hit song and a satellite revolution that has sidestepped previously existing layers of government censorship and enabled the videos to be readily available throughout the region.

Whatever one's opinion, all agree that music videos have given the visual element of the music an unprecedented dominance. It is common to hear people declare that physical beauty has become more important than the beauty of a singer's voice. A presentation that includes sexual titillation has become de rigueur. Earlier generations of singers did not face this expectation: Umm Kulthum and the Lebanese Fairuz performed in elegant gowns but moved little (or, in the case of Fairuz, virtually not at all) and gave no sense whatsoever of a sexualized presence. In the present day, individual singers have each had to negotiate their own path through this new territory. Some, like the Lebanese singer Haifa Wehbe (b. 1976), embraced a persona that featured voluptuous sexuality.[21] Others, like Nancy Ajram (b. 1983), also a Lebanese singer, have crafted a more nuanced image. Regularly coiffed to perfection and beautifully, even fetchingly, dressed, along with a smile that can be teasing and suggestive,[22] Nancy has also released two albums of children's songs and served as a Goodwill Ambassador for UNICEF.[23]

Nancy's song, *Ah wa-nuss* and accompanying video provides a rich example of a nuanced negotiation of sexuality and gender roles.[24] It may be argued that the words of the song suggest one stance, while the video visually offers another. The lyrics offer the voice of a woman who has become strong after putting up with too much for too long. She is ready to dictate the terms of her relationship with her beloved: "Calm down and listen to me – if you pamper me, I will give you everything; otherwise we're through and you will be the loser."

Refrain, part 1:

mā fīsh hāga tīgī kida	Things shouldn't be handled this way!
ihdā habībī kida	Calm down, my love,
wi-rga' zayyi zamān	And be yourself again.
yā bnī isma'nī hatdalla'nī	Listen to me, pal, if you pamper me,
takhud 'aynī kamān	I will give you my eyes [i.e., my heart].

Refrain, part 2:

habībī ʾarrab, buṣṣi wi-buṣṣi buṣṣ	Come close, my love, and listen
zaʿlān izʿal izʿal nuṣṣi nuṣṣ	Be reasonable even if you are upset,
l-aḥsan habʿad abʿad wi-nuṣṣ	Otherwise I will go away and I mean it!
wa-ḥtibaʾā inta akīd khasrān	And you will certainly be the only loser!

[Refrain, part 1.]

1st verse:

eh da kulli da	What is all that about?
khadti ʿalā kida	You got used to blaming me
inta mā btizhaʾshi malām	Do you never get tired?
taʿbti y-anā y-anā	You wore me out.
layālī ḥayrāna	I stay up long nights confused and frustrated
ihdā baʾa w-ikfāya ḥarām	Calm down and enough blame!

[Refrain, part 2.]

2nd verse:

di ḥāga mutaʿaba	This is a very tiring situation.
ikminnī ṭayyiba	Thanks to my good heart
mustaḥmilak wi-baʾā lī ktīr	I put up with your cruel attitude for years
ḥabībī shūf anā	My darling, look,
ṣuburti kam sana	How many years have I been patient?
khadti waʾti maʿāyā ktīr	I wasted so much time with you.

[Refrain, part 2.][25]

In the video, Nancy offers another persona. In a folkloric tableau, she is a *baladi* (local, folk) girl, who is very flirtatious with her suitor. The video begins with the rooster crowing and a young man looking up at Nancy's window. Finding no sign of her, he throws a small rock at the window, waking her up. She rises from her bed, quickly puts on a folk scarf, shuffles through the next room, which has five or six young children sleeping in close quarters, signaling that she is from a poor, working-class neighborhood. She gently jostles the children in an effort to wake them as she makes her way to the window. Here, looking down at her suitor, she flirts happily, smiling heartily, and playing with her hair.

In the remaining parts of the video she continues to flirt playfully as she washes the family's clothes in a small circular washbasin, among the chickens, and then proceeds to sing and dance suggestively as she hangs out the clothes on a series of clothes lines, with the boyfriend watching from a short distance. Interspersed are a series of companion shots of the boyfriend accompanying Nancy as she walks along a dirt road (perhaps returning from the market), singing and dancing with a basket on her head, he riding his scooter alongside her. In one brief scene, where we see the two interact among other people, she walks past an outdoor coffee/tea shop where he is sitting and goes up to buy vegetables from a young man's small vegetable cart. Nancy's friend quickly jumps on his scooter and rides up to her at the cart, offering her a ride home. She refuses, not willing, it seems, to be so obvious about their relationship in front of other people. The video ends back on the dirt road: when a village taxi comes by (an open-backed truck), she gets on, joining the many village women and children who are crowded in the back and on top of the vehicle. She continues to sing and dance, now on the back of the vehicle, with the women and children clapping along. The boyfriend is left to try to follow behind, but the road becomes increasingly rough and rutted. The scooter finally tips over on its side, leaving the boyfriend to look on as the taxi disappears further up the road.

While Nancy does keep her suitor at bay, especially at the market and in the final scene, she happily flirts with him throughout most of the video and, thus, there is little sense of the stern declaration of the song's refrain. We might imagine that the decision was made among Nancy and her managers to soften the refrain's message in the video, to present, instead, a more nuanced fun-loving image. This image is carefully crafted: dressed in modest folk clothes throughout, there is no sense of the blatant sexuality that Haife Wahbe and others regularly manifest. Nevertheless, with continual flirtation and sensual, if not explicitly sexual dancing, titillation remains. Nancy has achieved her own unique mix.

In building her career, it is abundantly clear that Nancy Ajram has understood the high premium given to beauty and sexuality in the modern-day pop scene. One of the dramatic ways she has openly participated in this aspect is with plastic surgery. Understanding the need for physical beauty, modern-day pop singers, male and female, have enthusiastically embraced plastic surgery to achieve the look that they feel is necessary. In a video accessed on YouTube, Nancy openly talks about her surgeries, with her manager sitting next to her. I quote the subtitles provided in the video:

> I had a surgery on my nose at 16 or 17. I was yo[u]ng and [my manager] [later] came and asked me[,] "You got a nose job?" I said, "Yes," and he told me, "It's not right (good)," and I said thank you (irony). "It was red

like this" [her manager momentarily enters the conversation, pointing to something nearby], so I went for a second time to do a surgery and when he saw me I still had a big bone[.] That's why I did it again[.] Then I saw him again and he said, "Hi, Nancy, how are you? u got another nose job?' And once again I said, "Yes, it's still not good?"

She goes on to say that she was quite shy at sixteen and seventeen, but changed a lot between seventeen and twenty. She asserts that the more beautiful look that resulted after the three surgeries made her feel more confident.

Cosmetic surgery has come to have a huge place in Lebanese society. It is widely believed that the expertise for this type of surgery was developed out of necessity during Lebanon's fifteen-year civil war (1975–90). Nose jobs, or rhinoplasty, is the most common form of plastic surgery in Lebanon today. Nancy Ajram's place in the movement is undeniable: when women get nose jobs, it is common for them to ask to have Nancy's nose.

Not everyone is comfortable with the situation. The 2011 song and music video by Muhammad Iskandar (b. 1960), *Ghurfit ʿamaliyat* (The Operating Room), is an earnest call for an end to the practice. The song and video start with a woman leafing through a fashion magazine and coming to a picture of a woman in a lipstick ad. Imagining herself with this woman's facial features, she signals to her husband her desire for cosmetic surgery, but he responds negatively. Successfully persuading her husband, we next see the two as the wife and another woman are being wheeled in for their operations at a hospital. The intent of the video is clear from the first moment. The lyrics, by the singer's son Faris Iskandar (with music by Salim Salemeh), begins immediately after the husband's initial refusal. "I am fearful for your entering of the operating room, seeing as three-quarters of all women now look alike. I will not love you more when your cheeks protrude or when your lips get bigger. You are beautiful the way God made you."[26] As the video proceeds, we watch the husband pacing the floor, waiting for his wife to appear after the operation. His wife finally appears at the exact same moment as the other woman who had come to have similar surgeries. Here the camera switches to a close-up of the two husbands, who are confused, since they cannot tell which one is their wife: they look so alike! Finally, the doctor, consulting his x-rays, makes the determination, and the husband and correct wife proceed to leave the hospital.

The video has a number of other hard-hitting moments, including a brief scene in which the couple's son rejects his mother's hug upon her arrival home, obviously uncomfortable with the new aspects of his mother's appearance. The activist nature of the video is reinforced again at the end as the credits are shown: we see live footage of an outdoor concert in which the singer, Muhammad Iskandar, leads the thousands in the audience as they sing the song along with him. The audience obviously knows the words and sings along with considerable enthusiasm. Clearly, Iskandar has succeeded in spreading his message. (Other singers have performed the song: YouTube includes a video of another singer performing *Ghurfat 'amaliyat* live on a TV program.) Despite the efforts of Iskandar and the adverse reactions of so many, the demand for physical beauty and heightened levels of sexuality both on stage and in music videos goes on unabated.

Conclusion

These six songs offer glimpses of a wealth of elements and issues that have helped shape the music of the Arab World. The songs range from a pair that were popular in the early nineteenth century (the two renditions of the same *muwashshah* poem, the first song above), and two that date from the middle of the twentieth century (*Ghanni li shwayya* and *Asma' Allah al-Husna*, the second and fourth songs above), to two from the early years of the twenty-first century (*is-Salamu 'alaykum* and *Ah wa-nuss*, the fifth and sixth songs). Additionally, one (*Sidi Mansur*, the third song) has existed as a vital part of a regional religious/folk music tradition for unknown decades/centuries. The songs cut across the Western categories of art, religious, folk, and pop music. While the *muwashshah* and *Ghanni li shwayya* would commonly be recognized as falling within the category of art music, *Ghanni li shwayya* took on many of the aspects of pop music fame: it is enthusiastically received, for example, at parties where it might accompany solo and communal dancing. Indeed, most of Umm Kulthum's music is understood to be art music, but much of it was also the popular music of its day. *Asma' Allah al-Husna* is clearly a religious song, but the complexity of the composition, a sophisticated exploration of a number of the intricacies of the melodic mode called *huzam*, lead many to consider it an art song. *Sidi Mansur* is also a religious song, but it holds an honored place in the world of Tunisian folkloric music. Meanwhile, the Saber el-Robaei version of the song became an international hit in the realm of pop music.

These songs were spread by a succession of mass media, starting with lithograph printing, and including records, radio, film, TV, cassettes, CDs, the Internet, video clips, and satellite television. Performance ensembles went through a number of changes, from the small *takht*, to the large orchestral *firqa*, to the modern-day keyboard-dominated ensemble. They also represent different moments in a long history of evolving genres, from the medieval Andalusian *muwashshah* and the transformation of the *wasla*-suite form, to the modern-day pop styles of *sha'bi* and *shababi* music.

The forces of Islam and Sufism have influenced music and musicians throughout the region. Musicians have had to negotiate appropriate levels of religiosity, as well as a great variety of other social and cultural issues, including appropriate levels of sexuality and engagement with national and international affairs and audiences. Individual songs can be seen as windows into a great variety of cultural realms. Six songs provide a wealth of issues to consider.

Notes

1　Muhammad ʿAli Abu Ziyan, in *Umm Kulthum: al-Naghm al-Khalid*, 1976, p. 11; quoted in Virginia Danielson, "Min al-Mashayikh": A View of Egyptian Musical Tradition," *Asian Music*, 22:1 (Autumn 1990–Winter 1991), p. 115.

2　Translated by Dwight F. Reynolds.

3　See www.youtube.com/watch?v=8hh5kc2UUDg.

4　See www.youtube.com/watch?v=6Ysx—e—rNJA. I thank the Israeli musician of Iraqi descent, Yair Dalal, for pointing out the *awshar* mode.

5　Translated by Dwight F. Reynolds.

6　Richard Jankowsky, *Stambeli: Music, Trance, and Alterity in Tunisia* (University of Chicago Press, 2010), p. 168.

7　See www.dailymotion.com: Saber Al Robai – *Sidi Mansour* ("Ya Baba").

8　Translated by Dwight F. Reynolds.

9　Michael Frishkopf, "Inshad Dini and Aghani Diniyya in Twentieth Century Egypt: A Review of Styles, Genres, and Available Recordings," *Middle East Studies Association Bulletin* (Winter 2000), p. 5.

10　Danielson, "Min al-Mashayikh," p. 114.

11　Michael Frishkopf, "Introduction," in *Music and Media in the Arab World* (American University in Cairo Press, 2010), p. 11.

12　Karim Tartoussieh, "Pious Stardom: Cinema and the Islamic Revival in Egypt," *Arab Studies Journal*, 15:1 (2007), p. 31.

13　See www.sufism.org: *Ninety-nine Names*.

14　While understood to be European in origin, the violin and accordion have long been accepted in Arab music performance. The violin was introduced in the second half of the nineteenth century and the accordion in the middle of the twentieth century. A number of the reeds on the accordion are altered so that the instrument can play the "non-Western" notes that occur in Arab music.

15 Personal communication, 2012; www.youtube.com: *Hakim es-salamu alaikum.*

16 Transcribed and transliterated by Magda Campo; translated by Mohamed Moharram.

17 See www.youtube.com: Mobinil Alo Dueto ad featuring Hakim; Mobinil commercial
    –Hakim; and, El Arousa Tea Hakim ad.

18 http://cinema.rotana.net/en/r/ali-spicy; accessed July 31, 2013.

19 Quoted in Scott Marcus, *Music in Egypt* (Oxford University Press, 2007), pp. 166–67.

20 Patricia Kubala, "The Other Face of the Video Clip: Sami Yusuf and the Call for al-Fann
    al-Hadif," *Transnational Broadcasting Studies*, 14 (Spring 2005).

21 See, for example, www.youtube.com: Haifa Wehbe *Habibi ya Einy.*

22 See, for example, www.youtube.com: Nancy Ajram, *Habibi ya 3ayni.*

23 www.unicef.org/media/media—51486.html.

24 Composer: Tariq Madrur; poet: Ayman Bahjat Qamar; see www.youtube.com: *Aah W
    Noss.*

25 Translation as provided in CD liner notes: Nancy Ajram, *Collector's Edition: Ah Wa Nuss*,
    EMI France, 2004.

26 I thank Pam Abi Najem, who introduced me to this video, provided this "rough
    translation" of the opening lines, and for bringing the issue of plastic surgery in
    Lebanon to my attention. She also introduced me to the *Ghurfat 'amaliyat* video and to
    Nancy Ajram's work as a UNICEF Ambassador.

8

Cinema and television

Cinema played a central role in the creation of modern Arab identity in the decolonization period. The "golden age" of Arab cinema is widely considered to be the period when Pan-Arabism as a political ideology was at its height from the 1940s to the 1960s and today's cinema is often judged unfavorably against films of that era. In subsequent decades, the Arab defeat in the war with Israel in 1967, the passing of the Nasser era, the decline of secular Arab Nationalism, the impact of a globalized economy, the rise of Islamist politics, and the wave of Arab uprisings since 2011 have all influenced developments in the Arab film industry and television production. The growing conservatism of Arab audiences has also made directors, actors, and state censors throughout the Arab World today acutely aware of the limits of what they can present to the general public and even to the elite festival circuit. Translating the cinematic language of Arab films for a global audience remains a major issue for the main movie industries that now exist in the Arab World (Egypt, Lebanon, and Morocco), since films that win praise abroad often get mixed reactions or a negative response at home. Since the mid-1990s, the satellite television revolution has contributed to the decline of Arab cinematic production in terms of international recognition by offering an outlet that bypasses some of the obstacles of state censorship and film distribution companies. These same privately owned satellite channels have created a space for non-governmental voices representing competing religious and political factions and have given rise to a host of new genres, including news broadcasts aimed at a pan-Arab (rather than national) audience, music videos, reality TV, and talk shows that deal openly with sensitive social and political issues that have long been banned from state-owned broadcasting systems.

The early years

Short and full-length films were made in Egypt, Tunisia, and Syria in the 1920s, but Egyptian entrepreneurs worked hard to see that an independent national industry developed in Egypt. It was partly Egypt's head start that led to the wide distribution and influence of Egyptian films and a familiarity with Egyptian dialect throughout the region. Indigenous industries elsewhere were later to make use of Egyptian technical and directing expertise. They also adopted genres of melodramatic movies and musicals that Egyptian cinema had made popular and at times even used Egyptian dialect, as was the case in many Lebanese films up until civil war broke out in 1975. Viola Shafik notes in her study *Arab Cinema: History and Cultural Identity* that, although Algeria had more movie houses than Egypt in 1933, not a single film was made by a native Algerian director before independence in 1962. In the 1940s, France set up various studios in North Africa to counter Egypt's indigenous and Arab-nationalizing cinema, but the Egyptian film industry maintained its dominant position in the region throughout the twentieth century.

The golden age

During the three decades of the 1940s, 1950s, and 1960s, a remarkable cinema flourished that fed the dreams of the entire Arab World. Its leading femmes included Su'ad Husni, Fatin Hamama (famed for her image of a passive moral girl who bears injustice rather than struggle against it), Laila Murad (whose films are adored to this day for their innocent exuberance), Tahiya Carioca (noted for her belly dancing and man-trap mystique), Hind Rustum (the only true sex symbol of Arab cinema), the great singing diva Umm Kulthum (who made six films between 1936 and 1947), and a host of others. Its male stars included Rushdi Abaza (Egyptian-Italian ladies' man), Omar Sharif (a star in the Arab World for a decade before his 1963 breakthrough in the West with *Lawrence of Arabia*), Anwar Wagdi (dashing Syrian actor and director, married for a time to Laila Murad), comic Ismail Yassin, singer-actor 'Abd al-Halim Hafiz (the first young male sex symbol of Arab pop culture), singer-composer Muhammad 'Abd al-Wahhab (strait-laced precursor of 'Abd al-Halim), Lebanese singer and *'ud* (lute) player Farid al-Atrash, Ahmad Mazhar (who played the lead role in Youssef

Chahine's epic *Saladin*), and others. This period produced dozens of films a year and they remain a huge presence in today's popular cultural memory. A large number are still shown regularly on terrestrial and satellite channels all over the region – a nationalist cultural canon that every Arab comes to know. Egyptian TV even has quiz shows where guests are required to display their detailed knowledge about famous scenes, bits of dialog and other Golden Age minutiae. Despite this, an Algerian film, Muhammad Lakhdar Hamina's *Chronicle of the Years of Embers* (*Waqāʾiʿ sanawāt al-jamr*, 1974), is the only Arab film ever to win the Palme d'Or at Cannes.[1] Tunisian-French director Abdellatif Kechiche won in 2013 with *Blue Is the Warmest Color*, but to all intents and purposes it is a French film.

Most critics agree that Egyptian cinema's high point was Shadi ʿAbd al-Salam's 1969 movie *The Mummy* (*al-Mūmiya*) – one of Arab cinema's few real contributions to world movie classics and the only serious attempt to critique modern Egypt's crisis of identity as the country negotiates its Pharaonic past and Arab-Islamic and secular Western present. "The film presents a complex set of symbols about the problems of modern Egypt, its relationship with its Pharaonic past, its perspective on the West, and its Arab identity," critic Mustafa Darwish writes in his portrait of Egyptian cinema, *Dream Makers on the Nile*.[2] *The Mummy* is set during the time of foreign archeological discoveries in Thebes in 1881. Two sons of a recently deceased clan leader are shocked to learn that for generations their family has made its living through robbing tombs. The family murders one of them for fear he will give away the tombs' whereabouts to foreign archeologists. The other – filled with wonder at the incomprehensible ancient language of his ancestors left on the walls of temples – is determined to render homage to the past, to "count the years" (as invoked by the film's alternate title, *The Night of Counting the Years*) by finding meaning in the monuments of Pharaonic Egypt. His search for identity reflects the search for identity that the entire nation should engage in, the film implies. As long as the natives fail to ascribe value to their own past and endeavor to preserve it, the foreigners will continue to disdain them. But doing so means overcoming Arab and Islamic political and intellectual barriers to examining this past. Film historian Viola Shafik writes, "History may be used as a weapon in the fight for political or cultural positions. The resulting historicism serves to strengthen the chipped identity, particularly when a society is subjected to rapid changes."[3]

Decline and revival

From the 1970s to the mid-1990s, the Egyptian-led Arab film production went into decline. Without the drive of the nationalist period, the
region's unreformed economic and political systems militated against
thriving movie industries. Lebanon's fifteen-year civil war and Iraq's
woes after it entered into war with Iran in 1980 impeded and squashed
their film industries. Egyptian cinema found a new niche in the 1980s
with the so-called contract films, made with little expense at the behest
of wealthy Saudi entrepreneurs, featuring formulaic, bawdy humor for
video distribution to Gulf Arab audiences. But the general trend over the
period was a drop in production while television culture took off, driven
by video ownership in the 1980s, and then the satellite boom in the 1990s.
In the mid 1980s, Egypt was still making some sixty films a year, but by
the late 1990s production had dropped to around twenty a year. By contrast, Iran, with a population similar in size to that of Egypt, in that same
period was producing up to sixty films a year and had over three hundred
cinema houses.

Egyptian cinema saw a revival in the late 1990s, partly as a natural
extension of the satellite television revolution and the money pouring
into music videos, but also due to a burgeoning youth population looking for new faces and films. It began in 1997 with *Ismailiya Back and Forth*
(Ismāʿiliyya rāyiḥ gāyy), a crudely made comedy produced on a tiny budget
that defied all expectations to become Egypt's biggest grossing film up
to that time. It made a star of Muhammad Heneidy, who then starred
in the made-to-order *An Upper Egyptian at the American University (Ṣaʿīdī*
fī al-gāmiʿat al-amrīkiyya), which broke previous records as the highest
grossing film, raking in the equivalent of eight million dollars. "Some
people hadn't been to the cinema for thirty years before these films," said
producer Medhat al-Adl.[4] A rash of other comedies did well on the back
of the "Heneidy phenomenon," as private-sector firms opened new cinema complexes and the government lowered taxes on ticket prices.

Prior to the new comedy films, Arab cinema was dominated by
Egyptian actor ʿAdel Imam and Egyptian actress Nadia al-Gindy. Imam
was the highest paid actor in the Arab World; Gindy was dubbed *nigmat*
al-gamaheer, or "the star of the masses." Such monikers are often the products of a star's publicity staff or dedicated team in the local media rather
than of an adulating press or adoring public, but they stick nevertheless.
Both Imam and Gindy played supposedly attractive thirty-somethings

well into the 1990s, when they were in fact sixty-somethings, but they pulled it off with a certain aplomb. Imam dominated cinema in the 1990s with a series of political comedies attacking the Islamist extremist groups that were in open warfare with the Egyptian government for a number of years. The films, penned by leftist screenwriter Wahid Hamid, formed part of a successful government propaganda campaign against the insurgents and attempts to demonize Islamist ideology. In return for that, the filmmakers managed to direct a fair amount of criticism at the state itself for corrupt, undemocratic practices, with implications about why radical Islam had gained so much sway in Egyptian society. The most celebrated of these films is *The Terrorist* (*al-Irhābī*), where Imam plays the role of an Islamist on the run, who is taken in by an unsuspecting family who lead the kind of liberal, middle-class lifestyle that his ideology has taught him to despise. In the process of living among them and experiencing their humanity, Imam's character comes to question his radical beliefs. Imam deserves some credit for challenging the public with these films. In one he even did a parody of popular religious preacher Shaykh Muhammad Mitwalli Sha'rawi, *Mahrus, the Minister's Boy* (*al-Wad Maḥrūs bitāʿ al-wazīr*, 1999).

Nadia al-Gindy, on the other hand, is famed for emotional roller coaster performances, where she overcomes all odds through the will-to-power that only a woman can muster to triumph over some form of social, economic, or political evil. For example, in 1999's *The Drug Baroness* (*al-Imberatōra*), Gindy appears in the guise of a maid, the luscious Zenouba, working in the home of a police officer who is rising in the ranks. When their love affair is uncovered by his mother, the policeman shuns the lowly maid, denying he could have any romantic feelings for someone from the lower castes, and our heroine is turfed out ignominiously. It is one of those soul-destroying moments when love turns to hate. So Gindy embarks on an epic voyage of revenge. She begins by building herself up as a drug "baroness" in poor districts of Cairo, taking the name Madame Zizi and wearing ever more outlandish costumes. She becomes a big shot in the state, cutting deals with Israelis to smuggle Lebanese heroin into Egypt. When Gindy's brother and husband are killed by policemen, she has her ex-lover's wife machine-gunned to death. At that point, the police officer telephones her to say, with laughable lightness considering the circumstances, "Let's stop this war between us and come to an understanding." So the final scene is set for a romantic resolution – but she has poisoned his drink and he has secretly placed a bug under the table. He dies in her arms and the scene freezes on the face of our heroine in the anguished realization that life in prison with neither family nor lover awaits her. It is because of films like this that Egypt's film industry went from being known as "Hollywood on the Nile" in the 1960s to "Bollywood on the Nile" today.

How to merge quality subject matter and execution with commercial success is the great issue that continues to tax the Arab movie industry. Youssef Chahine's glossy 2004 film *Destiny* (*al-Masīr*) was a disappointment at the box office, while *Ismailiya Back and Forth* (*Ismāʿiliya Rāyiḥ Gāyy*), one of the most inexpensive films in Egyptian cinema history, was the industry's biggest financial success. Serious directors and actors took fright. "When they saw a film like *Ismailiya Rayih Gayy* breaking all the records, they had to go back and rethink everything," Raghda, a Syrian actress, said.[5] Art films such as the late Radwan al-Kashif's lavish *Date Wine* (*ʿAraq al-balaḥ*) from 1998 tend to be well received abroad and do well on the international film festival circuit, but they are shunned in Egypt where distributors shy away from offering them to the public. Daoud ʿAbd al-Sayyid's *Land of Fear* (*Arḍ al-Khōf*, 1999) was nominated in the Best Foreign Film category of the 2001 Academy Awards, but it had only limited success at home. Muhammad Khan scored a major coup for independent cinema with his 2004 *Thief* (*Kleftī*), the Arab World's first major film made using digital camera technology, but Khan preferred to sell it to Arab TV channels rather than fight with distributors over a general release.

A 1998 movie by young Lebanese director Ziyad Doueiri, *West Beirut* (*Bayrūt al-gharbiyya*), became the first Arabic-language film to have a general release in North America, but it did not get a general release in Cairo and fared poorly when shown in Beirut. The film focuses on two teenagers growing up in Beirut during the civil war, and the acting and colloquial language are convincing in a way rarely achieved by mainstream Arab cinema. It manages to be politically subversive in showing the teenagers' disregard for the ways that political and religious realities supposedly circumscribe the lives of all those caught in the conflict. According to Egypt's film censor at the time, ʿAli Abu Shadi: "People can like many things, but they will still walk out of a film like that and say confidently that it shouldn't be shown in public. It's a form of schizophrenia, but it's a natural, inherited instinct in this culture. It touches on a very fundamental problem we have in this culture."[6]

Critics hoped that 2006's *The Yacoubian Building* (*ʿImārat Yaqūbiān*) could open new avenues for commercial cinema in Egypt. Based on a best-selling novel by Alaa Al Aswany, its subject matter was serious, political, even depressing. Set in the 1990s, the film examines the lives of diverse characters living in a grand belle époque building in downtown Cairo, exposing the police brutality, corruption, and repression that mark Egypt's descent into political, economic, and social malaise in the postcolonial era. Costing some $3 million to make, the film was an enormous box office success. Starring familiar faces in Egyptian cinema such as Adel Imam and written by veteran screenwriter Wahid Hamid, the film followed in the tradition of politically aware box office winners of the 1990s featuring the Imam–Hamid combination (such as *The Terrorist* and *Terrorism and Kebab* [*al-Irhāb wa-l-kabāb*], both penned by Hamid). *The Yacoubian Building* demonstrated that, as with any other cinema industry in the world, there's nothing like a good story and a good script to score success with critics and the public in one film.

Egyptian cinema witnessed a commercial revival in the early 2000s with a series of "low culture" blockbuster comedies that made huge stars of some young actors. These films are formulaic and heavily panned by critics, but they have nevertheless tapped into a desire among the burgeoning younger generation for new faces and films that deal with the realities of today's youth. These films bring in huge audiences and profits, but the number of productions is still low. The industry also remains shackled by a rigid star system whereby a small clique of actors and directors dominate the scene, stifling talent, and limiting the types of films produced. Age is no limit to the stars' longevity – their age is simply kept a closely guarded secret, masked by toupees and plastic surgery, unlike in the West where actors' ages are exposed in the press. Quality and depth of storylines and treatment remain a major issue, and what one critic called the "tawdry treatment of desire" continues to stand in for convincing or moving representation of sexual and romantic relations.[7] "The Egyptian state must take a stance and set up a fund to support films that want to get out of the commercial strait-jacket," Tunisian director Nouri Bouzid once said.[8] "The problem goes beyond cinema. It's about culture, Arab society and educating future generations. The day will come when being creative is considered heretical and that's what's frightening."

The 2011 protest movement in Egypt plunged the country into an era of instability as Islamists won out in the first parliamentary and presidential elections, and an array of opponents challenged them on the streets. The result for cinema has been a plunge in output and some actors leaving the industry or the country for fear of Islamist backlash.

The industry has been reduced to its bare bones: Gulf-funded productions and Gulf-promoted stars.

The role of censorship

Censors are as much prisoners of public taste as they are arbiters of what the public ought and ought not to see. Tunisia's relative liberalism during the years of Zine el-Abidine Ben Ali's rule was a "political decision," as Abu Shadi puts it, and the corollary is that there's absolutely no margin for politics. "In Egypt it's the opposite. There's quite a lot of freedom to discuss political issues, but sex is always a problem. The law forbids nudity and lovemaking in a big way." Egypt's stricter moral code in cinema is part of the state's attempt to appease religious conservatism, recognized as a powerful force in society. "This trend [political Islam] is there, and we can't deny its existence, so we have to appease this part of our public," Abu Shadi says.⁹ He hoped that Egypt would ultimately return to the liberal standards of the 1960s, but the rise of Islamist forces after the uprising of 2011 that ended Hosni Mubarak's rule has made that an even more distant dream. Until then, in his view, Arabs and the rest of the world collectively had the right balance of modesty in cinema. An Islamist critique would label the period before the 1960s as a postcolonial aberration in the Arab World, but for Abu Shadi and other members of the secular-nationalist intelligentsia it was a veritable time of renaissance, led by Egypt. "It was a time of freedom in the arts, but at the same time, there was no nakedness, for example. We were moving in the same direction as the rest of the world then," he says. "We will never go too far, as they have done in the West. Here maybe we can get back to where we were in the 1960s, but even that's being ambitious."¹⁰

Censors are also under constant pressure from society at large. In 1995, Egyptian actress Yousra was taken to court over a scene in *Birds of Darkness* (*Ṭuyūr al-ẓalām*) because her bare legs offended a well-known Muslim preacher, Yousef al-Badri. Two years later, Egyptian actress Maali Zayed received a prison sentence because a bedroom scene in the film *Abu Dahab* (1996) disgusted a member of the public who saw it with his little boy. In Morocco, attempts begun in the early 1990s by director Abd al-Qadir Laqtaa to portray sexual relationships have come up against problems. There was a ruckus over Laqtaa's 1991 film *Love in Casablanca* (*al-Ḥubb fī al-Dār al-Bayḍā'*) because an actress was shown in a nightgown; over Muhammad Lotfi's 1995's *Rhesus* (known in Arabic as *Dam al-akhir,* or *Blood of the Other*) because of French kissing; and Laqtaa's 1995 film *The Closed Door* (*al-Bāb al-masdūd*) was banned because of a scene in which a couple make love. The extent of kissing and cuddling in Egyptian films is seen as highly risqué in Morocco. Islamists in Morocco forced Youssef Chahine's 1995 *The Emigrant* (*al-Muhāgir*) to be pulled from screens because it was based on the story of Joseph, son of Jacob, and conservative religious figures opposed the depiction of Biblical prophets on film; it was for a while banned in Egypt for the same reason.

Arab popular media have also prominently featured stories of female actresses who have retired and taken the veil. The wave began in the late 1970s, with Syrian actress Shams al-Baroudy, star of the famous 1973 risqué film *The Malatily Bathhouse* (*Ḥammām al-Malāṭīlī*). Then followed golden age actress Shadia in the mid 1980s, and a host of others in her wake: dancer Sahar Hamdy; singers Mona ʿAbd al-Ghani and Hanan; actresses Shahira, Hoda Ramzy, Suhair al-Bably, and ʿAbeer al-Sharqawy; Syrian actresses Hanaa Tharwat and Nisreen; and another golden age actress, Zubayda Tharwat. Since 2000, a few more Egyptian actresses have taken the veil for periods of time – young actresses Mona Lisa, Ghada ʿAdel, ʿAbeer Sabry, Myrna al-Mohandis, Wafa ʿAmer, Hanan Turk, and Sabreen. The latest bout of public religiosity followed a particularly tense political period, including the Palestinian Intifada, 9/11, and the invasion of Iraq. Some took the veil and later stopped wearing it in well-publicized returns to the limelight, including actresses Sawsan Badr and Farida Seif al-Nasr. Some male actors have also turned to more religious lifestyles, such as the Egyptian soap actor Mahmud al-Gindy, who now does television interviews in the white robes of a Sudanese Sufi.

With the post-Arab Spring ascendance of Islamist movements, such as the Muslim Brotherhood in Egypt and Ennahda in Tunisia, the arts became a highly contested space. For example, Salafi Islamists attacked a Tunis cinema house showing a film they disapproved of and an Islamist-leaning culture minister in Egypt removed officials in state-run arts institutions governing opera and book publication. Censorship is likely to remain an issue.

The rise of television

Arab governments have made extensive use of audio and televisual media to further their political and development agendas since they first became a feature of modern life in the mid-twentieth century. Rebel, sectarian, and other political movements have more recently done their best to catch up. The importance of radio was well understood by the officers led by Gamal ʿAbd al-Nasser when they enacted a military coup in Egypt in 1952. The model for media as an instrument for state control in the Arab World was established by the Egyptians. Egyptian radio was part of a "media of mobilization" of the masses which made Nasser one of the Arab World's first radio stars. Cheap transistor radios spread in the 1950s soon after Nasser came to power. Nasser's nationalization of the Suez Canal in 1956 was carried out upon the live radio broadcast of a code word in a speech he gave in Alexandria. After the 1967 Arab defeat to Israel, Nasser also dramatically announced his resignation on radio – with TV cameras, the latest development in government media, filming him reading the speech. Because she had been a favorite of the deposed monarch King Farouk, classical singer Umm Kulthum was associated in the minds of the masses with the royal Egypt that the military sought to replace with a new order. But Nasser realized there could no better publicity for the republican cause than for Umm Kulthum herself to sing to the nation on state radio. She subsequently developed a close relationship with the regime and with Nasser personally, and to this day she is intimately linked in the minds of people all over the Arab World with Nasserist Pan-Arabism.

Egypt's most talented artists were drafted into the service of selling the Arab revolution in state media, from poet Salah Jahin, whose nationalist rhyme was put to song, to heartthrob singer ʿAbd al-Halim Hafez, who sang the praises of Nasser's Aswan High Dam and "the Arab dream." There were two distinct stages: first, 1956 to 1967, the golden age of Nasser, after his emergence as a Suez War hero up to the defeat of 1967; and then, 1967 to 1973, when Egypt prepared for war with Israel to try to recover the losses of 1967. Singers from around the region joined together to sing "al-Watan al-akbar," or "The Greater Nation," penned by celebrated composer Muhammad ʿAbd al-Wahhab, including Egypt's ʿAbd al-Halim Hafez, Nagaat, Shadia, and Fayda Kamel, the Algerian singer Warda, and the Lebanese singer Sabah. The use of singers on state media in the Nasserist manner continued elsewhere. Iraqi singer Dawoud al-Qaysi, famous for his songs in support of Saddam Hussein and the Baʿath Party, was shot dead in central Baghdad in May 2003 after his songs were played endlessly on state television during the 2003 invasion to bring down Hussein and the Baʿath Party. After the fall of Mubarak and Ben Ali, many artists who had been particularly associated with the

previous regimes engaged in forms of reinvention or ingratiating themselves with the public. Some, such as singer Tamer Hosni and actor 'Adel
Imam, had a bad reputation in the immediate aftermath of the revolts,
but ultimately the public forgave them, forgot, or were apathetic.

Arab satellite TV since the 1990s: the Al Jazeera revolution

Since the 1990s, Arab television has witnessed a revolution led by Gulf
and Lebanese satellite television, and the Egyptians soon followed. One
of the main political developments behind this was the establishment of
a Saudi pan-Arab media empire. The original catalyst was the 1990–91
Gulf crisis during which Saudi Arabia invited American forces to use its
territory to mount the invasion of Iraqi-occupied Kuwait and the realization that the future was in satellite media, as CNN showed during
that war. The crisis raised serious questions for the Saudi leadership concerning its image in the Arab and Islamic worlds, its legitimacy, its alliance with the United States, and its political system. Following the war,
Walid al-Ibrahim, a Saudi businessman married to a sister of King Fahd,
launched the Middle East Broadcasting Corporation (MBC), a news station that was billed as the Arab CNN. Its aim was as much domestic and
regional as it was international, an attempt to frame political events in
the Arabic language from a Saudi leadership perspective or to create a
Saudi discourse for the Arab World.

Saudi Arabia now commands a powerful position in the pan-Arab
media, encompassing political, entertainment, and religious programming. The media empire includes the entire MBC network, Orbit, ART,
the Rotana network including religion-lite channel al-Risala, LBC, and
the newspapers *al-Hayat* and *Asharq al-Awsat*. There are many others that
are essentially Saudi, including the religious TV network al-Majd, for
example, but those listed are the key channels through which a specific
political message is conveyed. It is Western-friendly on a political and
cultural level, promoting itself as "liberal," "reformist," "moderate,"
"modern," and against al-Qa'ida, Hizbollah, Iran, or any other groups or
states who present a challenge to American presence in the Arab World
and the Arab regimes who form part of that constellation. There is no evidence of any particular coordination of this position among these media
outlets – in fact they often reflect rivalry between different camps in the
regime – but they are owned by members of the royal family or non-royal
allies who share the same general outlook on the need to protect the

Al Saud state from foreign and domestic dangers. In addition to this, state-controlled media in Arab states friendly to Saudi Arabia filter out criticism of the country, particularly significant in the case of Egypt as the former mobiliser against Western hegemony. Egypt's "media of mobilization" in the 1960s gave way to Saudi Arabia's "media of pacification" – a new soporific media of arguably greater proportions and reach than anything Gamal ʿAbd al-Nasser ever had, where entertainment helps put the political mind to sleep.[11] Or, as Dawood al-Shirian, a Saudi liberal writer who became the MBC Group's manager in Saudi Arabia, would prefer it, the Saudi era "opened up the Arab world and revealed the falseness of ideologies such as Arab nationalism, communism and political Islam."[12]

In 1996, Qatar's new ruling elite, established after a coup within the royal family, started its own satellite channel, Al Jazeera (meaning "the Arabian Peninsula"), with the intention at the outset of establishing a policy independent of Saudi Arabia that would put Qatar on the map. With shows like *The Opposite Direction* (*al-Ittijāh al-muʿākis*), which brought together guests from all over the region to talk about domestic, religious, and pan-Arab issues, it was a huge success. Watched by millions of Arab viewers across the Middle East, Europe, and North America, it established itself as a forum for debate on human rights, fundamentalism, religion, and corruption. Presenter Faisal al-Qassem, like many of Al Jazeera's staff, was hired from a failed project that the Arabic section of the BBC's World Service Radio attempted with Orbit in 2005. The advent of Al Jazeera came amid the beginning of mass satellite penetration throughout the region, which allowed audiences to see players in their own societies slogging it out on television for the first time, in debates previously confined to the press. Egyptians, for example, could see Islamist preacher Youssef al-Badry face-to-face with Egyptian feminist writer Nawal El Saadawi in 1997. Libya's Colonel Gaddafi appeared on Al Jazeera with a draft version of the March 2001 Arab Summit resolutions, mocking them as not worth the paper they were printed on. "I think we've thrown a big rock into stagnant waters," Qassem says of his show. "I think it has helped to liberate Arabs from the fear of not being able to talk about things. Eight years ago when I began the programme I was looking around left and right for the intelligence people after me."[13]

Al Jazeera at various times managed to offend almost all Arab governments, who have in response closed down Al Jazeera offices for months on end, shut off electricity to prevent people seeing some shows, banned reporters from operating, and taken journalists to court. Egypt's patience ran thin after the Palestinians began the Second Intifada against the Israeli occupation in September 2000. The debate engendered by Al Jazeera obliged Mubarak himself to appear on Egyptian state television in November 2000 to explain to interviewers that he could not afford to take the nation into battle and risk losing everything it had gained politically and economically since making peace with Israel in 1979. The channel broadcast scenes of children parading in the streets of Bethlehem carrying a papier-mâché donkey with Mubarak's name daubed on its side. Not long after that, Egypt deported Faisal al-Qassem's brother Majd, a reasonably well-known pop singer, supposedly over visa irregularities. Of course, it offended the Arab governments' American supporters and the Western powers too. Defense Secretary Donald Rumsfeld once dubbed it "Osama bin Laden's mouthpiece" because it was Al Jazeera that broadcast video and audio messages from Bin Laden in his Afghan cave as the Americans prepared to invade after the September 11 attacks of 2001. Al Jazeera also took the editorial decision to air portions of videos made by Iraqi insurgents who had kidnapped foreigners to pressure governments to withdraw troops and cease cooperation with the Iraqi occupation, though they never showed the beheadings that these videos included, which were, however, shown on Islamist websites.

Al Jazeera's impact has been huge. Because of Al Jazeera and the other channels competing with it during the 1990s (MBC, Hizbollah's al-Manar, LBC), the Intifada arguably stoked passions in the Arab World to a more immediate degree than any other event in the long conflict between the State of Israel and the Palestinians since the 1967 war. Arab-American academic Hisham Sharabi writes: "In modern Arab history, including during the revolutionary period of the 1960s and 1970s, there has been nothing to equal the power of the Arab satellite channels to change the nature of popular consciousness and perhaps in the political attitudes of popular forces in the Arab world."[14] The satellite media with their unifying power across the Arab region, constituting an Arab message for the Arab peoples – contrary to past reliance on the BBC World Service or CNN – crystallized hostility to the American presence in Iraq. The Arab intelligentsia considered that it was not "regime change" in Iraq that would bring democracy to the Arab World, but a just solution to the Israeli–Palestinian conflict, and the satellite channels helped make this a central tenet of political discourse in the Arab World.

Saudi Arabia's response to Al Jazeera took time in coming. Prompted by the September 11 attacks and their aftermath – involving the demonization in Western countries of Saudi Arabia and preparations for war in Iraq – Saudi Arabia set up the satellite television channel Al Arabiya in 2003. Part of the MBC network, with financial input from Lebanese and Kuwaiti investors, al-Arabiya is displayed in Saudi embassies today as if it is Saudi Arabia's official mouthpiece. It came on air just in time for the Iraq invasion when Saudi leaders were correct in assuming they were due for a round of anti-Saudi sentiment similar to that which followed the 1991 Gulf War. Saudi Arabia wanted to present the United States with a vision of "moderation" in the Arab World to counter Al Jazeera's hip rejectionism and its willingness to treat the ideology of Islamist groups like al-Qa'ida seriously, as something worthy of discussion and debate and as a reflection of a legitimate trend in Arab politics.

Both Al Arabiya and Al Jazeera faced challenges in covering the post-war conflict in Iraq, and for some time the Bush administration placed both channels in the same basket of Arab "obstructionism" and "extremism." Both channels were banned for two weeks from covering official activities in Iraq in September 2003, but, by the time President Bush chose Al Arabiya over Al Jazeera for an Arab media interview in May 2004 answering charges of torture of Iraqi detainees at Abu Ghraib prison, Washington had clearly established who was on its side and who was not.[15] Salafi internet users came to brand Al Arabiya as *al-Ibriyya*, or "the Hebrew Channel," in a sign of this perceived desire to win American approval through granting considerable space to American officials and their allies in Iraq and elsewhere to explain their policies. Hizbollah's leader Hassan Nasrallah repeated the taunt in December 2008 when Al Arabiya's editorial line showed a clear slant towards blaming Hamas for Israel's month-long invasion of the Palestinian territory of Gaza (Saudi Arabia, Egypt, and other US allies saw Iran's hand behind resistance to Israel, part of the tectonic shift in regional politics brought about by 9/11 and the Iraq invasion).

Before Washington caught on to the nature of the channel, Al Arabiya's services to Saudi Arabia manifested themselves in its early days through its coverage of Islamist insurgency groups using the name al-Qa'ida as they appeared in Iraq, Saudi Arabia, and elsewhere. After the Iraq War, Al Arabiya ran numerous documentaries and discussion shows about mass graves and other human rights abuses in pre-invasion Iraq in what may have been taken by viewers as an effort to create a balanced debate about tyranny, democracy, and nationalism in the Arab World, but which appeared in part to be an effort to rubbish an insurgency that had wide support with public opinion throughout the Arab World. Most evidence suggested Saudi Arabia was not happy about America's plans to invade and occupy its northern neighbor, but its political leaders were at least content to get rid of what they viewed as another Arab Nationalist abhorrence in the form of Saddam Hussein.[16] In 2003, the Palestinian uprising that began in 2000 was still a major force in the region's politics and topping the Arab news agenda. Like Al Jazeera, Al Arabiya designed powerful montages of Israeli soldiers putting down the Intifada, set to a background of stirring music, but unlike Al Jazeera it did the same to discredit the activities of the Islamist insurgency movement in Saudi Arabia. One of these short pieces referred to a shootout in Mecca between Saudi police and Islamist rebels in June 2003, after which the Saudi authorities said they had found Qur'ans rigged with explosives. The words "Qur'ans booby-trapped with bombs" flicked across the screen, inviting Saudi viewers to consider the heretical *über*-violence of al-Qa'ida.[17] Al Arabiya aired some videotaped messages from Iraqi insurgent groups, but never anything from Osama bin Laden or his number two, Ayman al-Zawahiri. If they were lucky, they were mentioned in the news ticker along the bottom of the screen. On Al Jazeera, by contrast, by September 2003, two years after the attacks in New York and Washington, guests felt sufficiently confident to revert to reverential references to Bin Laden as "Sheikh Osama."[18]

The uprisings of 2011 were a watershed moment for the new TV media. Al Jazeera immediately seized the opportunity to promote a revolution in Egypt, which had been on bad terms with Qatar's rulers for many years. Al Arabiya, whose Saudi owners were aghast at the collapse of Mubarak's rule and American acquiescence in it, adopted a more skeptical line. With the violence used by the Libyan and Syrian governments against protesters, Qatar and Saudi Arabia came together in a political and media effort to direct the Arab Spring movement in different directions, and away from the Gulf: thus Al Jazeera and Al Arabiya became major propaganda outlets for rebels in both conflicts. It was Al Jazeera, the most popular channel region-wide, which stood to lose the most from this, and surveys began to appear in 2013 giving hard evidence that viewership had fallen off – though that was partly due to the emergence of independent media outlets in Egypt and Tunisia that were better able to discuss local issues.

Entertainment

Since the 9/11 debacle, which put Saudi Arabia, its rulers and its religion under an uncomfortable international spotlight, Saudi media changed tack and began to bring Lebanese-style liberalism into the Saudi living room. The agenda is often set by the key royals involved, not the liberal intellectuals who are drafted into the project, and in fact these media activities often contradict other policies and positions. For example, veteran Riyadh governor Prince Salman, made crown prince in 2012, promotes "liberalism" with *Asharq al-Awsat* while backing the religious police in Riyadh. Prince Alwaleed's Rotana channels show music videos that religious scholars consider beyond the pale, and MBC and LBC show reality television shows where single young men and women intermingle, flouting a fundamental rule of Saudi Islam. Alwaleed is referred to sarcastically on Islamist websites as *al-amīr al-mājin*, "the depraved prince." LBC ran a short-lived show in 2007 called *More Than A Woman* (*Imra'a wa-akthar*), where filmmaker Haifaa Mansour hosted panelists in a discussion of restrictions on women in Saudi Arabia. The discussions covered issues such as the absence of women in the national Shura assembly, gender segregation and how it can encourage homosexual behavior, and the all-male character of the Saudi judiciary. State television, where leading Saudi clerics are given wide space to offer social and religious guidance, avoids such issues. The satellite options for young Saudis contradict everything that the Wahhabi state is about; yet these satellite options are the work of Saudi princes who fear reducing the grip of clerics on Saudi society. Thanks to Lebanon, they can watch shows and pop video channels featuring Arab women in scanty attire, and they can even call the station and talk to them. Most of the callers on programs where viewers can chat to the beautiful hostess are Saudis. Some Saudi advertisers stipulate that their ads should not appear during such shows.

Alwaleed's Rotana also moved into pop videos and cinema, dominating the market for singers through record production as well as its stable of music channels, and moving into film production as well as its range of movie channels. This included an initial foray into producing full-length Saudi films, in a country which has no public cinema because of religious objections. Saudi Arabia has made an immense effort to control the flow of information in the Arab World and assure positive coverage of its politics and society, and often to assure no coverage at all. This effort involved saturating the Arab viewer in Arab and Western entertainment in the form of dramas, quiz shows, comedies, films, and "soft religion," with only as much politics as is necessary.

Once Egypt dominated Arab cultural production; Gulf financial clout has changed that as Saudi Arabia and then Qatar came to dominate television news and entertainment. Indeed, Qatar, with a far smaller population than its Saudi rival and massive natural gas wealth, has emerged as the wealthiest country in the world in recent years and, while it has left television entertainment to Saudi Arabia, in the lucrative arena of sports, Qatar has dominated through its successful Al Jazeera Sports network. The network won exclusive broadcasting rights in the Middle East for the 2010 World Cup soccer tournament, after acquiring rights for all the major world soccer league matches – domination that it sealed by buying the Saudi-owned ART network in 2009. Qatar's Doha Film Institute has entered the burgeoning Gulf cinematic arts scene (where Saudi Arabia is not a player), competing with Dubai and Abu Dhabi in promoting Arab film production and hosting glamorous international film festivals. Despite the boost that the Arab Spring movements have given to entertainment such as television, the Gulf largely remains the focus point of cultural activity as Egyptians, North Africans, and Levantines head there to produce news and entertainment for the Arab World, and for many it is a refuge as the region passes through a difficult period of political transition.

Notes

1 Cinema was the target of armed Algerian Islamist groups in the 1990s. Merzak Allouache's *Bab el-Oued*, shot under difficult conditions of civil war in Algiers in 1994, was one of the last films to be made in Algeria in the 1990s.
2 Mustafa Darwish, *Dream Makers on the Nile: A Portrait of Egyptian Cinema* (Cairo: Zeitouna/American University in Cairo Press, 1998), p. 42.
3 Viola Shafik, *Arab Cinema: History and Cultural Identity* (American University in Cairo Press, 1998), p. 164.
4 Medhat al-Adl, interview with author, November 1999.
5 Raghda, interview with author, April 1999.
6 'Ali Abu Shadi, interview with author, July 1999.
7 Khairiya El-Bishlawi, "Matrimony of Extremes," *Al-Ahram Weekly*, May 3–9, 2001.
8 Nouri Bouzid, *al-Hayat*, December 27, 2002.
9 'Ali Abu Shadi, interview with author, July 1999.
10 Ibid.
11 A term used by Egyptian political writer Salah Issa in an interview in June 2002.
12 Dawood al-Shirian, interview with author, August 6, 2007.
13 Faisal al-Qassem, interview with author, June 2004.

14 *Al-Hayat*, July 16, 2003.

15 Bush was interviewed on Al Arabiya and Alhurra, May 5, 2004.

16 Bob Woodward's book *Plan of Attack* (NY: Simon & Schuster, 2004) portrays then Saudi
    ambassador to the United States, Prince Bandar bin Sultan, as encouraging the Bush
    administration to attack Iraq; public statements from Foreign Minister Prince Saud
    al-Faisal opposed the war plans.

17 "Saudi militants rigged Koran with explosives: report," *Reuters*, November 13, 2003.

18 Comments by Hani Sibai and Abdel-Bari Atwan in a program on September 10, 2003,
    discussing an audiotape from Bin Laden and images of him with Ayman al-Zawahiri.

9
———

Theater

Non-Western drama and theatrical traditions of the global south have been performed for centuries, yet international scholars of drama and culture have continuously overlooked them. As a result, a general disinterest has developed towards the examination of the dramatic production of those regions. Arab theater, like the Arab World, is not a monolithic entity, even if there are parallel dramatic experiences that connect the different performance trends within each country and across the region.

The Arab World is comprised of twenty-two countries extending from the Persian Gulf to the Atlantic Ocean. In the pre-modern period, this region as a whole did not practice theater in the Western sense, which necessitated the existence of a stage, an auditorium, and a dramatic text. Instead there were numerous indigenous Arab dramatic forms; among the various performance arts that thrived prior to the colonial period are poetry recitations, ritual re-enactments, puppetry, shadow plays, *al-hakawati* (storytellers), dance, ritual, musical *rababa* (spike fiddle) performances, *maqama* (short outdoor dramatic pieces written in poetry and prose), street performances by traveling troupes called *al-muhabbizun* (either from *muḥabbidhūn*, "people who garner applause," or *muḥabbizūn*, "jesters"), and *al-samir* (village gatherings that included dramatizations). Some of those art forms are still extant, albeit in a state of decline, and many have faded away completely.

The inherent difference between Arab dramatic art and Western theater has made the study of Arab drama a daunting undertaking for Orientalists who insist on understanding Arab theater through a single lens: the Western model. However, as modes of perception and study change around the world in the new millennium, cultures are no longer being viewed as separate compartments, but rather as members of an extended community around the globe. Today, the study of non-Western drama and theatrical traditions of the global south is regarded as a necessity to enhance cross-cultural understanding and tolerance. To marginalize any cultural and theatrical phenomenon would be to insist on outdated approaches and the politics of influence in the examination of the arts and humanities of certain parts of the world.

In general, Arab dramatic traditions in the nineteenth century grappled with the notions and dictates of realism, which had been newly introduced by the colonial West. In Egypt, where the European theater tradition developed faster than in other Arab states, directors and playwrights in the second half of the nineteenth century were still trying to erect the "fourth wall," the imaginary wall between the actors on stage and the audience in the auditorium, whereby the actors "pretend" not to see the audience and the audience "pretend" not to be present by sitting silently in the dark. Egyptian audiences at that time adamantly refused to sit silently in the dark and watch the play unfold on a lighted stage without their participation or involvement in the event. Historically, the Arab and Egyptian audience had been an inherently interactive one for as long as there had been performance events, and Arab spectators had been used to interacting with the players in a very spontaneous fashion. They were accustomed to requesting changes in the plots and were frequently encouraged by the players to take part in the action, but, more importantly, early Arab audience members were not used to going to the theater. Rather, they were used to the theater coming to them, for pre-nineteenth century dramatic art was predominantly presented by street players who traveled from village to village and from one marketplace to another. Thus, attempting to attract audiences in the nineteenth century to bourgeois Western-style interior theater spaces, which had started to appear across the Arab World, was not an easy endeavor. Directors and theater managers had to incorporate singing and dancing with the dramatic action in order to lure in a larger number of spectators. In fact, it took years to adjust the Arab audiences' conduct and viewing habits to the newly introduced mimetic principles of realism and melodrama. Those new dramatic criteria were imported first by the French, after occupying Egypt in 1798, and then by the British, who officially occupied Egypt in 1882 and stayed until 1956. Throughout the mid-nineteenth and early twentieth centuries, theater directors continued to strive to silence the audience and acclimatize them to the notion of sitting quietly during the performances of plays. Thus, while Western theater in the early twentieth century was trying to destroy the fourth wall, Arab theater makers were trying hard to erect it.

The connection with European theater in the nineteenth century, by way of colonialism, missionaries, education, and translations, sparked major interest in the art form in the Arab World. In 1848, Lebanese writer Marun al-Naqqash (1817–1855) mounted stage adaptations of Molière's plays as well as tales from *A Thousand and One Nights* in a performance space that he set up in his own home. Al-Naqqash called his plays "foreign gold cast in an Arab mould," and added songs as well as improvised segments to his adaptations of French plays; in fact, this was his unique way of transplanting foreign texts into his Arab environment. This trend quickly moved to Damascus via Abu Khalil al-Qabbani (d. 1902), whose dramatic performances aroused the opposition of the conservative religious establishment. Al-Qabbani later moved to Egypt, where artists at the time were able to exercise their artistic expression with more freedom. In Egypt, Yaqub Sanu (d. 1912), who is considered the father of Egyptian theater, opened his theater in 1870 under the patronage of Khedive Isma'il, who dubbed Sanu "The Egyptian Molière." The theater was the first Egyptian playhouse built by an Egyptian national for local audiences. Being proficient in many languages enabled Sanu to adapt plays from French and Italian texts and tailor them to suit the sensibilities of his Egyptian society. Among his many contributions to the Egyptian stage were translating European texts into colloquial Egyptian and introducing women to the stage. Those aspects made his theater company an immediate success and in only three years he was able successfully to mount some seventy plays; however, his theater was shut down in 1873 on the grounds that his plays were politically subversive.

As European-style theater based on mimetic dramatic art and realism became popular in Egypt, new parameters had to be put in place in order to accommodate it. The most pressing issue was the use of women on stage; after all, previous dramatic performances of street theater did not require the actual presence of women in the skits, since young boys played the female roles. However, realism in Sanu's scripts dictated the incorporation of actresses. He therefore found two young Jewish women, taught them to read and write, then taught them acting; these ladies, Milia Dyan and her sister, became the first two Egyptian women on stage. The audience immediately embraced the presence of female actors as an integral part of the new art form. They even objected when, at the end of a melodramatic piece, the male and female protagonists did not marry. The spectators were so upset by the finale that they requested the director/writer to appear on stage to talk to them. They threatened not to attend his plays in the future if he did not change the ending. Realizing that Arab audiences (at the time) did not appreciate the division of space between stage and auditorium or a written unchanging text, Sanu accommodated his audience and changed the ending to suit their wishes. This practice was of course the residue of the spectators' viewing habits inherited from street theater where they used to call for a change in the plot, or even in genre, directly to the players, even in the midst of a performance.

With the dawning of dramatic performance produced in the European theatrical style in Egypt, a desperate need for a large number of new dramatic texts surfaced. Although a number of playwrights had already started writing Arabic adaptations of Western plays in Arabic as early as the 1870s, what the stage really needed was much more than those few playwrights could offer. It was argued by some artistic directors of the turn of the century that a new play had to be mounted every week in Egypt because there were huge eager audiences in both the big cities and the countryside. Since the art of playwriting in Arabic had not yet developed, and there were not many writers for the stage available (after all, the theater was not a profession in which educated middle-class families wished their sons to participate), the only option was to increase the activity of translating plays from the now familiar Western tradition. This tendency resulted in a huge wave of translations, Arabizations, and Egyptianizations of European plays.

It is important to point out that the period between 1870 and 1930 was a period of dramaturgy rather than a period of original playwriting. The need for dramatic texts propelled artistic directors regularly to commission writers to translate or adapt texts for the stage. The point was not to create a dramatic literary heritage, but rather to produce scripts for the stage. This emerging movement depended heavily on what came to be called "Arabization," which means to adapt Western plays to the Arab or Egyptian environment by way of changing names and geographies to local and familiar ones, and of course by transferring all dialog into the spoken Egyptian language. Many theater companies, however, opted to translate plays while maintaining the original Western names, geographies, and references. Another tendency was "Egyptianization," which was in part the result of a rising sense of nationalism in Egypt. This rapidly expanding movement, which was instigated by political organizations in response to colonialism, called on translators to transfer all spatial references in foreign plays to specifically Egyptian ones, not Arab or Oriental, just Egyptian. This practice of appropriating international plays was a process that many within the Egyptian literary milieu denounced vehemently. They also disapproved of the massive liberties that stage directors took with those plays in order to tailor them to the abilities of their leading actors or actresses and to appease their audience at any cost. The result was pure and simple mutilation of some great texts, such as *Romeo and Juliet* and *Hamlet*.

By the turn of the twentieth century, translating Shakespeare had become part of a nationwide movement of adapting and Arabizing international texts. Between 1870 and 1921, *Hamlet* was given three different translations; the most loyal to the original text was by the famous poet and litterateur Khalil Mutran. The most translated Shakespearean plays during the first half of the twentieth century were *Macbeth*, *King Lear*, *Romeo & Juliet*, *Anthony and Cleopatra*, and *Hamlet*. Obviously, the tragedies were the most appreciated. His comedies were not as popular, possibly because British humor did not entertain Egyptians as much; French comedies were more popular by far.

During the first two decades of the twentieth century, three major theater companies were in competition: George Abyad's company (founded 1912) produced stage adaptations of world literature and translated Western theater classics; al-Rihani's company (founded 1916) was the most successful of all, producing primarily comedies and a new trend of drama called "Franco-Arab" pieces (which were, in effect, Arabized comedies that included long segments of dance); and the Ramsis company (founded 1923), which was established by two theater greats, Yusuf Wahbi and 'Aziz 'Id, and produced both original Egyptian melodramatic texts as well as Western classics in translation. Many other small theater companies existed during the same period, as well as musical theater companies, such as those of Sayyid Darwish and Salama Hijazi, which were already big successes.

In dramatic literature, a number of attempts at writing original verse drama were well underway. Ahmad Shawqi (1868–1932), the poet laureate of Egypt, wrote five verse plays: *Qays wa-Layla* (Qays and Layla), *Masra' Kliobatra* (Death of Cleopatra), *'Antara*, *'Ali Bek al-Kabir* and *Qambiz*; those plays are considered great works of literature, but they have never been stage successes, as their poetic merit exceeds the quality of their dramatic construction.

The most remarkable figure and pioneer of original prose drama in Egypt and the Arab World is Tawfiq al-Hakim (1898–1986). Born to an upper-middle-class family in Alexandria, he was sent to university in Cairo; there he discovered theater and joined a theater troupe. Upon graduating, he was sent by his father to France to obtain a doctorate degree in law. Instead, he spent his time there attending theatrical performances and learning the European theater tradition. When he returned to Egypt, he took up writing for the stage under the pseudonym Tawfiq Husayn. His objective was to establish a modern Egyptian dramatic tradition based on Aristotle's notions of the unity of space, time, and action. He spent five decades of his life working to enrich the Arab dramatic literature tradition. In the course of his career he wrote more than seventy plays that included a very wide variety of themes and styles, which he divided up and classified as: theater of ideas, theater of social themes, and theater of the absurd. His play *Ahl al-kahf* (Sleepers of the Cave, 1937) marks a major turning point for drama in the Arab World. Written in *fusha* (Classical Arabic) and borrowing its subject matter from the Qur'an and the Bible, it admitted drama into the Arab literary canon and launched the emergence of an Arab theater movement that encompassed both philosophical ideas and accomplished dramaturgy. Those qualities allowed *Ahl al-kahf* to become the first Arabic play staged at the (then) newly established National Theater. From that point onwards, great Egyptian and Arab playwrights embarked on serious contributions to stage writing, and dramatic literature started to be produced abundantly throughout the region

Indigenous dramatic performances continued to be popular around the entire Arab World in the latter half of the nineteenth century, whereas European-style theater dominated the entertainment business and constituted a serious cultural movement in only a few Arab countries: Egypt, Lebanon, Syria, and Iraq, followed by Morocco and Tunisia. In the twentieth century, many Arab theater artists worked to incorporate traditional art forms and rituals into their stage events. Today, this movement continues to celebrate local cultural identities and traditions, and has become a prominent feature in Arab theaters throughout the region.

The postcolonial period (1950s and 1960s) marks a high point in Arab theater in general and particularly in the theatrical productions of Arab countries that advocated strong nationalist agendas, such as Egypt and Syria. Much of the theater that emerged during those decades explored local Arab performance traditions, and a number of notable playwrights and scholars theorized on the subject of indigenous art forms. Among those dramatists are Yusuf Idris, Saadallah Wannous, Tawfiq al-Hakim, 'Izz al-Din al-Madani, and al-Tayyib al-Siddiqi. While their approaches varied, their conclusions were quite similar. Their various investigations on the topic confirmed that traditional Arab performance arts in the different Arab countries – while each possessing its individual character and uniqueness – were all originally democratized spaces where audience members were active participants in the event and not just silent spectators. They also affirmed that quintessential Arab dramatic performances were not text-based, but rather depended on improvisations, singing, and dancing, as well as comedic skits.

During the 1950s and 1960s, many young Arab playwrights emerged, theaters were built, and theater troupes were established around the Arab World. The 1960s is regarded as the golden age of Arab theater for its impressive theatrical movement, which gave rise to great playwrights, actors, and directors throughout the region, including 'Ali Ahmad Bakathir, Nu'man 'Ashur, Yusuf Idris, Alfred Farag, Mahmud Diyab, Mikha'il Ruman, and Nagib Surur in Egypt; Saadallah Wannous, Mahmud al-Maghut, Walid Ikhlassi, and Yusuf al-'Ani in Syria and Iraq; 'Isam Mahfuz and Roger Assaf in Lebanon; and 'Izz al-Din al-Madani, Ahmad al-Ilj, and al-Tayyib al-Siddiqi in Morocco and Tunisia. In Palestine, under the vigilant eye of the Israeli armed forces, theater troupes like the Balalin, Hakawati, and Ashtar have continued to produce experimental dramas that comment on the predicament and plight of Palestinians under occupation.

Alongside the male dramatists, directors, and critics, a large number of Arab women have contributed to the modern Arab stage, including playwrights Fathiya al-'Assal, Nehad Gad, Andrée Chedid, and Nawal El Saadawi, directors Nayla al-Atrash and Nidal al-Ashqar, as well as critics Nehad Selaiha and Amal Bakir.

A growing trend in Egyptian theater today is storytelling. It started in 1998 with performances by members of the Women and Memory Forum, which consists of a group of women academics and activists who set out to revise and orally retell Arab culture and history from the point of view of women. The Forum performs and gives workshops with the objective of producing alternate accounts of popular traditional texts, for example, *A Thousand and One Nights*, in order to challenge historical sexism and chauvinism, and increase awareness of gender studies by performing, publishing, and disseminating their rewritten versions with a gender-sensitive perspective.

An increasing number of "socially conscious" performance groups have taken up storytelling as their primary approach in order to give voice to different causes and disadvantaged groups in society, whether they be women's issues, street children, minorities, or the sexually harassed and abused. Moreover, this trend has become particularly visible in the aftermath of the January 25, 2011, revolution, as many artists, activists, and laypeople performed monologues around the country in order to tell their personal stories and testimonies of the euphoric and/or traumatic revolutionary experiences of that public uprising. Those performances found wide and keen audiences both on stage as well as on the streets around all of Egypt, particularly during the first eighteen days of the revolution, but they continue to be popular to date.

For non-Arabs hoping to explore Arab dramatic literature, the first major obstacle is the availability of texts in translation. On this front, it is crucial to note that translations of Arab dramatic literature into other languages are scarce, and many are woefully inadequate. More importantly, the small selection that is available is neither a comprehensive representation of the region as a whole, nor does it give sufficient attention to the works of Arab women playwrights. This is a result of both the politics involved in choosing translations (why certain texts are translated rather than others) and the agendas of individual translators.

Furthermore, the process of locating secondary sources is equally difficult. These are virtually non-existent in English. This lack of critical texts creates another set of problems altogether, one of which is the use of Western literary theory for the analysis of Arab dramatic productions, an approach that rarely results in understanding these works on their own terms and usually leads instead to the evaluation of Arab drama according to the yardstick of Western influence. The initial impulse of some researchers is to treat Arabic texts as imitations of Western originals, thus dismissing their intrinsic value and authenticity, as well as the cultural difference they offer. Although Western scholars openly acknowledge that Western playwrights, such as Brecht and Artaud, used non-Western trends in constructing their drama, they do not necessarily deem those experiments as examples of the "influence" of Asian theater, nor do they dismiss them as imitative of the dramatic productions of other cultures, as they do in the case of Arab drama.

Among the critical issues that arise in discussions of Arab drama are "political commitment," orality and literacy, tradition and continuity, identity and hybridity. A number of other issues, such as dramatic style, levels of language, and the use of history and mythology, all need to be given particular attention as well. Arab theater needs to be studied within the sociopolitical contexts that have impacted and shaped the intellectual trends and artistic movements in Arab drama and theater. The Arab World is a region that has suffered colonialism, numerous wars, and revolutions, so it is necessary to follow the changes in thought, philosophies, and writing styles of dramatists as their political and social realities have continually changed around them. A deep look at the importance of religious beliefs of the peoples of this area is also much to be desired and it is imperative to ask how religion holds them together and pulls them apart. In the study of modern Arab theater, it is important to examine the thin line between ideological support and creating propaganda for state policies in the aftermath of independence from Western colonialism.

Since the tragic events of 9/11, Arab and Middle Eastern origin American artists have received more attention than in previous years. While this attention was tarnished with suspicion, it nevertheless admitted important Arab-American dramatists into mainstream American theater. Common themes in the works of these émigré and second-generation playwrights are nostalgia for an imagined homeland and the search for a literary identity that encompasses both the present and an ancestral consciousness. Among the many talented Arab-American dramatists today are: Yusuf el-Gindi, Betty Shemieh, Mona Mansour, Heather Raffo, and Jamil Khuri, to name just a few.

While many Arab-American artists working today are still defending their homelands by satirizing opinions that peg Arabs and/or Muslims as terrorists, their artistic productions are powerful and therapeutic for audiences across the world who might be confused about geopolitical issues, as well as for those who see hyphenated writers' works as intrinsically American in nature. In all cases, at its best art reveals the sensitivity, sense of beauty, and fairness of people; it also sheds light on their collective angst.

10
_____

Art

"Modern Arab art" refers here to the artistic production of the contemporary Arab states, most of which came into being after World War
II. Despite considerable variation, they share a common history under
the broader umbrella of Islamic civilization that produced particular
idioms in the arts. With the exception of Morocco, all were provinces
of the Ottoman Empire starting in the sixteenth century and were subject to fashions and policies emanating from the Ottoman capital of
Constantinople/Istanbul. The intensive modernizing reforms of the
nineteenth century altered the cultural sphere in the Ottoman center
and its major provinces, and institutionalized the association between
modern art and art in the Western modality that was enhanced during
the colonial period following World War I. Today "modern Arab art" continues to refer to art in this modality, albeit with the understanding that
generations of Arab artists have altered its trajectory and imbued it with
new content and identity. This chapter follows the major transformations of this art from its Ottoman beginnings to the present.[1]

Early transformations through World War I

In 1919, shortly after a popular revolt against British control, Egyptian
sculptor Mahmoud Mukhtar began work on the statue he titled *Nahdat
Misr* (Egyptian Awakening or Egyptian Renaissance) (see Figure 10.1).[2]
Carved out of pink granite quarried at Aswan and standing about
thirteen feet tall on a basalt plinth, the statue is of a sphinx and a
female peasant clad in long garb and headdress. The woman rests one
hand on the sphinx and raises her head cover with the other, revealing
a serpentine crown beneath.[3] A clear personification of the nation, the

Figure 10.1 Mahmoud Mukhtar, *Nahdat Misr* (Egyptian Renaissance), 1919–28, Aswan pink granite, Cairo.

figure embraces the past in which it is grounded while fixing a steady gaze on the future. This double move is repeated in the clean lines and solid yet simplified forms that speak a modern artistic language while simultaneously referencing ancient Egyptian statuary. Dubbed "Neo-Pharaonism," the statue's style reveals its conceit: it represents conscious choices in the melding of past and present, a neoclassicism that combines new techniques and sensibilities with concepts of ancient Egyptian art to arrive at a modern artistic language that embodies Egyptian identity.

Moukhtar's famous statue reveals primary factors in the development of modern art in the Arab World and belongs to an important early phase in this development. The statue was inaugurated in 1928 in its original location in front of Cairo's railway station and was part of the modern urban landscape implemented by the Khedival dynasty founded by Muhammad 'Ali, who had been dispatched to Egypt by the Ottomans to repel the Napoleonic invasion of 1798. Thereafter, Egypt was semi-independent but charted a course of modernizing reforms that paralleled the Ottoman center in importing European technologies and institutional practices. By the beginning of the twentieth century, local talents like Moukhtar could avail themselves of art studies at home under (mostly) French tutelage before completing their training in Paris or Rome, often with government sponsorship. Upon their return, they played an important role in art education, nourished by archeological activity and the contents of art museums, and began creating a new visual language as part of a general process of cultural regeneration that emphasized Egyptian identity.

Similar transformations occurred elsewhere in the region in the nineteenth century, albeit within the Ottoman modernizing framework. Early art practitioners from the Arab provinces studied at the palace schools in Constantinople/Istanbul or joined the ranks of soldier-painters, whose training in technical drawing enabled accurate topographic representation and depiction of events in the imperial domains. Some of these new artists/technicians, such as the Lebanese 'Ali Jamal al-Beiruti (fl. nineteenth century), settled in Istanbul as teachers. Others, such as 'Abd al-Qadir al-Rassam (1882–1952) of Iraq, carried the new artistic modes and techniques back to their home regions where they taught either at academies or independently in their own studios.[4] The novelty of the art they introduced resided in the incorporation of illusionistic space and mimetic three-dimensional representation. This mode contrasted dramatically with local artistic conventions that retained the two-dimensionality of the painted or decorated surface and emphasized abstract patterning and planar compositions – modes that came to be taught at schools of applied and decorative arts (and that are still associated with a historical Islamic art) and that remained in evidence in modern popular production, such as the reverse painting on glass made famous by the Damascene Abu Subhi al-Tinawi (1883–1973) (see Figure 10.2).[5]

Figure 10.2 'Antar, reverse painting on glass in the style of Abu Subhi al-Tinawi, Damascus, 1980s.

By the turn of the century, the tools, media, and techniques of art had changed within the established circles of formal instruction and patronage, especially with the founding of schools of fine arts (first in Cairo in 1908). Instead of inorganic watercolor pigment on paper, artists applied oil paint to canvas and sculptors created statues that displaced architecture as the major vehicle of commemoration and carrier of historical memory. The professionalization of artists through specialized training at home and abroad, often with government sponsorship, went hand in hand with the adoption of sculpture and easel painting, and – at least among elite sectors of society – changed the very definition and uses of art as well as the venues in which it was experienced and enjoyed, leading to the establishment of salons, art societies, and, eventually, museums of modern art.

Thematically, the new art incorporated all the European genres, from historical painting to still life, although landscapes and portraits enjoyed a special popularity even after they were freed from their documentary tasks by photography. The prevailing style was Academic Realism, where institutional grounding and affiliation with a specific (art) history meant that artists who skillfully absorbed the lessons of the earlier European Masters whom they studied and copied could be admitted into an international co-fraternity of art, thereby reflecting their – and their patrons' – modernity. The descriptive properties of this representational mode insured its usability as an educational tool, a rationale offered by progressive religious thinkers who defended the new art against conservative views or Islamic objections to verisimilitude in the representation of living beings.[6]

Alongside formal channels, artists working in the older vehicles of manuscript painting and wall decoration began experimenting with the new pictorial mode independently over the course of the nineteenth century, often through reference to print media (such as postcards) and in response to changes in taste and architectural fashions. In the elite residences of cities like Cairo and Damascus, panels with views of the holy shrines gradually incorporated three-dimensionality and spatial recession, and materials such as glazed tile and stone inlay were replaced by lacquer and oil paint on plaster. New subject matter, including fruit and flower compositions, steam ships, railways, and European cities, became part of a decorative repertoire that reflected new trends and international engagements through news and travel.[7] By the late nineteenth century, artists whose names are mostly unknown to us had spread this fashion – through experimentation and apprenticeship – to the walls of a variety of private and public establishments. Similar changes appeared among icon painters (best documented for Palestine and Lebanon), who deployed their skills in churches and relayed them to a younger generation of apprentices and interested amateurs.[8]

Thus by the first decades of the twentieth century and prior to World War I (when new arts and crafts schools were established in Syria and Lebanon),[9] a new art had spread in the Arab provinces that was evident at two levels of practice: (1) an informal one that adapted novel European representational and pictorial techniques and was accessible to larger publics (through display in churches and school rooms, or at public venues such as coffee houses, public baths, and local fairs), through independent instruction, apprenticeship, or experimentation; and, (2) an official one that was grounded in formal training and institutional support and found its way into the salons of the bourgeoisie. The formal strain, evident primarily in a Cairo that the Khedives had transformed into an Egyptian Paris, followed the French model and included the founding of art academies and private collections that embraced European art from the Renaissance to Monet. As a result, Impressionism defined the stylistic limits of academically trained artists in the Arab World, including ones who flocked to Cairo's academies, long after it was considered retrograde in France.

Interwar era through to independence

Following World War I, artists working in the realist modes began incorporating nationalist sentiments into their art. They were succeeded by a generation that apprehended style itself as a carrier of meaning and abandoned Academism in favor of Abstraction. In North Africa and Sudan this move was often accompanied by the rejection of easel painting altogether and its replacement with local media and techniques. These changes were partly propelled by anti-establishment and anti-colonial sentiments, and partly by engagement with developments in international art that a younger generation of artists carried back from their European training locales.

In addition to its association with the establishment, Academic Realism was the favored style of Orientalist painters even after the introduction of looser brushstrokes and vibrant coloristic effects learned in the North African light by French painter Eugène Delacroix (1798–1863). From the precision of Jean-Auguste-Dominique Ingres (1780–1867) to the pre-Impressionism of some of the Romantic painters, Orientalist painting relied on Academic Realism's ability to "mirror" the world in imagining and imaging an exotic and often decrepit Orient that became a justifying vehicle for colonialism.[10] The expansion of colonialism in the region following World War I (Egypt and Sudan were under British control after 1882 and France had colonized large parts of North Africa already in the nineteenth century) meant an increase in the number of Orientalist artists and images in the region, as well as the implementation of educational programs (extending to formerly peripheral parts of the Ottoman Empire) that incorporated their embedded messages. The establishment of new museums of antiquities at this time, in Cairo in 1902 and later in Damascus and Baghdad, fostered cultural particularism based on ancient roots and "ethnic heritage" (creating material for a number of neoclassicisms, from Pharaonic to Mesopotamian to Phoenician) and supported the geopolitical recreation of the region. The European collection and construction of "Islamic art" as a single, undifferentiated historical category that spanned several centuries further devalued living practices, but added to the mix of historical modes that would be available to new artists interested in constituting a new Arab art.[11]

Artists whose careers bridged this context began working nationalist sentiments into their realist modes. In 1930s Jerusalem (then under British Mandate), Daoud Zalatimo (1906–2001), a Muslim who had frequented the studio of icon painter Nicola Saig (1863–1942), applied the new pictorial manner to paintings of historical and mythological subjects that were displayed in schoolrooms and fostered both national pride and interest in the new art. Zulfa al-Sa'di (1910–1988), also a student of Saig, won a municipal competition for portraits that transformed contemporary and historical personalities into secular icons of the nation, and became the first artist to hold a one wo(man) exhibition in Palestine.[12] Mustafa Farroukh (1901–1957), who practiced and taught ideals associated with Academic Realism in Lebanon, created historical paintings that celebrated Arabic achievements (as in *Mu'awiya Embarks* and *Amir Beshir and Shaykh Nassif al-Yaziji at the Palace of Beit el-Din c. 1937,* which depicts two protagonists of the nineteenth-century *Nahda*). These works incorporated sentiments that lend new valence to his derivative triad of local scenes, types, and landscapes (see Figure 10.3).[13] While these artists focused on local subject matter, Muhammad Racim (1896–1974) of Algeria – a French colony from 1830 to 1962 – combined modes and techniques in works that, aside from the three-dimensional rendering of the central subject matter (itself based on local themes), continued the look of the manuscript painting in which he had been trained.[14] The tension between style and technique evident in this juxtaposition of contrasting modes typifies art in regions where colonial schools long barred local participants and where European art proceeded alongside local practices.

By the late 1930s, Egyptian avant-garde artists began adopting abstraction as part of their rejection of the ideals associated with Neo-Pharaonism. The *Declaration of the Post-Orientalists* published in 1937 announced their rejection of Academism for its establishment and

Figure 10.3 Mustafa Farroukh, 'Irzal (Lebanese mountain treehouse), c. 1934, water-color on paper.

colonial history as well as its association with Nazism. Among a number of movements, the Art and Freedom group led by poet George Henein (1914–1973) allied itself with André Breton and Surrealism, adopted the revolutionary stance of Mexican Diego Rivera's manifestoes, and operated under the slogan "long live low art." Despite opposition from the establishment and a public now attuned to figuration, the group's intent of expressing the psychic content of the nation with attention to individual expression and experimentation in art education, laid the path for the emergence of Social Realism and Expressionism in the 1950s and 1960s (as in the art of Hamid Oweis and Gazbia Sirry). In its manifestoes, Art and Freedom defined a new relationship to style by charting a reverse flow of the principles of abstraction from local idioms (as in Islamic art) to Europe. Although the Egyptian avant-garde did not invent a new style, their strategic repositioning of abstraction effectively naturalized it as Egyptian while internationalizing Egyptian art. In contrast, Iraqi artists attempted to invent an entirely new and inherently Arab international style.

In Iraq, where the British had established a Hashemite monarchy in 1921 and where formerly Ottoman artists such as al-Rassam trained younger ones and encouraged painting directly from nature, artists continued to create Iraqi art through subject matter until the emergence of the Baghdad Modern Art Group in 1951. The Group, founded by artists and intellectuals including the Palestinian Existentialist Jabra Ibrahim Jabra (1919–1994) and led by Jawad Salim (1919–1961), focused on searching for a new style that would synthesize different artistic expressions from various times and places to arrive at a unique and immediately recognizable Arab-Iraqi visual language. Ancient Iraqi art was an element of this language, but it also included Expressionism and Cubism, Arab painting as exemplified by the thirteenth-century Abu Yahya al-Wasiti (the famous painter of the *Maqamat* of al-Hariri),[15] and *turath*, the interiorized cultural heritage and experience of a living society.[16] The Baghdad Modern Art Group did not advocate a particular style or subject matter, but encouraged experimentation across a wide spectrum of visual practices in an effort to arrive at an entirely new language that was at once both local and international. By cutting across temporal, geographical, and social divides, the group also attempted to erase distinctions between "high" and "low" art, and between "traditional" (local) and "modern" (Western) practice. This position was emphasized by the Group's exhibitions, which were held in Baghdad's popular squares and cafes in order to engage art with its society.

Jawad Salim's best work in painting, graphic art, and sculpture is related to its "grassroots" in complex, analytical, and not immediately discernible ways.[17] But his most famous work – and the one that was meant to communicate with the largest number of Baghdadis – is the *Nasb al-Hurriyya* (Freedom or Liberty Monument) commissioned to commemorate the 1958 Republican Revolution (see Figure 10.4).

The monument's twenty-five cast bronze figures allude as much to Iraq's ancient relief sculpture as to Henry Moore's figural stylizations, while certain sections (such as the horse on the far right) and the monument's overall graphic quality also invite comparison with Picasso's

Figure 10.4 Jawad Salim's *Nasb al-Hurriyya* (Liberty Monument), 1958, cast bronze, Baghdad.

Guernica and with the rhythmic spacing and linearity of Arabic writing. The stylistic principles and multiple references visible in the Liberty Monument became hidden layers of meaning in the work of Iraqi and Arab artists of the revolutionary period and carried them through an optimistic era of secular Arab Nationalism following independence. Many of these artists also continued experimenting with the use of elements of the Arabic language in art, resulting in the *hurufiyya* trend that coalesced with the importance of Arabic as identifier and unifier of the new Arab states, as well as with revivals and continuations of the art of calligraphy.

Neither a movement nor a school, *hurufiyya* (derived from the Arabic word *ḥarf* for "letter") denotes a wide range of explorations into the abstract, graphic, and aesthetic properties of Arabic letters. Artists came to these explorations via different paths. Beginning in the late 1940s and early 1950s, Saloua Raouda Choucair of Lebanon began incorporating letters into paintings that engaged the Parisian art scene (where the Cubists had already experimented with letters as signs), but transformed them into entirely abstract "modules" in her mature work as a sculptor.[18] Hassan Massoudi of Iraq continues to create calligraphic paintings with direct reference to Islamic calligraphy, while in his work of the 1970s and 1980s, Palestinian Kamal Boullata deconstructed the geometric principles inherent in Islamic art and recreated them in silk screens composed

Figure 10.5 Mona Saudi, *Numuww/Shajarat al-Nūn* (Growth/Tree of *Nūn*), 1981, Lebanese stone.

of repeating word motifs and entirely new graphic qualities and meanings. Whereas the use of Arabic words and letters allows them to act as signs of identity, it also often plays with the tensions inherent in the migration of the linguistic sign into the visual realm. In *Growth* by the Jordanian artist Mona Saudi (see Figure 10.5), the Arabic letter *nūn* ("n") that forms the sculpture lends identity and provides additional layers of meaning for those who recognize its form, but without creating interpretive distance in relation to the work's conceptual content.

Whether obscure or evident, melded into international abstract styles or based on principles derived from an Islamic art perceived as a unifying historical phenomenon, the use of Arabic lettering has contributed to linking artists across the region and the writing of an art history that provides their work with temporal depth and unique-ness.[19] In North Africa and Sudan, *hurufiyya* and continuities in medium and technique were linked to anticolonial resistance from the start (as seen with Racim).[20] Houria Niati continues to question the links among medium, technique, and content in multimedia installations that replace Orientalism's views of Algerian women with an emphasis on women's labor in society; she incorporates language by reciting Arabic–French translations of her poetry. In Morocco, *hurufiyya* went along with the replacement of oil paints by dyes such as henna and by the study of tattoo, weaving, and jewelry design of local, Islamic, Arab, and Imazighen (Berber) origin (much of which can be seen in work by contemporary artist Lalla Essayde, who incorporates a feminist pos-ition). Calligraphy, along with local practices and designs that art his-tory usually classifies as "crafts," displaced the Western art curriculum at the École des Beaux Arts in Casablanca under artist-director Farid Belkahia in 1964. In Sudan (under British rule from 1882 to 1964), art-ists of the so-called "Old Khartoum School" shunned the academic art imported by a generation trained in Cairo, as well as the materials asso-ciated with it, and adopted media such as leather and wood alongside calligraphy in order to produce art with African and Islamic valence.

By the 1970s, when the North African countries had achieved inde-pendence, these practices were folded into debates on artistic *hadatha* (modernity) and *asala* (authenticity) that took place at gatherings of Arab artists (first in Damascus in 1971 and then Baghdad in 1973, followed by the Baghdad and Rabat Biennales of 1974 and 1976 respectively). The dialogues took place at a time when the post-revolutionary regimes that supported the arts (notably in Egypt, Syria, and Iraq) also increasingly claimed con-trol over their form and content. Consequently, between 1952 and 1982, the Lebanese capital Beirut, which boasted an open cosmopolitan atmosphere, displaced Cairo as cultural center. Rather than support the emergence of an Arab art (or groups in search for identity in art), Beirut supported the coexistence of a multiplicity of artistic experiments and identities, from the most vehemently individualistic forms of self-expression to the most ideologically driven. These contrasts appear not only in Lebanese art of the period but also in Palestinian art, which found a home in the city's slums and refugee camps as well as in its elite circles and galleries.[21] While residents of the former worked in figural modes that appealed to popular

Figure 10.6 Paul Guiragossian, *al-Raheel* (Departure), oil on canvas, 1970s.

nationalist sentiments, the latter often developed their work into complex adventures with abstraction. The most renowned artist to emerge from the period, Paul Guiragossian (1926–1993), an Armenian Palestinian from Jerusalem, cut across these contrasts with a highly personal style in which he created monumental figures with large sweeps of his multicolored brushstrokes. His *al-Raheel* (see Figure 10.6) is an icon of departure that evokes the flight of the Holy Family from Jerusalem while speaking of the multiple departures in the artist's life.

While modern art in Beirut began, as it did in other Ottoman provincial cities, through adaptation of new pictorial modes or institutionalization of borrowed European ones, and proceeded from Realism through Romantic Impressionism into Abstraction, by the 1980s it no longer had a single classification or "school" (whether "Arab," "Western," or "Lebanese"); Beirut's supremacy as art capital ended during the long Lebanese Civil War that was accompanied by profound changes within and outside the Arab World. Since then, "modern Arab art," a visually multilingual artistic mode, has found new visibility in newly founded museums and galleries, an active art market, and new narrations of its history.

Contemporary spaces of Arab art

This active art scene now extends to new locations in the Arab World, as well as to newly established institutions in older centers. In 2009, for example, Beirut inaugurated BAC (Beirut Art Center), a minimalist space that is dedicated to exhibiting contemporary art by Lebanese, Arab, and international artists, as well as to sponsoring art events and educational programs. BAC represents the first major exhibition venue dedicated exclusively to contemporary and modern art since the establishment of the Sursock Museum in a nineteenth-century Italianate villa that was bequeathed to the state in 1961. Strong private support for the arts, as was the case in Lebanon, has appeared elsewhere. In the Jordanian capital Amman, the Darat al-Funun, established by the Khalid Shoman Foundation in 1993, now occupies a premier position as both museum and research center. With its longer history of sponsoring modern art, Egypt inaugurated a new complex for visual and performing arts in 2005. The comprehensive presentations at Cairo's Museum of Modern Egyptian Art are complemented by contemporary art at the Gezira Art Center, as well as at specialized museums (such as the Mahmoud Mukhtar Museum nearby) and smaller museums in the provinces. While the Baghdad Museum of Modern Art awaits restitution and restoration of collections lost in 2003 (an objective that is actively pursued by Iraqi and Arab artists and publics), major new museums and numerous commercial galleries have appeared in the Gulf region. The latest of these is the Qatar Arab Museum of Modern Art that opened its doors under the name Mathaf (Arabic for "museum") in late 2010. Mathaf joins a number of new museums (and museum expansions both in the Arab World and elsewhere) housed in structures that are themselves showcases of the art of architecture. Accompanied by newly founded museums of Islamic art as well as "branches" of European museums (such as the Louvre), these new art spaces testify to the multidirectional flow of art as well as larger cultural trends.

Outside the Arab World, modern Arab art is showcased and supported by institutions such as the Institut du Monde Arabe in Paris and the Tate Modern in London, which inaugurated its new galleries with installations by Palestinian artist Mona Hatoum. In 2006, New York's Museum of Modern Art launched *Without Boundary* as an exploration of connections between contemporary art from the larger Middle East and historical Islamic practices, thereby reframing questions about artistic identity and "authenticity" in contemporary terms and addressing them to new audiences.[22] The current increased visibility of Arab modern and contemporary art on the international scene is partly a matter of scale and perception befitting the global age, and partly a reflection of the anxieties raised by the intensified migration of identities outside national space. Art from the Arab World – the "Arabness" of which has always been a matter of negotiation – is itself an exemplary "space" for addressing issues of identity. From its Ottoman beginnings, through its nationalist phases and nostalgic revivals, into its current global presence, this art has perennially engaged critical questioning of artistic identity in relation to art's histories.

The future (?) of Arab art

In 2008, the Graffiti artist/style writer Don Karl (aka Stone) organized the event "Bombing Beirut" that brought together a number of practitioners concerned with the aesthetic properties of letters and with street art. A few years later, he collaborated with Pascal Zoghbi, a Lebanese type designer trained in the Netherlands, on the book project *Arabic Graffiti*.[23] Together, event and book herald the formalization of a new Arab art form (graffiti) that is tenaciously, and sometimes anachronistically, connected to older practices of stylized Arabic writing or calligraphy. Short essays in *Arabic Graffiti* connect one to the other as well as to a variety of practices, from calligraphy in historical manuscripts and on buildings, to political slogans on walls, to shop signs and decorated trucks. The project exemplifies a process – the beginning and institutionalization of a new art with a specific letter-based aesthetic. It brings together a gallery of artists from around the world whose goals are to enrich graffiti art with the aesthetic qualities of Arabic lettering while injecting Arabic stylized writing with a variety of Latin-based features and formal properties (such as Gothic and italic forms), thereby creating a new art form with global resonance.

While the multidirectional flow of concepts and artistic practices is not new to the Arab World, this project differs from past collaborations in scale – following the ease of movement, communication, and new mass media – and in the multiple layers of identity of the participating artists, whether French artists who create light sculptures made of letter forms in various venues around Europe or the Middle East (such as Julien Breton), or artists of Arab heritage, born or raised elsewhere, practicing in yet another part of the world. The deterritorialization of artistic practices and expressions appears elsewhere as well (as in the art of Ghada Amer, Mona Hatoum, Shereen Neshat, Janaan el-Ani, among others). While many of these artists continue to address the colonial legacies of their home countries, most are involved with expressing universal ideas pertinent to current times focused through the lens of personal experience. As with the urban art project, artistic identity is increasingly a matter of choice or of the peregrinations and dislocations of contemporary life. These contemporary practices, concerns, and exhibition venues underscore the fact that Arab art, the product of a specific modernity, has entered a "post-Arab" phase.[24]

This "post-Arab" phase does not mean that Arab art and artists have become part of regular academic curricula in art history or surveys of modern art (and those few who have are often burdened by representing political or social issues of distant locations, or of representing distant local artistic practices). Even in the Arab World itself, modern art continues to be taught via its canonical Western locations and histories with little emphasis on the ways that Arab artists gave new life to European artistic modes and practices, a situation that might change with the establishment of new museums and research institutions, and with the appearance of a new generation of cosmopolitan art historians focused on Arab art.

The forces of globalization that have brought about some of these developments have also impacted art in the Arab World in varying ways. The recent large-scale entry of Arab art into the world market, propelled by the newly founded museums in wealthy states and accompanied by the interest and control of international dealers and auction houses, have commodified Arab art and pushed prices beyond the means of most individual collectors (in some cases leading to the appearance of forgeries). Whereas one result is that artists are more subject to dealers than before, many have also taken advantage of the new media in establishing their own websites and, sensitive to the beginnings of these changes, have undertaken the publication of catalogs documenting their careers, thereby providing important first-hand information on their work. These works, which often cover the period of high Arab art and beyond, stand as self-representations of practicing artists in the Arab World. They join yet to be systematically collected periodicals, gallery notices, exhibition reviews, and manifestoes in providing critical sources for the study of the modern art of the Arab World, of the ways in which it expresses modernity and articulates Arab identity, and of the ways it transcends restrictions of place and location to assume its position in modern art history.

Notes

1 The most accessible general introduction to the subject is Wijdan Ali, *Modern Islamic Art: Development and Continuity* (Gainesville, FL: University Press of Florida, 1997). See also, Nada M. Shabout, *Modern Arab Art: Formation of Arab Aesthetics* (Gainesville, FL: University Press of Florida, 2007).

2 Liliane Karnouk, *Modern Egyptian Art 1910–2003* (American University in Cairo Press, 2005), pp. 15–20.

3 This is the ureaus crown symbolizing ancient Egyptian kingship.

4 Ali, *Modern Islamic Art*, pp. 34–44, esp. 35–36 (Lebanon); 44–54 (Iraq); May Muzaffar, "Iraqi Contemporary Art," in S. C. Inati (ed.), *Iraq: Its History, People & Politics* (Buffalo, NY: Prometheus Books, 2003), pp. 63–89.

5 Abu Subhi is the most commonly used name of Harb al-Tinawi, whose son Subhi practiced the same art. The themes of the paintings derive from folktales recounted by the *hakawatis* (storytellers) of Damascus in coffee houses with similar wall paintings (Ali, *Modern Islamic Art*, p. 86).

6 Karnouk, *Modern Egyptian Art*, pp. 11–12 is one example.

7 Changes appear in both manuscript and wall painting in Istanbul as early as the 1830s; see Günsel Renda, *A History of Turkish Painting* (Seattle, WA: University of Washington Press, 1989); Damascene examples are found in Stephan Weber, "Images of Imagined Worlds: Self-image and Worldview in Late Ottoman Wall Painting in Damascus," in J. Hanssen, Th. Phillip, and S. Weber (eds.), *The Empire in the City* (Beirut: German Orient Institute, 2002), pp. 145–71.

8 Icon painting was practiced in Iraq, Syria, Egypt, Palestine, Lebanon, and elsewhere. It is usually related to the development of modern painting in Lebanon, as in Ali, *Modern Islamic Art*, pp. 34–44; see also *Lebanon: the Artist's View* (London: Quartet Books, 1989). The best documentation of the continuity and transformation of the art is in Kamal Boullata, *Palestinian Art from 1850 to the Present* (London: Saqi Books, 2009), chapters 1 & 2.

9 Arts and crafts schools in Syria and Lebanon were established by the Ottoman governor Cemal Pasha.

10 For the Orientalist trope that feminized the Orient see Linda Nochlin, "The Imaginary Orient," in *The Politics of Vision* (NY: Westview Press, 1989), pp. 33–57; for the "odalisque" and Delacroix's influence, Todd Porterfield, "Western Views of Oriental Women in Modern Painting and Photography," in S. Nashashibi (ed.), *Forces of Change: Artists of the Arab World*, (Washington, DC: National Museum of Women in the Arts, 1994), pp. 59–71.

11 These practices had already begun under the Ottomans (who also collected Islamic art), particularly as they adopted a more colonial model in relation to the Arab provinces. See Wendy Shaw, *Possessors and Possessed: Museums, Archeology and the Visualization of History in the Late Ottoman Empire* (Berkeley: University of California Press, 2003); Ussama Makdisi, "Ottoman Orientalism," *The American Historical Review*, 107:3 (2002), pp. 768–96.

12 Boullata, *Palestinian Art*, pp. 63–70.

13 Musée Nicolas Sursock exhibition catalogue, *Moustafa Farroukh 1901–1957* (Beirut: n.p., 2003).

14 Ali, *Modern Islamic Art*, p. 56.

15 The *Maqamat* of al-Hariri were a very popular series of picaresque tales centered on a clever conman who traveled widely and appeared in many different guises.

16 The concept is discussed in Shabout, *Modern Arab Art*, pp. 42–44.

17 The term was used by Jabra to indicate authenticity, see Jabra Ibrahim Jabra, *The Grassroots of Iraqi Art* (Baghdad: Wasit Graphic and Publishing, 1983).

18 For illustrations, see Joseph Tarrab, Hala Schoukair, Helen Kahl(English), and Jack Aswad (Arabic) (eds.), *Saloua Raouda Choucair: Her Life and Art* (Beirut: privately printed, 2002).

19 Accordingly, the Jordanian artist/art historian Wijdan Ali translates *hurufiyya* as "the Calligraphic School of Art"; an approach that allows her to group Turkish and, especially, Iranian artists who experiment with Arabic letters with Arab ones, and so to arrive at a "modern Islamic art." See Ali, *Modern Islamic Art*, especially p. 151.

20 Ali, *Modern Islamic Art*, pp. 55–62 (Algeria); pp. 63–70 (Tunisia); pp. 71–76 (Morocco); pp. 114–18 (Sudan).

21 The best short statement on Beirut in this period and the place of Palestinian art in it, is Boullata, "Artists Re-member Palestine in Beirut," reprinted in *Palestinian Art*, pp. 123–60.

22 The exhibition included Arab, Turkish, Iranian, and Pakistani artists, as well as North American ones who draw inspiration from Islamic art. Its record is Fereshteh Daftari, *Without Boundary: Seventeen Ways of Looking* (New York: Museum of Modern Art, 2006).

23 Pascal Zoghbi and Don Karl aka Stone, *Arabic Graffiti* (Berlin: From Here to Fame Publishing, 2011).

24 This does not mean that there are no longer any artists who identify as Arab but rather that the "high Arab" phase of modern art in the Arab World has run its course.

11

Architecture

Architecture in the Arab World has gone through a series of profound transformative phases in the last 200 years. The romantic conception of an Arabo-Islamic architectural character, which informed the architectural production of the nineteenth and early twentieth centuries, had lost a lot of its appeal by the middle of the twentieth century. National independence movements, which soon became ruling political parties, brought with them the more vocal and more aggressive categories of modernity, nationalism, and, later, socialism to represent the architecture of their newly formed states. The new framework engendered some grand architectural and urban projects, such as commemorative monuments, large governmental complexes, and whole new administrative and industrial cities. It also generated extensive debates about regionalism and vernacular architecture as authentic illustration of the nation's spirit, which resulted in the creation of idealistic villages, residential suburbs, and community centers in Egypt, Syria, Iraq, Morocco, and Tunisia, in addition to numerous villas for the artistically minded nationalist elites. This progressive stage, however, was succeeded and somewhat supplanted by the no less passionate discourse on religion as a framer of identity that sprang forth in the 1980s, primarily as a response to the failure of the nationalist regimes to fulfill the aspirations of their people. During the same period, triumphant Late-Capitalism and its regional clones began to promote a glitzy yet monotonous globalized architecture in order to satisfy a business ambition to homogenize all markets. Today, most new architecture constructed in the Arab World follows international standards of form and function, but pays homage to some notion of "Islamic architecture," if only in the form of pastiche.

Creating "Arab" architecture

The Frenchman Pascal-Xavier Coste (1787–1879) was the first architect to use the term "Arab Architecture" in the title of his impressive compendium, *L'Architecture Arabe ou Monuments du Kaire mesurés et dessinés de 1818 à 1826*, which focuses exclusively on a selection of monuments from Cairo. Every example is depicted in plans, sections, elevations, and interior and exterior perspectives, in addition to short, descriptive paragraphs. A concise historical introduction sums up the period's knowledge of the architecture of Islamic Egypt and contextualizes the architecture of the "Arabs" in general in relation to medieval Western architecture. The detailed analytical drawings seem to have been necessary for Coste to make the leap from studying historical examples to devising a basic vocabulary for a Neo-Mamluk style (based on the monumental architecture in Egypt during the Mamluk period, 1250–1517), which he considered the most appropriate for new buildings in Cairo. He showcased his views in two mosques he designed for Muhammad 'Ali, the semi-independent governor of Egypt (1805–48), to be constructed in the Citadel of Cairo and in Alexandria (see Figure 11.1). Though never built, these two mosques may be considered the pioneering examples of consciously designed Arab architecture.

The initial exploratory attempts to define Arab architecture were followed by studies authored by archeologists and philologists who built their careers working for colonial administrations in Arab capitals. Scholars such as K. A. C. Creswell, Martin Briggs, Ernst Diez, Ernst Herzfeld, Gaston Wiet, Gaston Migeon, Henri Saladin, and Jean Sauvaget produced copious handbooks on Arab architecture, sometimes subsumed under the larger category of Islamic architecture. They classified historical buildings into types and styles following a rather rigid dynastic periodization, which is still with us today. Despite their erudite and prodigious output, however, they, like their counterparts studying the architecture of other non-Western cultures, subscribed too uncritically to the canonic view of architecture as culturally stratified and linearly chronological, with Western architecture at the center and on top. This is best exemplified by the infamous "Tree of Architecture" of Banister Fletcher (see Figure 11.2) that appeared as the frontispiece in all the editions of his influential book, *A History of Architecture on the Comparative Method for the Student, Craftsman, and Amateur*, between 1896 and 1961. This unabashedly racist diagram reserved the trunk and the upper, healthy

Figure 11.1 Pascal-Xavier Coste, Project for Alexandria Mosque Façade, 1825.

branches of the tree to an uninterrupted succession of Western styles from Greece to modern America, and relegated the architecture of all other cultures to dead-end branches.

This oppressive conception of architectural history, which reduced all architectures outside the West to bygone and insular traditions, has affected the production of new architecture in the Arab World, as well as elsewhere outside the West, and still does today. Architects and their patrons have had one of two choices. They could copy directly from Western models to assert their modernity and "up-to-dateness" – hence the preponderance of Neoclassical, Art Nouveau, Art Deco, Modernist,

Figure 11.2 Banister Fletcher, "Tree of Architecture," 1896.

and Postmodern architecture in cities like Cairo, Alexandria, Beirut, Damascus, Aleppo, Baghdad, Tunis, Amman, and Jerusalem – or they could reference historical architecture in their design if they wished to relate to the culture and history of the place. They have had to filter their borrowings, however, through established Western revivalist methods, since they have been trained to regard Arab architecture as an artistic heritage of the past that was interrupted with the onset of modernity and the colonial age.

The examples of revivalist Arab architecture are many. The earliest date back to the middle of the nineteenth century when Khedive Isma'il of Egypt was trying simultaneously to articulate a nationalist image in the architecture he sponsored and to claim that the country belonged to "Europe and not to the Orient." Several projects designed for him by expatriate European architects reveal these two tendencies, such as the

Figure 11.3 Karl von Diebitsch, The Mausoleum of Suleiman Pasha al-Faransawi, Cairo, 1862.

work of the German architect Karl von Diebitsch. In the porticoes of the Palace of al-Gezirah (1869) and the Mausoleum of Suleiman Pasha al-Faransawi in Cairo (1862) (see Figure 11.3), he experiments with intricate patterns in cast iron modeled on examples from medieval Moorish Spain (in Arabic known as "al-Andalus," hence the term "Andalusian style").

Similarly, the al-Rifaʿi Mosque (1869–1916) in Cairo, designed by the Austro-Hungarian Max Herz, reflects the tremendous influence of the Mamluk Mosque of Sultan Hassan across the street, but still strives to produce logical and symmetrically arranged plan and façades in the manner of the Beaux-Arts school.

Figure 11.4 Fernando de Aranda, The Hijaz Railway Station, Damascus, 1912.

Comparable impulses undergirded the work of European architects of the next generation, who followed their predecessors in seeking work in colonized Arab countries, the economies of which became forcibly tied to the colonial metropolis in the early twentieth century. Among these architects was the Slovenian Antonio Lasciac, who lived and worked in Cairo until his death in 1946. In his later buildings, such as the Trieste Insurance building (1910) and the Bank Misr headquarters in Cairo and Alexandria (1927 and 1928 respectively), he reproduced themes of an open and colorful Arabic palatial architecture, especially in its Moorish (or Andalusian) variations. Another architect who spent most of his life working in an Arab city (Damascus, in this case), was the Spaniard Fernando de Aranda (1878–1969). His Hijaz Railway Station (1912–17) is one of the most monumental and most balanced Neo-Arab examples in the city (see Figure 11.4).

Similarly, several French architects, such as Henri Proust, Adrien Laforgue, and Albert Laprade, applied an Andalusian Neo-Arab style in their work on the cities of Rabat and Casablanca, which were modernized with a touch of Orientalist exoticism by General Louis Hubert Lyautey, who ruled Morocco between 1907 and 1925 first as a military governor then as Resident-General.

This generation also included Arab architects who studied in European schools of architecture and applied the lessons they learned there in the public buildings they designed in their home countries. Among these pioneers is the Lebanese Youssef Aftimos (1866–1952), who studied in the United States and built in Egypt, Palestine, Syria, and Lebanon. In Beirut, he is credited with several elegant buildings in a revivalist-eclectic style, such as his Neo-Arab clock tower in Hamidiyya Square (1897) and the Neo-Moorish Municipality of Beirut building (1923–33). Another pioneer is the Egyptian Mustafa Fahmi (1886–1972), who studied in Paris and returned to Cairo to follow in the footsteps of his father, Mahmud Pasha Fahmi al-Mi'mar, the chief architect of the Awqaf Ministry built in a strict Neo-Mamluk style in three stages between 1898 and 1929. Mustafa Fahmi built several public buildings in a rational Neo-Mamluk style, such as the Egyptian Engineers Society building (1930) and the Young Muslim Association building (1935). Still another pioneer is the Syrian 'Abd al-Razzaq Malas, who studied in Paris as well and built several revivalist-eclectic public buildings in Damascus, the most important of which is the wonderful Neo-Arab Fijeh headquarters building (1937–42).

To be sure, the Neo-Arab, Neo-Moorish, or Neo-Mamluk styles were sometimes presented as national choices, especially in the Arab states that began to take shape after the dissolution of the Ottoman Empire. They provided the visual connection to a historical period in which the country was either independent or the center of a larger empire. Khedival Egypt, for instance, was moving towards adopting the Neo-Mamluk style as a national style in the late nineteenth century. But colonization and the consequent loss of political and economic independence weakened that drive and turned these styles into mere visual choices among different available revivalist styles running the gamut from Neoclassical to Neo-Hindu, the latter exemplified by the unusual palace designed in 1905 by the French architect Alexandre Marcel for Baron Empain in Heliopolis.

Other nation states in the region that did not experience colonialism, such as Turkey and Iran, sought in the articulation of their public architecture to revive a pre-Islamic past as a means to construct a presumed historical continuity of a quintessential national identity. This historical realignment did not strike roots in the Arab World, probably because of the perceived interconnectivity between Arabism and Islam. But several political movements that sought a national identity independent of Islam, such as the Wafd Party in Egypt and the Ba'ath Party in Syria and Iraq, experimented for a short while with similar historical makeovers. This can be seen for instance in the Mausoleum of Sa'd Zaghloul (see Figure 11.5), the leader of the 1919 revolution and the "father of the

Figure 11.5 Mustafa Fahmi, The Mausoleum of Sa'd Zaghloul, Cairo, 1929.

Egyptian Nation," designed by none other than Mustafa Fahmi and built in a politically charged Neo-Pharoanic style in 1929, or the Liberty Monument (*Naṣb al-Ḥurriyya*) in Baghdad with its clear Assyrian references, built by the famous artist/architect Jawad Salim to commemorate the 1958 revolution.

With its hybrid nature, class associations, and veneration of the past, revivalist-eclectic architecture was unable to fulfill nationalist aspirations to establish a "new" and "pure" national style, which became particularly assertive after several Arab countries achieved independence in the 1940s and 1950s. But these calls did not have the time to develop architectural alternatives. Military coups brought to power impulsive regimes that espoused a mixture of supra-nationalism, or Pan-Arabism, modernism, and a distorted form of state socialism. The architecture they sponsored reflected their new political and socioeconomic orientation by concentrating on public projects such as government offices, factories, schools, and public housing, and by adopting a stripped down form of modernism as an expression of modernity and a rejection of tainted historicist architecture. Most architects working in the pure modernist medium produced derivative and banal buildings, but some, such as Sayyid Kuraym and Antoine Salim Nahhas from Egypt, Antoine Thabet, 'Asem Salam, and Pierre el-Khoury from Lebanon, and Jean

François Zevaco from Morocco, rose above the rest in their understanding of the socioeconomic functions, structural integrity, and minimalist aesthetics of modern architecture. Sayyid Kuraym also founded *al-'Imara* (Architecture) in 1939 as the first Arabic-language journal of architecture, which, during its twenty years of publication, advocated a straightforward adoption of modernism.

In the 1950s and 1960s, a hopeful and progressive Pan-Arabism was exuberantly spreading all over the Arab World. Numerous modernist architects subscribed to its ideals and searched for ways to incorporate "Arabic" historical elements in their essentially modernist compositions both as means to engage their local context and to assert a creative continuity with the past. Mohamed Makiya and Rifat Chadirji, Iraqi architects who studied in England, are unquestionably the master contextual modernists. Their elegant, rational, streamlined, yet symbolically rich and historically evocative architecture mediates between the universal principles of modern architecture and the rich heritage of their Arab nation. The Egyptian Salah Zeitoun, a Taliesin Fellow greatly influenced by Frank Lloyd Wright, the Moroccan 'Abdelrahim Sijelmassi, trained in France, the Syrian Burhan Tayyara, who studied in the United States, and the Jordanian Ja'far Tukan, who studied at the American University of Beirut, can be cited as younger Arab architects, steeped in the tenets of modern architecture, who subtly introduced spatial or decorative local and historical elements in their designs.

By the 1970s, cities like Cairo, Damascus, Baghdad, and Algiers had acquired large, standardized "cookie cutter" buildings to house the expanding branches of the state and their associated bureaucracies. Some regimes, especially in Iraq, Algeria, Morocco, and Saudi Arabia, often commissioned international firms to create their modern image, a routine that limited local practices to small projects and contributed negatively to the growth of Arab architecture. Others, especially Nasserite Egypt, but also Syria, Jordan, Kuwait, and Lebanon, patronized foreign as well as Arab firms, which invigorated the profession in these countries.

Simultaneously, and resolutely in opposition to international modernism, two visionary Egyptian architects, Hassan Fathy and Ramses Wissa Wasef, advanced vernacular architecture as the most authentic representation of the people's architecture. Their principal projects, New Gourna village (1948–61) by the former and Harraniyya village (1957–74) by the latter, cast the vernacular through a mixture of objective social and environmental experiments and lyrical interpretations of an unlikely mix of traditional Mamluk Cairene and southern Egyptian Nubian styles that they admired. Their projects received ample praise in international architectural circles as ingenious and successful expressions of indigenously developed architecture with clear cultural contours, environmental responsiveness, and place rootedness. In fact, Fathy later became the most famous Arab architect in modern times, especially after the publication of his *Architecture for the Poor* by Chicago University Press in 1973. He also was the first Arab architect practicing in the Arab World to build in the United States with his Dar al-Islam Community Center, Abiquiu, New Mexico (1981–86). His disciples continued to use the formal language he had devised but did not build on its social, environmental, and economic underpinnings. Instead they brandished it as a kind of native response to both the blandness of modernism and the Eurocentrism of the nascent postmodernism and, in some cases, exported it as an expressive regional, that is, Arabo-Islamic, style.

The next significant historical shift, which came after the catastrophic defeat of the so-called progressive regimes in the 1967 war with Israel and evolved intermittently during the 1980s and 1990s, was the formation of an ideology that saw "Islam" as identity. This badly understood and still-evolving process has been promoted by at least two economically, historically, and politically dissimilar, though ultimately mutually reinforcing, phenomena. First was the re-emergence of Islamic political movements in most Arab countries after an apparent dormancy of some thirty years during which Pan-Arabism dominated the political scene. Coming on the heels of the victorious Iranian Islamic Revolution of 1979, and perceived as a response to the failures of the nation-states to face up to foreign interference, economic corruption, and moral decadence, the fundamentalist movements sought a return to more authentic political and social foundations to govern the Islamic community. Yet, despite relentless and violent attacks on what they saw as the depravity of all Western cultural imports, the fundamentalist movements showed surprisingly little interest in the conceptual contours of visual culture, including architecture.

By contrast, the second group to wield a vision of Islam as a framer of identity, the ruling elite of the many recently formed states of the Gulf region (Saudi Arabia, Kuwait, Qatar, Bahrain, UAE, and Oman), has had a tremendous impact on the trajectory of architecture in the Arab World in recent decades. Having lain on the edge of the desert outside the centers of Arabic culture for so long, and, with the exception of Saudi Arabia and Oman, not having achieved independence until the 1960s and even 1970s, these countries had no role in the early developments of modern Arab architecture. But things changed first in the wake of oil discovery in the 1940s and then, more spectacularly, after the 1970s oil price surge: the poor countries suddenly became super rich. With the massive cash flow and its concomitant socioeconomic empowerment came the desire to develop fast and big. Cities had to be expanded and modernized and up-to-date infrastructure had to be installed in record time to serve the growing population of natives and foreign workers, and to satisfy their sociocultural needs and newly acquired expensive tastes (Beirut, which had previously fulfilled this need, was mired in a nasty civil war between 1975 and the early 1990s). The wealth of the Gulf patrons, their deeply religious and conservative outlook, and their fervent quest for political and cultural identity combined to create a demand for a contemporary, financially beneficial, yet visually recognizable, Islamic architecture. Sincerely at times, but opportunistically at many others, scores of architects, mostly Westerners but also a few Arabs, responded by incorporating in their otherwise state-of-the-art designs various historical elements dubbed "Arabic" or "Islamic," which they often used as basic diagrams for their plans or splashed on the surfaces as ornament.

The 1980s thus became the decade of readily identifiable Islamicized postmodern architecture everywhere in the Arab World. There were the post-traditionalists who, like Hasan Fathy before them, looked for inspiration in the vernacular architecture of the region. The Egyptian Kamal al-Kafrawi, for instance, deployed the *badgir*, or windcatcher, both as a visual referent and an environmental device in his inspired University of Qatar complex (1985). Similarly, in the Great Mosque of Riyadh (1984–92), the Palestinian-Jordanian Rasem Badran used a rationalizing approach to reference the local Najdi architecture. There were also the free and often arbitrary melanges of diverse historical forms and patterns from a wide range of Islamic styles. This is seen for instance in the high-quality sculptural work of the Egyptian 'Abd al-Wahid al-Wakil, particularly in the series of mosques he built in Jeddah in Saudi Arabia in the late 1980s. A bit more colorful is the work of the Iraqi Basil al-Bayati, who dips into the exuberance of postmodernism to produce loud formalist compositions, such as his al-Nakheel Mosque in Riyadh (1985) and his castle-like Scotland Great Mosque in Edinburgh (1988–98). This trend culminated with grand structures by large international firms, which garnered the lion's share of all new projects in the

Figure 11.6 Jørn Utzon, Kuwait National Assembly Complex, Kuwait, 1972–82.

Gulf. They reinterpreted visual symbols and historical motifs and used them in otherwise ultra-sleek designs, such as the gigantic Hajj Terminal in Jeddah by SOM[1] (1982), inspired by the Bedouin tent, or the Ministry of Foreign Affairs in Riyadh by Henning Larsen (1982–84), which employs both the notions of a covered *suq* (bazaar) and courtyard, or the Kuwait National Assembly Complex by Jørn Utzon (1983), which evokes the sail of the traditional *dhow* (see Figure 11.6).

Despite short halts caused mostly by the tragic series of adventures that the regime in Iraq plunged into between 1980 and the early 2000s and the savage destruction of that country since its invasion in 2003, development in the Arabian Gulf continued apace. It, in fact, grew exponentially under the dual influence of an unstoppable global late-Capitalism looking for new, underexploited, and profitable outlets after its decisive victory against the Socialist camp in 1989 and the reorientation of the accumulated oil wealth to seek easy and safe investments at home. Rising suspicion of Arab and Muslim investors in the West and new restrictive American and European security measures after the attacks of 9/11 brought back further fresh assets to the region. The combined capital found its ideal conduit in real estate development of gargantuan business parks and malls, luxury housing and hotels, and touristic and entertainment complexes. Architecture at once assumed the role of branding instrument and spectacular wrapping for these new gigantic business enterprises.

Dubai, with its entrepreneurial spirit, unrestrained economic laissez-faire, and aggressive pursuit of investments, was the first to ride the new tide and eventually to guide it. The entire city, its surrounding desert, and even its coastal water became the world's most phenomenal visual laboratory where the only check on architectural and urban flights of fancy seems to be the ability of the designers to push the limits of size, height, eccentricity, and desire. In this milieu, the fantastic architecture of what Mike Davis has called the "utopian capitalist city" seems to have emerged as a tacit design objective shared by the designers and the patrons to lure in more investors. Thoughtful regionalism, traditionalism, revivalism, and even postmodernism were hastily given up in favor of a new architecture that loudly, and often too loudly, bespoke the ambition to endow a global pursuit of luxury aimed at the wealthy with sanitized but recognizable local flavors. This is most stunningly represented by the self-styled most luxurious, tallest, and only "seven-star" hotel in the world, the Burj al-'Arab Hotel, which evokes the form of the traditional *dhow* sailing ships of the region, designed by Tom Wright of W. S. Atkins in 1999. It extravagantly exploits all the clichés of the fabulous Orient in the service of the super-wealthy jetsetters.

The trend spread to many other cities in the Gulf, especially Doha, Abu Dhabi, Manama, Riyadh, and recently Kuwait, and beyond into the major cities of neighboring Arab countries, such as Cairo, Beirut, Aleppo, Amman, and Rabat, that cannot sustain this kind of financial, urban, or social pressure. However, the most alarming recent change in these older cities is not the proliferation of Dubai-style exclusive "new cities" around them or in their commercial cores, such as the Solidere rebuilding of war-torn downtown Beirut (see Figure 11.7) or the 'Abdali development in the heart of Amman. Nor is it the urban decay of their historic centers under the weight of severe population explosion and heavy rural emigration, accompanied by an assortment of governmental neglect and corruption, greedy real estate markets, and chaotic zoning and overbuilding. It is rather the fading away of their civic quality that was slowly acquired over the last two centuries and its replacement by a double-headed market-driven commodification

Figure 11.7 Solidere, Suq Area, Beirut, 1994–2009.

process, which is splitting the city into two extremes. On one end, the old, poor quarters are robbed of the last vestiges of urban life and turned into contiguous village-like neighborhoods living by their own informal codes. On the other end, the new rich suburbs acquire a consumerist, neo-liberal, and globalized identity that has no local feel or connection.

Architects are responding differently to this state of affairs. The majority is, of course, getting by on small projects and ignoring the big picture. But a few are taking sides. Some are turning to conservation as a means to revitalize the old urban centers. Projects such as the rehabilitation of Old Aleppo, Old Sanaʿa, Shibam in Yemen, Old Jerusalem, Kairawan in Tunisia, and the Darb al-Ahmar in Cairo, funded by various international agencies, are notable efforts in this direction. Other architects, mostly graduates of American schools, such as Bernard Khoury and Nabil Gholam from Lebanon, Sinan Hassan from Syria, Sahel Al-Hiyari, and Ammar Khammash from Jordan, and many more, are focusing on improving and even revolutionizing the quality of design without necessarily engaging the larger socioeconomic context. Some, such as Tarek Naga and Hani Rashid from Egypt, but especially Zaha Hadid from Iraq, have managed to break into the global stage as iconic international architects. It remains to be seen, however, whether architecture in the Arab world can keep on functioning within these dichotomous conditions or whether it should challenge them by assuming an environmentally and socially proactive role.

Notes

1 Skidmore, Owings & Merrill LLP.

12

Humor

A man is sent to prison and finds that the inmates have told the jokes they know so many times that they have ended up assigning them numbers. That way, they can simply use the numbers as references, saving the time and effort of telling them all over again. "Eighteen!" one yells out from his cell and the others laugh. "Twenty-seven!" – the others laugh. But then one yells, "Eighty-seven!" The other inmates break into fits of uproarious laughter; it is quite some time before they quieten down. The new inmate asks his neighbor why they laughed so much the last time and he replies, "'Cause that was a new one!"

This anecdote is not unique to Egypt, but certainly fits well within the parameters of Egyptian and Arab humor in general. Jokes are a common and ordinary part of social interaction, like etiquette and formulas of politeness. They are an essential and ubiquitous part of popular culture in the Arab World, as important as soccer, movies, and tea. Their frequency varies, nevertheless, across cultures within the Arab World, and even within one nation. Egyptians, for example, are thought to joke incessantly, relatively more than is customary in some other Arab societies. They often joke with complete strangers as a way to test whether they are generally good-natured, whereas in the north of Morocco, in contrast, it is seen as inappropriate to joke with strangers (southern Moroccans, however, are more like Egyptians when it comes to joking). In Egypt, the definition of a "great guy" is someone who can come up with a joke, humorous quip, or anecdote in response to any remark or situation, whether sanguine, dire, or even disastrous. Such a person is termed *ibn nukta* (literally, "son of a joke") and is in many ways viewed as the quintessential Egyptian. Jokes are told in the midst of extreme poverty, hardship, and difficult circumstances – in fact, many Egyptians insist that this is the only way they can muddle through an otherwise barely tolerable existence. Whatever the reason for their proverbial appreciation for humor, Egyptians export jokes throughout the Arab World and beyond, together with music, films, and much-too-predictable soap operas.

Categories of jokes

Jokes in the Arab World, as elsewhere, often fall into familiar large categories, including political jokes, jokes about current events, jokes about various ethnic or regional groups and minorities, jokes about sex, and so on. Some belong to genres that are also found in Europe and the United States, *mutatis mutandis*, while others do not. The particular constellation of salient joke genres varies a great deal from country to country within the Arab World. Jokes about "stupid people," for example, are found in nearly all nations around the globe, including the Arab nations. The French tell their "stupid" jokes about Belgians, the Spanish about the inhabitants of the southern town of Lepe, the Italians about the *carabinieri* (their own police), Syrians tell "stupid" jokes about the inhabitants of the town of Homs (halfway between Damascus and Aleppo), Egyptians about Saʿidis, Moroccans about peasants called ʿArubis, Algerians about the inhabitants of Mascara (a country town 50 miles southeast of Oran in the west of the country), Tunisians about Libyans, Lebanese about Syrians, Palestinians about the natives of al-Khalil (Hebron), Iraqis about Kurds, and so on. Another very widespread type of jokes is about "stingy people." Just as the English tell stingy jokes about the Scots and the Italians about the inhabitants of Genoa, the Egyptians tell stingy jokes about the inhabitants of Dumyat, the Moroccans about the Soussis (Berbers from the southern region of the country), Iraqis about the inhabitants of Mosul, and so on. But in genres that are shared across cultural divides, some distinct features often exist, so that not all Egyptian Saʿidi jokes can be "translated" into Iraqi jokes about Kurds, because they simply do not fit. Among the most widespread categories of jokes in the Arab World are political jokes, identity jokes (including jokes about misers, numbskulls, and various ethnicities), and dialect jokes that play on both regional and social distinctions in language use.

Political jokes

Politics is an extremely fertile area for jokes in the Arab World, in part as a function of the frustration of Arab citizens who feel that they have little or no say in national or international affairs. An Iraqi friend remarked that bathroom graffiti are very instructive about the differences between cultures and the nature of people's frustrations. In American bathrooms, he found that nearly all graffiti were about sex; in Iraq they were all about politics.

The rulers of the various Arab countries are the butts of constant jokes and this includes presidents who are often presidents for life. Other high officials appear with some frequency, depending on the political scandals of the day, but ministers of the interior appear very regularly, as they are closely associated with the power, oppression, corruption, and foibles of the current regime. Political jokes act as a counterbalance of sorts to the rather heavy-handed propaganda regularly produced by the government-controlled media. Many jokes about international politics and even national politics feature current foreign heads of state, especially the President of the United States, the British Prime Minister, and the President of France, usually more as representatives of those nations' power or culture than as representatives of their particular personalities, just as Moses and Jesus often represent Jews and Christians in American jokes ("Remember, Jesus saves, but Moses invests!").

In Egypt, jokes about the former president, Hosni Mubarak, emphasized his ineffectual nature and the corruption of the government, including particularly him, his cronies, and his eldest son, ʿAlaʾ. The story is told of three people arriving at Cairo airport without their passports. The first is Umm Kulthum, the most famous Egyptian singer of all time. When she arrives at passport control, they ask for her papers. She explains that she has lost her passport but that she is Umm Kulthum, the famous singer. "Surely you recognize me?" They say, "Well, prove it. What can you do?" So Umm Kulthum sings *Inta ʿUmrī* (You are my life), one of her best-known songs. They say, "OK, you can go through." Next, the famous actor ʿAdil Imam comes and he, too, has lost his passport. "But surely you recognize me?," he says. "I'm ʿAdil Imam, the famous actor." They say, "Well, prove it. What can you do?" ʿAdil Imam then performs some of his comedy sketches and they, now convinced that he is in fact who he purports to be, let him through. Next comes Hosni Mubarak. "Surely you recognize me?" he says. "I'm the president of the Arab Republic of Egypt."

They say, "Well, prove it. What can you do?" He thinks for a while and then admits, "But I can't do anything." Convinced, they let him through.

In another joke, Hosni Mubarak returns from a trip abroad and has missed his wife tremendously. Rather than driving straight home with her in the limousine, he takes her out to the Pyramids at the edge of the desert to park. Unfortunately, the vice squad catches them making out in the car and hauls them off to the police station, where they are separated for questioning. After questioning them, the police officer talks to Mubarak: "I'm sorry, Mr. President, but we must enforce the law equally for everyone. No one is above the law." Mubarak says that he understands but wants to know what they are going to do with them. The officer says, "You're free to go, but you have to pay a fine of ten pounds and your wife has to pay a fine of fifty pounds." Puzzled, Mubarak asks, "Why do I have to pay ten pounds and she has to pay fifty? That doesn't make sense." The officer replies, "But, Mr. President, it's only your first offense!" Mubarak is generally viewed as clueless, in general, and a cuckolded husband as well.

A typical joke of the international sort tells the story of a contest between the secret services of the United States, the Soviet Union, and Egypt. The contest involves locating a rabbit in a huge tract of the harshest desert imaginable. The Americans go first: the CIA finds the rabbit in six hours. The Soviets go next: the KGB finds the rabbit in eight hours. Then comes the turn of the Egyptian secret service. An entire day goes by, then a second day. No news. On the third day, they send a search party into the desert to find the Egyptian secret service team. When they find them, the Egyptians are beating a tied-up gazelle, yelling at it, "Say, 'I'm a rabbit!' Say, 'I'm a rabbit!'"

Many jokes focus on corruption in the government and political repression in general rather than on a specific political figure: A Jordanian minister had to spend a night in a hotel at the Dead Sea. His personal secretary sent a telegram to the hotel manager, asking them to prepare a nice room, a good meal, etc., etc., etc., for His Excellency. As soon as the minister arrived at the hotel, the manager took him to a room where there were three lovely girls waiting for him. The minister asked who they were, and the hotel manager said: "They're etc., etc., and etc.!"

A Libyan minister visits an Italian colleague and sees that his home is very luxurious. He asks him how he can afford such a high standard of living. "Use your head!" the Italian replied. Then he showed him the drawings for a bridge. He opened the window and there was a bridge, but it differed slightly from the drawings. "The difference between the draw-ings and the bridge is here," he comments, patting his pockets. Some time later, the Italian returns the visit and notices that his Libyan colleague is now even better off than he is. "How did you manage to get so rich?" he asks him. The Libyan shows him the drawings of a bridge, then opens the window. "But I can't see anything!" exclaims the Italian. "Exactly!" cries his colleague. "I used my head better than you did!"

'Ala' Mubarak, Hosni Mubarak's eldest son, was widely considered to be an extremely corrupt businessman who took advantage of his influence in the government to demand bribes and payments from for-eign and local businessmen. He was often called "Thirty-Percent-'Ala'" because of his alleged practice of demanding a 30 percent stake in any for-eign company wanting to do business in Egypt in return for signing off on their business license. In one joke, a tourist goes to a cafe in Cairo and sees three portraits on the wall, showing the presidents of the Republic, Gamal 'Abd al-Nasir (i.e., Nasser), Anwar al-Sadat, and Hosni Mubarak. He asks who the first one is. The cafe owner explains, "That is *al-za'īm al-khālid* (the Eternal Leader), Gamal 'Abd al-Nasir." "Who is the second one?" "That is *al-ra'īs al-mu'min* (the Pious President), Anwar al-Sadat." "Who is the third one?," asks the man. The cafe owner replies, "That's the father of our partner in the cafe."

Identity jokes

One of the main functions of jokes, beyond simple amusement, is to define the identity of a particular group, often the "national" character, and this is most often done by contrast. Jokes define the characteristics of "real" or "authentic" Lebanese, Iraqis, Algerians, Egyptians, and so on by distinguishing them from other groups, either from neighboring coun-tries – such as Syrians for the Lebanese or Libyans for the Tunisians – or marginal groups from inside the national borders – such as Sa'idis for Egyptians and Homsis for Syrians. These types of jokes generally attrib-ute negative traits to the group in question and, in doing so, imply that the joke tellers themselves or their group of "ordinary" people are free of these negative qualities. As mentioned above, many Arab countries have important genres of jokes about "stupid people" – usually portrayed as country bumpkins – and "stingy people," and they all serve to stress that the true representatives of the national character are urban, modern, and sophisticated, as well as generous and hospitable.

Misers and stingy people

Jokes and stories about misers belong to a very old tradition in Arabic: one of the most famous works in the history of Arabic humor is *The Book of Misers* by ʿAmr ibn Bahr al-Jahiz (d. 868), which provides story after story about champion penny-pinchers, skinflints, freeloaders, and cheapskates. Stinginess is all the worse in Arab culture because generosity is considered the noble trait par excellence, especially as demonstrated through hospitality to guests. In fact, the adjective *karīm* (generous) in Arabic (or *jawād*, and other synonyms) comes to be nearly synonymous with "noble." In modern Arab humor, the butts of miser jokes are generally regional groups within the national borders.

In Morocco, the Soussis (Berbers from the south of the country) are often portrayed as penny-pinchers by other groups. Many Soussis have moved to the major cities of northern Morocco in search of economic opportunity and many own small grocery stores, which figure prominently in the jokes about them. It is told that a Soussi has a spot on the left side of his forehead. Why? Because when he prays, his cash box is on his right. (It is common for Muslim men to develop a spot or callus on middle of the forehead from repeatedly touching the forehead to the ground in prostration while praying. This mark is called a *dīnār* [gold coin] in Morocco and a *zibība* [raisin] in Egypt. Even while he is prostrating in prayer, the Soussi can't let his eyes wander from his cash box.)

In another story, two brothers from Sous who live in the city (Casablanca or Rabat) are getting angry with their father. Whenever they phone him, the first thing he asks is, "How many hours did you work today?" No matter how long they work, he says, "That's not enough." They discuss the matter and decide that the next time he asks this question, they will say that they worked twenty-four hours that day. One calls and his father asks, "How many hours did you work today?" The son answers, "Twenty-four hours." Then the father says, "Sell the door (*bī ʿr-rīdu*)." In other words, if they are working twenty-four hours a day, they will never close, so they won't need the rolling steel door used to lock up the shop (from the French *rideau*, "curtain").

Numbskull jokes

Jokes about "stupid people" are even more common than jokes about misers and in several Arab nations make up the largest of joke genres. The Syrians tell "stupid" jokes about the inhabitants of Homs, who have stores that are open "only seven days a week" and sell "refrigerated ice":

One Homsi says to the other, "I was born in Lebanon." The other asks, "Oh really, what part?" The first replies, "All of me, you fool!"

How do you make a Homsi laugh on Saturday? – Tell him a joke on Wednesday.

Why did eighteen Homsis go to the cinema? Because "under-eighteen" was not allowed.

Why can't Homsis make ice cubes? They keep forgetting the recipe.

Similar jokes from Morocco feature ʿArubis, peasants, especially those from the area surrounding Casablanca:

An ʿArubi went to the cinema and found the auditorium full – by the time he finished greeting all of them and shaking their hands, the movie was over.

An ʿArubi took the bus and left his sandals by the door when he got on.

Similar jokes about Kurds come from Iraq:

A Kurd saw an ad for Marlboro. The ad worked so well on him that he went out and bought a horse.

A Kurd found a buried treasure and exclaimed, "Now if I only had the map!"

The largest joke category in Egypt and the largest genre of jokes about "stupid peasants" in the Arab World is that of the Saʿidi joke. The Saʿid, literally "high plain," refers to Upper Egypt (that is, southern Egypt). Since Pharaonic times there has been a cultural divide between southern and northern Egypt. The Old Kingdom was formed through the unification of the two kingdoms. Later, there were two main dialects of the Coptic language: southern, called Saiditic, and northern, called Bohairitic. Even today there is a clear split between Saʿidi Arabic dialects in the south and the dialects of the Nile Delta in the north, which are, on the whole, closer to the urban dialects. Political power is concentrated in the north and the south gets a relatively small portion of investment and state funds. The Saʿid is also hotter, harsher, and poorer than the rest of the country. For these and other reasons, the Saʿidis get singled out as representative of rural backwardness by middle-class, urban Egyptians, particularly in Cairo.

Many Saʿidi jokes harp on the idea that Saʿidis are physically different from "ordinary" Egyptians, the former being bigger, harder, stronger, and endowed with a sort of brute animal force:

> A Saʿidi entered the mosque to pray, and when he came out he found a tow-truck carting off his shoes.
> A Saʿidi was throwing his baby son up in the air and knocked down two airplanes.
> A Saʿidi scratched his head and put a hole in his skull.
> A Saʿidi missed the train – he ran to catch it and passed it.

Other Saʿidi jokes are simple stupid jokes. For the following jokes, it helps to know that Haridi is a typical Saʿidi name, much like Billy-Bob or Bubba for rednecks in the United States.

> Someone asked a Saʿidi, "What's your name?" He answered, "Is my brain an account book?"
> A Saʿidi was walking down the street going "Akh! Akh!" and hitting himself on the forehead. A friend met him and asked, "Haridi, what's wrong?" He yelled, "That's it! Haridi!"

The Saʿidis' lack of understanding often occurs in particular contexts: those of the modern, urban environment. The Saʿidi cannot function in train stations, doctors' offices, department stores, and so on, because his experience is limited to the countryside and he lacks the mental agility required to adjust to new situations. A typical stupid joke is told of a Saʿidi here, but is heard in many other cultures:

> A Saʿidi goes into a store and asks, "How much is this refrigerator?" The salesman answers, "We don't sell to Saʿidis." The Saʿidi is offended by this blatant discrimination and decides to outwit the salesman. So he comes back disguised as a cowboy and asks, "How much is this refrigerator?" The salesman's answer is the same: "We don't sell to Saʿidis." Even more upset, the Saʿidi comes back in a series of disguises – a policeman, a soccer player, and so on, but the result is always the same. Finally, fed up with these failed efforts, the Saʿidi asks, "How did you know I'm a Saʿidi?" The salesman says, "That's not a refrigerator. It's a stove."
> A Saʿidi got sick and went to the doctor. The doctor gave him medicine and sent him home. The Saʿidi came back after a few days and his condition was much worse. "What happened? Didn't you take the medicine I gave you?" The Saʿidi explains, "I couldn't get the spoon in the bottle!"

Language and dialect jokes

An important sub-class of jokes focuses squarely on language and the specific linguistic features that set the dialect of the marginal group apart from the prestige dialect of the nation, in the Egyptian case Cairene dialect. Some Saʿidi jokes turn on the fact that some Saʿidis (certainly not all; a small percentage in fact) pronounce the letter which in Cairo is pronounced *g* as *d*:

They asked a Saʿidi, "Are you from the town where they pronounce *g* as *d*?" He said, "No, from the one next to it." He pronounces "next to it" as *DANbaha*, which in the north is pronounced *gamBAha*, thereby proving that he is in fact Saʿidi, because he said it with *d* for *g* and with the emphasis on the first instead of the second syllable.

A similar Iraqi joke tells that a Kurd got a fake passport in order to leave the country and go to Europe. The name on the passport was *Ḥasanēn*, a name which is a dual noun referring to "the two Hasans" (i.e., Hasan and Husayn, the grandsons of the Prophet). When they stopped him at the border and asked him his name, he said *"ithnēn Ḥasan"* ("two Hasans"). The Kurdish language, in contrast to Arabic, does not have the dual form, so he is inept at using it.

Foreign languages, especially English and French, often figure in language joke genres because, as the Homsi or Saʿidi is meant to represent country bumpkin, one of the main signs of his lack of sophistication is his lack of familiarity with European languages, or at least the naive use of that language. It is told that a pretty Lebanese girl was stopped by a Syrian soldier at a checkpoint. He called her *madame* and she said that, no, she was *mademoiselle*. Standing erect with pride, he announced that he, too, was *mademoiselle*. In this joke, the Syrian soldier knows that *mademoiselle* means that she is unmarried and he wants to tell her that he is also single. He fails to realize, however, that the term *mademoiselle* only applies to females. Other jokes of this type include the following:

A Syrian man goes to a Lebanese restaurant in Beirut. He asks the waiter for the location of the restrooms. The waiter points toward the back of the restaurant. The Syrian goes there and sees two doors. He stands there looking at the first door and then at the second door. He stays there looking at these doors back and forth for ten minutes, while people go in and out. Finally the waiter comes and asks the Syrian, "Is there a problem, sir?" "Well, one of the doors is for people from Damascus (Dames) and the other is for people from Homs (Hommes). I am from Aleppo, so I don't know where to go!"

An Egyptian is being inducted to the army. The sergeant shouts to all the young men, "Those who didn't finish high school go in this line, those who have a high school diploma in this second line, and those who have a Baccalaureus (B.A. degree) go in this third line." One asks, "If you have a Magister (M.A. degree), where do you go?" The sergeant responds, "Magister or Bilharzia [a common disease in Egypt], it doesn't matter. Everything will come out in the urine analysis."

At the opposite end of the social spectrum is the Egyptian genre of *fafi* jokes that also deploy special types of language for their humor. *Fafi* means "sissy" or "effete": the protagonists of these jokes are young, effeminate men who belong to the upper class and are overly influenced by European culture.

A *fafi* goes to the grocer and asks, "Do you have zucchini-flavored ice cream?" He says, "No." The next day the *fafi* comes back and asks, "Do you have zucchini-flavored ice cream?" "I told you, no." He keeps coming back, asking the same question. Finally, the grocer has had it. The next time the *fafi* shows up and asks for zucchini-flavored ice cream, he says, "Yes, we do," just to see what happens next. The *fafi* says, "Yuck!"

A *fafi* is walking along the Nile with his mother and sees a guy selling *tirmis* (small yellow beans the size and shape of lima beans, sold as a common snack). He says, "Eew! [Ar. *yāy*] Mommy, what are those yellow buttons?" The Arabic interjection *yāy* is marked as feminine speech, something like the "Eew!" used by American teenage girls, and "Mommy" (*māmi*) is also marked as upper class and effeminate. More common ways of addressing one's mother are *māma* or *ya-mma*.

Where do jokes come from?

Everyone has probably wondered at one time or another where jokes come from. As a folk genre, jokes do not have recognized authors. If one were to follow a joke back to its origin, where would one end up? Egyptians and many other Arabs identify the primordial joke factory with the hashish-smoking gathering. According to popular theory, there is something special about the effect of hashish – it somehow loosens the synapses in the brain, allowing linguistic connections to be made which defy ordinary logic, turning the mild-mannered, ordinary Egyptian into a philosopher king of humor. He rises above the plane of mundane thought and becomes able serenely to observe and comment on the foibles of society and humanity. Individual sparks of humorous genius are compounded by the social nature of the gathering. This is not to say that Egyptians across the board smoke hashish. Nevertheless, the mental agility or flexibility that is associated with hashish consumption is highly valued in Egyptian society. The association between cannabis and humor is so strong that someone who laughs uncontrollably, or an extremely funny person who causes the audience to double over in fits of laughter, is termed *ḥashshāsh*, "a veteran hashish smoker." The ability to play with and to manipulate language and thereby the perceptions of the audience is equated with Egyptians' particular forte, their specific brand of intelligence, termed variously *fatāka*, *fakāka*, *ḥadāʾa*, and so on, which we may render as "cleverness" or "ingenuity." Its opposite, mental rigidity and a consequentially rigid view of language, is associated with naivety, gullibility, and stupidity.

Even though these jokes poke fun at hashish smokers, the protagonists demonstrate the mental and linguistic flexibility that is so prized. Therefore, they are seen, at least partially, in a positive light.

Two hashish smokers are going home very late one night. One says to the other, "Is my left eye, this one here, very red?" "Yes, very red," the other one answers. The first asks, "Does it hurt?"

One hashish smoker asks another, "Is today Tuesday or Wednesday?" The other one answers, "Monday." The first one asks, "At the same time?" (This is based on a pun: *il-itnēn*, which means *yom il-itnēn*, "Monday," also means "both.") This joke works in a manner opposite to that of Saʿidi jokes. Whereas the Saʿidi generally is stuck interpreting a word in one rigid sense, the concrete or mundane meaning, failing to understand the second or figurative meaning, the hashish smoker readily jumps to the second or figurative meaning even when it is not intended, creating an unexpected connection or interpretation.

The following are some similar hashish smoker jokes from Iraq:

> A hashish smoker saw his sister with a man. He said, "Today with a man; who knows? Tomorrow she might start smoking!"
> Two hashish smokers were playing chess. A pawn died, so they held a funeral.
> A hashish smoker sneezed and his friend coughed. He asked him, "Why are you changing the subject?"

Wordplay and double-entendre

Much humor in Arabic depends on wordplay: puns, double-entendre, rhyme, and the like. This sort of humor is seen frequently in retorts and rhyming extensions, some of which are used so frequently as to become automatic. In Egypt, the statement *insa* (Forget [it]) is often followed by the extension *wi-khud il-binsa* (and take the plyers). There is no real, logical connection between the two phrases; the latter is merely a rhyming extension of the first, the oddity of which makes it funny.[1] A common retort occurs following statements ending in feminine adjectives or nouns that are at the same time common female names. For example, the statement *di sitt laṭīfa* (she's a nice lady) provokes the retort *mish Laṭīfa tgawwizit* (Didn't Latifa get married?). The adjective *laṭīfa* in the first statement becomes *Laṭīfa*, the girl's name, in the second. The masculine version of this type of retort is as follows: *di kānit ayyām ʿizz* (those were days of glory [i.e., the good old days]) provokes the response *mish ʿizz māt* (Didn't ʿIzz die?), where the noun *ʿizz* (glory) becomes the male given name. Verbal ingenuity, inventiveness, and variety are prized. While many retorts and other jokes are standard or automatic, the best ones are generally recognized as spontaneous and unique. The result is a strong incentive to produce constant variations on a theme. For example, a smooth talker is called in Egyptian dialect *bayyāʿ kalām*, "an (inveterate) seller of speech." If the rhetorical effect of this clever epithet is considered to have worn off, then one may substitute *fakahāni kalām*, "a fruit seller of speech." This adds to the meaning in some fashion because fruit sellers have many different types of fruit to sell, representing the different types of speech the smooth operator is adept at using. In addition, fruit sellers are notorious for varying their prices a great deal according to the customers buying from them. An even more novel epithet for the smooth talker is *mikanīki ḥanak*, which one might translate as a "jaw mechanic."

In some cases, a phrase is changed in an unexpected way to render it amusing. As a flattering expression of welcome, the following is often heard: *ḥa-nidbaḥ-lak kharūf*, "We will slaughter a sheep for you!" or *ḥa-nidbaḥ-lak dakar baṭṭ*, "We will slaughter a male duck for you!" The comic version is *ḥa-nidbaḥ-lak dakar ʿads*, "We will slaughter a male lentil for you," emphasizing either the lack of means to do more or the commonplace nature of the visit. Another example takes the common expression for "good night," *tiṣbaḥ ʿala khēr* (literally, "may you wake up in goodness," i.e., well, in good health), and renders it with a twist: *tiṣbaḥ ʿala khashaba*, "may you wake up on a plank," i.e., dead as a doornail.

A related type of statement is one in which, after a brief pause, something extra is added that changes the meaning of the underlying statement completely, as in:

Allāh yinawwar bētak ... bi-ḥarī'a, "May God light up your house ... with a fire".

Inti amar ... amar bi-s-satr, "You are a moon (i.e., very beautiful) ... God commanded that it be covered up" (meaning something frightful, ill-omened, dreadful, embarrassing, or scandalous).

An example from Moroccan Arabic is based on the common phrase *thella f-rāsek*, which means "take care of yourself," but may be changed by extension to *thella f-rāsek ... bi-shampwan* ("take care of your head ... with shampoo"), for *rāsek,* literally "your head," also means "yourself."

A series of vulgar, juvenile expressions provide automatic retorts to the cardinal numbers, all using the verb *nāk, yinīk* (to f**k). Whenever someone says *arbaʿa* (four), as you would when answering the question, "What time is it?" – "Four," for example, the retorter chimes in *nakūk ʿala arbaʿa* ("They f**ked you on all fours!"). The retort to "ten" (*ʿashara*) is *nakūk fi n-nashra* ("They f**ked you on the evening news!").

Some jokes in Arabic, while adopting similar strategies of punning and distortion, are based on the specific characteristics of the writing system. In the Arabic alphabet certain letters share a basic shape with other letters but are distinguished by additional dots written above or below the letter. For example, "s" and "sh" have the same exact shape, but "s" has no dots while "sh" has three dots arranged in a triangle over the letter. There are many jokes that play on this fact, making what are actually visual – as opposed to aural – puns. One joke of this type involves a poor man whom a rich, older woman marries because she is sexually attracted to him. With his new wealth, he builds an apartment building, putting a prominent plaque on it with the Qur'anic phrase, *hādhā min faḍli rabbī* (This is from the bounty of my Lord), as people often do in order to ward off the evil eye. An acquaintance of his, who knew him before his good fortune, changed the sign by adding a single dot above the "r," so that the plaque now read, *hādhā min faḍli zibbī*, "This is from the bounty of my penis."

Religious jokes

These last jokes bring up the fact that many jokes in the Arab World express irreverence toward religion, something that may come as a surprise to a Western audience. A boy whose father had hired a religious scholar to teach him the Qur'an once tried to stump his teacher. "O Shaykh, you say that the Qur'an contains all knowledge, right?" The teacher replied, "Yes." "Then where in the Qur'an does Coca-Cola appear?," asked the boy. The teacher thought a moment and then replied, "In the verse *a-mā tarakūka qā'iman.*" This is a pun. In the original sense, the verse means, "Did they not leave you standing?" Dividing up the words differently, however, gives a different sense, as the same phrase sounds like *a-mā tarā Kūkā qā'iman* ("Do you not see Coca standing there?").

An Egyptian answer to the exclamation *Allāhu akbar* ("God is greater/bigger") is the retort *ṭīzak bitikbar,* "Your ass is getting bigger." Another is the expansion of the phrase *Allāhu akbar* to *Allāhu akbar ... mi-l-Hiltun* ("God is greater ... than the Hilton!"). (The Hilton hotel in downtown Cairo was long the largest building in Egypt, though this is no longer the case.) Most examples of irreverent Arab humor, and not just that involving religion, adopt a similar strategy of creating a surprising or incongruous mixture of high and low registers, of the sublime and the mundane.

It is nevertheless true that irreverent humor can get one in trouble, particularly when it has to do with religion or an Arab head of state. In December 2006, a weekly magazine in Morocco, *Nichane,* published an article with the title, "Jokes: How Moroccans Laugh about Religion, Sex, and Politics." The article included ten jokes, obviously derived from oral sources and culled from the thousands of jokes circulating at the time, apparently chosen to be representative of irreverent humor regarding three topics: Islamic religion in general, Islamists, and the rule of the former king, Hasan II (1961–1999). The article provoked a strong and immediate conservative backlash and all involved in the publication of the article were accused of blasphemy. In January 2007, the editor of the magazine and the author of the article were convicted of denigrating Islam, given three-year suspended sentences, and fined 80,000 dirhams (about $9,320). The journal was banned temporarily. The jokes, some of which appear below, were rendered mostly in standard written Arabic but retaining some colloquial vocabulary and features. (The first involves Abu Hurayra, who was a Companion of the Prophet and one of the most important transmitters of *hadith,* or reports of the Prophet's deeds and statements.)

Abu Hurayra died and stood before the angel responsible for the consequences of his deeds on earth. The angel looked at the computer and told him, "Hell." Abu Hurayra protested and demanded that the Prophet come. The Prophet came and looked in the computer and told him, "I can't do anything about it. For you, it's Hell." Abu Hurayra began to scream and blame the Prophet. Then God came down and Abu Hurayra started complaining to him, crying. Upon this, they patted him on the shoulders and told him, "Look over here! You're on Candid Camera!"

A guy asks, "Who was the prophet who spoke with the animals?" The second one answers, "The Prophet Mowgli, peace be upon him." (In the Qur'an and Islamic literature in general, King Solomon is a prophet endowed with the ability to understand the speech of animals, so that would be the expected answer. The joke pokes fun at the lack of religious cultural knowledge on the part of the youth and its replacement by knowledge of Disney cartoons.)

Three Islamists meet in the civil status office to register their newborn sons. The first one asks the second, "What did you name him?" "Abu Hamza. And you?" "Abu Ja'far. And you?" The third replied, "Abutagaz." (*Butagaz* is the name given to the canisters of butane gas that are used to fuel stoves in kitchens in Morocco and most other Arab countries. The prefix *A-* can be interpreted here as the Berber prefix for masculine nouns, which occurs at the beginning of many masculine Berber given names, such as *Amellal* [white, fair], *Amzin* [junior, the younger], *Azerwal* [blue-eyed], etc.)

An Islamist plays with his little girl, saying, "My little bomb-let ..."

An Islamist discovered that he was homosexual, so he now wears a veil.

After Idris al-Basri (the much-feared Minister of the Interior under King Hasan II) died and arrived in the Afterlife, he tried to bribe the angels in order to get into Paradise, but he couldn't because the angels all insisted that they were above such things and that "the corruption of the world stays in the world." When he was on his way to Hell, he saw King Hasan II in Paradise and exclaimed, "By God, bribery works even here!"

Irreverence and mixing of registers is particularly evident in parodies of popular songs, which can become almost as popular as the songs themselves. It is unclear who invents the song parodies and in the Arab World there does not seem to be the equivalent of the American comic Weird Al Yankovitch, who makes his living by inventing new lyrics for pop songs – "Eat It" for Michael Jackson's "Beat It," and so on. The anonymous Arab heroes of this genre often come up with exceedingly clever "versions" of popular songs, the humor of which turns, as one might expect, by inserting irreverent material into serious or emotionally charged love songs and the like. One favorite is based on an Umm Kulthum song that includes the line,

> *yāma kunt atmanna aʾablak biʾbtisāma*
> "Oh how long I've wished to meet you with a smile."

And the parody begins,

> *yāma kunt atmanna aʾablak biʾl-bijāma*
> "Oh how long I've wished to meet you in pajamas."

In the parody, which maintains the exact same rhyme and rhythm as the original, an emotionally charged lovers' tryst becomes a comic scene. One imagines the two chasing one another around the bedroom and having a pillow fight before jumping into bed.

Much Arab humor depends on *badīha*, improvisation or extemporaneous verbal cleverness. An Egyptian who was invited to a wedding of a bride with a large nose remarked that she was beautiful *raghm anfaha*, a pun meaning both "despite herself/whether she likes it or not," or "despite her nose."

The late Coptic patriarch, Pope Shenouda III (1971–2012), was asked at a public event to give advice to an older woman who had to travel to Germany with her family. She didn't know any German and was reluctant to go to a strange country where she wouldn't understand anyone. He responded, *ana ma-aʿrafshi ʾalmāni – wil-ḥikāya di miʾalmāni,* "I don't know German, and this situation upsets me" (lit., is causing me pain), where the words *almāni* (German) and *miʾal(l)māni* (causing me pain) match nearly exactly. (One can even interpret the prefix *mi-* here as the preposition *min/mi-,* meaning "from" German.) The crowd, even at this serious Christian religious gathering, exploded in laughter.

An Egyptian high school student told a pretty girl with a slender waist, *bamūt fi-wisṭik,* "I am dying for your waist." She answered *mūt fi-wisṭ ahlak,* literally "Die for the waist of your family," but also, "Die amidst your own family," using *wisṭ,* "waist," with the sense "in the middle of."

The term *ʾafya* means several things in Egyptian Arabic, all of them having to do with humor. In one sense it means joking around in general, particularly in the form of retorts. It is from this meaning that the phrase *bala ʾafya* (all joking aside/seriously) derives. In another sense, it refers to garden-variety puns. In yet another sense, it refers to a specific genre of jokes that we might term put-downs. They follow a strict form of exchange, reminiscent of knock-knock jokes. The equivalent of "your mother wears army boots" in Egyptian Arabic is the following:

> *ummak – ishmi'na? – ismaha Hasan.*
> Your mother – What about her? – Her name is Hasan. (Hasan is, of course, a man's name.)

Other typical examples are the following:

> *abūk – ishmi'na? – biyirkab il-ḥimār wi-yibaddil.*
> Your father – What about him? – He rides a donkey and pedals.
> *abūk – ishmi'na? – biyishtaghal ḥarāmi ba'd iḍ-ḍuhr.*
> Your father – What about him? – He moonlights as a thief.
> *sittak – ishmi'na? – libasha damanhūr*
> Your grandmother – What about her? – She wears burlap underwear.

A pan-Middle Eastern trickster

Emblematic for Arab folk humor is the folkloric figure of Juha, an average man who is portrayed alternately as a fool, a wise fool, or a trickster. Similar figures are found in other Middle Eastern cultures, including Hoca Nasruddin in Turkey and Molla Nasruddin in Iran. Juha is relentlessly local: while he appears in the folk culture of every Arab nation, he is an Iraqi in Iraq, an Egyptian in Egypt, and a Moroccan in Morocco.

They asked Juha if a ninety-year-old man could father a child if he married a young wife. He thought a moment and then said, "Of course." They asked, "How?" "If he has a neighbor about twenty years old."

Once Juha was walking in the city and he watched as a beggar went up to the grill of a kebab seller to smell the kebab cooking. The seller grabbed the man and demanded that he pay for smelling the food. Juha intervened and asked how much he wanted. "Five dirhams." Juha took the coins in his hand, jingled them in the ear of the kebab seller, and said, "Hear that? That's your payment."

A modern character who resembles Juha closely is Abu l-'Abed, the protagonist of a prolific joke genre in Lebanon. Abu l-'Abed is from one of the old quarters of Beirut, al-Basta. He has a wife, Emm el-'Abed, and a buddy Abu Steif, with whom he spends time in *'Ahwet il-izēz* ("The Glass Café"), a well-known hangout in Beirut where men traditionally play cards and backgammon, drink tea and joke. Abu al-'Abed, like Juha, is portrayed as a simpleton who is alternately a fool and a trickster:

Abu al-'Abed decided to visit Amsterdam after he heard a lot about it at the Glass Café. He went around looking for a girl. "How much per hour?"

"100," she answers. He says, "I'll give you 200 if you do it the Lebanese way." "No thank you." Abu al-ʿAbed went to the next one and asked her, "How much?" "200." He says, "I'll give you 400 if you do it the Lebanese way." She refuses. Abu al-ʿAbed went to the next one and asked her, "How much?" She said, "500." "I'll give you 1,000 if you do it the Lebanese way." The girl accepted, and after they finished she looked at him and asked, "Abu al-ʿAbed, what's the Lebanese way?" "I'll pay you later."

Abu al-ʿAbed is going on a bus to Tripoli. He looks at the girl sitting next to him and says, "Allow me to introduce myself – your servant, Abu al-ʿAbed. Please excuse me, are you Chinese?" "No, Abu al-ʿAbed, I'm not Chinese." After a while, Abu al-ʿAbed asks the girl, "Is your father Chinese, perhaps?" "No, my father is not Chinese." After a while, he asks, "Is your mother Chinese, perhaps?" "No, my mother is not Chinese." After ten minutes, he says, "Are you sure that there isn't anyone Chinese in your family?" In exasperation, and in a final effort to shut up Abu al-ʿAbed, the girl replies, raising her voice in annoyance, "Yes, I'm Chinese, my father's Chinese, my mother's Chinese, and my whole family is Chinese! What do you want now?!" "Don't get angry. It's just funny that your eyes aren't like Chinese people's eyes."

Jokes on current events

On December 14, 2008, at a press conference in Baghdad where President Bush was speaking along with Iraqi Prime Minister Nuri al-Maliki, an Iraqi journalist, Muntazer al-Zaidi of Al-Baghdadia TV, hurled his size 10 shoes at Bush, shouting, "This is a farewell kiss, you dog!" Bush skillfully dodged the missiles, twice, and shrugged off the attack, but the dramatic incident was quite poignant because shoes are viewed as dirty and throwing them or hitting someone with them a sign of profound contempt. This incident is an excellent example of the type of political event that produces, almost immediately, scores upon scores of new jokes, spreading like wildfire through email and text messages. Egyptians lost no time in producing a series of fake newspaper headlines based on the incident, poking fun at Bush, the US invasion of Iraq, the War on Terror, and US allies in the Middle East.

> US occupation forces comb areas throughout Iraq in search of terrorist shoe factories.
> A man wearing a shoe-belt around his waist has been arrested by a US patrol in Baghdad as a would-be shoe-icide bomber.

Washington adds footwear to its terror list and passes a bill allowing wire taps on shoe stores and factories.

Several international shoe manufacturers deny US charges of aiding terrorist organizations.

A top US intelligence official, saying Zaidi's shoes were made in Syria and Iran, calls for their invasion.

An emergency Arab League meeting elects to shut down all shoe stores when Western officials visit.[2]

Humor in other media

Arab humor of course occurs in other media besides the spoken word, the focus of our exploration thus far. Street comedians and performers of farces at weddings have a long history. The modern counterparts of these professionals have for decades sold their sketches on phonographic disks, then cassettes, and now CDs. In Morocco, there is a strong tradition of comedic duos, similar to Laurel and Hardy or Abbott and Costello, but drawing more directly on the French tradition of comedic duos, such as *Les Frères Ennemis* (Teddy Vrignault [1928–1984] and André Gaillard [1927–]), *Grosso et Modo* (Guy Grosso [1933–2001] and Michel Modo [1937–2008]), Pierre Dac (1893–1975) and Francis Blanche (1921–1974), and others. They include the Tiqar duo and Bziz and Baz (Houssine Benyaz and Ahmed Snoussi). An outstanding Egyptian comedian is Musʿad al-Qass, one of the few comedians who can accurately imitate Saʿidi accent. Al-Shawish Bu ʿAzza is an important Moroccan comedian who is not part of a duo. His humor focuses on the plights of the Moroccan lower and middle classes in a global economy. He confesses to a friend that he is in love with Guadelupe, the star of the Mexican soap opera of the same name, but has no hope of winning her affections. His friend suggests that there shouldn't really be any obstacle to their union, because both Mexico and Morocco are in the Third World. He explains to her, *lā hūmā l-ʿālim it-tālit il-fūqī wi-hnā l-ʿālim it-tālit s-suflī* ("No. They are the 'upstairs' Third World, and we are the 'downstairs' Third World").

Comedy has been a standard part of Arab nightclub acts, theater, radio, and cinema, the histories of which have been tightly interrelated since their beginnings in the nineteenth and early twentieth centuries. In Egypt, Syrian and Lebanese immigrants such as Naguib al-Rihani (1889–1949) and ʿAbd al-Salam al-Nabulsi (1899–1968) played a large part in the development of comedy in the theater and the cinema. A high point in the history of Egyptian comedy was the popular radio show *Sāʿa li-ʾalbak* (An Hour for Your Heart), a play on the popular proverb *sāʿa li-ʾalbak wi-sāʿa li-rabbak* (Some time for your heart and some time for your Lord), which means that one should enjoy some light entertainment and not spend all one's time in religious devotion or chores. This variety show, which began in 1953, had brilliant writers such as Yusuf ʿAwf, Ahmad Tahir, and Amin al-Hineidy, and featured a number of talented comedians, including ʿAbd al-Munʿim Madbuli (1921–2006), Fuʾad al-Muhandis (1924–2006), Mary Munib (1905–1969), Khayriyya Ahmad (1937–2011), and others, who produced scores of brilliant sketches and hilarious characters such as Abu l-Lamaʿ, the inveterate braggart and teller of tall tales. Many of these also acted in comedic plays and films. Fuʾad al-Muhandis and Shiwikar (1938–) were brilliant in *al-Sikirtēr al-fannī* (The Technical Secretary), *Hawwāʾ al-sāʿa itnāshar* (Eve at Twelve O'Clock), and *Sayyidati al-gamīla*, the Egyptian version of *My Fair Lady*.

Nearly as emblematic of Arab humor as Juha is Ismaʿil Yasin (1912–1972), a comic actor in the mode of Jerry Lewis, France's Jacques Tati, and Italy's Totò (Antonio Gagliardi, 1898–1967), who was in his heyday in the 1950s. He was similar to Totò in his odd appearance, his exaggerated facial expressions, depiction of visceral emotions, and physical gags. Like Totò, he appeared in a series of films featuring his name: *Ismaʿil Yasin in the Police*, *Ismaʿil Yasin in the Army*, *Ismaʿil Yasin in the Navy*, *Ismaʿil Yasin in the Airforce*, *Ismaʿil Yasin in the Wax Museum*, *Ismaʿil Yasin in the Mental Hospital*, and *Ismaʿil Yasin in Prison*.

The most famous comedic actor in Egypt today is ʿAdil Imam (1940–), who worked with the greats of the earlier generation, but became famous on his own, along with Salah Subhi, in ʿAli Salim's play, *Madrasat al-mushāghibīn* (Trouble-Makers' School, 1973), in which he plays Bahgat il-Abasiri, the domineering ring-leader of the school's troublemakers, who yells at one point, "After I've served fourteen years in high school, the principal tells me 'Sit down?!!'" Another runaway success was the play *Shāhid ma-shaf-shi hāga* (A Witness Who Saw Nothing), in which he is hauled in for questioning, the hapless neighbor of a murder victim. He has appeared in over a hundred films and plays, and continues to act in leading roles although he is in his seventies. Noteworthy are his performances in anti-Islamist films as part of a public awareness or government propaganda campaign devoted to the dangers of Islamic extremism: *Terrorism and Kebab* (1992), *The Terrorist* (1994), and *Birds of Darkness* (1995).

His willingness to star in these films reflects his own distaste for the Islamists.

Another very famous comedic actor is Syrian Duraid Lahham (1934–), who starred in the television series *Sahret Dimashq* (Damascus Evening Party) when Syrian television began in 1960. From that time he formed a comic duo with established stage actor Nihad al-Qalʿi (1928–1993) and the two dominated comedy on Syrian television for decades, creating *Ṣaḥḥ in-nōm* (Wake Up!), *Ḥammām al-Hanā* (Bath of Bliss), *Maʾālib Ghawwār* (The Tricks of Ghawwār), *Mughāmarāt Carlo* (Carlo's Adventures), and other series. Duraid created the character Ghawwar il-Tosheh (a comic name meaning someone who dives into a quarrel), which he continued to play on television and in many films. He later acted in a number of Arab Nationalist plays, including *Kāsak ya waṭan* (Your Glass, O Nation) and *Ḍayʿit Tishrīn* (October Village). His comedy often focuses on the effects of political crises and decisions on the lives of ordinary citizens. In *al-Ḥudūd* (The Border), he plays a man whose house is divided by the new borderline separating the fictional nations Sharqistan and Gharbistan ("East-Land" and "West-Land"). The movie brings out the absurdity and arbitrary nature of political conflict.

American influence has been strong in the Arab cinema and television nearly since the beginning, especially in Egypt, and this is true of comedy as much as technology, music, and other aspects of the entertainment industry. In the 1970s, Candid Camera was adapted to Arab television as *il-kamira al-khafiyya* (The Hidden Camera), and many hilarious skits were produced. In one, interviewers in Zamalek, the posh island neighborhood of Cairo where most of the foreign embassies are found, accosted passers-by and asked for directions to the Egyptian Embassy. They were given many detailed directions: "It's next to the Italian Embassy"; "Take a right here, take the third left, and it will be on your right," and so on. In another episode, a man picking up photos from the photographer suddenly has to explain to his wife he has no idea why the photo shows him with a strange woman (a fake, of course); his wife does not believe his explanations, exclaiming *kān ʾalbi ḥāsis!* ("My heart felt it," i.e., "I just knew it!"). The couple seemed headed for a serious row until the fake photographer reveals that it is a hoax. The Moroccan version of *il-kamira al-khafiyya* was less successful, as the participants often did not take the humor in their stride and took revenge on the camera or the crew.

Another recent trend in Egypt and elsewhere that draws heavily on American examples is stand-up comedy. Distinguished from earlier comedians by venue, technique, and genre, the new stand-up comics are consciously following the models of American comedy clubs, open-mike nights, and so on, which they are familiar with chiefly through satellite television, and they consciously use the English word "stand-up" to refer to their art. In 2009, Hashim al-Gahry founded Ḥizb al-kumidi, the Comedy [Political] Party, an act of defiance toward the political powers that be. When not performing, they teach the art of stand-up to other aspiring comics, instructing them on things like timing and body language. This particular form of comedic art has caught on in other Arab nations, even in Qatar, where a few young comics have come together to form SUCQ (Stand-Up Comics of Qatar). One of them, Mohamed Kamal, notes that they have to be careful with their material: "We can't talk about politics, or very sensitive topics, like sex or religion." An Egyptian comic reported that a taxi driver complimented him on doing stand-up: "It's so great that you guys are doing that, and not insulting people and using foul language." (While the taxi driver seemed to have heard of the new phenomenon of stand-up [istand-ap] comedy, he didn't understand the foreign word and interpreted it as meaning istanḍaf, "to clean up").

In 2011, in the midst of the Arab Spring, Egyptian Bassem Youssef created Barnāmig il-barnāmig (The Program, or "The Show Show"), a satirical commentary on the politics of the day inspired by Jon Stewart's The Daily Show. He has gained a huge and loyal following and his arrest in April 2013 at the order of Islamist President Morsi for allegedly insulting Islam only added to his popularity.

Humor in Morocco, Algeria, Tunisia, Syria, and Lebanon, while also showing signs of American influence, still has strong ties with France. The Moroccan leftist, political weekly publication al-Usbūʿ al-ḍāḥik (Humorous Week) is modeled to a large extent on the French satirical weekly Le Canard enchaîné, which, ever since it was founded in 1915, has featured humorous pieces on political scandals, social issues, and the trials and tribulations of the working class. As in Le Canard enchaîné, al-Usbūʿ al-ḍāḥik reports regularly on, and satirizes, corrupt government officials, such as Hasan Tabit, the corrupt police chief who was executed in 1993 for using his power to rape and molest scores of women over the preceding twenty years.

Named after a theater in Paris that dates back to 1925, the Theatre de Dix Heures in Beirut, which was founded in 1962, closed in 1978 after several years of the Civil War, and revived in 1986, has been a major center for the production of contemporary comedy and has become a Lebanese institution. One of the most talented and popular comedians who has performed there is the Lebanese Armenian actor Pierre Chammassian (1949–), who is well known for his characters Batal Schvaradzian, a Lebanese Armenian, and Emm Georgette, a controlling busybody whose daughter is living in Los Angeles. While imitating a politician, Chammassian was asked why he turned down standing for election as a member of parliament and responded that, since his brother was a minister, being a member of parliament would be somewhat embarrassing, adding, with biting satire, *ish-sheghel mish ʿayb bass quand même!* (Working is nothing to be ashamed of, but really [there are limits]!), in what has become a nearly proverbial statement.

Comedic writers also abound in the Arab World, publishing in newspapers, magazines, and books that are usually collections of newspaper columns. The comic press has long roots in Egypt, going back to writers such as nationalist reformer ʿAbd Allah al-Nadim (1844–1896), who, beginning in Alexandria in 1881, published a weekly with the title *al-Tankīt wa-l-tabkīt* in which he wrote humorous and satirical pieces that protested against abuses of power and foreign control. This was succeeded by *al-Ustādh*, which began in 1892. Particularly influential was the humorous magazine *al-Kashkūl*, published by Sulayman Fawzi 1925–30, which featured many cartoons showing corrupt government fat cats in fezzes plotting to embezzle funds and sell out to foreign interests.

Among the funniest contemporary writers is the Egyptian Ahmad Ragab, who has a regular column in the newspaper *al-Akhbār*. One of his most enjoyable works, *al-Aghānī lil-Argabānī* (The Book of Songs by al-Argabani), has a parodic title referring to the famous medieval work *Kitāb al-Aghānī* (The Book of Songs) by Abu al-Faraj al-Isbahani, but giving as the author a scrambled version of Ahmad Ragab's own name). In the work he discusses Egyptian songs, revealing that, as a child, he thought that the orchestra music he heard accompanying singers on television was actually coming out of their mouths as well. When he tried to produce the same effect at the kitchen table, opening his mouth and waiting for the orchestra music to pour forth, his mother remarked to his father, "It looks like the kid is growing up retarded." In a brilliant exposition, as perceptive as it is side-splitting, he examines the physical world portrayed in Egyptian love songs, in which eyelashes are deadly weapons, hearts bite like German shepherds, and eyeballs carry loved ones around like so many pick-up trucks.

Cartoons and caricatures have also provided fertile ground for Arab humor. Political cartoons abound, but many are overt propaganda pieces that cannot be considered humorous. A few artists such as Salah Jahin (1930–1986), who was also a well-known poet and lyricist, have produced more clever and amusing work, particularly his series of pieces depicting the *fahhāma* (roughly, "the Understanderator"), a contraption in the shape of a large C-clamp or vise clamped to the skulls of various representatives of Egyptian social types – politicians, bureaucrats, and so on – in a vain attempt to get them to use their brains. Ahmad Ragab has created a panorama of characters – 'Ali al-Kumanda, Kambura, al-Kahhet, Captain Uzu, Qasim al-Samawi, 'Aziz Beg al-ʾalit, 'Abduh al-'Ayiʾ – that together provide a critical dissection of Egyptian society in the Mubarak era.

Regional variation

It is difficult to do justice to a topic as broad as Arab humor in a short space, particularly since there are many Arab countries, and the humor of each could be studied in detail. Many features of Arab humor are shared across national boundaries to such an extent that one may hear the same exact joke told about Saʿidis by Egyptians, Homsis by Syrians, and Khalilis by Palestinians. As seen above, the genres of "stupid" jokes and "stingy" jokes are widespread throughout the Arab World and the specific national examples of these often share many of the same strategies, not to mention the jokes themselves. Jokes about Arab rulers and international politics of the day are also widely shared throughout the Arab countries. There are a number of other widely shared genres that we have not discussed here, such as jokes about mothers-in-law. There is nevertheless a great deal of variety and even stark contrasts between the use and styles of humor from one Arab country to another. Certain genres are more developed in one country than their counterparts in other countries: Soussi jokes are a large and varied genre of jokes in Morocco, while Dumyati jokes form a relatively modest joke genre in Egypt, though both focus on stingy people. Jokes like the Saʿidi jokes that focus on physical features are not as common in stupid joke genres in other Arab countries. Some joke genres are limited to specific countries. Though Juha is shared among Arab countries, Abu al-'Abed is exclusively Lebanese.

The examination of humor is important as a window into Arab culture that is not colored by government and official propaganda and the perceived need to whitewash everything for presentation to an out-side audience. Understanding Arab humor involves learning not just the structure and vocabulary of the various Arabic dialects but also the stereotypes, concepts, foibles, and assumptions prevalent in the national cultures of the Arab World.

Notes

1 These are similar to the expressions, "See you later, alligator!" "In a while, crocodile!"
2 Sana Abdallah, "Shoe-Throwing Journalist Inspires Arab Jokes," *Middle East Times*, December 17, 2008.

13

Folklore

Folklore is the art of everyday life. It is the customs, traditions, beliefs, and habits of a community rendered in daily phenomena that include greetings and modes of politeness; concepts such as hospitality and friendship; practices such as clothing and foodways; verbal art forms such as proverbs, jokes, insults, stories, and poems; beliefs about supernatural beings, health, and diseases; physical art forms such as vernacular architecture and handmade furniture; and many other aspects of the ways in which we conduct ourselves and make sense of who we are on a daily basis. Most folklore is not written down or recorded, but is more typically communicated orally in face-to-face contexts from one individual to another, by performers to audiences, and transmitted from one generation to the next. In essence, folklore is the nitty-gritty detail of culture that we often hope to glimpse by reading novels, watching films, or viewing theatrical productions: the way people actually live their lives.

Although all classes of society participate in a given culture's folklore, some groups live a more cosmopolitan and international lifestyle that is enmeshed with the consumption of written texts and various forms of mass media, while others live in ways that are typically labeled more "traditional." It is common for members of a society to be able to point out certain practices and beliefs within their culture that they consider "traditional," even ones they themselves have never engaged in, but with which they nevertheless identify culturally.

The Arabic-speaking peoples of the Middle East possess rich and vibrant regional folk cultures that include some widespread features such as the privileged place given to oral poetry as an art form, the esteem given to hospitality as one of the highest virtues, and the popular veneration of holy figures ("saints") across Jewish, Christian, and Muslim communitarian boundaries. They also share a number of genres and customs including folktales about supernatural beings such as jinn, ghouls, angels, demons, and water spirits, many similarities in the celebration of weddings and holidays, as well as a variety of practices regarding food, greetings, folk remedies, and other aspects of daily life. But these same regional folk cultures also show a great deal of diversity.

Some of the regional differences in folk culture in the Arab World stem from the varied topography of the region. Arabs live in steep, mountainous regions in northern Yemen, the Atlas Mountains of Morocco, in Lebanon, and in northern Syria and Iraq, but also in ancient river valleys such as those of the Nile, the Tigris, and the Euphrates. They inhabit coastal areas such as the North African littoral, the Eastern Mediterranean, and the shores of the Indian Ocean and Persian Gulf, where fishing and pearl-diving are common livelihoods, as well as desert regions such as the interior of the Arabian Peninsula, central Iraq, southern Syria, and parts of Palestine and Jordan. Arabs live in some of oldest inhabited urban centers on the planet such as Damascus, Jericho, and Byblos (modern Jubayl), as well in the great medieval capitals that they founded such as Baghdad, Cairo, Tunis, and Fez. It is no wonder then that peoples whose geography, lifestyles, and primary occupations are so diverse should have developed equally diverse forms of traditional housing, music and dance, proverbs and tales, clothing and cooking, and much more. In short, the realm of Arab folklore is a perfect demonstration of both the unity and diversity of the Arab World as a whole.

Oral poetry

No art form is more central to Arab identity than poetry and even a brief survey of the social uses of oral poetry demonstrates the crucial role it plays in everyday life. Poetry is recited or sung to celebrate weddings and other festive occasions, to express deep-felt personal emotions, to criticize social and political situations, as a form of artistic competition in improvised "poetic dueling," in historical ballads that recount famous murders, crimes, and other noteworthy events, as oral history to preserve tribal genealogies and accounts of past conflicts, as a form of stand-up comedy for entertainment, in religious worship including the veneration of saintly figures and the celebration of sacred festivals, to accompany agricultural work and children's games, and on many other occasions. Composing, reciting, singing, and listening to poetry is an extraordinarily widespread activity in the Arab World.

To take but one example, in the Tihama region of Yemen, three contrasting genres of men's oral poetry exist side-by-side for use on different occasions.[1] The *bala* is a short, rather simple form of poetry composed spontaneously and sung by young men at weddings. The performance takes place in concentric rings of onlookers with the poet-singer standing in the center, surrounded by an inner circle of other young men, who participate by clapping the rhythm with their hands and by singing refrains made up of the last few words of the poet's verses. Beyond them is an outer ring of onlookers, the listeners who will judge whether the poet has acquitted himself well or not. Once a theme has been established by the first singer, each man who jumps into the circle to sing his own improvised verses must respond to those who have preceded, both in subject matter and in rhyme. It is a skill that males hone when they are younger, first by listening and imitating, and that they later perfect by joining in the chorus circle and finally by stepping into the ring and performing before the assembled wedding guests. This is not, however, merely entertainment, for the ability to compose and sing *bala* poetry is a badge of manhood in this regional culture.

In the following brief excerpt, different poets take turns extending greetings to the guests while the chorus chants the refrain, "O night of the *bala*!" between the verses, all of which are sung to the same melody and spontaneously composed in the same meter and rhyme:

> *Chorus:* O night of the *bala*!
> *Poet 1:* Long life to all of you, and may you not see any calamities [in
>   life];
>   O thousands of welcomes innumerable
> *Chorus:* O night of the *bala*!
> *Poet 1:* I serve the two groups [i.e., the chorus] who are wearing their
>   daggers and scabbards;
>   They who meet in the bulwarks of every fortified mountaintop.
> *Chorus:* O night of the *bala*!
> *Poet 2:* Long life and health to you [as many times as] they press the
>   grain on the grinding stone;
>   Generosity to the guest, even in lean years.
> *Chorus:* O night of the *bala*!
> *Poet 3:* O blessed evening when a friend meets a friend;
>   Welcome to the guest far and wide!

> *Chorus:* O night of the *bala!*
> *Poet 4:* I serve the happy groom fine perfume;
>   And I serve guests from afar melon and grapes.[2]

These improvised verses are ephemeral and soon forgotten. They are composed for and in the moment and are not meant to be memorized or preserved. The skill and ingenuity demonstrated lies precisely in their extemporaneous and spontaneous nature.

Another genre of poetry in this same region, the *zamil*, is, in contrast, meant to be remembered and retained by listeners, for it is a form that is used, for example, when giving testimony in front of tribal judges who assemble to settle disputes. In Arab culture it has long been recognized that poetry is easier to memorize and preserve than prose is. The strict meter and rhyme help to hold the words into place and to make it more difficult to accidentally forget or change a phrase. In Arabic, poetry has traditionally been termed *manzum*, or "organized" words, while prose is termed *manthur*, or "scattered" words. This idea goes back to an ancient image of stringing pearls or beads on a string to form a necklace, for *manzum* literally means "strung." Thus verses are likened to strung pearls, whereas ordinary talk is seen as "unstrung" or "scattered." The *zamil* genre is longer and more difficult to compose than the *bala*, for the composer must try to make a persuasive case with powerful images and references to accepted ideas, sometimes encapsulated in adages and proverbs. The judges and listeners act as "court stenographers," remembering and weighing the testimony of plaintiffs and defendants. The requirement that official speech in these tribal courts be restricted to poetry also effectively bars participants from making angry outbursts and maintains a sense of decorum throughout the proceedings.

Finally, in this same region there are also longer, carefully crafted "odes" called *qasidas* that can deal with many different topics, but are often compositions that address social or political issues. In the past, these long poems were carefully taught to others so that they might recite them publicly and transmit them widely. In more recent times, however, such odes have been broadcast on radio, distributed on cassettes, and are even featured in televised poetry competitions.[3] These three genres – *bala*, *zamil*, and *qasida* – coexist within a single region of Yemen, but similar clusters of interacting genres of oral poetry can be found in almost every region across the Arab Middle East, for there are literally hundreds of different genres of oral poetry composed and recited or sung by women, men, and children in different contexts.

Two interesting genres of women's poetry are the *ghinnawa* (little songs) composed among the Bedouin of the Western Desert in Egypt and the *hawfi*, an urban poetic genre from the city of Tlemcen in western Algeria. Among the Awlad 'Ali Bedouin studied by Lila Abu-Lughod, it is considered shameful to complain about one's lot in life or to publicly display one's emotions in normal speech; the ideal is to be forbearing and endure the hardships of life with silent fortitude. However, one *is* allowed to voice a certain amount of protest and complaint *if* one couches those sentiments in verse. It is as if the act of controlling one's words with meter and rhyme demonstrates that although one has intense feelings, one still maintains the culturally valued stance of strength in the face of hardship. The emotions found in these women's poems are, in addition, often partially concealed by the use of traditional metaphors or images, to the extent that one might not be able to tell what a particular poem means until one knows who composed it, at which point the intent becomes clear from the poet's personal circumstances. These poems can also be recited in two very different manners. The first is spoken in a normal voice and the words are given in straightforward order:

> Tears increased, O Lord
> The beloved came to mind in the time of sadness

The second, more emotionally powerful, style of recitation involves unveiling the images of the poem one by one in a mournful cantillated melody, and only allowing the complete image to emerge at the end:

> In the time
> In the time
> In the time of sadness
> In the time
> The beloved in the time of sadness
> In the time
> In the time
> The beloved in the time of sadness
> In the time
> In the time
> In the time tears
> Tears increased, O Lord
> In the time
> In the time
> The beloved came to mind
> The beloved came to mind in the time of sadness.[4]

The result is a powerful evocation of the emotions described, in this case, intense sadness at remembering a lost loved one.

In the city of Tlemcen in western Algeria, the genre of *hawfi* poetry was traditionally sung by women while on all-female outings to streams, pools, or waterfalls, often while swinging back and forth on a makeshift swing made of rope thrown over a tree branch (*joghlila* in Tlemcenian dialect), with a sheepskin or cushion to form a makeshift seat. There are *hawfi* poems about a number of different themes, but many poems express the longings and frustrations of women and unmarried girls in a remarkably overt manner. Here, for example, is a poem that tells of a woman who has seen a young man whom she found so attractive she swears she would give up her family and destroy her hometown to be with him:

> I was sitting in the garden, hiding behind the almond tree,
> And there passed by me a handsome youth holding a blue staff.
> His cap was cocked to one side and his hair was gleaming.
> For him I would abandon my children, for him I'd be divorced,
> For him I would destroy the town and turn it into a caravanserai.[5]

Another poem expresses a young woman's desire to choose her own husband, a man she finds attractive, and not just a man who has money:

> While I was watering the basil, he was tossing lemons at me.
> Your son I will not marry, even if he covers me in riches.
> I will marry a handsome youth whose figure pleases me![6]

This third example expresses the anger and frustration of an unmarried girl at the unwanted attention she receives from men, even in her own quarter, whenever she goes out:

> O my mother, O mistress, I will certainly die betrayed,
> The people of our quarter are all in league against me
> When I go out they discuss me like a bull [for sale]
> When I return they cry out, "[Come here] you who want your part!"
> O my mother, O mistress, my flesh is too dear for envious dogs [such as these]![7]

If the Bedouin *ghinnawa* allows women to express emotions that would be shameful to give voice to in regular speech, the traditional *hawfi* (which has now almost entirely disappeared) clearly gave voice to women's desires, longings, frustrations, and even anger at the restrictions placed on them by the male-dominated society they lived in.

Epic poetry

A truly remarkable form of oral poetry and storytelling is found in the tradition of Arabic folk epics: extraordinarily lengthy tales of heroes and heroines, tribal wars, conquests, romances, and occasional struggles against supernatural powers told in alternating passages of prose and verse. In the Middle Ages, there were over a dozen such epics, but there is now only one that survives in purely oral tradition, the epic of the Bani Hilal Bedouin tribe (*Sirat Bani Hilal*). Some Arabic epics from previous centuries had their roots in oral tradition, but were primarily propagated as a type of "popular literature," where a public storyteller would read the tale from a written text in a coffee house or other public place, often embellishing it with improvised additions and commentary. This type of performance is still found today, though in a steadily decreasing number of venues. The epic of the Bani Hilal is unique in that it seems always to have existed predominantly as an oral, musical, sung tradition.

This epic recounts the history of the Bani Hilal Bedouin tribe who, in the tenth century, migrated out of their homeland in the Arabian Peninsula, crossed through Egypt, conquered much of North Africa, and established themselves in their new homeland, but were later destroyed in a series of cataclysmic battles. Historically, those final battles were fought against the Moroccan Almoravid dynasty in the twelfth century, though most versions of the epic portray the tribe's destruction as the result of a civil war in which rival clans killed each other in internecine combat. The main outlines of the story are rooted in history, but the epic tells the larger tale as an ongoing drama among a constellation of central characters, including the cunning, silver-tongued black hero Abu Zayd; the brash, powerful, but temperamental warrior Diyab; the astute diplomatic leader of the tribe, Hasan, who struggles to keep the various factions and clans unified; the extraordinarily beautiful and wise heroine, al-Jazya; and the archvillain, al-Zanati Khalifa, who, in the end, proves to have some human qualities and dies a tragic figure. The various sub-plots of rivalries, love affairs, adventures, and feats of arms all play out, however, against the backdrop of the cataclysmic final demise of the tribe that occurs at the end of the story.

The main figures of the Bani Hilal epic have become symbols for various types of behavior – Abu Zayd, for example, is cited in proverbs, folktales, poems, and modern novels as an image of bravery and cunning. In the past, this epic was performed by specially trained singers, often from families who performed this art form as their primary occupation, while accompanying themselves on the Egyptian spike-fiddle (*rabāb*) in cafes, at harvest festivals, weddings, and other celebrations. Although traditional performances by hereditary epic singers have now all but disappeared, recordings from older performances are still sold on cassettes and CDs, and new adaptations of the epic have been produced in film and TV serials in recent years.

Here is a short excerpt from a performance of "The Birth of Abu Zayd" in which the character Rizq the Valiant, son of Nayil, bemoans the fact that he has sired many daughters, but does not yet have a son to be his heir:

> I am the servant of all who adore the beauty of Muhammad,
>   Taha [i.e., Muhammad] for whom every pilgrim yearns.
>
> Listen now to what Rizq the Valiant, son of Nayil, sang,
>   While tears from the orb of his eye did flow:
>
> "Ah! Ah! The World and Fate and Destiny!
>   All I have seen with my eyes shall disappear!
>
> I do not praise among the days one which pleases me,
>   But that its successor comes along, miserable and mean.
>
> O Fate, make peace with me, 'tis enough what you've done to me,
>   I cast my weapons at thee, but my excuse is clear.
>
> My wealth is great, O men, but I am without an heir;
>   And wealth without an heir after a lifetime disappears.
>
> I look out and catch sight of Sarhan when he rides,
>   His sons ride with him, princes and prosperous.
>
> I look out and catch sight of Zayyan when he rides,
>   His sons ride with him and fill the open spaces.
>
> I look out and catch sight of Ghanim when he rides,
>   And his sons ride with him and are princes, so prosperous.
>
> But I am the last of my line, my spirit is broken,
>   I have spent my life and not seen a son, prosperous.
>
> I have taken of women, eight maidens,
>   And eleven daughters followed, princesses true!
>
> But this bearing of womenfolk – Ah! – has broken my spirit,
>   I weep and the tears of my eyes on my cheek do flow."[8]

The many different genres of oral poetry in the Arab World, ranging from short lyric verses to lengthy epic narratives, and the multitude of contexts in which poetry is recited, from impromptu verses composed in conversation to formal odes recited at solemn occasions, attest to the central role that oral poetry plays in the life of Arabs throughout the Middle East.

Greetings

This cherished role of poetry and verse-making may also have contributed to the widespread appreciation of the art of greetings and salutations in Arab culture. There are a number of passages in the Qur'an and in the *hadith* (sayings) of Muhammad that deal with greetings, but perhaps the most important is found in Qur'an 4.86: "When you are greeted with a greeting, return it or respond with one better than it."

This verse commends the act of returning a greeting with one more beautiful than that which was received. The most common morning greeting throughout the Arab World, for example, is "Morning of goodness!" (*ṣabāḥ al-khayr*), to which the immediate response is "Morning of light!" (*ṣabāḥ al-nūr*). At this point, the basic exchange of greetings is complete, but it does not take much to lead people into a more extended or more poetic exchange that can include images such as the following:

> Morning of roses! (*ṣabāḥ al-ward*)
> Morning of Arabian jasmine! (*ṣabāḥ al-full*)
> Morning of jasmine! (*ṣabāḥ al-yasmīn*)
> Morning of honey! (*ṣabāḥ al-ʿasal*)
> Morning of dew! (*ṣabāḥ al-nadā*)
> Morning of the moon! (*ṣabāḥ al-qamar*)

To which many other examples might be cited such "milk and dates," "cloves," "cream," and so on. Some such greetings are regional and some are spontaneous poetic images composed on the spur of the moment.

Later in the day, the most common greeting among Muslims is "Peace be upon you" (*al-salāmu ʿalaykum*), to which one responds "And upon you be peace" (*wa-ʿalaykum al-salām*). This greeting is specifically mentioned in Qur'an 6.54: "When those who believe in Our revelation come unto you, say: 'Peace be upon you!'"

Because this greeting is mandated specifically for Muslims, in non-Muslim communities there are often alternative greetings, such as "May your day be happy!" (*nahārak saʿīd*), a greeting used by many Christian Arabs.

One widely shared aspect of greetings, however, is the understanding of who should greet whom first. Unlike in many Western cultures, the person entering a house or room greets those already inside first, and they then respond. If there is a group of people assembled, it is considered polite to move around the room greeting and shaking the hand of each and every person before accepting an invitation to take a seat (at least among groups of the same gender – more pious Muslim women sometimes prefer not to shake hands with men). Even in public spaces such as cafes in rural areas it is not uncommon to hear each person who enters call out a greeting to all of those present before taking a seat.

Folk narrative

Oral storytelling traditions are found throughout the Arab World in a variety of genres and performed in many different contexts. Some narratives are oral history recounting events set in the distant or recent past, others, such as what are often called "folktales" or "fairy tales" in English, are set in a non-historical, fictional world of their own. Unfortunately, when most Westerners think of Arab folktales, they are likely to think first of the *Thousand and One Nights* (also known as the *Arabian Nights*). This is unfortunate only in that this collection of tales, fascinating though it may be, is only partially based on Arabic stories and, in its modern form, owes more to European than to Arab creativity. It is a perfect example of what is termed "Orientalism," the portrayal of Eastern cultures in an exoticized and overly romanticized fashion that has little to do with reality; an image of the East created by the West for its own entertainment and enjoyment.[9]

The origins of the *Arabian Nights* probably stretch all the way back to ancient India, for several of the main features of these tales (such as talking animals and the use of frame-tales) are found in Sanskrit literature, and a number of the tales are also found in parallel versions in Sanskrit texts. The first documented written version, however, was in Old Persian. Although that text has not survived, it is described in several medieval Arabic sources and this is why the names of many characters are Persian rather than Arabic (such as King Shahriyar, Sheherazade, Dunyazade, and others). By the tenth century, the collection had been translated from Persian into Arabic and a series of new stories had been added set in the

Baghdad of the Caliph Harun al-Rashid (r. 785–809) and his vizier, Ja'far. Later, another series of new tales set in Cairo of the twelfth to fourteenth centuries was added, including references to buildings, street names, and marketplaces from that period. For several centuries thereafter, the collection circulated as one of a number of collections of fantastic tales, but was not particularly well known, nor did it attract a great deal of attention from Arabs or Europeans, until a Frenchman named Antoine Galland (1646–1715) obtained an Arabic manuscript and published a French translation in seven small volumes from 1704–6.

In France this was the heyday of the French *contes des fées* (fairy tales) and these new fairy-tale-like stories set in the exotic East quickly became wildly popular. So popular, in fact, that Galland's publisher begged for more material. The problem was that there was no more material – the extant Arabic manuscripts of the *Arabian Nights* do not include more than 282 nights. But Galland eventually gave in to the demands of his publisher and starting adding new material from a variety of different sources, without ever acknowledging publicly that they were not from the Arabic text. The collection was expanded until it finally reached 1,001 nights and Galland created an ending to the massive work. All of the added stories (including the ones most famous in the West – Ali Baba and the Forty Thieves, Aladdin and the Magic Lamp, Sindbad the Sailor, etc.) have ever since continued to be part of the *1,001 Nights*. In the nineteenth century, the work was reintroduced into Arabic complete with the tales that Europeans had added (many of the tales had to be translated from French into Arabic since there was no original Arabic text). Though in the Arab World it has never achieved the popularity and status that it gained in the West, it is nevertheless now a well-known work of "Arabic" literature. The collection is, without doubt, a masterpiece of literature, but it should not be read as an unadulterated work of Arab folk narrative. To cite but one glaring example, previous to the reintroduction of the *1,001 Nights* from Europe to the Middle East, there appears to have been no mention of "flying carpets" or "magic lamps" in Arabic literature. Thus two of the most famous images of Arab culture in the West turn out to have been introduced into Arab culture by Westerners.

More authentically Arab folktales deal with many of the same themes as the tales in the *1,001 Nights* (the quirks of fate, the inevitability of destiny, amazing journeys, encounters with magicians, beggars who become kings, and vice versa, tales of happy or tragic love, and so forth), but there are also many tales on other patterns. In some regions of the modern Arab World, the telling of different types of tales is deeply gendered, with women more often performing tales of the "fairy tale" type in the privacy of homes and men more commonly performing tales of battle and heroism in public spaces such as cafes. Because the traditional folktale is often a primarily female tradition, the protagonists of the tales are frequently female as well, and it is not a rare thing to find male hegemony being subtly, or not so subtly, criticized.

One common category of folktale of this type focuses on encounters with ghouls (Ar. *ghūl* or *ghūla*). These supernatural creatures are rather different from their English progeny, though the word "ghoul" does derive from the Arabic. In Arabic, the ghoul is a female creature, sometimes call "Mother Ghoul" (*umm ghūla*) or some other relational term such as "Our Aunt Ghoul." She is able to change her form and appear to humans as anything she wishes and she does so to trick hapless characters (usually men) into her power or abode, so that she can eat them. In many such tales, the male figure (husband/father) is fooled by the ghoul who appears to him, for example, as an innocent old woman or poses as a long-lost female relative and offers to guide him to a place where there is a lot of food or great riches. His wife or daughter attempts to warn him, but he does not heed them, and the whole family is placed in peril. The female character is smart enough to figure out how to escape, and sometimes the entire family is able to get away, but other times only the women escape and the unfortunate gullible male is eaten. It is easy to read these tales as admonitory tales about female acumen and sagacity versus male ineptitude (especially when greed or gluttony is involved), recounted by wiser, older women for the benefit of their younger, unmarried daughters.[10]

Other supernatural figures that inhabit Arab folklore are the jinn and angels, both of which are mentioned in the Qurʾan and therefore enjoy a certain amount of official religious recognition. In Arab culture, however, jinn do not come in lamps and offer to grant their liberator three wishes; instead, they exist invisibly in the same spaces as human beings and interact with us in various ways. The common Arabic word for "crazy" is *majnūn*, which literally means "possessed by jinn." One category of spirit related to the jinn is the *zar* spirits. These figures vary from region to region, but are typically known by titles such as "the Sultan," "the English officer," "the Red spirit," etc. Once a spirit enters a human host and possesses her/him, the spirit can often never be fully exorcised and instead must be negotiated with and appeased. The process of dealing with the spirits is a ceremony that is itself called a *zar*. A skilled leader, male or female, works with a group of musicians to call forth and mediate with the possessing spirits, for they are highly susceptible to specific rhythms and melodies. Once the music appropriate to a particular spirit is played, it will make itself known, usually by dancing and exhibiting the movements associated with that spirit. Sometimes the spirit simply dances and at other times it may speak to the leader and make demands. The spirit might demand that it be given certain foods or types of clothing or it will wreak havoc in the household of the possessed person. Western observers sometimes view these trances as expressions of psychological illnesses within a local cultural form, while others also see a deeply rooted power dynamic in which the weakest members of society can, at least temporarily, make demands of those who are more powerful.[11]

Popular religion

Among many different religious communities of the Arab Middle East there exist traditions of saintly intercessory figures that are referred to as "Righteous Ones," "Friends of God," or, among Christians, "Saints." Their burial places often become shrines and the sites of pilgrimages (see Figure 13.1), and many, in addition, are celebrated in popular festivals, some of which can attract hundreds of thousands of attendees, such as the enormous *mūlid* (festival) of al-Sayyid al-Badawi in Tanta in the Nile Delta of northern Egypt. In the past, the Jewish Arab pilgrimages of Morocco attracted similarly huge crowds. Such festivals can include musical performances, the consumption of special foods and sweets, games for children, along with more overtly religious practices such as Sufi *zikrs* (or *dhikrs*). Whether at the time of the festival or during other seasons of the year, these saintly figures are the object of prayers asking them to intercede with God for the supplicant who may be asking for a child, the safety of a loved one, the healing of an ill relative, a marriage, or other requests.

Although Westerners are usually most familiar with Sufism in the rather rarified form that has been marketed for non-Muslim consumption, which carefully picks out "universalist" passages by Sufi poets and authors, Sufism in the Arab and larger Islamic world is a much broader phenomenon. Almost no practicing Sufi would imagine that one could somehow be a "Sufi" without first becoming a Muslim, for the rites and rituals of Sufis are deeply imbued with texts that praise Muhammad as

Figure 13.1 A rural saint's shrine, Northern Egypt.

the final prophet and enshrine the Qur'an as the unimpeachable Word of God, even while promulgating somewhat tolerant and unorthodox interpretations of its text. In most places, Sufism is organized into different "orders" or "brotherhoods," each with its own set of teachings and practices derived from a lineage of shaykhs. One of the most widespread rituals is the *zikr*, a rhythmic and sometimes musical recitation of key texts or phrases, accompanied by bodily movements such as swaying from side-to-side or jumping in place, or, most famously, spinning, as do the Mevlevi "whirling dervishes." Some orders perform very sober *zikr*s accompanied only by a single percussion instrument, while others use a number of musicians, a solo singer, as well as a chorus.

Some Sufi practices, such as walking on hot coals or eating ground glass, have attracted harsh criticism from established religious authorities, but the primary cause of the current tensions with Islamist groups is the Islamist rejection of the entire category of "saints" who possess intercessory powers with either Muhammad or with God. In addition, Islamists usually point to a variety of superstitious and other folk practices common among Sufis, especially in rural areas, as ignorant and un-Islamic. Where Islamist groups have come to power, they have often destroyed shrines and forbidden pilgrimages, saints' festivals, and the practice of *zikr*.

Vernacular architecture

The varied geography of the Arab World has given rise to numerous different forms of vernacular architecture, each rooted in the raw materials available in that region. In the Nile Delta of northern Egypt, for example, where wood and stone are both rare, houses and other structures have traditionally been made from sun-dried brick (Arabic *at-ṭūb*, which passed into Spanish as *adobe*). A common house type consists of one and a half stories. The lower story is divided into a central living space that is entered from outside through a wooden doorway. This is where women during the daytime do household tasks such as preparing meals and where the family sits together to eat if there are no outside guests. To one side is a separate room, locally termed the *mandara*, which is where males who are not members of the family or very close friends are received, and where the men may gather in the evening. To the other side or the rear will be one or more small bedrooms. Until recently the floors were of pounded earth, over which reed mats or rugs would be rolled out as needed, and then rolled up and placed in the corner when not in use (see Figure 13.2).

The upper half-story of the house is a room used primarily for raising small animals such as chickens, ducks, and pigeons, as well as rabbits, all of which are basic foodstuffs. The remaining open area of the roof is used for the drying of grains such as wheat, rice, and corn (maize), as well as for hanging washing lines for drying clothes. Along the sides of the roof are low walls that have rounded silos in them, in which grain is stored and protected against both rain and rodents. Along the tops of the walls patties of animal dung mixed with straw or dried rice stalks are placed to dry hard in the sun, which are later used as fuel in the communal bread ovens. Since the Nile Delta is close to the Mediterranean, and therefore experiences heavy winter rains, such adobe houses require annual repairs, and eventually, after several decades, need to be partially or fully knocked down and rebuilt.

Beginning in the 1980s, these traditional adobe houses, however, began to be replaced at increasingly faster rates with new urban house forms constructed of red baked brick. Since adobe brick can be made by hand at virtually no cost and red baked brick must be bought from a factory, these new houses represent an extraordinary investment of money, usually supplied by a son or relative who has returned home after working abroad. The new red-brick houses were of a different pattern than the old mud-brick homes: they were raised above the level of the street rather

Figure 13.2 A traditional adobe brick house, Northern Egypt.

than opening directly onto an alleyway or passage and therefore had
to be entered by walking up a flight of steps; the floors were of cement,
sometime covered in tiles, which are harder and colder than the traditional pounded-earth floors and necessitated the purchase of cushions
and furniture since reed mats no longer provided enough cushioning to
sit on. In quick succession a variety of traditional social practices began to
change under the influence of the new house forms.

In contrast to these adobe homes of northern Egypt, in the swampy
regions of southern Iraq, groups sometimes referred to as the "Marsh
Arabs" traditionally constructed extraordinary large "guesthouses"
entirely from bundles of bound reeds. These guesthouses served as a
space to receive, entertain, and even house male guests and were held
in common by extended families and clans. By binding long reeds
together, first in small bundles that one can hold in one's hand, and
then bundling several of those together into a "beam" a foot or so across,
and then bundling several of those together to form even larger pillars
and girders, they succeeded in creating structural elements that could
support surprising amounts of weight and could be used to construct
large "halls" several meters high and wide and many meters in length.

Northern Yemen, on the other hand, particularly the capital city of
Sana'a, is famous for its extraordinary "tower houses" up to seven stories

high, the doorways and windows of which are beautifully decorated with white plaster giving them a "gingerbread" effect. These remarkable structures of stone and red brick contain an ingenious system of pulleys and ropes that allow loads to be raised and lowered, and even allow one to unlock the front door from several stories up. The houses contain indoor wells from which water can be drawn from different levels, which also permits a remarkably modern form of indoor plumbing, with all waste being washed downwards by simply pouring water down the plaster-lined shafts. Different levels of the house contain spaces for the family, the kitchen, sleeping quarters, and a special sitting room where male guests are entertained, often with poetry and music, while admiring views out over the city and the mountains.

From region to region, the basic building materials and house forms differ, and these in turn shape a number of social practices such as where one entertains guests, how one serves food, and the etiquette for approaching and entering someone else's home.

Proverbs

Although it is difficult to isolate and study shared values across a complex society, one of the places in a culture where values are expressed succinctly is in common proverbs and adages. Proverbs can at times be contradictory (cf. English "He who hesitates is lost" versus "Look before you leap"), but large clusters of sayings that express a similar idea usually reflect a core value in a given community. This is certainly the case with hospitality, which is almost everywhere in the Arab World held up as one of the basic pillars of Arab culture and one of the most highly esteemed virtues.

Hospitality was already central to Arab culture in ancient accounts of Bedouin life in pre-Islamic Arabia. Not only was a host obliged to provide any guest both food and water, but additional practices of hospitality included not asking guests their name or tribal affiliation for three full days and also defending them against attack or harm. In the harsh climate of the Arabian Peninsula, access to water and provisions could often be a matter of life and death, and the ability to reside as an anonymous guest for up to three days allowed needy travelers to seek nourishment even in the camps of groups with whom they might be in a state of feud or enmity. Thus, on a practical level, the custom of hospitality benefitted everyone.

The concept, however, runs deeper than simply a practical solution to life in a harsh environment. It is also tied to a worldview that sees hospitality, the giving of goods, and the sharing of wealth as an unending cycle in which the giver eventually becomes the receiver, similar to the English expression, "What goes around, comes around." This ethos was heartily embraced by Islamic culture and the "guest," already honored in the pre-Islamic era, was raised in status almost to that of an emissary from God. One of the most common Arabic phrases about guests is, "A guest is the guest of God."

> *A guest is the guest of God, who provides his provisions*
> The hospitality that a host offers a guest will eventually be returned by
>   God at some point in the future.
> *Food offered by a worthy man to a worthy man is but a loan*
> Again, the food that is offered will eventually come back to the host.
> *A guest is inviolable, even if he is an enemy*
> The status of guest and the relationship of a host to his guest
>   supercedes enmity.
> *A guest's right is three and a third days*
> For three and a third days the guest has the right to remain
>   anonymous, revealing neither name nor tribal affiliation. If the
>   guest leaves before that time, the host might never be certain of
>   the guest's identity.

Although such Bedouin customs as allowing a guest to remain anonymous are now found only in a tiny number of nomadic communities in the Middle East, the overall role of hospitality and generosity continues to be almost universally revered.

Conclusion

In a world that is daily more and more linked by social media, online websites, satellite broadcasting, reality TV shows, and other mass-mediated art forms, it is not surprising to find that even in these new conduits of culture, images and values drawn from Arab folklore are being adapted and re-presented. Many television and radio shows, as well as online sites, are based on the idea of the *hakawati*, or traditional Arab storyteller. Great stories such as the frame-tale of the *1,001 Nights* and the story of the Bani Hilal Bedouin tribe are continually being adapted and retold as plays, soap operas, and films. Societies for the preservation of traditional architecture have sprung up in many regions, and some of the Arab World's most modern architects and artists turn to folk art and architecture for inspiration. Even in a time of Twitter and SMS text messaging, the Arab love of poetry, proverbs, and greetings appears to continue unabated.

Notes

1 See Steven Caton, *"Peaks of Yemen I Summon": Poetry as Cultural Practice in a North Yemeni Tribe* (Berkeley: University of California Press, 1990).

2 Adapted from Caton, *Peaks*, p. 91.

3 See W. Flagg Miller, *The Moral Resonance of Arab Media: Audiocassette Poetry and Culture in Yemen* (Cambridge, MA: Harvard Center for Middle East Studies, 2007).

4 Lila Abu-Lughod, *Veiled Sentiments: Honor and Poetry in a Bedouin Society* (American University in Cairo Press, 1986), p. 179.

5 Mourad Yelles-Chaouche, *Le Hawfi: poésie féminine et tradition orale au Maghreb* (Algers: Office de Publications Universitaires, 1990), p. 245

6 Ibid., p. 285.

7 Ibid., p. 328.

8 See Dwight F. Reynolds, *Heroic Poets, Poetic Heroes: The Ethnography of Performance in an Arabic Oral Epic Tradition* (Ithaca, NY: Cornell University Press, 1995). This text was sung by Shaykh Taha Abu Zayd on June 1, 1987. The complete text can be found in the Sirat Bani Hilal Digital Archive (www.siratbanihilal.ucsb.edu) in Arabic, English, and in "Virtual Performance" mode.

9 Dwight F. Reynolds, *Arab Folklore: A Handbook* (Westport, CT: Greenwood, 2007), pp. 77–86.

10 Two such tales are found in Ibrahim Muhawi and Sharif Kanaana, *Speak, Bird, Speak Again: Palestinian Arab Folktales* (Berkeley: University of California Press, 1989), pp. 234–37, and Haya Bar-Itzhak and Aliza Shenhar, *Jewish Moroccan Folk Narrative from Israel* (Detroit: Wayne State University Press, 1993), pp. 93–97.

11 See, for example, Janice Boddy, *Wombs and Alien Spirits: Women, Men and the Zār Cult in Northern Sudan* (Madison, WI: University of Wisconsin Press, 1989) and Barbara Drieskens, *Living with Djinns: Understanding and Dealing with the Invisible in Cairo* (London: Saqi Books, 2008).

14

Food and cuisine

Food and cuisine are not synonymous. Humans are omnivorous and on a global level the human diet allows for a seemingly endless list of items prepared in a variety of ways and consumed for nutritional and other purposes – therapeutic, affective, expressive, social, religious, and political. Food is a matter of selection of a limited range of edible (and sometimes not so edible) items, while cuisine involves above all the preparation and presentation of foods in a variety of ways as determined by culinary canons embedded in culture. Geography and climate certainly set limits on the range of possibilities, but they are not unconditionally determinative, given the dynamics of ongoing historical processes such as trade, conquest, and migration, not to mention human invention and ingenuity in the domestication and hybridization of plants and animals. Food's connection with identity is evident in how people define themselves as members of a group through its preparation and consumption, when and with whom they share it, and the ways in which particular tastes and dishes become emplaced in individual and collective memory. Food is a central focus of a society's sacred stories, rituals, and symbolic life; it may bring it closer to the divine world, or alienate it from it. The interrelationship of food and identity is also evident in the ways cultural agents interact with each other, or stereotype one another, as becomes readily apparent in travel literature and modern advertising.

Determining the cuisines of the Arabs is made difficult by the wide variety of foods and culinary taxonomies present in the Middle Eastern region. It must be considered in relation to Persian, Turkish, Amazigh (Berber) cuisines, and those of smaller ethnic groups, as well as in relationship to the differentiated foodways practiced on the local level by

Arabic-speaking people living in a variety of geographic zones – deserts, plains, mountains, river valleys, and seacoasts. The general aridity of the climate has not inhibited the desire to vary cuisine or adapt the food traditions of others. The culinary practices of city dwellers differ from those living in the countryside, and the cuisines of each are further differentiated internally according to social class and other factors. In modern times, moreover, indigenous Arab cuisines find themselves contending with the inroads made by European and American "industrialized" foods and agricultural technologies. Additionally, for people living in the region, like those in other parts of the world, thinking of food cannot be separated from the tastes and smells produced at the family hearth – "our food" is not an abstraction that can readily be equated with a race or nation. Rather, it is more likely what a mother, grandmother, aunt, or a male relative has prepared in accordance with recipes that have been passed through the generations, invested with memories of holidays, births, marriages, deaths, and the accidents of everyday family life. Seen from this perspective, identity is conveyed in whether a lamb is roasted or boiled, what kind of thyme (za'tar) mixture is used to make mana'ish (flatbreads topped with spices), whether stuffed grape leaves are flavored with whole or cut garlic, how many times coffee is brought to a boil, and whether cardamom is added to it or not. Arab cuisines, therefore, must be situated in the interstices of such memories, contingencies, processes, and everyday practices.

Cookbooks are important sources for exploring the nature and history of Arab cuisines. The first such books in the Arabic language were composed in the tenth century in Abbasid Iraq.[1] They reflect the *haute cuisine* of Arab elites in the Caliphal court and the bourgeoisie rather than the mundane cuisine of the lower urban classes, peasants, and nomads, though there have doubtlessly been interactions among these different cuisines over time. Some of these cookbooks were of a literary character, containing poetry and amusing anecdotes, others were dietetic, while others still were intended for practical use in the kitchen. This tradition of writing continued well into the fourteenth century, when it largely died out until the late nineteenth. Although there were recipes for simple dishes that had been enjoyed by Arabs for centuries, such as *tharid* (a meat and bread stew, reportedly a favorite of the Prophet Muhammad), *'asida* (a wheat porridge mixed with fat), *harisa* (a meat and flour porridge), and *hays* (dates with curds and butter), these books also celebrated the rich cuisine of Sassanid Iran, abundant with aromatic ingredients, almonds, pomegranates, sweet and sour combinations – all intended for conspicuous display. Many dishes were known by their Persian names, such as the famed *sikbaj* (a meat dish prepared with vinegar and sweetenings), *sanbusak* (stuffed dumpling), *faludhaj* (an almond sweetmeat), and *jurjaniyya* (a meat dish named after an Iranian city and prepared with sour pomegranates, sweet almonds, raisins, and several spices). With the passage of time, however, Arabic terms were increasingly used for dishes once known by their Persian names, such as *akhbisa*, a collective name for jellied dishes and sweets, and *ibrahimiyya* (a sweet and savory meat dish named after an eighth/ninth century Abbasid prince). Surprisingly, none of the medieval Arabic cookbooks used "Arab cuisine" (*al-tibakha al-ʿarabiyya*) or "Arab food" (*al-akl al-ʿarabi*) as a culinary classification. Many were simply entitled *Kitab al-tabikh* (Cookery Book) or *Kitab al-atʿima* (Book of Foods), or bore more lyrical titles, such as *Kitab ila l-habib li-yastaghna bihi ʿan ʿilaj al-tabib* (The Book of Bonding with the Beloved to Spare Him from Need for a Doctor's Cure) and the fifteenth-century Egyptian *Kanz al-fawaʾid fi tanwiʿ al-mawaʾid* (Treasure of Benefits Concerning the Variety of Dining Tables). None of these titles made reference to "Arab" food or cookery.

Cookbooks featuring Arab food as a self-identifying culinary tradition do not really begin to make their appearance until the late nineteenth/early twentieth century as part of the print revolution that swept the Middle East in the wake of European colonial expansion and the modernization policies of regional powers. By the mid-twentieth century, cookbooks had begun to appear with titles referring to specific Arab nations, such as "Egyptian cooking" and "Lebanese cuisine." Only in the 1970s and 1980s do cookbooks published in the Middle East begin to carry titles that identify them clearly as "Arab" cookbooks.[2] The self-identification of an "Arab" cuisine therefore appears to be a recent phenomenon, the outcome of centuries of interaction between Arabs and non-Arabs, coupled with the disembedding of food traditions from their local contexts and their reformulation in a globalized framework of commerce and migration. Cookbooks written in North America and Europe tend to favor "Middle Eastern" and "Mediterranean" or national designations, rather than "Arab" in their representations of Arab culinary traditions. This is due largely to marketing considerations, as is also the case with restaurants. There are no doubt underlying ethnic and political factors that come into play, particularly those associated with the conflicts between Arab countries and Israel.

Arab macro-foodscapes and their transformations

Given the varying and often contested notions associated both with what is "Arab" and what is "Arab cuisine," we propose a heuristic definition that is conducive to identifying general patterns, as well as local and national specificities. We define Arabs as a people who claim the Arabic language as their own, are conscious of their historical or genealogical ties to a collective past, and establish their individual and shared identities through their culinary traditions and memories associated with them. We address Arab cuisine as situated in four Middle Eastern macro-foodscapes. Admittedly, these overlap with each other, and with those of neighboring cultures in the Middle East and Africa. In addition, there exist multiple local micro-foodscapes within each that also beg further study. Each of the Arab macro-foodscapes has distinctive contours that have been determined by historical, sociocultural, and ecological processes. From west to east, they are:

1. *The Maghrib*: The North African Maghribi macro-foodscape is the result of the interaction of Arabs and Imazighen (Berbers), the indigenous peoples of this region, beginning in the seventh century. It was further enriched by the influx of Andalusian Jews and Muslims, who carried their culinary practices from Spain, particularly in the wake of their expulsions between 1462 and 1614. The savory pigeon pie known as *bastila* was likely introduced to Moroccan cuisine this way.[3] Additionally, traces of later Ottoman influence can be found along the Mediterranean shores of this region, as well more recent French and Italian dishes, especially among the upper classes. Situated on both the Atlantic and Mediterranean and encompassing the modern states of Morocco, Algeria, Tunisia, and Libya, the diversity of the Maghrib's people and landscape – plains, mountains, desert, and seashore – contributes to the complexity of its culinary cultures. For example, in Morocco, the former capital cities of Rabat, Fez, Meknes, and Marrakesh developed into major culinary centers where the kitchens of elite households were the domains of the *dada*s, female slaves imported from sub-Saharan Africa as domestics. These women carried the oral tradition of Maghribi cooking from generation to generation, but with their passing there is danger of this culinary heritage being lost. Middle Eastern culinary expert Claudia Roden has identified two primary culinary regions in this country: a northern one encompassing Tangier and Tetouan, where Andalusian and Ottoman influences are most pronounced, and a southern one centered

in Marrakesh, Safi, and Essaouira, where the influence of African and Atlantic foods are marked. These two regions, with their own distinctive styles of cooking, intersect in Fez.[4]

The food *par excellence* for the Maghribi foodscape is couscous – small grains of steamed semolina served variously with sauce, vegetables, fruits, meat, chicken, or fish. Its name is thought to be derived from the Amazigh *kesksou*, but it has been embraced for centuries by all North Africans. Variants are made from barley and maize. Couscous is served at all important social gatherings, holidays, and celebrations. Other identifying components of Maghribi cuisine are sweet and savory meat stews (*tajines*) simmered slowly in a delicate spice mixture over fire or charcoal in special earthenware cooking pots, hardy flour-based soups known generically as *harira*, as well as the aforementioned *bastila*. The Maghribi fondness for cooking with aromatics, nuts, fruits, and sweet and sour flavorings is most certainly a survival of culinary practices carried there by Arabs from the medieval courts of Baghdad and Persia. Dishes prepared in Algeria, Tunisia, and Libya are similar to those of Morocco, though they often are made spicier with the addition of a condiment of crushed New World chili peppers called *harisa*.

2. *Egypt*: The Egyptian (*Misri*) macro-foodscape extends southward from the shores of the Mediterranean along the Nile Valley to northern Sudan, bounded by Cyrenaica (eastern Libya) in the west and the Sinai Peninsula in the east. The landscape is not as varied as that of Morocco, but the Nile Valley's rich alluvial soils resulting from centuries of annual inundations until completion of the Aswan High Dam in 1970, together with its hot climate, have yielded abundant food crops since the days of the Pharaohs. Indeed, this resource made Egypt an essential source of alimentation for the ancient Roman and Byzantine empires. For centuries Egyptian culinary culture remained relatively stable, consisting of grains, meat from cattle and poultry, fish, shellfish, and assorted indigenous fruits and vegetables.

Although little is known about the preparation of food in ancient Egypt, available evidence indicates that Egypt's culinary culture advanced significantly during the medieval era and beyond as a result of the interaction between its people's indigenous food traditions with those of the Mediterranean, the Levant, Arabia, the Indian Ocean Basin, and, more recently, Europe and North America. The city of Cairo, the location of several Islamic dynasties in the past and Egypt's present capital, became the center of culinary achievement for this macro-foodscape.

Praised by Ibn Khaldun (d. 1406) as "the metropolis of the world," Cairo for centuries possessed an Islamicate palace culture that produced an elaborate cuisine that benefitted from the culinary revolution that had occurred in Abbasid Baghdad. Indeed, city dwellers across the Middle East enjoyed the fruits of transregional trade networks and the introduction of new crops and agricultural technologies by the Arabs.[5]

Contemporary sources indicate that medieval Cairenes commonly ate flatbreads, vegetables, pulses, salted fish, river mussels, stews, and sour milk preparations. A very popular (and ancient) dish was *mulukhiyya*, a green herb (Jew's mallow) prepared in a soup with meat, onions, and other herbs. A variation of this soup is still prepared in Egyptian households today. The haute cuisine of the elites, however, was comprised of dishes such as those described in the medieval Arab cookery books, copies of which were reproduced, read, and expanded in Egypt. Even though the dynasties ruling Egypt after the Fatimid era (909–1171) were non-Arab, the foods Cairenes consumed continued to be largely products of Abbasid Arab court culture combined with indigenous Egyptian food traditions. Marketplace street kitchens and vendors offered customers from different walks of life a wide array of food preparations, both simple and elaborate, which were eaten at home or in the workplace; restaurants are a modern phenomenon. The Ottoman Era in Egypt (1571–1867) witnessed the introduction of new food traditions, such as stuffed vegetables and coffee house culture.

Today, Egyptian food is known for its simplicity, though the fare of the middle and upper classes offers more variety than that of peasants and blue collar workers. Flat bread made of barley or wheat is so essential to the Egyptian diet that it bears the name of "life" (*'aysh*) itself. Grilled meat – lamb and chicken – is a leading food for those who can afford it, as well as stuffed pigeon. Among peasants, goose, duck, and rabbit are popular, but vegetable dishes are more common. A mashed fava bean dish (*ful mudammas*) is eaten for breakfast by all Egyptians, usually with onions, a bit of oil, and cumin. Its rival as the national dish of the country is *ta'miyya* (similar to *falafel* in the Levant), spiced balls of fried fava bean paste served with flat bread and *tahini*. Lentil soup is popular, but it is surpassed by *mulukhiyya*, which is today commonly served with okra (*bamya*), onions, and rice. Sweetbreads and veal, beef, lamb or camel joints (*kawari*) are also favored. *Kushari* is a popular street food made of a mixture of pasta, rice, and lentils, topped by caramelized onions and a spicy tomato sauce. Some scholars have proposed that this dish was brought by British troops from India in the early twentieth century, but others find evidence that even though it may have originated in India, it has been present in the Middle East region long before Britain was on the scene.[6] As a result of colonization, economic modernization, and tourism, European fare has had a growing influence in the country, accelerating in the 1980s and 1990s with the introduction of American fast food chains, which the country's rising middle and upper classes find appealing. Cairene cuisine also prevails to the north in Alexandria, but seafood is especially esteemed there, as it is in Mediterranean coastal cities of the Maghrib, despite the declining fish populations. In addition, because Alexandria looks out to the Mediterranean basin and is home to immigrants from that region, Greek and Italian culinary traditions have been incorporated into its local foodscape. Following upon the popularity of sugary desserts in medieval Cairo, Egyptians today are especially fond of sweets like baklava, *basbusa* (semolina cakes), *kunafa* (layers or rolls of vermicelli stuffed with nuts and raisins or cheese, baked, then soaked in syrup), and *qata'if* (small folded crepes filled with clotted cream or nuts, fried, then soaked in syrup). *Umm 'Ali* – a rich pudding of layered filo dough, shredded coconut, nuts, and milk – has become a favorite among Egyptians in recent years, but its origin is uncertain.

3. *The Arab Levant*: The Arab Levantine macro-foodscape extends from the Tigris and Euphrates river valley in Iraq to the eastern shore of the Mediterranean, southward from the Taurus Mountains in southern Turkey to the northern part of the Sinai Peninsula. It consists of a diverse topography, allowing for the cultivation of a wide variety of crops and livestock. It has an equally diverse population of ethnic groups. The modern countries of Syria, Lebanon, Israel,[7] Palestine, Jordan, and large parts of Iraq and southwestern Turkey lie within it. Also known as the Fertile Crescent, this was the region where plants and animals were probably first domesticated, where the first cities were created, and it was home to a number of ancient peoples and civilizations that contributed to the formation of the culinary traditions that exist there today, particularly those of the Lebanese, Syrians, Iraqis, and Palestinians. Damascus and Baghdad, the two former capitals of the Umayyad and Abbasid empires, are located there, together with other major urban areas, including Jerusalem, Aleppo, Homs, Beirut, Antioch, as well as the more modern city of Tel Aviv. Baghdad was the focal point of a medieval culinary renaissance between the ninth and thirteenth centuries that was carried to many outlaying regions, most notably Egypt,

the Maghrib, and Spain. Baghdad's golden age of culinary innovation, however, was abruptly ended by the invasion of the Mongols in the thirteenth century. Today, its cuisine is not as famous as it once was, but it can still be characterized as representing a mixture of Arab Levantine, Turkish, and Persian tastes.

Between the sixteenth and early twentieth centuries the Levantine region was administered by the Ottoman Empire. The palace kitchens of the sultan in Istanbul produced an endless variety of dishes for royal and public feasts, inspired by the many local foodways of the vast territory that he ruled. As a consequence, the culinary cultures of the Arab Levant underwent profound change. They were also affected by the decades of European colonial influence, especially by the French in Syria and Lebanon. The leading culinary centers for this foodscape are Beirut and Aleppo, but households and eateries in smaller cities and towns also offer dishes that delight the palate. For example, the resort town of Zahlé in the Bekaa Valley is celebrated by the Lebanese as the birthplace of their *mezze* tradition.

Mezze, for which Levantine Arabs are famous internationally, are usually served as hors d'oeuvres and, among Arab Christians and Jews, with 'araq, a potent alcoholic beverage made from distilled grape juice. An essential component of Arab hospitality, the number of dishes served at any one meal varies, but they are divided into cold and hot, as well as vegetable and meat dishes. Popular cold *mezze* include olives, *tabuli* salad, hummus and tahini dip, assorted garden vegetables and salads with olive oil dressing, bread salad (*fattush*), pickled vegetables, cucumber and yogurt, spiced eggplant and tahini dip (*mutabbal* or *baba ghanuj*), meatless stuffed grape leaves, and steak tartare (*kibbe naye*). Hot *mezze* include falafel, grape leaves stuffed with ground lamb or beef, stuffed filo pastries (*sambusek*), meat pizzas (*sfiha*), spinach or cheese pies (*fatayir*), chicken liver, and grilled quail. Signature main course foods in the Levant comprise fried or grilled meat balls or patties (*kibbe*), stuffed zucchini and green peppers (*mahashi*), grilled kebabs, and a meat and yogurt soup served on rice and bread (*mansaf* or *laban ummuh*). *Mujaddara* – a mixture of rice, lentils, and fried onions – is a traditional domestic dish similar to *kushari* in Egypt. It has become an essential component in the diet of Palestinian refugees because its ingredients are inexpensive and made available by international relief agencies. Flatbreads topped with a mixture of thyme, oil, and sesame seeds (known as *mana'ish*) are a favorite breakfast food in Lebanon. In coastal areas, seafood dishes are favorites, like *sayyadiyya* (fisherman's catch), a layered rice dish with fried fish and pine nuts. Baghdadis enjoy sharing in a meal of barbequed carp from the Tigris River known as *masguf*. One of the most popular street foods, aside from falafel sandwiches, is *shawarma* – layers of marinated beef or lamb roasted on a vertical rotating spit. The most famous sweets in Levantine cuisine, all of diverse origins, are baklawa, *kunafa*, crepes (*qata'if*), date pastries, nut-filled cookies (*ma'mul*), rice pudding, and an ice cream made of gum Arabic known as *buza*.

4. *The Arabian Peninsula and the Gulf*: This Arab macro-foodscape encompasses a vast desert area bounded by highland ranges to the west and south and nearly surrounded by the waters of the Red Sea to the west, the Arabian Sea to the south, and the Persian (Arab) Gulf to the east. Saudi Arabia, Yemen, Oman, the United Arab Emirates, Qatar, Bahrain, Kuwait, Jordan, and southern Iraq are the modern states located there. The pastoral nomadism of the Bedouin was once the primary mode of subsistence for much of this region because of its climate. These tribal groups live throughout the Peninsula, extending into the desert regions of Iraq, Syria, Jordan, Israel, Palestine, the Sinai, Egypt and North Africa. Their way of life, which is rapidly disappearing, always existed in symbiotic relationship with settled societies in oasis towns and on the margins of cultivated lands. Although much of the agriculture of the Peninsula has depended on subterranean water sources and run-off from sporadic winter rain, year-round cultivation is possible in Yemen's Sarawat Mountains, which receive southwest monsoon rains from May to September. In southern Iraq, the Tigris and Euphrates supply water for irrigated farmlands where dates and grains are grown. The Peninsula is home to Mecca and Medina, the two holiest cities in Islam; they are major pilgrimage centers, receiving visitors from around the world. Other prominent cities in the region are Jeddah, the Red Sea gateway to the holy cities, Sana'a and Aden in Yemen, Muscat, and Basra, Iraq's Persian Gulf port. New cities have arisen from fishing towns and villages along the Peninsula's east and west coasts as a result of the growth of the oil industry during the latter part of the twentieth century. These include Kuwait City, Dammam and Khobar, Manama, Doha, Dubai, and Abu Dhabi.

Bedouin are dependent on their livestock for food, particularly camels, sheep, and goats. In addition to meat and cooking fat, livestock provide milk and hides. Trade with settled Arab populations provides dates, barley, wheat, and rice. Flatbread is a basic staple, together with dates.

Meat, used mainly for festive occasions, is roasted or boiled and served on a bed of bread or rice. Key meat dishes are *mansaf* (meat and yogurt broth) and *tharid* (meat and bread broth). Variations on both of these became favorites among Arabs in the Levantine and Egyptian regions. Camel milk is consumed whole, but milk from goats and sheep is used to make butter, yogurt, and *jamid*, a rock-hard ball of cheese derived from yogurt that can be reconstituted with water for cooking. Bedouin fare also includes small game animals, jerboa, lizards, roasted locusts, and desert truffles.[8] Urban areas have developed a more differentiated cuisine, influenced by foods originating in Persia, Turkey, India, and the Horn of Africa. With the arrival of the oil industry in the mid-twentieth century, this macro-foodscape became fundamentally transformed, featuring European continental fare, American fast foods, north and south Indian dishes, as well as Levantine and Persian cuisine. Mecca's cuisine developed from a Bedouin base, always supplemented by food traditions brought by caravans from afar, including India (especially after the seventeenth century). May Yamani has documented the heterogeneity of foods that currently constitute Meccan cuisine, enriched by the many different ethnic and racial groups that have gone there to worship, live, and work, including domestic cooks (Filipinos, Lebanese, Sudanese, Egyptians, and Moroccans). In addition to traditional lamb, bread, and rice dishes, she notes some of the foreign dishes that have been adapted to local tastes: Bukhara rice, Indian *laddu* sweets, and Indo-Pakistani *biryanis* (a savory layered rice and meat dish).[9] Historically, Basra, known for its seafood, has benefited from the combination of Arab and Persian traditions, as well as Indian curries.

This South Asian component of the Arabian Peninsula's foodscape has become increasingly present because so many South Asians have gone there in recent decades for employment in the blue and white collar sectors. Shopping malls in Dubai, for example, include Indo-Pakistani food stands and restaurants feature menus in both English and Arabic, indicating that their fare is enjoyed by natives as well as foreigners. Some mix Arab with South Asian cuisine. Yemen constitutes a historically distinct culinary corner (or micro-foodscape) in the peninsula, separated from neighboring countries by high mountains and the desert expanses of the Empty Quarter. On the other hand, its ports have linked it for centuries to the wider Indian Ocean basin. This may be why fenugreek paste (*hulba* and *hilbeh*) and a hot paste made of fenugreek and chilies became leading condiments on the Yemeni table, unlike other native cuisines in the peninsula. They are often served with one of several different kinds of Yemeni flatbread, including one that resembles Indian *chapati*.

Points of Arab culinary unity

The foregoing classification and description of the four primary Arab macro-foodscapes suggests that, alongside the distinct features of each, there are areas of commonality. This is less a manifestation of an Arab ethnic or national essence, or a deep cultural structure, than the result of historical contingencies, sociocultural differentiation, irrigation techniques, and cropping patterns, interaction with non-Arabs, geographic contiguity and patterns of migration and acculturation. Perhaps one of the most important underlying factors is that Arab cuisine became embedded in a milieu where the written word was embraced, allowing a vast body of ideas and practices to become organized over time and great distances, east and west. With respect to food, the Arabic written corpus includes not only the cookery books discussed above, but also histories, legal texts, travel accounts, dietary and medical treatises, and literary works (including *A Thousand and One Nights*), as well as books on botany and zoology.

A listing of features shared among all the Arab macro-foodscapes should include preference for meat, especially mutton and lamb, the ubiquity of flatbreads made of wheat or barley, the combination of meat and grains or breads in cooking, the use of aromatics (e.g., rose water) and spice mixtures (e.g., *baharat* and *ras al-hanut*), preference for dates and other dried fruits and nuts, the use of dairy products like ghee, yogurt, and cheese, and the development of an elaborate selection of confections. Added to this would be Islamic taboos against pork and alcohol.

A major beverage that first gained widespread use among Arabs was coffee. It originated as a beverage in Yemen during the fifteenth century, then rapidly spread with the help of Sufis and merchants to the Hijaz, Egypt, Syria, the Ottoman Empire, and from there to the world. Its close connection to Arab culture is signified by its modern Linnean classification, *Coffea arabica*, where the genus name is derived from the Arabic *qahwa* and the species name links it directly to Arabia. It is also reflected in the importance coffee houses hold in all four Arab macro-foodscapes and in the hospitality customs of Arabs from all walks of life.[10] Tea, which was only introduced to the Middle East in the seventeenth century, is consumed in greater quantity (even in coffee houses), in part because it is less expensive, but it has not been as successful in becoming linked with Arab identity as coffee.

Olives are consumed in all four regions, even in localities where they cannot be grown easily, such as Egypt and the Arabian Peninsula. Rice was probably introduced to the Middle East by the Persians before the appearance of Islam, but its cultivation from Iraq to North Africa and Spain was an achievement of the Arabs.[11] It nonetheless holds a secondary place at Arab tables compared with flatbread, except in places where it grows in abundance, such as southern Iraq. Couscous appears to be a markedly Maghribi staple, but it did travel eastward to Mamluk Egypt and to the Levantine Arab foodscape, where it developed into a variant known as *mughribiyya* as early as the thirteenth century. It never gained the prominence in the east that it had in the Maghrib, however.

Historical changes

At least four major historical transformations have shaped the Arab foodscapes. The first is the early Islamic expansion, which occurred with the spread of Islam from Arabia to the rest of the Middle East and North Africa in the seventh and eighth centuries CE. This resulted in the introduction of Qur'anic dietary rules and the eventual embedding of Muslim feasting and fasting traditions first among the Arab Muslim elites, then more widely among the local populace.

The second was the Abbasid culinary revolution, which occurred between the ninth and thirteenth centuries CE. This involved a number of significant developments, which included:

- the interpenetration of indigenous, Arab, and Persianate culinary traditions;
- the launching of an Arab agricultural revolution with the introduction of new agricultural technologies and food crops, mainly from Asia, such as rice, sugar cane, citrus fruits, bananas, watermelons, spinach, eggplants, and artichokes;
- the circulation of cookbooks with recipes for exotic dishes using a variety of spice combinations;
- a concern for the healthful properties of food and the science of dietetics.

The Abbasid phase also involved the transplanting of its culinary fashions to Egypt, the Maghrib, and the Iberian Peninsula, where they took on a life of their own, especially after the fall of Baghdad to the Mongols in 1258.

The third phase was the Ottoman Era of culinary synthesis and elaboration (fifteenth to early twentieth centuries), which brought the dissemination of refined Ottoman palace cuisine to urban areas in all four Arab foodscapes, including the Mediterranean shores of the Maghrib. Ottoman fare such as shish kebab, stuffed vegetables, savory filo pastry dishes, pastries like baklawa, and the use of bulgur wheat became widespread. It was also during this phase that New World foods were introduced, such as potatoes, tomatoes, maize, and the turkey.

The fourth, most recent, phase is that of the global, characterized by European foods and industrialized food production technologies introduced initially as a consequence of French and British imperialism in the region. European foods were embraced by westernizing classes of the native population, as reflected in cookbooks and the proliferation of European-style eateries, but they also provoked communal and nationalist resistance, leading to revivals of more traditional foodways and calls for food sovereignty.[12] Periodic campaigns have been launched to enforce Islamic dietary laws, especially with regard to consumption of pork and alcohol. Postcolonial globalized commodification, accelerated by the influx of petroleum revenues and arrival of large numbers of workers (especially from South Asia) with their own food preferences, are other characteristics of this phase. Concomitantly, the new commercial media have helped market non-traditional food industry products among the emergent middle and upper classes. One has only to visit the food courts in the monumental, air-conditioned shopping malls that have sprouted up in the Gulf region, Egypt, and Lebanon to see the concrete impacts of these developments at the local level. Restaurants and caterers featuring Arab (usually Levantine) cuisine and cafes offering water pipes vie with American fast food outlets, Starbucks and Costa coffee shops, and eateries serving European, South Asian, and East Asian fare, even across the street from the Sacred Mosque in Mecca. The best Arab cuisine is still, of course, to be found at home, but, even there, globalized food commodities are finding a place at the table and, in the homes of the moneyed classes, cooks hired from abroad prepare European cuisine or dishes from their native countries, as well as Arab recipes given to them by the female head of household.

Foods sacred and profane: dietary rules

The Qur'anic dietary code emphasizes the binaries of the lawful (*halal*) and the forbidden (*haram*), which intersect with the pure and impure.

It proclaims a general dispensation to "eat from the land what is tasty [or good; *tayyib*] and permitted [*halal*]," but not to "follow in the footsteps of Satan" (Q 2.168). "Tasty" food is what has been provided by God (Q 2.172). From other verses we know that "tasty" food included both plants (namely, dates, grapes, olives, pomegranates, and grains) and animals (particularly domestic sheep, cattle, goats, and camels, as well as seafood), with meat – especially mutton – being traditionally most highly valued among all Muslims. Muslims are also permitted to eat the food of Christians and Jews (Q 5.5). On the other hand, God has forbidden (*harrama*) believers from eating carrion, spilt blood, pork, and what has been sacrificed in the name of any being other than God (Q 2.173). The taboo against eating pork is no doubt inspired by the Jewish prohibition, but is not embedded in the same cosmologically based system of clean and unclean creatures as it is in the Biblical books of Deuteronomy and Leviticus. Wine (*khamr*), which was represented ambiguously in the Qur'an as both a reward for the faithful in Paradise (Q 47.15) and as a Satanic device for sowing discord among humans (Q 5.90–91), was finally subject to prohibition in the latter part of Muhammad's career in Medina. The ambiguous status of wine in the Qur'an overall made it the subject of ongoing commentary, debate, and elaboration in Islamic tradition, evidenced in the commentaries, *hadith*, legal, and historical texts. The consensus reached by most jurists was that wine and wine-trading was forbidden (*haram*) and that this prohibition extended to all intoxicants (unless used for medicinal purposes). While this may have initially helped set observant Arab Muslims apart from Arab pagans, Jews, and Christians, it did not prevent the enjoyment of wine by Muslim elites and, on occasion, commoners. It was also celebrated in poetry and song, to the extent that wine and its consumption became metaphors for mystical experience.[13] Until today, the production of wine in Arab lands has remained largely in the hands of Christians and Jews.

The dietary rules pertaining to meat, like wine, have also been subject to much discussion and legislation. Permitted (*halal*) meat includes domestic cattle, sheep, goats, and fowl sacrificed or slaughtered by making an incision across the throat and invoking God's name. Jurists recommend that camels be slaughtered by stabbing the upper chest. The Qur'an bans eating that over which God's name has not been invoked, and proclaims that doing so is a transgression inspired by demons (*shayatin*) and their human agents (Q 6.118–121); it relegates the transgressor to the status of being a pagan (*mushrik*). Fishing and hunting wild animals is licit as long as the quarry is lawful (Q 5.94–96). Muslims are forbidden from eating carrion (*mayta*), which includes anything that has been strangled, beaten, or gored to death, or animals that have died by falling. A creature that has been partly consumed by predatory beasts is also forbidden, unless it has actually been killed by ritual slaughtering or by a trained hunting animal (Q 5.3–4). Such prohibitions inevitably begged questions: Does food become unfit if it comes into contact with alcohol, a menstruating woman, or an impure animal like a dog? What are the precise requirements for slaughtering an animal? Is it lawful to consume meat sacrificed by a Christian or Jew for one of their feast days? Is meat imported from a country like Australia, where there is a Christian majority, or India, where there is a Hindu majority, lawful? Is the flesh of an animal that has been mortally injured and left for dead by a predator lawful? Are the eggs of wild birds? Are shrimp and lobsters?[14]

The observance of other formal Islamic requirements, such as fasting during Ramadan, performing the hajj pilgrimage to Mecca, celebrating feast days, and giving food in charity also provided occasions for consideration of questions pertaining to which culinary practices and substances were lawful and unlawful. Taking up such questions is a matter not only of religious law and ethics, but also of positioning in a social world of intersecting, changing, and conflicting identities. It is also a matter of taste.

Fasting and feasting

In addition to the food taboos of Islam, religion has also shaped and given meaning to the feasting and fasting traditions of the Arabs. Of the two major Muslim feasts, '*Id al-Adha* (Feast of Sacrifice) marks the end of the annual pilgrimage to Mecca with the slaughtering of pastoral livestock – sheep, goats, camels, and cattle. This ritual is performed by the hajj pilgrims and is also celebrated by Muslims around the world between the tenth and thirteenth of the twelfth Islamic lunar month with the consumption of a variety of savory meat dishes, commonly accompanied by distribution of food by individuals, civic, and religious organizations to the poor. Recipes for this holiday vary from region to region – mutton is a favorite: whole-roasted, cooked in stews, and grilled as kebabs. *Tharid* and *fatta* (meat and bread mixtures) are very common, as are cooked liver, brain, and sweetbreads. A traditional

Moroccan food prepared for this holiday is *mrouzia*, a lamb stew sweetened with raisins, honey, saffron, cinnamon, almonds, and spiced with a blend known as *ras al-hanut*. The other major Muslim feast is *'Id al-Fitr* (Feast of Fast-Breaking), a three- to four-day feast that breaks the end of the month-long Ramadan fast. Meccans prepare a dish called *minazzala*, consisting of whole lamb cut in pieces and roasted. In addition to such festive meals, this holiday is marked by the preparation of abundant quantities of sweet baked goods, such as date- or nut-filled cookies (known as *kleicha* in Iraq, *ma'mul* or *ka'k* in Syria, Palestine, and Egypt). Arab Christians prepare similar dishes for their Easter holiday celebrations. Euro-American foods may also be included in holiday menus, including French fries and pastries.

Despite its being a month of fasting involving the ban of all food and drink for healthy adults during daylight hours, Ramadan has evolved into also being a time for the preparation of favorite holiday dishes, especially for *iftar*, when the fast is broken at the end of each day. While some people adhere to the requirement of daytime fasting and the principle of moderation throughout the month, for many, Ramadan evenings are a time for large celebratory gatherings of family, friends, and neighbors, requiring the preparation of extraordinary quantities of food. Shopping begins in the previous month, often driving prices up on popular ingredients, especially rice, sugar, dates, nuts, dried fruits, and pastries. Governments in some countries, such as Egypt, become involved in price regulation and providing key staples at subsidized prices. In addition, the media provide advice on healthful eating and avoiding weight gain. According to a nutritionist quoted in an Egyptian newspaper, "Ramadan can be an ideal time to try to normalize one's weight."[15] In recent decades, luxury hotels and restaurants have hosted lavish *iftar* dinners throughout the month. Some establishments arrange for food to be served in stylized "traditional" settings: a club in Cairo provided guests with "Bedouin," "Moroccan," and "Arab" (of the Arabian Peninsula) air-conditioned tent options. In Dubai, expensive Ramadan meals are served in lavish Bedouin-style tents set up by the emirate's leading hotels. On the other hand, mindful that Ramadan is also a month for fulfilling the duty of charitable giving (*zakat*), companies, wealthy individuals, and non-governmental organizations in the United Arab Emirates and other Arab countries sponsor free Ramadan banquets (*mawa'id al-rahman*: "tables of the All-Merciful") that are open to the public, especially orphans and the poor. Those organized by religious organizations feature short sermons before the meal.

There is great variety in Ramadan cuisine embraced by the Arab cultures of the Middle East. Before the sun rises, a light meal known as *suhur* is served, consisting of nourishing foods like yogurt, *kishk* (a yogurt-based soup), cheese, dates, rice pudding, bread and jam, *mana'ish* (in Lebanon), *rghaif* (Moroccan stuffed bread), and *sahlab* (warm thickened milk with sugar and spices), with tea or milk as a beverage. At the end of the day, the fast is traditionally broken with dates and a glass of water, following the example of Muhammad. An elaborate variation of this practice consists of filling large bowls with a mixture of dried fruit, assorted nuts, water, and sugar, aromatically enhanced by rose water and orange-blossom water. Families tend to have their own favorite recipes for this delicious specialty, which is known as *khoshaf* in Syria and Egypt and *ramadaniyya* in the Arabian Peninsula. In Morocco, the fast is broken by a serving of the soup *harira*, which may consist of a variety of ingredients depending on the region, season, and cook's preferences.[16]

The *iftar* meal proper usually consists of a variety of dishes, depending on the family's socioeconomic status. For example, in Egypt, lentil soup, *ful mudammas*, falafel, flat bread, or rice are commonly prepared by low-income families and at free Ramadan banquets for the poor. Wealthier households enjoy more variety, mixing traditional favorites with those of a markedly European flavor. For example, an *iftar* dinner for family and guests in a middle-class district of Cairo might feature several soups (tomato, chicken, and *kishk*), calamari salad, stuffed pigeon, rice with chicken liver, beef liver, beef sausage (*mumbar*), *fatta* with beef trotters, filo pastry stuffed with meat and hummus, chicken *escalope panée*, along with pickles, condiments, and hot and cold beverages. Mecca's native population makes a special meal of barley soup, *ful mudammas*, cheese and meat-filled *sambusak*, and *fatta*. Hotels and restaurants, including American fast-food outlets, have also developed an array of special Ramadan fixed menus for those who can afford to break their fast at a commercial establishment. Like meals at home, these combine traditional favorites with non-traditional dishes. McDonald's, on the other hand, simply packages a soup and salad with an American-style burger, fries, soft drink, and fried apple pie for about six US dollars.

Among the most common Ramadan desserts in Egypt and the Arab Levant (including Iraq) are the same date- and nut-filled cookies that are baked at the end of the month in celebration of *'Id al-Fitr*, together with *kunafa* and *qata'if*. Until recently, when many homes did not have ovens, women would prepare these desserts at home and then send them to the local bakery for baking. Instead of making plain *kunafa* and *qata'if* dough from scratch, they could also buy (and they still buy) it from sweet shops, then finish assembling them at home with the help of other family members and servants. Nowadays, these desserts can be purchased ready-made from local vendors. A favorite Moroccan Ramadan dessert is *halwa shabakiyya* (also known as *mharka*), a flower-shaped honey and sesame fried cookie customarily eaten with *harira* for the *iftar*. The Lebanese Ramadan specialty called *kallaj* is made of a very thin rice paper that can only be obtained from bakery shops. This paper is stuffed with cream, nuts, dates, or halloumi cheese, then pan fried and soaked in sweet syrup.

Other sacred times are recognized in relation to foods associated with them. They include the *mawlid* of the Prophet Muhammad, which commemorates the anniversary of his birth, and is observed in many Muslim countries, Arab and non-Arab, with the enjoyment of roasted chickpeas and sweets. In Mecca, the holiday is celebrated with a meal of whole roast lamb served on rice with side dishes. The *mawlid*s of Muslim saints also provide occasions, especially for pilgrims who visit the saints' shrines and people living in the vicinity, when food is shared among family, friends, and even needy strangers. Sufi organizations erect hospitality tents (*khidamat*) for serving food and beverages to all comers. Sweets obtained at a shrine are considered indications of the saint's *baraka* (blessing power). When the Shi'ites of Iraq commemorate the martyrdom of Husayn ibn 'Ali, the grandson of Muhammad, during the first ten days of the lunar month of Muharram (*'Ashura*) they prepare cauldrons of a meat porridge comprised of lamb or chicken, chickpeas, wheat, salt, sugar, and cinnamon. This specialty, known as *harisa* (not to be confused with the spicy condiment used in North African cooking), is distributed to households in large bowls and provided free to pilgrims who flock to the major Shi'ite shrines in Iraq, especially in Karbala, Najaf, and Samarra. Neighborhoods save money throughout the year in order to accumulate sufficient quantities of ingredients for this holiday dish. Religious organizations also distribute fruits, juice, cookies, cake, and hot tea to pilgrims at this time.

Coexisting with Sunni and Shi'ite Arabs in the Middle East are Arab Christians, particularly in Egypt, Lebanon, Syria, Jordan, Israel, and Palestine. Most of them are affiliated with one of the Eastern Orthodox churches (Coptic, Greek, Syrian, Assyrian, or Armenian) or the Roman

Catholic Church (including Maronites, Melkites, Chaldeans, and Armenians), where the celebration of the Eucharistic meal of bread and wine is a sacramental ritual conducted throughout the year. This practice, in which the bread and wine come to mystically constitute the body and blood of Jesus Christ, developed from the life of the first-century Christian community based in Syro-Palestinian lands; it became institutionalized as a sacrament in later centuries. Easter is the most important religious feast for these churches, preceded by the forty-day fasting period of Lent. Strictly observing the fast requires replacing meat, fish, eggs, and dairy dishes with vegetarian ones. Olive oil or another vegetable oil is used in cooking instead of butter or animal fat. Arab Christian fasting foods have a long history in the Middle East, perhaps extending to pre-Islamic times, and they were included in medieval Arab cookery books. Indeed, they may have contributed to the array of vegetable dishes found in the typical Lebanese *mezze* menu. Arab Easter feasting dishes vary according to local custom, and mirror the feasting traditions of Arab Muslims, often with a focus on mutton recipes. There are differences, however. Many Christians have fish and hard-boiled eggs, or make *ma'mul* and *ka'k* cookies, the shapes of which are said to represent Jesus' crown of thorns and the sponge used to quench his thirst as he was dying on the cross. Christians, unlike observant Muslims, consume alcoholic beverages on feast days.

Important events in the life of the individual, the family, and the community also provide occasions for celebration and feasting. Medieval Arabic literary texts indicate an impressive lexicon of specific terms for meals associated with occasions such as the birth of a child, thanksgiving for having a flock of more than one hundred animals, the birth of a domestic animal, receiving a guest, a child's first hair cut, the arrival of a traveler, completion of memorization of the Qur'an, circumcision, betrothal, a wedding, a funeral, and the building of a house. Although some of the terms have fallen out of use, many of these events are still celebrated with meals today. Other life occasions that are celebrated include the naming of a child, the return of pilgrims from Mecca, recovering from an illness and returning from the hospital, death anniversaries, and, for Arab Christians, baptism and First Communion.

Modern Arab food diasporas

American diasporas: Arab immigrants to the Americas were typically peddlers and proprietors of small businesses. Some opened grocery stores in Arab neighborhoods where imported foods were sold; others opened food stands and restaurants featuring "oriental" cuisine. As early as 1895, Arab men were observed in New York's Syrian neighborhood gathering in "restaurants" (actually common rooms in boarding houses) to drink Turkish coffee and smoke *nargileh*s, while women worked at home.[17] Detroit was another important center for the establishment of Arab culinary culture in North America. Restaurants and groceries there catered to the needs of a Syro-Lebanese immigrant population, followed by other Arabs from Palestine, Yemen, Iraq, and Egypt. Some of the early businesses closed as the first immigrants moved away and second-generation Arabs assimilated into American culture, but others continued to be established with the arrival of new groups.

The 1990s and 2000s have witnessed significant commercial growth for Arab foods in North America, coinciding with the increased media attention given to the Middle East and Islam, and the growth of the North American Arab population, together with other ethnic groups from the Middle East. The low cost of many Levantine dishes has helped popularize them among the wider, non-Arab, populace. Moreover, Armenians from Lebanon, Copts from Egypt, Chaldeans from Iraq, Greeks, and Israeli immigrants have contributed to this process, often claiming Levantine dishes as their own. Large metropolitan areas now boast Middle Eastern markets and eateries offering "Mediterranean" dishes, serving not only Arab clienteles but other immigrant groups from the Middle East, Southeastern Europe, South Asia, and the wider North American public. Middle Eastern grocery stores, bakeries, markets, and food stands have also flourished.

Many of these enterprises are overtly Arab in identity, with names like Byblos, Alfanoose (The Lantern), Amir's Felafel, Al Bustan (The Garden), Beirut Palace, Damascus Bakery, Zaytoon (Olives), and Marrakesh Restaurant. Throughout North America, flatbreads, kebabs, hummus, and other such foods have become so popular that they have found their way onto the menus of non-Middle Eastern restaurants and university residence hall dining commons, as well as onto grocery store shelves. A recent development is the emergence of Arab chefs with training in both Middle Eastern and European cuisine. For example, Farid Zadi, a French chef of Algerian parentage, was trained at l'École hotelière Eragny in Paris and now teaches at the California School of Culinary Arts, where he promotes Maghribi dishes along with French cuisine.

The migration of large numbers of Levantine Arabs to Latin America has left its mark on the culinary landscape there, as it has to the north. Although intermarriage and assimilation into the local cultural milieus took its toll, the development of immigrant community institutions and networks helped preserve traditions from their homelands. In Brazil, which has by far the largest number of citizens of Arab descent in the Western hemisphere (estimated to be 9 million or more), accounts of early immigrant life indicate that spices, dates, and lentils were available in the early 1900s, and that households prepared lamb dishes and enjoyed Levantine pastries and *'araq*, even as far inland as the Amazonian city of Manaus. Syro-Lebanese social clubs, such as the Clube Monte Libano in Rio de Janeiro (founded in 1946), provide a setting where business, travel, and family matters can be discussed over appetizers and entrées selected from a richly varied Levantine menu. During the 1950s, restaurants featuring explicitly "Arab" food opened in Saõ Paulo. Indeed, Arab food has become so popular in Brazil, that it is used in biting political satire directed at corrupt politicians of Arab descent.[18]

In Colombia, Arabs first settled in the country's Caribbean coastal cities and towns, and then spread throughout the country. As in other lands where they migrated, their food was what linked them with their families and memories of life back home, but, for some, it became their livelihood. Today bakeries, restaurants, and eateries featuring Levantine cuisine can be found in many of Colombia's upscale neighborhoods and towns. Arab foodways also became indigenized in Mexico. Syro-Palestinian Arabs began to arrive by boat at Vera Cruz in the 1870s and soon spread throughout the country, establishing immigrant bases in the Yucatan Peninsula, central Mexico, and the northern borderlands.[19] When ingredients for traditional recipes were lacking, Arab women improvised with local ingredients, which eventually contributed to their widespread acceptance beyond immigrant community circles, thus enhancing Mexico's rich culinary landscape. In Yucatan, which already possesses a distinct cuisine based on its mixed Mayan–Spanish heritage, Arabs substituted beef for mutton in preparing *kibbe*, and introduced variations made with fish or venison, until it became a popular appetizer and street food in the region. They used chard (*silq*) to make stuffed grape leaves when the latter were in short supply. *Tabbouleh* (*salad árabe*) and *fattush* also underwent adaptation in the Peninsula. In central Mexico, especially around Puebla and Mexico City, the most popular dish of Levantine origin is *shawerma*, which is known locally as *tacos al pastor* (shepherd style), *tacos árabe*, and *tacos de trompo* (spinning top). This dish is prepared from meat, often marinated pork instead of lamb, grilled on a rotating, vertical spit. It is usually served with tortillas instead of Arab flatbread, along with one or more other condiments, including chipotle or guacamole, instead of *tahini*. Arab flatbread (*pan árabe*), once made at home, is available in supermarkets, as it is in the United States and Canada. The Arab pastries *baklawa* and *kunafa* are sold in upscale patisseries.

Arab diasporas in Britain and Europe: In the case of Britain, sizeable numbers of Arabs started to arrive in the first decades of the twentieth century.[20] It is a heterogeneous population, comprised of Egyptians, Iraqis, Moroccans and other North Africans, as well as Saudis, Palestinians, Jordanians, and Lebanese. They are concentrated in London, where Arab restaurants, nightclubs, grocery shops, and cafes can be found on Edgware Road in the Westminster area, as well as Bayswater and Shepherd's Bush. Also known as "Little Cairo" and "Little Beirut," Edgware Road's eateries cater to wealthy Gulf Arab vacationers as well as to British Arabs and, of course, the British. The Shepherd's Bush area is known as "Little Syria" because of the number of Syrian-owned restaurants and businesses. Many of London's Middle Eastern restaurants combine Levantine and Moroccan dishes on their menus, along with Persian.

France has the largest population of Arabs in Europe, and, as is the case for Arabs in Britain, most come from countries where they were once subject to colonial rule by the host country. This means that its Arab population is largely North African, and that the Arab culinary culture carried by the immigrants is Maghribi. These mostly working-class immigrants are concentrated in some 1,000 neighborhoods throughout the country. Although socially marginalized, a sign of their growing presence and cultural influence is evident in the popularity that couscous has enjoyed in many French households since the 1960s. Other North African foods are now produced in France, such as the spicy condiment *harisa* and the spice mixture *ras al-hanout*. Couscous, *bastila*, *tajine* dishes, and *harira* soup are featured on the menus of pricey Moroccan restaurants in Paris. Bakeries specializing in North African foods have opened in many cities. There is also a heavy representation of Lebanese foods in France as a result of immigrants from that country and secondary immigrations of Lebanese via Egypt and other countries in Africa.

Conclusion

Claudia Roden recounts an impassioned debate among Moroccan restaurateurs that occurred at a culinary arts festival in Fez in 2001. On one side were those concerned about preserving the traditional Moroccan cuisine in the face of all the challenges with which it was being confronted. They took issue with Moroccan chefs working abroad, who felt that they should be free to improvise with traditional dishes as they saw fit. A third group took a median position in advocating "modernizing" the cuisine in order to make it healthier.[21] That food should be a focal point for debate and contestation is not surprising, especially when it becomes a means through which identity is articulated. Debates also occur on the field of religion, particularly in regard to the dietary laws. One of the most important questions debated in the sixteenth century was whether coffee should be banned as an intoxicant or not. Those who argued that it was not an intoxicant eventually prevailed.[22] Similar debates continue today around intoxicants, pork products, and foods produced or prepared by non-Muslims. National identities have also come to play in these, as evidenced in competing claims between Arabs and Israelis to falafel as a national dish.[23] Coffee, hummus, baklawa, and even couscous have also become points of contention in nationalist debates, extending beyond Arabs and Israelis to Turks, Greeks, Iranians, and Europeans. It is a challenge to foresee the ways in which Arab identities will be reimagined and articulated through their cuisines in the decades to come, but they will no doubt continue to both develop their culinary traditions and influence the culinary cultures of others around the world.

Notes

1 For a survey of this genre of Arabic literature, see Nawal Nasrallah, *Annals of the Caliphs' Kitchens: Ibn Sayyar al-Warraq's Tenth-Century Baghdadi Cookbook* (Leiden: Brill, 2007), pp. 15–29. H. D. Miller includes a chapter-by-chapter description of al-Khatib al-Baghdadi's *Kitab al-tabikh* in his discussion of the subject: "The Pleasures of Consumption: The Birth of Medieval Islamic Cuisine," in Paul Freedman (ed.), *Food: The History of Taste* (Berkeley: University of California Press, 2007), pp. 135–61.

2 For example, Suha al-Kiyali, *Al-Tabkh al-'arabi al-asil* (Beirut: al-Mu'assasa al-'Arabiyya li-l-Dirasat wa-l-Nashr,1988). Heine identifies the author as S. Kuhayli. This book, like others, also included some European recipes, but it decries their invasion of Arab kitchens.

3 The Arabic *bastila* is derived from the Spanish *pastilla* "pastry." Pies of various sorts were popular in medieval Europe, including *empanadas*, stuffed pastries that originated in northern Spain. These savory pastries were sometimes coated with sugar, as is *bastila*.

It is possible that these in turn were inspired by *sanbusik*, a stuffed pastry introduced to Spain by the Arabs and later gave birth to the South Asian *samosa*. See further Clifford A. Wright, *A Mediterranean Feast* (New York: William Morrow, 2000), pp. 294–95; David M. Gitlitz and Linda Kay Davidson, *A Drizzle of Honey: The Lives and Recipes of Spain's Secret Jews* (New York: St. Martin's Press, 1999), pp. 222–24.

4 Claudia Roden, *Arabesque: A Taste of Morocco, Turkey, and Lebanon* (New York: Alfred A. Knopf, 2006), p. 15; cf. "Saveurs d'hier et d'aujourd'hui," www.lematin.ma/Actualite/Journal/Article.asp?idr=110&id=8900, September 25, 2010.

5 On new crops and technologies, see Andrew Watson, "The Arab Agricultural Revolution and Its Diffusion, 700–1100," in David Waines (ed.), *Patterns of Everyday Life* (Aldershot: Ashgate, 2002), pp. 247–74.

6 Wright, *Mediterranean Feast*, pp. 600–1, and p. 754, n. 78. Iraqis have a similar dish called *kujari*, and both dishes are like the Levantine *mujaddara*; Nawal Nasrallah, *Delights from the Garden of Eden: A Cookbook and a History of Iraqi Cuisine*, 2nd ed. (Sheffield: Equinox Publishing, Ltd., 2013), p. 254.

7 The creation of the State of Israel in 1948 brought large numbers of European Jews into this region, followed by Sephardic Jews from the Maghrib, Egypt, and Turkey, plus Yemeni, Ethiopian, and Persian Jews, thus establishing several new culinary traditions, in addition to a local Jewish one that was already present. The history of their interactions with the Arab Levantine traditions and each other is a topic that deserves further inquiry. Some aspects of these culinary encounters are considered below. The publications of Claudia Roden reflect a Levantine Jewish perspective on culinary practices of the wider Middle Eastern region, including those of the Arabs. See also Poopa Dweck, *Aromas of Aleppo: The Legendary Cuisine of Syrian Jews* (New York: Harper Collins, 2007).

8 Alan Davidson, *Oxford Companion to Food*, Tom Jaine, ed. (Oxford University Press, 2006), 33, 68–69. On desert truffles, see John Feeney, "Desert Truffles Galore," *Saudi-Aramco World*, 53:5 (September/October 2002), pp. 22–27.

9 Mai Yamani, "You Are What You Cook: Cuisine and Class in Mecca," in Sami Zubaida and Richard Tapper (eds.), *A Taste of Thyme: Culinary Cultures of the Middle East* (London: Taurus Park Paperbacks, 2000), pp. 171–84.

10 Ralph S. Hattox, *Coffee and Coffeehouses: The Origins of a Social Beverage in the Medieval Near East* (Seattle: University of Washington Press, 1985).

11 Andrew M. Watson, *Agricultural Innovation in the Early Islamic World: The Diffusion of Crops and Farming Techniques, 700–1100* (Cambridge University Press, 1983), pp. 17–21; Davidson, *Oxford Companion to Food*, p. 663.

12 Rami Zurayk, *Food, Farming, and Freedom: Sowing the Arab Spring* (Charlottesville, VA: Just World Books, 2011).

13 For a recent treatment of the early Islamic literature on wine, see Kathryn Kueny, *The Rhetoric of Sobriety: Wine in Early Islam* (Albany: State University of New York Press, 2001). See also Ignaz Goldziher, *Muslim Studies*, ed. S.M. Stern (London: Allen and Unwin, 1966), p. 27ff; Ignaz Goldziher, *Introduction to Islamic Theology and Law* (Princeton University Press, 1981), pp. 59–63, and A. J. Wensinck and J. Sadan, "Khamr," *Encyclopedia of Islam*, 2nd ed.

14 See further Yusuf al-Qaradawi, *The Lawful and the Prohibited in Islam*, trans. K. El-Helbawi, M. M. Siddiqui, and S. Shukry (Indianapolis: American Trust Publications, 1960), pp. 39–78; Maxime Rodinson, "Ghida'," in *Encyclopedia of Islam*, 2nd ed.; Muhammed Hocine Benkheira, *Islam et interdits alimentaires*; Muhammed

Hocine Benkheira, "Chairs illicites en Islam. Essai d'interprétation anthropologique de la notion de mayta," *Studia Islamica*, 84 (1996), pp. 5–33.

15   *Al-Ahram Weekly* (Cairo), August 19–25, 2010.

16   A detailed cultural analysis of this soup is provided in Abdelhai Diouri, "On Leaven Foods: Ramadan in Morocco," in Sami Zubaida and Richard Tapper (eds.), *A Taste of Thyme: Culinary Cultures of the Middle East* (London: Taurus Park Paperbacks, 2000), pp. 233–55. See also Fatéma Hal, *Ramadan: Le cuisine du partage* (Paris: Éditions Agnès Viénot, 2006), pp. 47–60.

17   Alixia Naff, *Becoming American: The Early Arab Immigrant Experience* (Carbondale: Southern Illinois University Press, 1985), p. 135.

18   John Tofik Karam, *Arabesque: Syro-Lebanese Ethnicity in Neo-Liberal Brazil* (Philadelphia: Temple University Press, 2007), pp. 57–60. The estimate of *sfihas* consumed daily in Saõ Paolo is quoted on p. 128.

19   See Roberto Marin-Guzman and Zidane Zeroui, *Arab Immigration in Mexico in the Nineteenth and Twentieth Centuries* (Austin, Mexico: Augustine Press, 2003); and Theresa Alfaro-Velcamp, *So Far from Allah, So Close to Mexico: Middle Eastern Immigrants in Modern Mexico* (Austin: University of Texas Press, 2007).

20   See C. El Solh, "Arab Communities in Britain: Cleavages and Commonalities," *Islam and Christian Relations* 3:2 (1992), pp. 236–58; and Ghada Karmi, *The Egyptians of Britain: A Migrant Community in Transition* (Durham: Center for Middle East Studies and Islamic Studies, University of Durham, 1997).

21   Roden, *Arabesque*, p. 21.

22   Hattox, *Coffee and Coffeehouses*, Chap. 3.

23   Jody Kantor, "A History of the Mideast in the Humble Chickpea," *New York Times*, July 10, 2002.

15

Migration and diaspora

Modern political and religious conflicts, as well as economic disparities and shifts, have led to significant migrations of Arabs both within the Arab World and well beyond its borders. The Arabic terms *al-mahjar* (the place of migration), *al-manfa* (the place of exile), and *al-shatat* (dispersal; the diaspora) are used to refer to the locations in which Arabs live but experience *al-hanin ila al-watan* (nostalgia or longing for home) and *al-ghurba* (separation and estrangement experienced when away from home). Yet because of the ethnic, religious, and linguistic diversity within the Middle East, the term "Arab" itself must be understood as a loose shorthand referring to people from countries that are predominantly Arabic speaking, though some of them speak Arabic as a second language and may not identify ethnically as Arab at all.

In addition to this mosaic of identities, the Arab diaspora includes many forms of migration: stateless refugees who fled in pursuit of survival; internally displaced refugees; exiles who departed to escape personal threat or censorship; intra-regional and extra-regional immigrants largely motivated by economic factors; return migrants; students who spend a finite period away; and transnationals who split their time between their country of origin and their home abroad. Likewise, host country status ranges from legal resident and citizen to officially registered refugee, to temporary worker or student, to "illegal." All of these disparate groups have in common their participation, both indirectly and directly, in the key questions and struggles of modern Arab culture: conceptions of modernity and tradition; how such conceptions pertain to gender and sexuality; the building of identities with multiple class, ethnic, religious, national, and linguistic allegiances; a sense of loss for

Arab cultural ascendance and/or for faraway or destroyed homelands; and a search for paths to resiliency.

The Arab diaspora is the result of many different historical waves of migration. Yemenis began establishing themselves as merchants via international maritime trade routes in East Africa, South Asia, and Southeast Asia several centuries ago. In the nineteenth and early twentieth centuries, large numbers of Arab emigrants left the Ottoman Empire, particularly the Levant (Syria, Lebanon, and Palestine), for North and South America. Estimates indicate that between 1860 and 1914, among the more than a million émigrés that left the Ottoman Empire for the Americas, there were roughly 600,000 Arabic speakers from the Levant.[1] The 1948 establishment of the State of Israel, as well as the 1967 war and subsequent conflicts, resulted in displaced Palestinians arriving in the Americas, Europe, and Australia, as well as in Arab countries. Currently more than half the total number of Palestinian nationals lives outside of historical Palestine.[2] The establishment of Israel also triggered another population movement, though one of much lower numbers: the migration of Arab Jews. Jews who had lived for centuries in North Africa, Egypt, Iraq, Syria, and Yemen emigrated to Europe, the Americas, and Israel. Roughly one million Lebanese left during the prolonged civil war (1975–90), and subsequent conflicts, primarily the 2006 war between Israel and Hezbollah, led to further displacement.[3] The majority went to other Arab countries and the Americas (notably the Triple Frontier area of Paraguay, Brazil, and Argentina), while others went to France, West Africa, and Australia. Estimates suggest that 12 to 15 million Lebanese and their descendants live abroad; at least 16 percent of Lebanon's citizens live outside Lebanon.[4]

Since the early twentieth century, North Africans (Maghribis) have been emigrating to France and other European countries in a migration pattern that is closely tied to the colonial history with France. By 2004, there were an estimated 2.6 million Maghribis in Europe and over 3 million worldwide in communities that include Arabs, Imazighen (Berbers), and North African Jews. The most recent population shifts within the Arab World are those of the Iraqis and the Syrians. The 2003 US invasion of Iraq and subsequent intersectarian violence created a refugee crisis of major proportions. As of 2007, over 4 million Iraqis had been displaced. Similar to the Palestinian situation, the Iraqi crisis became a pressing local issue in neighboring Jordan and Syria, which together received more than 2 million Iraqi refugees. In addition to these and the internally displaced, more than 140,000 Iraqi refugees are in Europe, though less than 20,000 have been admitted to the United States.[5] In 2011, as part of the Arab Spring, the uprisings began in Syria that later grew into a civil war. So far the Syrian conflict has forced over 2.4 million people to flee and seek safety in neighboring countries, only exacerbating the insecurity of Palestinians that had been living in Syria as well as the concentration of regional refugees in Lebanon and Jordan.

As with all immigrant and diaspora groups, Arab émigrés are involved in two key relationships: that with the "host" country and that with their country of origin. The challenges faced by Arab communities abroad are intense and the difficulties of these cultural negotiations affect, albeit in largely indirect ways, Arab cultural expression and identity formation around the world. This essay focuses on how Arab émigrés outside of the Middle East and North Africa impact their region of origin; that is, it addresses the relationship of the migrant – including returnees and descendents of émigrés – with the cultures of Arab countries.

One very direct avenue of impact is return migration. Though it is often very difficult to calculate the numbers of returnees, their presence is palpable in their home villages, towns, and cities. Khater extrapolates that around 45 percent of the original turn-of-the-nineteenth-century émigrés from Mount Lebanon returned to that region.[6] The new experiences and wealth that they brought back changed styles of home-building, schooling patterns, and gender relations, and thus contributed to the emergence of a new middle class.[7]

Whether upon returning or while abroad, money is a significant element of the émigré–home country relationship. While immigrants and their descendents often offer financial support during a particular crisis or to address a specific humanitarian need back home, many migrants support the daily needs of family members by regularly sending them a portion of their earnings. As part of a global trend, these remittances play an important role in the national economies of the receiving countries, by encouraging economic growth and providing a livelihood for poorer citizens. Another type of return includes the "cultural remittances" of the Arab diaspora.

Literature and intellectual life

In the early twentieth century, the Arab writers who had emigrated to the Americas, known as the *mahjar* or émigré writers, developed their own literary style that had a deep impact on the trajectory of Arabic literature. Writing in a language that was completely outside of the mainstream of the countries in which they settled, these writers formed societies to cultivate their Arabic literary enterprise and founded journals to provide them with venues for publication. Although often referred to as a single group, the *mahjar* writers consist of distinct communities primarily in the United States and South America, in particular in Brazil and Argentina. Prose fiction writers in both the north and south *mahjars* experimented with short and long Arabic narratives in the first two decades of the twentieth century, a time when in the Arab World the short story had just begun to be cultivated and there were only a handful of accomplished novels. Whereas most of the Latin American *mahjar* poets were more traditionalist in view and poetic style than their brethren to the north, some did participate in the innovations of the US *mahjar* poets. The pioneering US *mahjar* school, as a direct contributor to the Arabic free verse movement, is one of the most important schools of modern Arabic literature.

The North American émigré writers were typically more universalist in perspective (believing that all persons and creatures are linked to, and will be reconciled with, the divine), whereas their counterparts to the south tended to be more nationalist or pan-Arabist. The northern *mahjar* writers drew freely from Biblical themes and language in their work and in this way opened the door to experimentation with the literary style of the Bible within Arabic letters in general. They are sometimes described as having taken from North American and European writers in order to offer the Arab World a new style of poetic expression, while simultaneously offering to their US and international readership a stereotyped version of "Eastern" spirituality. Yet these poets also tapped into specific aspects of their Middle Eastern heritage: some *mahjar* poetry seems to draw from popular Syro-Lebanese music and certain *mahjar* writers (Gibran, ʿArida, and Abu Madi) were groundbreakers in the incorporation of Phoenician and Arab myths into modern Arabic literature.[8]

One of the earliest North American *mahjar* writers was Amin al-Rihani (1876–1940), who emigrated from Lebanon to New York in 1888 and published prose and poetry in both English and Arabic. Al-Rihani sought in his Arabic writings to release the Arabic literary tradition from the constraints of classical formulas and grammar. Although some have claimed that al-Rihani's pioneering efforts led to the earliest free verse in Arabic poetry, his clearest contribution was to be the first to consciously craft

Arabic "prose poetry." Al-Rihani represents an important shift from the Neoclassical concept of the writer to a Romantic vision of the socially committed writer.

The *mahjar* writer most credited with literary innovation and intellectual leadership is the famed Jubran Khalil Jubran (Kahlil Gibran) (1883–1931). After initial emigration from Lebanon to Boston and periods in Beirut and Paris, Gibran settled in New York as a writer and artist. In 1920, together with twelve other Syro-Lebanese writers, he founded the literary group *al-Rabita al-qalamiyya* (The Pen Society) and served as the group's president. Gibran's most famous work, *The Prophet* (1923), a collection of mystical prose poems, has been translated into some twenty languages and, after the Bible, was the bestselling book of the twentieth century in the United States. In spite of the small size of Gibran's Arabic (versus English) corpus, and what many commentators consider a weak style in Arabic, his popular appeal and his great influence on other *mahjar* writers made him a highly significant figure. The Arabic work that garnered him the most attention as a poet was the long poem *al-Mawakib* (The Processions, 1918). Like most of the poetry of the US *mahjar* school, it breaks from the monorhyme form and fixed meter of traditional Arabic poetry and treats philosophical questions. In a metaphysical, Romantic vein, the poem presents human society as corrupt and calls for a return to nature. In other works, Gibran also experimented with prose poetry and prose narrative, producing early attempts at the short story and the novel.

Mikhail Naimy (Mikha'il Nu'aima) (1889–1987), one of the other key figures of the US *mahjar*, made a significant contribution to Arabic literary criticism. Naimy published in, and later edited, the New York-based Arabic periodical *al-Funun* (The Arts), which together with *al-Sa'ih* (The Traveler), was one of the main publication venues of US *mahjar* writers and circulated in the Americas and the Middle East. Later Naimy returned to Lebanon and continued to publish in both English and Arabic, including translations of his own English works into Arabic and vice versa. In the realm of prose fiction, in addition to an early attempt at the novel and one of the earliest efforts at Arabic drama, Naimy produced some of the earliest well-developed Arabic short stories.

Whereas his literary works, including poetry and prose, are concerned with alienation and mysticism, his critical essays attack the orthodoxies of the Arabic literary tradition. Among Arab litterateurs, Naimy is most well known for *al-Ghirbal* (The Sieve, 1923), a collection of critical essays published in Cairo. In this collection Naimy presents the task of the literary critic as that of using his own particular sieve to sift through works and determine their literary merit. *Al-Ghirbal* is considered one of the most important critiques of Arabic letters of its time.

Two other prominent writers connected to The Pen Society were Nasib 'Arida (1887–1946) and Iliya Abu Madi (1889–1957). The Syrian 'Arida established an Arabic publishing house and various periodicals in New York, among them the literary review *al-Funun* (The Arts). 'Arida also wrote introspective, symbolic poetry with structural innovations. In many works he experimented with the strophic form and refrain of the *muwashshah* (a poetic form developed in medieval Muslim Spain in the tenth century and revived in the early twentieth century). Elsewhere 'Arida contracted the unit of meaning from full lines to what would have been only a short segment (a foot) of traditional metered verse. This innovation came decades before the recognized inauguration of Arabic free verse poetry in 1947, leading some to regard 'Arida as the earliest composer of free verse. Following a more precise definition of this term, he is certainly a precursor to the flourishing of free verse in the 1950s.

Abu Madi, a Lebanese poet who spent more than a decade in Egypt before emigrating to the United States, did not consistently follow the new forms and themes espoused by The Pen Society. Nonetheless, according to critic Salma Jayyusi, in the Arab World he is the most widely read *mahjar* poet and during the mid-twentieth century was one of the most popular contemporary Arabic poets in general.[9] Many Arab critics consider Abu Madi to have been the best poet of the group precisely because of his combination of a strong command of Classical Arabic prosody with some innovation. The collection *al-Jadawil* (Streams, 1927) is considered his most important work; many of its poems are made up of short strophes that have their own rhyme schemes.

The most prominent woman writer within the North American *mahjar* was 'Afifa Karam (1883–1924). She worked as an editor and later founded and edited her own journal, *al-'Alam al-Nisa'i al-Jadid* (The New Women's World), that addressed female readers throughout the diaspora, and also published the novel *Badi' wa-Fu'ad* (Badi' and Fu'ad, 1906). In all of her writing, she criticized gender oppression and defended women's rights.

While some of the *mahjar* writers, particularly those in the north, profoundly changed the meter, form, and language of Arabic poetry and greatly enriched the symbolic language and tone of Arabic literature, thus ushering in Romanticism, other *mahjar* writers, primarily those in South America, participated in significant ways in the cultural and political aspects of either Arab Nationalist movements or Pan-Arabism. Émigrés in Latin America were particularly active in the politics of the Arab region through their Arabic journals, political organizing, and poetry. Father and son immigrants Khalil Saʿadeh (1857–1934) and Antun Saʿadeh (1904–1949), who lived in both Argentina and Brazil, stand out for their nationalist writing and activism in pursuit of an independent Greater Syria. Similarly, the Syrian Nationalist Jubran (Yubrán) Massuh (1884–1977) wrote political essays in Argentina that he published in Cairo, Beirut, and Damascus newspapers.

Although the *mahjar* writers of Brazil and Argentina included poets and prose writers, it was the poets among them who attained renown. The poets of the southern *mahjar* were much more prolific than those of North America, yet on the whole they were more moderate in their attitude toward Classical Arabic poetry. With regard to form, although the émigrés in South America did make some use of shorter meters and a type of strophic verse (*muwashshah*), they continued largely with the classical verse structure of two hemistichs and monorhyme. For this reason, their literary groups were not schools with distinct principles, but rather associations that fulfilled practical publishing and cultural needs. In 1933, a group of Arab writers in Brazil established the literary society *al-ʿUsba al-Andalusiyya* (The Andalusian League, a reference to medieval Muslim Spain, known in Arabic as *al-Andalus*). By the 1920s, Arab writers were actively publishing in Argentina, largely in local Arabic and bilingual periodicals as well as in individual volumes; but it was not until 1949 that a group of Syro-Lebanese writers in Buenos Aires formed *al-Rabita al-adabiyya* (The Literary Union).

A common topic of South American *mahjar* poetry was Arab Nationalism, usually expressed with the rhetorical, declarative tone typical of Neoclassical Arabic poetry. In contrast with their counterparts to the north, who seldom wrote poems on social or political events, the Brazilian and Argentine *mahjar* writers focused on public and political occasions and issues. As a result, although the works of most of the southern *mahjar* writers, in contrast with that of The Pen Society in North America, did not have much of an impact on the direction of Arabic poetry, their works played a significant role in Arab culture because of their support for, and even direct involvement in, homeland national politics or the Pan-Arabist movement.

The two most well-known *mahjar* Arab Nationalist poets are the Lebanese writers Ilyas Farhat (1893–1976) and Rashid Salim al-Khuri

(1887–1984), better known as *al-Shaʿir al-Qarawi* (The Village Poet), or simply al-Qarawi, both of whom emigrated to Brazil. Farhat, who strongly criticized what he considered the radicalism of The Pen Society in North America, generally wrote with attention to correct, refined language and maintained the structure of the traditional classical poem (*qasida*). Farhat penned passionate occasional and nationalist poems that were so widely read throughout the Arab World that he became famous among Arabs as a defender of Arab interests. Additionally, he expressed anti-clerical ideas similar to those of his colleagues in New York. Like Farhat, al-Qarawi became known throughout the Arab World as a poetic chronicler of communal Arab events and issues. Al-Qarawi was strongly opposed to the US *mahjar* writers' rebellion against Classical Arabic models, because he saw it as a loss of trust in Arabness and thus a departure from Arabism. As a result of his nationalist and Arabist verse, al-Qarawi was invited to tour the Middle East, and stay in Syria with a government stipend, and was decorated by Egyptian President Nasser.

In contrast with Farhat and al-Qarawi, another Lebanese Brazilian, Fawzi al-Maʿluf (1889–1930) was a supporter of The Pen Society, an admirer of Gibran, and a participant in the renovation of Arabic poetry. Al-Maʿluf became famous in the Arab World for his romantic poetry that presents an idealized suffering poet. Many Arab writers responded to his early death with elegies. Other writers associated with The Andalusian League included Fawzi's brother Shafiq al-Maʿluf (1905–1976) and Shukrallah al-Jurr (1903–1975).

In Buenos Aires, The Literary Union included Argentine Syro-Lebanese writers who, like most of their brethren in Brazil, wrote poetry about Arab identity, Arab Nationalism, or Pan-Arabism.[10] In addition, Argentine émigré writers produced early attempts at Arabic novels, short stories, and dramas. Notable among these is *Daʿas wa-Fadʿus* (Daʿas and Fadʿus, 1923) by Najib Baʿqlini and Samʿan al-Hamati. The text is of interest because of its extensive use of colloquial Arabic. Such a use of the colloquial was not seen again in Arabic narrative until largely marginalized experimental works of the 1960s.

During the 1910s and 1920s, while the North American *mahjar* school was developing, literary activity in Egypt was also moving toward a break from the diction, themes, and rigid structure of Neoclassicism. In Cairo, this activity centered around the *Diwan* group. The two movements, although part of a broader shift in Arab culture toward Romanticism, did not have any contact until after both had already developed their core ideas. The outcome of both groups' path-breaking work was the creation of the Apollo Group in 1932. This Romantic literary movement, though based in Cairo, involved writers from around the Arab World – diaspora included – in the renovation of Arabic letters. Both North and South American *mahjar* writers, such as Abu Madi, Shafiq al-Maʻluf, and al-Jurr, contributed to the Apollo movement by publishing their work in its influential eponymous journal.

Although in Europe there were no Arab literary groups akin to those of the Americas, during the 1800s and early 1900s, many Arab intellectuals resided in Europe, usually for limited, but formative and productive, time periods. Most notably, Ahmad Faris al-Shidyaq (1804–1887) left Lebanon in his early twenties and lived the rest of his life in Cairo, Malta, England, Paris, Tunis, and Istanbul. His vast oeuvre includes translations, travel narratives, poetry, and also philological and grammatical treatises geared toward the modernization of Arabic. Prominent among these is *Al-Saq ʻala al-saq fi ma huwa al-Faryaq* (*Leg Over Leg*, 1855), a foundational text of modern Arabic literature that presents a semi-autobiographical Arab protagonist's encounter with Europe. The Egyptian poet Ahmad Shawqi, the foremost Arabic Neoclassical poet and a pioneer in Arabic verse drama, after studying in France for a few years, was exiled when the British deposed his patron, the ruler of Egypt (the Khedive). Shawqi chose to spend his exile in Spain, where he wrote nostalgic and nationalist poetry, as well as poems inspired by *al-Andalus*, medieval Muslim Spain.

In later periods, countless Arab émigrés and their descendants have become prominent writers and intellectuals in the languages and literary circles of their new homes in the Americas, Europe, and Australia. However, many of these have maintained or cultivated a role in the cultural life of the Arab region, and also the Arab World at large, by continuing to write in Arabic or French, by having their works translated into these languages, through return migration, or via joint literary projects. In the United States, Syrian-born Yusuf al-Khal (1917–1987), a major contributor to the modernist movement in Arabic poetry, made his literary career in Beirut and also New York City, where he lived from 1948 to 1955. After returning to Beirut, al-Khal co-founded in 1957 the magazine *Shiʻr* (Poetry), which for several years was the heart of avant-garde Arabic poetry. The distinguished writer and artist Etel Adnan, after a few years in Paris, moved to the United States in 1955, yet her work remains an integral part of Lebanese culture. Her famous novel *Sitt Marie Rose* (1978) decries the Lebanese Civil War with an innovative form and *L'apocalypse arabe* (*The Arab Apocalypse*, 1980) experiments with joining poetry and drawing. Palestinian–American poet (and actress) Suheir Hammad, who became prominent through her performance in an award-winning Broadway spoken word poetry event, has conducted writing workshops in Dheisheh refugee camp in the West Bank (and stars in a feature-length Palestinian film). One of the most internationally well-known Arab intellectuals is the Palestinian literary and cultural critic Edward Said (1935–2003), who is connected to various strands within Arab migration: the great Levantine immigration through his father, who was a return migrant in that movement, the Palestinian diaspora, as well as the "brain drain" phenomenon. From his base in the United States, Said ultimately had a significant impact on Arab intellectuals in the Middle East through translations of his books and his regular contributions to the Arabic press.[11]

In Europe, a number of the émigré intellectuals that remain a vital part of Arab culture are Maghribi writers who reside (or resided) in France and published their landmark works there. Kateb Yacine (1929–1989) is most famous for his novel *Nedjma* (1956), which was highly influential within Francophone North African literature, and for his later plays in Algerian dialect. Moroccan novelist Driss Chraibi (1926–2007) was labeled a traitor by Moroccans because of *Le Passé simple* (1954; *The Simple Past*), which was published at the height of the Moroccan struggle for independence and criticized not only French colonial rule but also the Moroccan bourgeoisie and patriarchy. Chraibi nonetheless became the leading Moroccan writer of his generation; some of his novels depict the experiences of Moroccans in Europe or relations between Arabs and Europeans. Tunisian Jewish intellectual Albert Memmi wrote, in addition to acclaimed novels, a classic study of colonialism, *Portrait du colonisé, précédé par Portrait du colonisateur* (1957), translated as *The Colonizer and the Colonized*. Algerian novelist, historian, and filmmaker Assia Djebar is famous for narratives in which she offers a feminist critique and a revision of Algerian history through multiple perspectives. Moroccan poet, playwright, and novelist Abdellatif Laâbi's highly political works led to the banning of his influential journal, his imprisonment and torture, and subsequent exile to France, where he has continued to be a major figure in experimental Maghribi writing. Moroccan Abdellah Taïa resides in Paris but, as the first openly gay Moroccan writer and the author of works that both criticize the Moroccan regime and graphically portray homosexuality, he has become a center of controversy in the Moroccan cultural scene.

Beyond the Maghribi sphere, Sudanese Tayeb Salih's years in Britain yielded the classic postcolonial novel *Mawsim al-hijra ila al-shamal* (*Season of Migration to the North*, 1966), which examines the impact of British colonialism and years spent in Britain on two Sudanese men and their village. The acclaimed Palestinian poet Mourid Barghouti, after being forced to settle in Egypt, spent seventeen years exiled in Budapest. After the Oslo Accords allowed him to return to the West Bank for the first time in thirty years, he wrote the autobiographical novel *Raʾaytu Ram Allah* (*I Saw Ramallah*, 1997). The Syrian–Lebanese poet and literary critic Adonis (ʿAli Ahmad Saʿid), years after co-founding the magazine *Shiʿr* (Poetry), escaped the Lebanese Civil War by moving to Paris, where he continues to be a highly influential figure in Arabic letters. A Lebanese who lived in England, Mai Ghoussoub (1952–2007) was the co-founder of Al Saqi Bookshop, a center of Arab culture in London and an important publisher, along with Beirut's Riad El Rayyes Books, of diaspora writers. Also within the London Arab diaspora, Lebanese novelist Hanan al-Shaykh, well known for her novels *Hikayat Zahra* (*The Story of Zahra*, 1980) and *Misk al-ghazal* (*Women of Sand and Myrrh*, 1989), also wrote *Innaha Landan ya ʿazizi* (*Only in London*, 2001) about Arab immigrants in that city. Other notable contemporary Arab cultural figures based in Europe include Francophone North African novelists Mohammed Dib, Tahar Ben Jelloun, and Malika Mokkeddem, Lebanese novelist Hoda Barakat, and Iraqis Haifa Zangana (also a painter) and Alia Mamdouh.

As seen in some of the titles mentioned above, migration itself is the topic of myriad works of Arab literature produced by both émigrés and those within the national borders. Among these texts, many focus specifically on the effects of emigration and return emigration on the Arab village. Besides Salih's *Season of Migration*, various Lebanese authors have written on this topic: Farah Antun's novels, *al-Hubb hata al-mawt* (*Love till death*, 1898) and *Al-Wahsh, al-Wahsh, al-Wahsh* (*The Beast, The Beast, The Beast*, 1903); Naimy's "Saʿat al-Kuku" (*The Cuckoo Clock*, 1927); various mid-twentieth-century short stories by Saʿid Taqiyy al-Din; and Emily Nasrallah's *Tuyur aylul* (*Birds of September*, 1962), *Al-Iqlaʿ ʿaqs al-zaman* (*Flight against Time*, 1981), and *Al-Jamr al-ghafi* (*Sleeping Ember*, 1995).

Visual and performing arts

Many artists within the Arab diaspora, despite extensive periods or permanent settlement abroad, have contributed to the cultural life of the Middle East and North Africa. After a group of Syrian and Lebanese painters were sent to Istanbul for training in the mid 1800s and upon their return established a school of marine painting, in the late nineteenth and early twentieth centuries, several Lebanese painters studied art in Europe. Among these was the Lebanese academic portraitist Daoud Corm (1852–1930), who spent eight years abroad studying art in Rome and serving as the official painter of the Belgian royal family. Corm returned to Lebanon and trained a generation of Lebanese painters. Many other Arab visual artists have lived abroad and then returned to play an influential role in the arts scene of the region. For instance, Yusuf Saʿadallah Huwayyik (Youssef Hoyeck, or Howayek) (1883–1962), a Lebanese painter and sculptor, spent twenty years studying art in Rome and Paris before returning to Lebanon. There he established the first sculpture studio in Beirut and became known as the "father of modern Lebanese sculpture." Also from Lebanon, Labiba "Bibi" Zoghbi (1890–1973), who emigrated to Argentina and began her professional life in South America, is known for her colorful flower paintings. After periods in Paris and Dakar she held several shows in Beirut where she was well received and established a model for Lebanese women artists. The Egyptian Mahmoud Mukhtar (1891–1934) and the Iraqi Jawad Salim (1919–1961) both studied art in Europe for several years and then returned to their home countries to develop aesthetics that incorporated, respectively, Pharaonic and Babylonian elements and thus were integral in the creation of nationalist Egyptian and Iraqi artistic styles. Algerian Mohammed Racim (1896–1975), who spent the 1920s in Paris, developed a hybrid, modern version of the traditional Islamic miniature and thus founded the Algerian school of miniature painting (that continues today), and contributed greatly to the first national Algerian arts movement. Syrian-born Madiha Omar (ʿUmar) (1908–2005) spent periods in England and Iraq and then moved to the United States in 1942. Soon after, she became the first artist to use Arabic calligraphy in modernist painting. Her pioneering work with abstract elements of a traditional Islamic art form developed into a significant trend in contemporary Arab and Muslim art.

The work of Lebanese Nadim Karam bridges art and design. Born in Senegal, raised in Beirut, educated for several years in Tokyo, and

now based in Beirut, Karam practices architecture and creates installations that are exhibited internationally. Other noteworthy figures
in design are award-winning Iraqi–British architect Zaha Hadid,
whose structures have been built in Europe and the Arab Gulf, and
Egyptian–British–Canadian designer Karim Rashid, who, from his base
in New York, has risen to fame for his industrial and interior designs,
ranging from luxury goods to innovative yet accessible household
products. Karam, Hadid, and Rashid were on the advisory board of the
International Design Initiative (organized by pan-Arab business venture
Moutamarat) that hosted a 2007 design forum in Dubai that aimed to
develop and promote Arab industrial and urban design.

In the realm of performance, many Arabs have gone abroad to train in
the dramatic arts and have stayed on for significant periods. Whether via
re-migration or visits, they often continue to contribute to Arab theater.
Egyptian Hassan El-Geretly studied in the UK and France, and worked
in France for years as an actor, director, and head of a theater company.
El-Geretly returned to Egypt and began working in theater and film,
eventually founding in 1987 Al-Warsha (The Workshop), an internationally recognized experimental theater company, known for its incorporation of Egyptian folk arts. Similarly, Lebanese Munir Abu Dibs studied
and worked in France for fifteen years before returning to Lebanon where
he co-founded a theater school and theater company, becoming a major
force in Lebanese theater. Awni Karoumi, a leading Iraqi theater director,
after studying in Germany returned there years later as an exile. From his
base in Germany, Karoumi held a theater workshop in Cairo's Hanager
Center in 2002 and has staged several plays in the Cairo Experimental
Theater Festival.

Members of the Arab diaspora have contributed to the development of another art form that is at the intersection of literature and visual art: *la bande dessinée* (Francophone comic books or graphic novels).
Iraqi–Lebanese Charles Berberian established himself in France and has
become one of the leading *bande dessinée* authors. Farid Boudjellal, who
emigrated from Algeria to France, is also a prize-winning comics author.
Both graphic novelists participated in the first international *bande dessinée* festival, held in Algiers in 2008. Through their works and this type of
collaboration they enrich the Middle East's growing interest in graphic
novels. In a project more akin to US-style comic books, Naif al-Mutawa,
a Kuwaiti who grew up spending summers in the United States and
received his university education and postdoctoral training there,

developed *The 99*, a comic book featuring superheroes that represent Muslim virtues. *The 99*, which is published in both English and Arabic editions, is currently the most popular – and controversial – comic book in Arabic-speaking countries. At the juncture between art and politics, the prolific and renowned Palestinian political cartoonist Naji al-'Ali (c. 1938–87) lived in exile in Lebanon, the Arab Gulf, and finally London, where he worked for the international edition of a Kuwaiti newspaper until his assassination.

Cinema

Given the technical knowledge and specialized production facilities that cinema requires, many Arab filmmakers have trained outside the Middle East and North Africa. Whereas some left as students and then stayed abroad, others emigrated or went into exile after their careers had already begun in their home countries. These filmmakers' location in Europe or North America offers them not only technical resources, but also financial support and freedom of expression that are often difficult to find in their home countries. Since film is an extremely costly art form, many Arab films – by émigrés and non-émigrés alike – arise from co-productions with European production companies; being abroad can facilitate access to these funding sources. Similarly, being abroad provides freedom from censors, at least until distribution in Arab countries is sought. Thus, residence abroad allows filmmakers to contribute works with high production values and critical viewpoints or sensitive topics to Arab cinema.

Perhaps not coincidentally, some of the countries with those most active in filmmaking – Algeria, Egypt, Lebanon, Morocco, Palestine, Syria, and Tunisia – are also (with the exception of Syria) some of those with the largest diaspora populations. Prominent Algerian director and screenwriter Merzak Allouache studied filmmaking in Paris and later spent a period in exile there. Allouache is most known for *Omar Gatlato* (1976), a highly successful film that affected the development of Algerian cinema, and the acclaimed *Bab el-Oued City* (1994). Allouache finished his sixth feature, *Salut cousin!* (Hello Cousin!, 1996) in France; the film is a light-hearted look at the lives of Algerian immigrants in France, one of them second generation and the other freshly arrived from Algeria. Algerian Mahmoud Zemmouri also studied filmmaking in Paris and then stayed on, eventually directing his first feature film there, *Prends dix mille balles et casses-toi* (*Take Your Ten Thousand Francs and Get Out*, 1981), which humorously portrays the results of the French policy of offering 10,000 francs to immigrants who would return to their "home" country. Another Algerian immigrant to France, Mehdi Charef, is famous for his film *Le Thé au harem d'Archimède* (*Tea in the Harem*, 1985), an adaptation of Charef's own novel. Together they are some of the inaugural works in a new form of cultural expression in France that focuses on the social issues of two partly overlapping communities: that of the *beur* (second-generation North Africans in France) and the *banlieue* (French public housing project neighborhoods). Charef has gone on to create various other films with migrant-related themes. The distinguished Palestinian filmmaker Michel Khleifi left for Belgium as a young adult and ended up studying film and settling there. His prize-winning *'Urs al-Jalil* (*Wedding in Galilee*, 1987) is the best-known Palestinian narrative film. Lebanese Ziad Doueiri, who left war-torn Beirut for the United States at age of twenty, directed the award-winning *Bayrut al-gharbiyya* (*West Beirut*, 1998). This humorous, though ultimately heart-wrenching, portrait of adolescence in a war zone was wildly popular in Lebanon. Nazareth-born Palestinian Elia Suleiman emigrated to New York and, during his approximately ten-year stay, directed two well-received short experimental films (one co-directed with Lebanese–Canadian multi-media artist Jayce Salloum). In the early 1990s, he moved to Jerusalem where he has taught and continued to make films, among them the award-winning, surreal dark comedy *Yad Ilahiyya* (*Divine Intervention*, 2002). Annemarie Jacir, a Palestinian who grew up in Saudi Arabia, received her formal education and taught in the United States, and now lives in Jordan. In addition to curatorial work and creating prize-winning short films, she wrote and directed the first feature-length film by a Palestinian woman. This film, *Milh hadha al-bahr* (*Salt of this Sea*, 2008), Palestine's submission to the Foreign Language Film category of the 2009 Academy Awards, stars Suheir Hammad as a US-born Palestinian who visits Palestine for the first time.

As with literary narratives, many Arab films address the topics of migration and exile. In addition to those by the émigré filmmakers mentioned above, such films include: *Dhil al-Ard* (*Shadow of the Earth*, 1982, by Tunisians al-Tayyib al-Wuhayshi and Taieb Louhichi), which presents the effects of modern life, including emigration, on a rural clan; *Le marriage de Moussa* (*Moussa's Wedding*, 1982, by Algerian Tayeb Mefty), which depicts the alienation experienced by a return émigré; *Bab al-sama' maftuh* (*A Door to the Sky*, 1989, by Moroccan Farida Benlyazid), which presents the spiritual quest that ensues when a young Moroccan woman returns from Paris to visit her dying father; *Lalla Hobby* (*Madam Hobby*, 1997, by Moroccan Mohamed Abderrahman Tazi), which, in a sequel to a wildly popular comedy, presents the misadventures of a Moroccan illegal immigrant in Belgium; and *al-Medina* (*El Medina*, 1999, by Egyptian Yousry Nasrallah), which follows the protagonist from Cairo to Paris and back again, as he searches for fulfillment and a sense of identity.

Music

The Arab diaspora has also helped develop transnational musical cultures. When Algerian authorities censored and banned *rai*, the North African community in France provided a haven for exiled *rai* singers (e.g., Cheb Hasni, Cheb Mami, Cheba Fadela, and Cheb Khaled) and also opened the door to a European fanbase. By the late 1990s, *beur* (persons of North African heritage born in France) and Maghribi immigrant musicians were creating innovative *rai* fusions, such as the funk, hip hop, reggae, and flamenco-influenced music of Faudel and the rock, punk, techno blend of Rachid Taha. Franco-Maghribi singers also brought immigrant themes to *rai* lyrics: racism, unemployment, and nostalgia. Additionally, in France, *rai* musicians were able to record albums with higher production standards and thus gained wider appeal. Within Arab countries, *rai* musicians have had a great deal of visibility and influence in Arabic pop music, producing duets with recording artists from the Mashriq and inspiring *rai* sounds in the songs of Arab musicians outside the Maghrib (e.g., Kazem al-Saher). On a broader scale, Gross, McMurray, and Swedenburg point out that, by the late 1980s, *rai* had become part of the US world music scene, which until then had barely included music from the Arabo-Islamic world.[12] The entry of *rai* paved the way for other Arab musicians and singers to reach a broader audience. In these ways, the French North African community has played an integral part in the survival, development, as well as international success of *rai*.

In a more indirect way, Arab émigré musicians support the budding hip hop scenes in Palestine, Egypt, Algeria, and Morocco. These recording artists, who rap in Arabic, French, English, and other European languages, include the Marseille-based Algerian break dancer and rapper Freeman (Malek Brahimi) of the group IAM; Rim'K (Abdelkarim Brahmi-Benalla), the French-born son of Kabyle Algerian immigrant parents, who is part of the group 113; Palestinian–British musician Shadia Mansour; Moroccan–Danish Isam Bachiri from the trio Outlandish; Iraqi–Canadian rapper The Narcicyst (Yassin Alsalman); Moroccan–Dutch rapper Salah Edin; and Cilvaringz (Tarik Azzougarh), a Moroccan–Dutch rapper and hip hop producer. Together with rappers in the Middle East and US black Muslim musicians, these diaspora musicians are creating transnational Muslim hip hop and Arabic hip hop networks.[13] Natacha Atlas, a Belgium-bred, London-based recording artist of mixed Arab Jewish, Arab Muslim, and British heritage, who creates an equally difficult to categorize global fusion dance music, also participates in these networks to some extent.[14] In addition to opening "Western" ears to Middle Eastern sounds, much as *rai* did, she has collaborated with Arab musicians, most notably with popular Egyptian singer Hakim. Although within the Arab region interest in her music was initially limited to westernized audiences, her popularity has increased.

The Colombian pop superstar Shakira (Shakira Mubarak), of Lebanese origin on her father's side, not only brought Middle Eastern rhythms and belly dance to the mainstream of the Americas and Europe, but has also influenced popular culture in Arab countries. Having already recorded one song ("Ojos así" [Eyes like that]) with Arabic lyrics in an earlier album, Shakira covered two songs by Lebanese superstar Fairuz in her 2002–3 and 2006–7 concert tours. The second of these tours included a Middle Eastern leg in which Shakira held a very well-attended concert in front of the Giza Pyramids. Shakira's belly dancing outfits have caused such a sensation that even cabaret performers in Cairo have copied Shakira's outfits, which Egyptian entertainment industry censors then deemed indecent. Shakira's influence and popularity are also notable in the Arab music industry: singers such as Nawal al-Zoghby and Mariam Fares echo the Lebanese-Colombian's music and look, while male Arab singers vied to be the first to perform a duet with Shakira.

Other networks and other maps

There are other networks or channels of contact and exchange. Although these are sometimes difficult to gauge, they clearly have a role in creating transglobal Arab communities. These include the Internet, pan-Arab newspapers (e.g., *al-Hayat*) and satellite television (e.g., Al Jazeera), the phenomenon of "homeland tourism" (in which descendents of Arab immigrants go on vacation tours designed as a return to the home country), and the more informal channels of visits and phone calls between friends and family across national and regional boundaries.[15] These, together with economic links, literary and critical texts, the visual and performing arts, cinema, music, and the overlapping realm of popular culture, create different forms of national, ethnic, religious, and linguistic communities that extend beyond the boundaries of the Arab states and the region they form.

In one sense, the Arab diaspora is another consequence of the forces that shape Arab countries: colonial and postcolonial relations; sectarian, ethnic, and linguistic differences; and social, religious, economic, and political power struggles. At the same time, though, migrant Arabs are not just an end result. Rather, they are often both the source of answers to questions regarding all of these key issues and their bearing on the directions of Arab cultural expression, and the source of new questions that help in understanding these issues further. Thus, Arabs abroad are an integral part of contemporary Arab culture – of both their home countries and the Arab World that transcends regional boundaries. Accordingly, many scholars note that the term "diaspora" itself is problematic. In addition to other concerns, the term suggests that those outside of the physical space of the country of origin are severed from networks that may indeed be integral to their construction of identity. Inversely, it also suggests that diaspora communities are not part of the identities constructed within the Arab region. The term may inadvertently support the idea that "authentic" culture is limited to a specific geographic space. Yet the interaction between many Arabs and their descendants outside of that space, with those within it, belies such a conception of Arab migration. For many Arabs, the "map" of their identities (national, religious, etc.) includes the coordinates of Arab communities abroad. Reframing the term diaspora, or even replacing it in given contexts with terms such as "transnational migration" (a network based on social rather than territorial spaces), highlights the need to reconceptualize the term "Arab World" as well.[16] Rather than a single territorial region, the term "Arab World" must include those who participate in defining and developing Arab culture (from the arts to daily practices) regardless of geographic location.

Notes

1   Kemal Karpat, "The Ottoman Emigration to America, 1860–1914," *International Journal of Middle East Studies*, 17: 2 (May 1985), p. 185.

2 Philippe Fargues, "International Migration in the Arab Region," p. 9. [Downloaded from: www.un.org/esa/population/migration/turin/Symposium—Turin—files/P09—Fargues.pdf.] Also: Helena Lindholm Schulz with Juliane Hammer, *The Palestinian Diaspora: Formation of Identities and Politics of Homeland* (London/New York: Routledge, 2003), p. 45.

3 Albert Hourani and Nadim Shehadi (eds.), *The Lebanese in the World: A Century of Emigration* (London: The Centre for Lebanese Studies/I.B. Tauris, 1992), p. 610.

4 Philippe Fargues, "International Migration," p. 9.

5 UNHCR, "Statistics on Displaced Iraqis around the World," September, 2007. [Available at: www.unhcr.org/470387fc2.html.]

6 Akram Khater, *Inventing Home: Emigration, Gender, and the Middle Class in Lebanon, 1870–1920* (London: University of California Press, 2001), p. 110.

7 Ibid., Chapter 5.

8 Shmuel Moreh, *Modern Arabic Poetry 1800–1970* (Leiden: Brill, 1976), pp. 24–32.

9 See Salma Khadra Jayyusi, *Trends and Movements in Modern Arabic Poetry*, 2 vols. (Leiden: Brill, 1978), vol. II, p. 535, and p. 791, n. 1.

10 Prominent members included Jurj Saydah (1893–1978), Jurj 'Assaf (1883–1957), Jurj Sawaya (1888–1959), Yusuf al-Ghurayyib (José Guráieb) (1896–1988), Zaki Qunsul (Konsol) (1916–1994), and Ilyas Qunsul (Elias Konsol) (1911/1914–1981).

11 See Sabry Hafez, "Edward Said's Intellectual Legacy in the Arab World," *Journal of Palestine Studies*, 33:3 (Spring 2004), pp. 76–90.

12 Joan Gross, David McMurray, and Ted Swedenburg, "Arab Noise and Ramadan Nights: Rai, Rap, and Franco-Maghrebi Identities," in Smadar Lavie and Ted Swedenburg (eds.), *Displacement, Diaspora, and Geographies of Identity* (Durham, NC: Duke University Press, 1996), pp. 121 and 125.

13 See H. Samy Alim, "A New Research Agenda: Exploring the Transglobal Hip Hop *Umma*," in Miriam Cooke and Bruce B. Lawrence (eds.), *Muslim Networks: From Hajj to Hip Hop* (Chapel Hill and London: University of North Carolina, 2005), pp. 264–74.

14 Ted Swedenburg, "Islamic hip-hop vs. Islamophobia: Aki Nawaz, Natacha Atlas, Akhenaton," in *Global Noise, Rap and Hip-Hop Outside the US* (Middletown, CT: Wesleyan University Press, 2001), pp. 57–85.

15 On "homeland tourism" see John Tofik Karam, *Another Arabesque: Syrian-Lebanese Ethnicity in Neoliberal Brazil* (Philadelphia, PA: Temple University Press, 2007), Chapter Six.

16 See Anja Peleikis, *Lebanese in Motion: Gender and the Making of a Translocal Village*, (Bielefeld: Transcript, 2003), pp. 13–22.

Glossary

effendi/effendiyya – the Turkish term *effendi* was used in many parts of the Arab World in the late nineteenth and early twentieth centuries to refer to (or address) men of the newly emerging educated, professional class, particularly those who adopted Western-style dress. It is still in use in some regions as a form of address indicating high social status, education, and/or wealth. The class as a whole is referred to as the *effendiyya*.

fatwa – a formal legal opinion pronounced by a qualified Islamic legal scholar; the extent to which such opinions are authoritative or binding for the individual(s) to whom they are issued depends on a wide variety of factors and, because Sunni Islam is not hierarchically organized, such opinions can be attenuated or contradicted by opinions issued by other scholars with different views. Shiʿite Islam recognizes a more rigid hierarchy of authority, such that the followers of particularly high-ranking scholars may consider such scholars' opinions to be incontrovertible.

fiqh – the general term for the substantive rules of Islamic law as elaborated by qualified Islamic legal scholars; in general, rules of *fiqh* are derived from the Qurʾan, the exemplary behavior of the Prophet Muhammad (see *hadith* and *sunna* below), and the legal writings of Muslim jurists; the term literally means "full or deep understanding."

hadith – literally "speech," but specifically used to refer to reports of the utterances and actions of the Prophet Muhammad; these reports were initially transmitted orally from eyewitnesses to others, and then on to following generations; eventually large collections of *hadith* were compiled and written down in now authoritative works along with the "chain of transmission" (Ar. *isnad*) detailing who had heard the report from whom from the compiler of the written work back to the original eyewitness. The *hadith* are an important body of legal precedents that collectively are considered to comprise the totality of Muhammad's exemplary behavior (see *sunna* below).

hakawati – traditional Arab storytellers who narrate folktales to audiences, whether in the open air or in coffee houses. Performances are often accompanied by music.

haram – that which is forbidden or deemed morally harmful, unacceptable, or unlawful in Islam.

ijtihad – a self-conscious exercise of legal interpretation by a highly qualified religious scholar, usually in regard to a legal question not directly addressed by the Qurʾan or the *hadith*, that results in the issuing of a legal ruling or interpretation.

Levant – the Eastern Mediterranean region between Egypt and modern Turkey (Palestine/Israel, Lebanon, Jordan, Syria); from the French term for "rising," referring to the rising of the sun in the east, which parallels the Arabic term *mashriq*, meaning "where the sun rises."

madhhab – "school of thought." From the tenth century on, Sunni jurists have been divided into four schools of legal thought (*madhhabs*), named after four important early jurists who died between 767 and 855. The Hanafi school, for example, is named after Abu Hanifa (d. 767) and was the official school of the Ottoman Empire. The Maliki school, which predominates in North Africa, is named after Malik ibn Anas (d. 795).

mahjar – the Arab diaspora; literally the "place of migration."

Maghrib (Maghreb) – the Arabic term for North Africa, and in particular Morocco; literally, "where the sun sets."

maqama – often translated as "picaresque narrative," the *maqama* is a genre of Arabic literature that emerged in the Middle Ages; early examples consisted of witty tales of scoundrels and conmen couched in highly erudite, even florid, rhymed prose (*saj'*) and Classical Arabic poetry; it has remained popular for centuries and has spawned many modern adaptations that treat a variety of different topics.

Mashriq (Mashreq) – the Arabic term for the Levant or Eastern Mediterranean littoral; literally, "where the sun rises."

muwashshah – a complex, rhyming strophic form of poetry originating in medieval Muslim Spain that originally mixed literary Arabic, colloquial Arabic, and Romance dialect. The *muwashshah* has influenced vernacular poetry and music in many regions.

Nahda – the Arab "Renaissance" or "Awakening" of the late nineteenth and early twentieth centuries; the term comes of verb meaning to "get up" or "stand up" from a prone position.

Nakba – the "Catastrophe"; a term used in Arabic to refer to the creation the Jewish State of Israel in 1948 in Palestine, despite the opposition of all Arab states, through a process that did not give Palestinians any voice in the matter.

Naksa – the "Setback"; a term used in Arabic to refer to the defeat of Arab forces in the 1967 war with Israel.

rihla – literally, "journey" or "travel"; the rich genre of travel writing in pre-modern Arabic literature that offered geographical and cultural descriptions and sometimes included a vivid portrayal of the author-traveler as well.

saj' – rhymed prose; along with prose and metrical verse, one of three major modes of Arabic literature; much of the Qur'an is composed in *saj'*.

salafi/salafiyya – Islamists who wish to return to the model of governance they believe was practiced in the time of Muhammad and the first generations of the Islamic era; from the Arabic term *salaf*, meaning predecessors, forebears, or ancestors.

shari'a (sharia) – a blanket term for Islamic law; if *fiqh* is the usual term for the rules of Islamic law as elaborated by qualified Islamic legal scholar, then *shari'a* refers to Islamic law in its capacity as the divine revelation of the law.

Shi'ite – Shi'ite Islam is one of the two main branches of Islam, which generally recognizes a more hierarchical and centralized structure of religious authority; also, a practitioner of Shi'ite Islam. Shi'ites are a minority in the Arab World overall, but are a majority in certain regions of Iraq, Bahrain, Lebanon, Saudi Arabia, and Yemen.

sunna – in this context, the behavior or practices of the Prophet Muhammad during his lifetime, especially those depicted in the *hadith*, and which are sought to be emulated by pious Muslims.

Sunni – Sunni Islam is one of the two main branches of Islam and has a more decentralized and diffuse structure of religious authority than that found in Shiʿite Islam; the majority of Muslims in the Arab World are Sunni Muslims.

tarab – "ecstatic engagement" between listeners and a performer, usually a singer or musician; *tarab* is usually achieved through a style of performance in which the singer or musician engages in extensive improvisation or repetition in response to audience reactions.

turath – literally "patrimony" or "heritage"; in Arabic the term is used most often to refer to cultural or artistic heritage, such as art, architecture, music, literature, and poetry, especially to the pre-modern literary and religious heritage.

ʿulama (ulema) – Muslim religious scholars or clerics.

umma – a term denoting "community" or "people," but not a "nation state"; it is commonly used to denote the community of all Muslims, but has also been used in modern political discourse to refer to the Arabs as a single "people."

Guide to further reading

Modern Arab culture: introductory remarks

Fromkin, David. *A Peace to End All Peace: The Fall of the Ottoman Empire and the Creation of the Modern Middle East*. New York: Holt and Co., 2009.

Gelvin, James L. *The Arab Uprisings: What Everyone Needs to Know*. Oxford University Press, 2012.

Kraidy, Marwan. *Reality Television and Arab Politics: Contention in Public Life*. Cambridge University Press, 2010.

Chapter 1: The question of language

Beeston, Alfred Felix Landon. *The Arabic Language Today*. Washington, DC: Georgetown University Press, 2006.

Haeri, Niloofar. *Sacred Language, Ordinary People*. New York: Palgrave Macmillan, 2003.

Holes, Clive. *Modern Arabic: Structures, Functions and Varieties*. Washington, DC: Georgetown University Press, 2004.

Stetkevych, Jaroslav. *The Modern Arabic Literary Language: Lexical and Stylistic Developments*. Washington, DC: Georgetown University Press, 2006.

Versteegh, Kees. *The Arabic Language*. New York: Columbia University Press, 1997.

Chapter 2: Ethnic and religious minorities

Bailey, Betty Jane, and J. Martin. *Who Are the Christians in the Middle East?* Grand Rapids, MI: Eerdmans, 2010.

Bengio, Ofra, and Gabriel Ben-Dor. *Minorities and the State in the Arab World*. Boulder, CO: Lynne Rienner Publishers, 1999.

Cleveland, William L., and Martin Bunton, *A History of the Modern Middle East*. Boulder, CO: Westview Press, 2009.

Collins, Robert O. *A History of Modern Sudan*. New York: Cambridge University Press, 2008.

Held, Colbert C., and John Thomas Cummings. *Middle East Patterns: Places, Peoples, and Politics*. Boulder, CO: Westview Press, 2011.

Chapter 3: *Nahda*: the Arab project of enlightenment

Bashkin, Orit. *The Other Iraq: Pluralism and Culture in Hashemite Iraq*. Stanford University Press, 2009.

Binder, Leonard. *Islamic Liberalism: A Critique of Development Ideologies*. University of Chicago Press, 1988.

Commins, David. *Islamic Reform: Politics and Social Change in Late Ottoman Syria*. New York: Oxford University Press, 1990.

Hafiz, Sabry. *The Genesis of Arabic Narrative Discourse: A Study in The Sociology of Modern Arabic Literature*. London: Saqi Books, 1993.

Hamzah, Dyala (ed.). *The Making of the Arab Intellectual, 1880–1960: Empire, Public Sphere and the Colonial Coordinates of Selfhood*. New York: Routledge, 2013.

Haykel, Bernard. *Revival and Reform in Islam: the Legacy of Muhammad al-Shawkani*. New York: Cambridge University Press, 2003.

Hourani, Albert. *Arabic Thought in the Liberal Age, 1798–1939*. Cambridge University Press, 1989.

Irwin, Robert. *Dangerous Knowledge: Orientalism and its Discontents*. Woodstock, NY: Overlook Press, 2006.

Kassab, Elizabeth Suzanne. *Contemporary Arab Thought: Cultural Critique in Contemporary Perspective*. New York: Columbia University Press, 2009.

Maghraoui, Abdeslam. *Liberalism Without Democracy: Nationhood and Citizenship in Egypt, 1922–1936*. Durham, NC: Duke University Press, 2006.

Mishra, Pankaj. *From the Ruins of Empire: The Intellectuals Who Remade Asia*. New York: Farrar, Straus and Giroux, 2012.

Pollard, Lisa. *Nurturing the Nation: The Family Politics of Modernizing, Colonizing, and Liberating Egypt, 1805–1923*. Berkeley: University of California Press, 2005.

Sedgwick, Mark. *Muhammad Abduh*. Oxford: Oneworld, 2010.

Chapter 4: Law

Bechor, Guy. *The Sanhuri Code, and the Emergence of Modern Arab Civil Law (1932 to 1949)*. Leiden: Brill, 2008.

Bernard-Maugiron, Nathalie, and Baudouin Dupret (eds.). *Egypt and its Laws*. The Hague: Kluwer, 2002.

Brown, Nathan J. *Constitutions in a Nonconstitutional World: Arab Basic Laws and the Prospects for Accountable Government*. Albany, NY: State University of New York Press, 2002.

   The Rule of Law in the Arab World: Courts in Egypt and the Gulf. Cambridge University Press, 1997.

Hill, Enid. "Al-Sanhuri and Islamic Law: The Place and Significance of Islamic Law in the Life and Work of 'Abd [*sic*] al-Razzaq Ahmad al-Sanhuri, Egyptian Jurist and Scholar, 1895–1971," *Arab Law Quarterly*, pt. 1 in 3:1 (1988): pp. 33–64; pt. 2 in 3:2 (1988): pp. 182–218.

Lombardi, Clark B. *State Law as Islamic Law in Modern Egypt: The Incorporation of the Sharī'a into Egyptian Constitutional Law*. Leiden: Brill, 2006.

Mallat, Chibli. *Introduction to Middle Eastern Law*. Oxford University Press, 2007.

Saleh, Nabil. "Civil Codes of Arab Countries: The Sanhuri Codes," *Arab Law Quarterly*,
      8:2 (1993): pp. 161–167.

Sfeir, George N. *Modernization of the Law in Arab States*. San Francisco, CA: Austin &
      Winfield, 1988.

Vogel, Frank E. *Islamic Law and Legal System: Studies of Saudi Arabia*.
      Leiden: Brill, 2000.

Chapter 5: Poetry

Abu-Lughod, Lila. *Veiled Sentiments: Honor and Poetry in a Bedouin Society*.
      Berkeley: University of California Press, 1986.

Akash, Munir, and Khaled Mattawa (eds.). *Post-Gibran: Anthology of New Arab-American
      Writing*. West Bethesda, MD: Kitab, distributed by Syracuse University
      Press, 2000.

Allen, Roger. *The Arabic Literary Heritage: The Development of its Genres and Criticism*.
      Cambridge University Press, 1998.

Badawi, M. M. (ed.). *Modern Arabic literature*. Cambridge University Press, 1992.

Caton, Steven C. *"Peaks of Yemen, I Summon": Poetry as Cultural Practice in a North Yemeni
      Tribe*. Berkeley: University of California Press, 1990.

Handal, Nathalie (ed.). *The Poetry of Arab Women: A Contemporary Anthology*.
      New York: Interlink Books, 2001.

Jayyusi, Salma Khadra. *Trends and Movements in Modern Arabic Poetry*, 2 vols.
      Leiden: Brill, 1978.

Jayyusi, Salma Khadra (ed.). *Modern Arabic Poetry: An Anthology*. New York: Columbia
      University Press, 1987.

Reynolds, Dwight F. *Heroic Poets, Poetic Heroes: The Ethnography of Performance in an Arabic
      Oral Epic Tradition*. Ithaca, NY: Cornell University Press, 1995.

Starkey, Paul. *Modern Arabic Literature*. Edinburgh University Press, 2006.

Chapter 6: Narrative

Allen, Roger. *The Arabic Novel: An Historical and Critical Introduction*. Syracuse University
      Press, 1995.

Badawi, Muhammad Mustafa. *The Cambridge History of Arabic Literature*. Cambridge
      University Press, 2006.

Brugman, J. *An Introduction to the History of Modern Arabic Literature in Egypt*.
      Leiden: Brill, 1984.

Cooke, Miriam. *War's Other Voices: Women Writers on the Lebanese Civil War*. Cambridge
      University Press, 1987.

El Sadda, Hoda. *Gender, Nation, and the Arabic Novel: Egypt, 1892–2008*. Syracuse
      University Press, 2012.

Musawi, Muhsin. *The Postcolonial Arabic Novel: Debating Ambivalence*. Leiden: Brill, 2003.
      Reprint 2005.

   Islam on the Street: Religion in Modern Arabic Literature. Lanham, MD: Rowman and
      Littlefield, 2009.

Meyer, Stefan G. *The Experimental Arabic Novel: Postcolonial Literary Modernism in the Levant*. Albany, NY: State University of New York Press, 2001.

Said, Edward. "Arabic Prose and Prose Fiction after 1967." In *Reflections on Exile and Other Essays*. Cambridge, MA: Harvard University Press, 2000.

Siddiq, Muhammad. *Arab Culture and the Novel: Genre, Identity and Agency in Egyptian Fiction*. London and New York: Routledge, 2007.

Chapter 7: Music

Burkhalter, Thomas. *Local Music Scenes and Globalization – Transnational Platforms in Beirut*. London and New York: Routledge, 2012.

Danielson, Virginia. *The Voice of Egypt: Umm Kulthūm, Arabic Song, and Egyptian Society in the Twentieth Century*. University of Chicago Press. 1997.

Danielson, Virginia, Scott Marcus, and Dwight Reynolds (eds.). *Garland Encyclopedia of World Music, Volume 6: The Middle East*. New York: Routledge. 2002.

Frishkopf, Michael (ed.). *Music and Media in the Arab World*. American University in Cairo Press. 2010.

Goldman, Michal, producer, director, and writer. *Umm Kulthum: A Voice Like Egypt*. A video recording, a production of the Filmmakers Collaborative, 1996.

Lohman, Laura. *Umm Kulthum: Artistic Agency and the Shaping of an Arab Legend, 1967–2007*. Middletown, CT: Wesleyan University Press, 2010.

Marcus, Scott. *Music in Egypt*. Oxford University Press. 2007

Racy, Jihad Ali. *Making Music in the Arab World: the Culture and Artistry of Tarab*. New York: Cambridge University Press, 2003.

Shannon, Jonathan. *Among the Jasmine Trees: Music and Modernity in Contemporary Syria*. Middletown, CT: Wesleyan University Press, 2006.

Stone, Christopher. *Popular Culture and Nationalism in Lebanon: The Fairouz and Rahbani Nation*. London and New York: Routledge Studies in Middle Eastern Literatures, 2007.

Chapter 8: Cinema and television

Armes, Roy. *Arab Filmmakers of the Middle East: A Dictionary*. Bloomington, IN: Indiana University Press, 2010.

Darwish, Mustafa. *Dream Makers on the Nile*. American University in Cairo Press, 1998.

El-Nawawy, Mohammed, and Adel Iskandar. *Al-Jazeera: The Story of the Network that is Rattling Governments and Redefining Modern Journalism*. Boulder, CO: Basic Books, 2003.

Lynch, Marc. *Voices of the New Arab Public: Iraq, al-Jazeera, and Middle East Politics Today*. New York: Columbia University Press, 2006.

Miles, Hugh. *Al-Jazeera: The Inside Story of the Arab News Channel that is Challenging the West*. New York: Grove Press, 2006.

Sakr, Naomi. *Arabic Television Today*. London: I.B. Tauris, 2007.

Seib, Philip. *Real-Time Diplomacy: Politics and Power in the Social Media Era*. New York: Palgrave Macmillan, 2012.

Shafik, Viola. *Arab Cinema: History and Cultural Identity*. American University in Cairo
    Press, 1998.
Shaheen, Jack. *Reel Bad Arabs: How Hollywood Vilifies A People*. New York: Olive Branch
    Press, 2001.

Chapter 9: Theater

Allen, Roger. "Arabic Drama in Theory and Practice: The Writings of Sa'adallah
    Wannus." *Journal of Arabic Literature* 15 (1984): pp. 94–113.
    "Drama and Audience: The Case of Arabic Theater." *Theater Three* 6
    (1989): pp. 25–54.
    "Egyptian Drama after the Revolution." *Edebiyat* 4:1 (1979): pp. 97–134.
Amin, Dina A. *Alfred Farag and Egyptian Theater: The Poetics of Disguise*. Syracuse
    University Press, 2008.
    "Egyptian Theater: Reconstructing Performance Spaces." *Arab Studies Journal* 14:2
    (Fall 2006): pp. 78–100.
Awad, Louis. "Problems of the Egyptian Theatre." In R. C. Ostle (ed.). *Studies in Modern
    Arabic Literature*. Warminster, England: Aris & Phillips, 1975, pp. 179–93.
Badawi, M. M. *Early Arabic Drama*. Cambridge University Press, 1988.
    Modern Arabic Drama in Egypt. Cambridge University Press, 1987.
al-Ra'i, 'Ali. "Some Aspects of Arabic Drama." In R. C. Ostle (ed.). *Studies in Modern
    Arabic Literature*. Warminster, England: Aris & Phillips, 1975, pp. 167–78.
Rubin, Don (ed.). *The World Encyclopedia of Contemporary Theatre: The Arab World*. London
    and New York: Routledge, 1999.
Selaiha, Nihad. "Voices of Silence: Women Playwrights in Egypt." In *Egyptian Theatre,
    A Diary: 1990–1992*. Cairo: Dar al-Kutub, 1993.

Chapter 10: Art

Ali, Wijdan. *Artworld: Contemporary Art in the Middle East*. London: Black Dog
    Publishing, 2009.
    Contemporary Art from the Islamic World. London: Scorpion Publishing, 1989.
O'Brian, David and David Prochaska (eds.). *Beyond East and West: Seven Transnational
    Artists*. Illinois: Krannert Art Museum, 2004.
Eigner, Saeb. *Art of the Middle East: Modern and Contemporary Art of the Arab World and Iran*.
    Forward by Zaha Hadid. London and New York: Merrel Publishers Ltd., 2010.
Faraj, Maysaloun (ed.). *Strokes of Genius: Contemporary Iraqi Art*. London: Saqi
    Books, 2001.
Hale, Sondra, "Imagery and Invention: Sudanese at Home and In the World." In
    Sherifa Zuhur (ed.). *Images of Enchantment: Visual and Performing Arts in the Middle
    East*. American University in Cairo Press, 1998, pp. 187–203.
Khal, Helen. *Lebanon: The Artist's View II 1975–2004*. London: The British Lebanese
    Association, 2004.
    The Woman Artist in Lebanon. Washington, DC, and Beirut: The Institute for
    Women's Studies, 1987.
Lloyd, Fran (ed.). *Contemporary Arab Women's Art: Dialogues of the Present*.
    London: Women's Art Library, 1999.

Displacement and Difference: Contemporary Arab Visual Culture in the Diaspora.
London: Saffron, 2001.

Nashashibi, Salwa Mikdadi. "Gender and Politics in Contemporary Art: Arab Women
Empower the Image." In Sherifa Zuhur (ed.). *Images of Enchantment: Visual and
Performing Arts in the Middle East.* American University in Cairo Press, 1998,
pp. 165–82.

Porter, Venetia. *Word into Art: Artists of the Modern Middle East.* London: The British
Museum Press, 2006.

Saudi, Mona. *Mona Saudi: Forty Years in Sculpture.* Beirut: 2006.

Winegar, Jessica. *Creative Reckonings: The Arts of Politics and Culture in Contemporary Egypt.*
Stanford University Press, 2006.

Chapter 11: Architecture

Bianca, Stefano. *Urban Form in the Arab World: Past and Present.* London: Thames &
Hudson, 2000.

Chadirji, Rifat. *Concepts and Influences: Towards a Regionalized International Architecture.*
London: KPI Ltd., 1986.

Easterling, Keller. *Enduring Innocence: Global Architecture and its Political Masquerades.*
Cambridge, MA: MIT Press, 2005.

Fathy, Hasan. *Architecture for the Poor: An Experiment in Rural Egypt.* University of Chicago
Press, 1973.

Holod, Renata, and Hasan-Uddin Khan. *The Contemporary Mosque: Architects, Clients, and
Designs since the 1950s.* New York: Rizzoli, 1997.

Kultermann, Udo. *Contemporary Architecture in the Arab States: Renaissance of a Region.*
London: McGraw-Hill, 1999.

Makiya, Kanan. *Post-Islamic Classicism: A Visual Essay on the Architecture of Mohamed
Makiya.* London: Saqi Books, 1990.

Rabbat, Nasser. *Thaqafat al-Bina' wa-Bina' al-Thaqafa: Buhuth wa-Maqalat fi Naqd
wa-Tarikh Al-'Imrah, 1985–2000.* Beirut: Riyad al-Rayyis, 2002.

Shafei, Farid M. *Al-'Imara al-'Arabiya al-Islamiya: Madiha wa-Hadiruha wa-Mustaqbaluha.*
Riyadh: Imadat Shuun al-Maktabat, 1982.

Volait, Mercedes. *L'architecture moderne en Egypte et la revue al-'Imara (1939–1959).*
Cairo: CEDEJ, 1988.

Chapter 12: Humor

Caubet, Dominique. "Jeux de Langues: Humor and Codeswitching in the Maghreb."
In Aleya Rouchdy (ed.). *Language Contact and Language Conflict in Arabic: Variations
on a Sociolinguistic Theme.* London and New York: RoutlegeCurzon, 2002,
pp. 233–58.

Göçek, Fatma Müge (ed.). *Political Cartoons in the Middle East.* Princeton University
Press, 1998.

Jayyusi, Salma Khadra, Matthew Sorenson, and Christopher Tingley. *Tales of
Juha: Classic Arab Folk Humor.* Northhampton, MA: Interlink Books, 2006.

Kanaana, Sharif. "Humor of the Palestinian Intifada." *Journal of Folklore Research* 27:3
(1990): pp. 231–40.

"Palestinian Humor During the Gulf War." *Journal of Folklore Research*, 32:1 (1995): pp. 65–75.

Kazarian, Shahe S. "Humor in the Collectivist Arab Middle East: The Case of Lebanon." *International Journal of Humor Research* 24:3 (2011): pp. 329–48.

Kishtainy, Khaled. *Arab Political Humor*. London: Quartet Books, 1986.

Mednicoff, David. "Cultural Apathy in the Service of Stability?: Cultural Politics in Monarchist Morocco." *North African Studies* 3:4 (1998): pp. 1–27.

al-Muhawi, Ibrahim. "Language, Ethnicity and National Identity in the Tunisian Ethnic Joke." In Yasir Sulaiman (ed.). *Language and Identity in the Middle East and North Africa*. New York: Psychology Press, 1996, pp. 39–60.

Rosenthal, Franz. *Humor in Early Islam*. Leiden: Brill, 1965.

Shehata, Samer S. "The Politics of Laughter: Nasser, Sadat, and Mubarak in Egyptian Political Jokes." *Folklore* 103:1 (1992): pp. 75–91.

Stewart, Devin. "The Humor of the Scholars: The Autobiography of Niʿmat Allāh al-Jazāʾirī (d. 1112/1701)." *Iranian Studies* 22 (1989): pp. 47–50.

Chapter 13: Folklore

Abu-Lughod, Lila. *Veiled Sentiments: Honor and Poetry in a Bedouin Society*. American University in Cairo Press, 1986.

Boddy, Janice. *Wombs and Alien Spirits: Women, Men and the Zār Cult in Northern Sudan*. Madison, WI: University of Wisconsin Press, 1989.

Cachia, Pierre. *Narrative Ballads of Egypt*. Oxford: Clarendon Press, 1989.

Caton, Steven. *"Peaks of Yemen I Summon": Poetry as Cultural Practice in a North Yemeni Tribe*. Berkeley: University of California Press, 1990.

Drieskens, Barbara. *Living with Djinns: Understanding and Dealing with the Invisible in Cairo*. London: Saqi Books, 2008.

Miller, W. Flagg. *The Moral Resonance of Arab Media: Audiocassette Poetry and Culture in Yemen*. Cambridge, MA: Harvard Center for Middle East Studies, 2007.

Muhawi, Ibrahim, and Sharif Kanaana. *Speak, Bird, Speak Again: Palestinian Arab Folktales*. Berkeley: University of California Press, 1989

Reynolds, Dwight F. *Arab Folklore: A Handbook*. Westport, CT: Greenwood, 2007.
Heroic Poets, Poetic Heroes: The Ethnography of Performance in an Arabic Oral Epic Tradition. Ithaca, NY: Cornell University Press, 1995.

El-Shamy, Hassan. *Folktales of Egypt*. Chicago University Press, 1980.

Chapter 14: Food and cuisine

Benkheira, Mohammed Hocine. *Islam et interdits alimentaires: Juguler l'animalité*. Paris: PUF, 2000.

Bsisu, May S. *The Arab Table: Recipes and Culinary Traditions*. New York: William Morrow, 2005.

Davidson, Alan. *The Oxford Companion to Food*. 2nd edition. Oxford University Press, 2006.

Gelder, Geert Jan van. *God's Banquet: Food in Classical Arabic Literature*. New York: Columbia University Press, 2000.

Lewicka, Paulina B. *Food and Foodways of Medieval Cairenes: Aspects of Life in an Islamic Metropolis of the Eastern Mediterranean*. Leiden: Brill, 2011.

Nasrallah, Nawal. *Annals of the Caliphs' Kitchens: Ibn Sayyar al-Warraq's Tenth-Century Baghdadi Cookbook*. Leiden: Brill, 2007.

Delights from the Garden of Eden: A Cookbook and History of the Iraqi Cuisine. 2nd edition. Sheffield: Equinox Publishing, 2013.

Roden, Claudia. *The New Book of Middle Eastern Food*. New York: Alfred A. Knopf, 2003.

Rodinson, Maxime, A.J. Arberry, and Charles Perry (eds.). *Medieval Arab Cookery: Essays and Translations*. Devon: Prospect Books, 2001.

Waines, David. *In a Caliph's Kitchen*. London: El-Rayyes Books, Ltd., 1989.

Wright, Clifford A. *A Mediterranean Feast*. New York: William Morrow, 2000.

Zubaida, Sami and Richard Tapper (eds.). *A Taste of Thyme: Culinary Cultures of the Middle East*. London: Taurus Park Paperbacks, 2000.

Chapter 15: Migration and diaspora

Alfaro-Velcamp, Theresa. *So Far from Allah, So Close to Mexico: Middle Eastern Immigrants in Modern Mexico*. Austin, TX: University of Texas, 2007.

Brand, Laurie A. *Citizens Abroad: Emigration and the State in the Middle East and North Africa*. Cambridge University Press, 2006.

Bunt, Gary R. *iMuslims: Rewiring the House of Islam*. Chapel Hill: University of North Carolina Press, 2009.

Civantos, Christina. *Between Argentines and Arabs: Argentine Orientalism, Arab Immigrants, and the Writing of Identity*. Albany, NY: State University of New York Press, 2006.

Cooke, Miriam, and Bruce B. Lawrence (eds.). *Muslim Networks from Hajj to Hip Hop*. Chapel Hill: University of North Carolina Press, 2005.

Hargreaves, Alec G. *Immigration and Identity in Beur Fiction: Voices from the North African Community in France*. New York and Oxford: Berg, 1991.

Hourani, Albert, and Nadim Shehadi (eds.). *The Lebanese in the World: A Century of Emigration*. London: The Centre for Lebanese Studies/I.B. Tauris, 1992.

Karam, John Tofik. *Another Arabesque: Syrian-Lebanese Ethnicity in Neoliberal Brazil*. Philadelphia: Temple University Press, 2007.

Khater, Akram. *Inventing Home: Emigration, Gender, and the Middle Class in Lebanon, 1870–1920*. Berkeley/Los Angeles/London: University of California Press, 2001.

Lloyd, Fran. *Displacement and Difference: Contemporary Arab Visual Culture in the Diaspora*. London: Saffron Books, 2001.

Nashashibi, Salwa Mikdadi. *In/Visible: Contemporary Art by Arab American Artists*. Dearborn, MI: Arab American National Museum, 2005.

Peleikis, Anja. *Lebanese in Motion: Gender and the Making of a Translocal Village*. Bielefeld: Transcript, 2003.

Schulz, Helena Lindholm with Juliane Hammer. *The Palestinian Diaspora: Formation of Identities and Politics of Homeland*. London and New York: Routledge, 2003.

Shohat, Ella, and Evelyn Alsultany (eds.). *Between the Middle East and the Americas: The Cultural Politics of Diaspora*. Ann Arbor: University of Michigan, 2013.

Index

CPSIA information can be obtained
at www.ICGtesting.com
Printed in the USA
LVOW13s1032050917
547587LV00015B/291/P